The Challenge of
Global Capitalism

*

The Challenge of Global Capitalism

THE WORLD ECONOMY IN THE 21ST CENTURY

*

WITH A NEW PREFACE BY THE AUTHOR

ROBERT GILPIN

AND WITH THE ASSISTANCE OF

JEAN MILLIS GILPIN

PRINCETON UNIVERSITY PRESS

PRINCETON AND OXFORD

Copyright © 2000 by Princeton University Press
Published by Princeton University Press, 41 William Street,
Princeton, New Jersey 08540
In the United Kingdom: Princeton University Press,
3 Market Place, Woodstock, Oxfordshire OX20 1SY
All Rights Reserved

Fifth printing, and first paperback printing, with a new preface, 2002
Paperback ISBN 0-691-09279-6

The Library of Congress has cataloged the cloth edition of this book as follows

Gilpin, Robert.
The challenge of global capitalism : the world economy
in the 21st century / by Robert Gilpin ; with the
assistance of Jean Millis Gilpin.
p.   cm.
Includes bibliographical references and index.
ISBN 0-691-04935-1 (cl. : alk. paper)
1. International economic relations.   2. International relations.
3. Structural adjustment (Economic policy).   4. International trade.
I. Title.   II. Gilpin, Jean M.
HF1359.G5515 2000
337 21—dc21   99-044906

British Library Cataloging-in-Publication Data is available

This book has been composed in Berkeley Book

Printed on acid-free paper. ∞

www.pup.princeton.edu

Printed in the United States of America

7   9   10   8

Contents

✳ *Illustrations* ✳

Preface to the Paperback Edition *

A NUMBER of important developments have altered the economic and political landscape since publication of this book in April 2000. On the whole, these developments have reinforced the themes and concerns expressed there, particularly those concerning the increasing importance of economic globalization, the growing negative reactions in many countries (including the United States) to globalization, and the continuing threat of economic regionalism, trade protectionism, and unilateralism. In this preface, I consider important new developments transforming "The Second Great Age of Capitalism" (also see chapter 1). No preface or book, however, can do justice to either the scope or the rapidity of the economic, political, and technological developments transforming human affairs.

The American economy suffered a serious setback in 2000–2001. Throughout much of the 1990s, the American economy experienced the most extended period of high rates of economic growth in the history of the world. Productivity growth, the major determinant of economic growth and wealth, was much higher than most economists had thought possible, and the American stock market soared to an unprecedented level. As I comment in the opening pages of this book, however, there were good reasons to be concerned over the sustainability of what enthusiasts called the "New Economy." Many economists considered the buoyant stock market mainly a speculative boom that would, like other such financial extravagances, one day collapse and cause considerable economic misery (see chapter 5). Moreover, Americans in the 1990s were living far beyond their means; indeed, they had been doing so for several decades. Nevertheless, in the 1990s the American urge to consume accelerated even more and became a major factor propelling rapid economic growth.

Americans were, to a disturbing extent, financing their extraordinarily high level of consumption by drawing down their personal savings, borrowing heavily from abroad, and mining the appreciation of stocks and other assets. The high dollar made imports of oil, raw materials, and consumer goods relatively inexpensive, and thereby contributed to a low inflation rate that enabled the Federal Reserve to pursue an expansionary economic policy. The American economy owed its success in the 1990s to the fact that much of the rest of the world was in recession or experiencing low economic growth. As I write these lines, the tide has turned, the speculative boom of the 1990s has ended, and Americans are facing the prospect of a Biblical "seven lean years."

The New Economy began to falter in the early months of 2000. The overall growth rate of the American economy slowed, the dot-com companies, the centerpiece of the New Economy, began to fail one after another, and the stock market declined precipitously while the technology stock–heavy Nasdaq lost half its value by early 2001. Contrary to the assertions by proponents of the New Economy, the "boom and bust" cycle of capitalism had not been transcended after all. Fears of a full-blown recession began to be expressed as the Administration of George W. Bush replaced that of William J. Clinton. Yet despite this economic reversal on the domestic front, the value of the dollar remained strong against most major currencies and continues to be so as of this writing (August 2001). Due in part to the high dollar, the trade / payments deficit of the United States has continued to grow alarmingly; so has the country's international debt. In 2000, the American trade deficit grew an extraordinary 40 percent to approximately $1 billion a day. As a percentage of gross domestic product, the trade deficit had increased from less than 1 percent in 1992 to nearly 4 percent in 2000.[1] As a consequence of these deficits, the foreign debt of the United States, by at least one estimate, has risen to more than 20 percent of gross domestic product.[2]

Most disturbing of all, the "consumption binge" of the 1990s caused the personal savings rate of Americans to plunge to approximately zero. The low personal savings rate and the high corporate investment rate, financed in part by borrowing from abroad, resulted in the unprecedented trade and payments deficit that is still increasing as I write this preface. With huge trade / payments deficits year after year, the foreign debt of the United States has reached an all-time high. On the positive side of the national economic ledger, the rapid growth of the economy and a significant tax increase put through by the Clinton Administration enabled the United States to eliminate the federal budget deficit, begin repaying America's huge accumulated public debt of $5.7 trillion, and pass on a large budget surplus to the Bush Administration, which has decided to give rich and especially super-rich Americans substantial tax cuts rather than address the serious social and economic problems of the nation. The Bush Administration's failure to take adequate initiatives to reduce the huge and growing U.S. public and foreign debt is of particular importance from the perspective of this book. As economists warn, the damage to the American economy would be substantial if in response to concerns over the U.S. debt and the value of the dollar, lenders abroad were to liquidate their loans. It has become imperative that the American people learn to live within their means and that the national debt be reduced.

This situation of Americans living beyond their means cannot last; they cannot indefinitely consume more than they produce. Americans cannot realistically expect others to make up the difference through investing in American stocks, bonds, and other assets forever. Dollar-denominated assets, however, will continue to be favored over yen- or euro-denominated assets as long as the Japanese economy remains in recession and the West European economy has its own serious economic problems such as a high level of unemployment and low rates of economic growth. Yet the tide must turn one day, and when it does, Americans will find themselves in a highly uncomfortable position. When the $1 billion a day that flow into the United States dry up and the flight from dollar-denominated assets begins, the dollar will weaken and the economy will suffer. Although the growth of imports would slow eventually and the level of exports would increase, the trade / payments deficit and the debt build-up would probably continue for some time because of the low American personal savings rate. Such developments would cause both employment and the American standard of living to fall, or at least to grow much less rapidly than during the 1990s.

When this book was first published in 2000, I concluded that the combination of a significant decline in the rate of growth of the U.S. economy, a continuing substantial American trade / payments deficit, and an elevated rate of unemployment could trigger a powerful protectionist reaction in the United States, and that such a development would seriously damage the global economy. Although the United

States is the world's largest exporter, it is also the "importer of last resort" for many countries around the world. An American recession and accompanying trade restrictions could set off a vicious cycle of protectionism and trade contraction around the world. Even in the good times of the late 1990s, a number of American economic sectors (notably steel) were demanding and receiving protection against imports. If protectionist demands were to increase and the American government were to lead the way in a global revival of trade protection, "The Second Great Age of Capitalism" would certainly suffer a severe setback.

The fraying of political ties between the United States and its major allies—Japan and Western Europe—is a particular concern of mine. It is regrettable that American international leadership has weakened substantially. The shift from multilateral leadership to unilateralism and to a disregard for the opinions and interests of other nations began in the Reagan Administration with its multitrack trade policy and commitment to North American regionalism (NAFTA). The Clinton Administration continued this shift in its attempt to impose a policy of "managed trade" on Japan. The George W. Bush Administration in its first six months, however, has been even more extreme than its predecessors in its aggressive pursuit of unilateral initiatives, many of which other nations have deeply resented. The most egregious example is its abrupt and callous abandonment of the Kyoto Treaty, which was planned to control both the emissions that most experts consider responsible for "global warming" and the possibly extremely serious consequences of those emissions.

Efforts to strengthen the European Union continue. The West Europeans, for example, have launched a major initiative to create a unified rapid deployment force under European command; however, it is not yet clear whether they will be willing to pay the high cost of such a force. Economic and Monetary Union (EMU) continues on track as the euro replaces national currencies and the European Central Bank takes command over monetary affairs. Yet a number of Northern European nations have decided not to become members of the EMU, and Great Britain, one of the three largest economies in Western Europe, has not joined as of this writing, a situation that could lead to fragmentation of the unification movement. It is doubtful that the EMU can long survive without much greater political unity, at least regarding fiscal policy and other related matters. Moreover, there are increasing political differences between France and Germany, as well as among other countries, over a number of crucial issues. Such important and contentious issues as institutional reform, voting rights, the "democratic deficit," and enlargement of the European Union to include Eastern European countries, make achievement of political unity more difficult. While I continue to cheer for the European Union, I still have reservations regarding its ultimate success. In 2001, Western Europe continues to be a region composed of nation-states with many differing economic and political interests.

In East Asia, one of the most important developments since publication of the book was the decision of the United States in 2000 to support the admission of China to the World Trade Organization (WTO). This major shift in American policy was in large part the consequence of a realization that China and the United States share important economic interests. It was also based on recognition that China has made and is continuing to make major strides in transforming its command economy and introducing important market reforms. Yet abuse of human rights and lack of political freedom continue as serious problems. Despite these political and other issues dividing the two major economies, both nations appreciate the importance of working together for mutual benefit. Nevertheless, it would be foolish to underestimate the difficulties of achieving a long-term harmonious relationship and the need for both sides to respect the interests and concerns of the other.

At the same time that China's presence in the global economy has grown, Japan has continued to wallow in a self-made economic malaise. Although Japan remains a formidable competitor in world markets and a major exporting nation, its economy has continued in recession. As I argue in the book (see chapter 9), Japan's economic problems are fundamentally political. The political and bureaucratic leadership of the country has been unwilling to initiate the basic economic, institutional, and other reforms required to re-ignite economic growth and to create a dynamic entrepreneurial economy based more on domestic-led rather than export-led growth. On a more positive note, the economic tensions between Japan and the United States have eased, largely as a consequence of America's outstanding economic success throughout most of the 1990s. Yet, as I warn in this book, the combination of a recession with growing unemployment and a continuing large trade deficit with Japan and other countries could trigger a strong protectionist movement in the United States.

With respect to the Newly Industrializing Economies of East Asia seriously harmed by the post-1997 East Asian financial crisis, some countries such as South Korea and Thailand have made impressive economic recoveries and have initiated needed structural reforms. Yet these countries have not overcome their economic and political troubles, and many observers fear that they have failed to make the reforms necessary to prevent another serious economic crisis. In Indonesia, the economic and political situation has deteriorated further and is pulling apart this devastated land. Furthermore, little progress has been made in reforming the international financial system to ensure that similar financial crises will not occur in the future.

The economic and political situation of most less developed countries (LDCs) has hardly changed since the book's initial publication. International concern is intensifying over the continuing poverty of much of the human race, and there is a growing tendency to blame the problems of poor countries on globalization, international institutions, and the rich countries, especially the United States. Some reforms have been instituted, including reduction of the debt burden of the poorest countries. Yet, as I argue in another book, *Global Political Economy: Understanding the New International Economic Order* (Princeton 2001), the LDCs are, for one reason or another, actually *insufficiently* globalized rather than harmed by globalization. The three major regions of intense poverty—sub-Saharan Africa, rural India, and rural China—are scarcely integrated into the global economy. Unlike the economies of East Asia, they have neither pursued successful export-led growth strategies nor opened their economies to capital and technology. Moreover, the principal sources of the troubles of many LDCs lie in the countries themselves: war, corrupt or incompetent governments, and, especially in Africa, debilitating diseases. While the industrialized countries can and should do much more to assist the LDCs, such assistance would not have more than a marginal impact unless many LDCs enact major reforms. As demonstrated by the East Asian Newly Industrializing Economies, economic development is primarily the responsibility of each national society.

This book argues that an open and successful international economy based on free markets is dependent on a secure and hospitable political foundation. Domestic or international markets do not just appear but are dependent on international political stability and the supportive policies of national governments. The political prerequisites for an open and stable international economy are three-fold. One or more nations must provide economic and political leadership, and leaders must provide a stable international currency, promote free trade, and establish fair and impartial rules to govern international commerce. A stable international economy must also be based on cooperation among the major economic powers; the economic leader, however powerful it might be, cannot manage the world economy alone (at least not for long), but must work in concert with other important economic powers. And finally, the peoples of the world must believe that free trade and other forms of international commerce work to their advantage; support for openness and free trade would rapidly evaporate if the American, West European, or other peoples began to believe that the global economy worked to their disadvantage.

Since the end of World War II, the political foundations of the international economy have rested on American leadership, close cooperation among the United States and its Cold War allies, and the belief of the American people and others that the open world economy did and would continue to serve their economic and political interests. A number of developments raise doubts that these secure foundations will continue. With the end of the Cold War, both American leadership and the willingness of others to support the U.S. waned appreciably. Little effort has been invested to encourage such rising economic powers as China and other rapidly industrializing economies to become more active in the governance of the international economy. Moreover, as economic globalization has widened and deepened, important economic interests in the United States, Western Europe, and elsewhere have begun to question whether an open international economy is to their advantage; for example, public opinion polls at the turn of the century revealed that more than half of the American people were skeptical of the benefits of economic openness and economic globalization.

Questions surrounding these political and economic developments are especially pertinent to the current Bush Administration. Whereas the Clinton Administration—after much stumbling and vacillation on trade matters—eventually committed itself (albeit not wholeheartedly) to American participation in the global economy, the position of the Bush Administration on trade and other economic matters remains deeply disturbing at this halfway point in its first year in office. One questionable economic development is the Administration's commitment to extend NAFTA to include Latin America; this idea is essentially a revival of President George H. W. Bush's June 1990 "Enterprise for the Americas" proposal. While it is too early to assess this initiative, it would be unfortunate if it distracts the Bush Administration from pursuing more global trade initiatives through the WTO. Without strong American leadership, prospects for the liberal trade regime are dim.

The collapse in November 1999 of the WTO summit in Seattle was an especially worrisome development because it challenged the stability of the political foundations of the world economy. That meeting was convened to deal with the many issues left unresolved in the Uruguay Round of trade negotiations and to launch the Millennium Round. The ambitious agenda before the assembled trade ministers included such items as significant reductions in overall trade barriers, review of WTO anti-dumping and anti-subsidy rules to curb abuse (especially by the United States) of these otherwise legitimate trade rules, and granting of duty-free access for the poorest countries to the markets of the industrial economies. Unfortunately, that trade summit was devastated by a number of unprecedented political developments. To understand the most dramatic aspect of the Seattle debacle—the violent street protests—one must appreciate the importance, at least in the United States, of what has been labeled the "new trade agenda."

As the volume of world trade has expanded and as trade has penetrated more and more deeply into national societies, it has become increasingly entwined with politically sensitive matters and has come into conflict with powerful domestic interests, especially in the United States. This development has produced the "new trade agenda," which includes such highly controversial issues as labor standards and human rights, the environment, and national sovereignty. Some proponents of the new trade agenda on both the political Left and Right are unalterably opposed to free trade and are outright protectionists; indeed, parts of American organized labor provide a prime example. Most advocates of one or another of the issues on the new trade agenda want radical changes in the WTO that would greatly weaken the effectiveness of that institution and would undermine the trade regime. Examination of the new trade agenda and the intense political controversy surrounding various items reveals serious threats to the trade regime that will be difficult to counter.[3]

Considerable conflict has arisen regarding whether the important and politically sensitive issues of "fair" labor standards, human rights, and environmental protection should be treated together with conventional trade issues or in a different venue. Powerful groups, especially in the United States and Western Europe, strongly believe that these matters should be incorporated into the international trade regime and that trade liberalization should be made subordinate to achievement of such specific objectives as human rights and environmental protection. On the other hand, most economists, governments, and business groups are strongly opposed to integrating these issues into international trade negotiations and fear that, however well intended some groups may be, the important issues of labor standards, human rights, and environmental protection will be and are being exploited by outright protectionists. Indeed, the political stalemate generated by these clashing positions led to the 1997 defeat of President Clinton's request for "fast track" authority, an authority that could have greatly facilitated negotiation of trade agreements. Thus far President Bush has been hesitant to ask Congress for such authority.

In the United States and elsewhere, the opposition of environmentalists to the trade regime has grown intense.[4] Environmentalist critics fall into two major camps. One accepts the principle of free trade but believes that environmental protection should be incorporated into trade negotiations and given equal, if not higher priority than trade liberalization itself. This group also believes that the WTO and its dispute-settlement mechanism should be more open to the public. Advocates of a more radical position believe that free trade and the globalized economy itself are a threat to the environment; they reject the WTO because they consider the WTO an instrument of powerful corporate interests; this group also agrees with American neo-isolationist conservatives that WTO actions infringe upon American sovereignty. The environmentalists have become a formidable force in the political struggle over trade policy.

The issues initially raised by environmentalists and other protest groups in Seattle are serious and must be addressed by national governments. Yet, with a few particularly important exceptions such as global warming and pollution of the oceans, almost every environmental issue can be dealt with most effectively on a domestic or regional basis; moreover, the serious problems of nuclear and other hazardous wastes, water contamination, air pollution, toxic dumps, and carbon dioxide emissions have little or nothing to do with international trade. One of the most vehement groups of protesters in Seattle consisted of opponents of logging and especially of "clear cutting." This problem is primarily the result of high government subsidies to timber companies (as in Alaska), inadequate governmental regulations, and land-hungry farmers and national development strategies in many LDCs. Although the responsibility for over-cutting belongs to national governments, the WTO has been made the whipping boy of many environmentalists in this and many other matters. Moreover, even when environmental issues do relate to international trade (as in the cases of ocean oil spills and trade in endangered species), the WTO has neither the authority nor the power to deal with such matters. These pressing problems, however, can be dealt with most effectively through such other mechanisms as international conventions. The international agreement on safety rules for genetically modified foods, despite its imperfections, provides an example of such an alternative procedure.[5]

The issue of labor standards has become a major impediment to trade liberalization, especially in the United States, where this issue has been raised forcefully by organized labor and, to a lesser extent, by human rights advocates genuinely concerned over child labor in LDCs generally and in China particularly. It is worth noting that a disproportionate number of the street protesters in Seattle were union members mobilized by the American AFL-CIO, whose president, John Sweeney, rejoiced at the collapse of the meeting. Although the International Labor Organization (ILO) has established labor standards, most advocates of labor standards and opponents of child labor believe that the ILO is incapable of enforcing its standards; moreover, the United States and a number of other countries have not even ratified all ILO standards. Furthermore, even though many advocates of labor standards and of prohibitions against child labor are genuinely concerned over the oppressive conditions of labor in many countries, others use the issue as a protectionist device.

Most economists, businesses, and national governments reject the idea that labor standards and human rights should be incorporated into trade negotiations. Economists are concerned that inclusion would unduly complicate the already overwhelming task of achieving agreement on trade liberalization, and that it would provide a convenient and effective rationale for protectionist measures against low-wage economies. Developing countries themselves have strongly denounced efforts to impose "Western" standards on them. They have reason to believe that such proposals are frequently motivated by protectionist interests and would be used to reduce the principal comparative advantage of developing countries based on low-wage labor and provision of only minimum welfare benefits.

The closely related issues of labor standards, human rights, and child labor are legitimate and need to be addressed. Also, some countries are undoubtedly guilty of "social dumping," that is, of gaining competitiveness through their denial of workers' fundamental rights and decent working conditions. Remedying these problems, however, will be extraordinarily difficult. As almost every LDC is strongly opposed to incorporating labor standards and human rights into the WTO, a concerted effort to do so could destroy the effectiveness of the organization. It is particularly ironic that many protestors at Seattle denounced the rulings of the WTO as an infringement of American sovereignty at the same time that they and others advocated that the WTO impose labor and human rights standards on delinquent LDCs! Needless to say, reconciling the positions of those who support and those who oppose incorporation of workers' rights within the trade regime will be difficult indeed.

Ultimately, a combination of education and economic development is needed to provide solutions to the associated problems of labor standards, human rights, and child labor. In general, the countries with the highest labor standards and respect for human rights are the most developed countries; this is, at least partially, because they are wealthy and have a strong and concerned middle class. In societies with low per capita income where parents frequently need the wages of their children, such outside interventions as trade sanctions are unlikely to succeed.[6] In the short term, the best solution is to exert organized consumer pressure against those business firms that violate human rights, use child labor, and abuse other labor standards.

A particularly disturbing aspect of the new trade agenda is that the WTO and other international economic institutions have come under heated attack from an alliance of environmentalists and human rights advocates with protectionist trade unions and even ultra-conservative neo-isolationists. In the vehement protests surrounding the WTO's November 1999 meeting in Seattle, the International Monetary Fund (IMF) / World Bank meeting in April 2000 in Washington, D.C., and the Group of Eight meeting in August 2001 in Genoa, and during other such protests, the WTO, other international agencies, and wealthy countries became the enemy for concerned and frustrated groups around the globe who want the world to be different from its present unfortunate state. The demands of protesters have included abolishing the WTO and other international economic organizations because they are undemocratic and unresponsive to the needs of the world's poor. Those groups and individuals who blame globalization for their own and the world's problems now view the WTO, the World Bank, and the IMF as symbols of feared and predatory global capitalism.

The Seattle protest was a crucial watershed in the politics surrounding the global economy. It constituted the first major attack on what many consider the evils of economic globalization and on those international institutions and national governments, especially the U.S. government, that promote a more open and integrated global economy. Growing global inequalities, environmental degradation, and other problems that protestors associate with global capitalism, were put on the international agenda by many protests. Because it was the Seattle protest that launched this wholesale attack on economic globalization, the rest of this preface will concentrate on the Seattle events and the issues they raised.

Although the Seattle street protestors and their vehement attacks on the WTO attracted most of the attention at the November 1999 WTO meeting, primary responsibility for the abysmal failure of that meeting belongs to the major economic powers and to the Clinton Administration in particular. For domestic political reasons, President Clinton tried to force the conference to include the issue of "labor standards" on the agenda of future trade negotiations; his irresponsible reference in a newspaper interview to the possible imposition of economic sanctions on countries that did not meet certain labor standards was especially infuriating to developing countries who, quite correctly, viewed the president's motives as politically motivated and protectionist. Another factor in the breakdown of the negotiations was the inexperience of the then recently appointed WTO director-general, Mike Moore. Still other factors were inadequate preparation for the meeting, no previously agreed agenda, and the unwieldiness of a meeting composed of 135 member-nations,

The unwillingness of the major economic powers, especially the United States and the European Union, to contemplate serious trade liberalization was critical in the Seattle fiasco. All of the major economic powers had different agendas that conflicted with one another and precluded a successful outcome. High on the Clinton Administration's formal agenda were such issues as the elimination of European and Japanese agricultural subsidies and the protection of intellectual property rights. At the conference, however, the President subordinated even this formal agenda to the issue of labor standards. Furthermore, the President refused to discuss the outrage in Japan and other countries over his Administration's extensive and improper use of the WTO's anti-dumping provision as a protectionist device.[7] The Administration also opposed the European Union's strong desire to put competition (anti-trust) policy on the agenda, and instead supported a narrow agenda favoring American export interests—financial services, information technology, aircraft, and agriculture—and did so with little regard for the interests of others.

At Seattle both Japanese and West Europeans, also for domestic political reasons, adamantly opposed opening their economies to American and other nations' agricultural exports. Within the European Union, protection of agriculture through large subsidies to farmers is considered essential to the achievement of European economic and political integration. In Japan, the ruling Liberal Democratic Party, needing the votes of rural Japan, opposed opening its market to imports of rice and other agricultural products. The inability of the major economic powers to find compromises of these fundamental differences doomed the conference to failure. For all three major participants, domestic political objectives took precedence over trade liberalization.

Because these issues have not yet been resolved or even seriously discussed, prospects for a major breakthrough in trade negotiations are not especially promising as I write this. Trade barriers have declined in such sectors as textiles and agriculture, but only to a level politically acceptable to powerful domestic constituencies in the United States and other industrialized countries. The United States and Western Europe—the two largest trading powers—are at odds over a number of difficult issues, including genetically modified food, European trade discrimination, and American corporate tax policies. Moreover, public opinion in the United States and European Union has grown increasingly concerned about the impact of imports, especially from low-wage economies. LDCs have also become increasingly disillusioned with opening their markets. The experience of the East Asian economic crisis increased concerns about the dangers of opening national economies.[8] Re-energizing the process of trade liberalization will require strong political leadership and international cooperation.

One important result of the meeting and the accompanying protests was a widespread sense that the international institutions governing the world economy, such as the WTO, the World Bank, and the IMF, have become totally inadequate for a highly integrated global economy. Clearly, these and other international institutions face a number of critical issues whose solution will greatly affect their future. One pressing issue given public prominence by the Seattle protestors is the "democratic deficit," that is, international economic institutions are criticized because they are not accountable to any democratic electorate. Closely tied to this issue is the gap between the authority of existing institutions and the changing distribution of economic power in the international system. Despite the significant shift in economic power that occurred in the last half of the twentieth century, especially the shift toward East Asia, decision-making authority and responsibility in the IMF, WTO, and World Bank continue to reside mainly with the United States and, to a lesser extent, with Western Europe. Still another issue is the question of institutional reform.

In the interest of efficient decision-making and in deference to member governments' desires to keep their national affairs confidential, every important international organization operates largely in secrecy; the predilection toward secrecy is reinforced by fears that negotiations on trade, monetary, and other economic matters could roil and seriously destabilize global markets; a proposed change in exchange rates, for example, could raise havoc in currency markets. Still, more and more people are coming to believe that their daily lives, cultures, and social well-being are subject to secret decisions made by faceless international bureaucrats. Such growing concerns feed the backlash against globalization and undermine the foundations of the global economy.

The Seattle meeting of the WTO illustrated the difficulties encountered in the search for a solution to the democratic deficit. In addition to launching the Millennium Round of trade negotiations, the conclave of trade ministers was expected to begin a concerted effort to reform the organization and strengthen the WTO's authority over trade-dispute settlement procedures and other matters. The WTO has more authority over national policies than does any other international economic organization. Whereas the IMF and the World Bank do have significant influence over LDCs needing financial and other forms of assistance, the WTO's authority over trade matters extends to every one of its members, including the United States, Western Europe, and Japan. Unlike any other international organization, the WTO has the authority to penalize and impose a monetary fine on any country that defies the decisions of its dispute-settlement panels. Indeed, WTO judicial and regulatory powers are unprecedented among international organizations.

Moreover, despite what many Seattle protesters believe, the WTO is the most democratic of the important international institutions, with the possible exception of the United Nations General Assembly. In the

WTO, every one of the more than 130 members has a single vote; the major economic powers have no formal privileged position. Both the World Bank and the IMF do have a system of weighted voting that greatly favors the United States, Western Europe, and, to a lesser extent, Japan. Yet despite its more democratic nature, doubters still question the WTO's legitimacy.

One of the most important demands of the Seattle protestors was that the WTO's decisions and, by implication, those of other international institutions, be made transparent to the public. In addition to openness, many demanded that non-governmental organizations (NGOs) (especially those dealing with human rights, labor, and environmental problems) should be permitted to participate in the decision-making process of the WTO and of other international organizations; private groups and individuals should be permitted to submit briefs and provide testimony regarding matters under consideration. Superficially, these demands for greater democratic accountability appear reasonable. Indeed, if the larger public is to accept as legitimate the international institutions and their decisions, then greater openness and accountability are necessary. Yet formidable obstacles block the achievement of increased openness. Some international organizations are notoriously inefficient, and inclusion of additional participants would greatly complicate decision-making. Also, the decisions of international organizations involve sovereign nations. Making the WTO's dispute-settlement mechanism more transparent would mean that the states party to these disputes would have to reveal sensitive information that they and powerful domestic constituents would prefer to keep secret. In such a situation, member governments could lose confidence in the WTO and be tempted to move outside the organization to resolve their differences.

Although a serious effort must be made to solve the democratic deficit, it will be extremely difficult to achieve both increased efficiency and greater transparency, the two seemingly contradictory goals set forth by the EU trade commissioner, Pascal Lamy, following the Seattle debacle. The WTO is indeed undemocratic in the sense that it is not directly accountable to any electorate; however, it is difficult to envisage an electorate to which it and other international institutions could be made accountable. Although the NGOs at Seattle insisted that international institutions be made accountable to them, they themselves are not accountable to any public electorate. Moreover, it is important to recognize that nearly every international, regional, and even national organization responsible for managing our highly complex and integrated world is also characterized by a democratic deficit and is not directly accountable to citizens; this group includes the Security Council of the United Nations, the International Court of Justice, the World Health Organization, the European Commission, NATO, and the American Federal Reserve as well as a multitude of others. These organizations, however, as well as the WTO and other international organizations, are ultimately accountable to national governments that, at least in democratic systems, are themselves accountable to an electorate. Until the peoples of the world come together in one global society, the ultimate responsibility for governing the world has to rest with national governments and their representatives.

Another important problem confronting international institutions is the growing gap between the distribution of authority within existing international institutions and the international distribution of economic power. When the original Bretton Woods institutions—IMF, World Bank, and GATT / WTO—were established in the early postwar era and when they were subsequently modified, authority over these organizations was in essence vested in the United States and Western Europe. By custom, selection of the director of the World Bank became the prerogative of the United States, and selection of the head of the IMF, the prerogative of Western Europe; furthermore, these major powers did and do have the ability to block any appointment or action of which they disapprove. As they themselves have developed and gained greater economic strength, Japan and the LDCs, especially the larger LDCs, have increasingly resented this arrangement and have demanded more authority and more leadership roles. This issue came to the fore in early 2000 in efforts to decide on the appointment of a new director of the IMF after the resignation of Michel Camdessus. Following tradition, the West Europeans proposed their nominee (German finance official Caio Koch-Weser) whom they assumed would be chosen. Unexpectedly, both Japan and an unusual coalition of LDCs nominated alternate candidates.[9] Although the United States did not contest the "right" of the Europeans to choose the head of the IMF, it did raise serious questions about Koch-Weser's qualifications. Eventually, the dispute was settled when an "acceptable" German (Horst Kohler) was nominated.

Underlying this seemingly minor dispute was the more fundamental question of which nation(s) will control or predominate in those institutions responsible for managing the global economy.[10] This issue has long divided the United States and Western Europe; in this instance, even though many Europeans also had reservations about Mr. Koch-Weser, they (especially the French) regarded his candidacy as a means to prevent growing American domination of the IMF and other international institutions. In addition, West Europeans had become increasingly concerned that their position in the international economic and political system was diminishing. German insistence that it was their turn to select the IMF director reflected their desire to be recognized again as a great power. Alas! National pride is still very much with us.

In practice, the United States has been the dominant power in the IMF as well as in the World Bank and the GATT / WTO. In the several financial crises that have afflicted the international economy, including the 1994–1995 Mexican crisis and the post-1997 East Asian crisis, the United States in effect dictated IMF responses. In the realm of trade, the United States initiated every round of trade negotiations and largely set the agenda. West Europeans and other powers have frequently opposed the United States as it performed its leadership role; the United States had to put considerable pressure on the West Europeans to get them even to participate in the Uruguay Round. Nevertheless, West Europeans have also exercised inordinate influence in both the GATT and the WTO. It is not excessive to say that the United States and Western Europe, because of their sheer economic strength, have been and continue to be the dominant players in the international economic system.

The continuing American and West European dominance in the WTO, IMF, and World Bank has become more and more distasteful to a Japan increasingly unhappy about its subordinate role in these institutions. Although Japan is the second largest donor to such international institutions as the Organisation for Economic Co-Operation and Development and the IMF, no Japanese has ever been elected head of, or even been seriously considered for the directorship of any important international economic institution other than the Asian Development Bank. Japan is also very resentful of the IMF's handling of the 1997 Asian financial crisis and the ways in which the IMF has operated in that region. The Japanese, as well as other East Asians, believe that the IMF is too much under American influence. In 1999, Japan proposed its own candidate to be the next director general of the IMF and requested support for that candidate from other Asian nations. Japan's new assertiveness highlights the fact that leadership of the international institutions responsible for managing the global economy continues to reside with the West despite the shift in the global balance of economic power toward non-Western powers. This discontinuity between authority and power must one day be rectified if these institutions are to survive.

For the first time, Western dominance of the WTO was successfully challenged by the LDCs when they blocked major items on the Seattle agendas proposed by the Americans and Europeans. The Seattle conclave witnessed a new and potentially important development in the governance of the WTO. Led by Brazil, Egypt, and India, LDCs that by then possessed an overwhelming majority of the votes in the WTO were successfully mobilized. Although they were not able to achieve their own agenda, they did thwart the efforts of the United States to incorporate labor standards and environmental protection into the trade regime. The LDCs discovered that they could influence the rules governing the international economy and could prevent adoption of rules contrary to their interests. How the LDCs will choose to exercise this newfound power remains unclear. Obviously, China will play a large role in these matters.

The various developments surrounding the Seattle disaster could have the unfortunate consequence of encouraging the major economic powers to abandon the WTO's multilateral approach to lowering trade barriers and to turn toward trade negotiations conducted on a bilateral or regional basis on terms highly favorable to the major powers. Abandonment of multilateral trade negotiations would be highly detrimental to the world trading system and especially to the LDCs. Although the protesters in Seattle believed that the WTO was a prisoner of corporate interests, it is actually the weak, rather than the strong, who benefit most from the rule of law. If bilateralism and regionalism were to replace the WTO's multilateralism, more restrictive trading arrangements would undoubtedly increase and eclipse the postwar effort to achieve a multilateral trading system based on generally accepted rules.

In fact, growing evidence suggests that the movement from multilateral trade negotiations to bilateral and regional negotiations has been accelerating since the collapse of the Seattle meeting. The European Union is continuing to create a regional economic sphere, and, as I point out in the book, trade discrimination has tended to accompany enlargement of the European Union. For its part, the United States appears to have retreated from its former leadership role in multinational trade negotiations. There are other examples of the global de-emphasis on multilateral trade negotiations that I could cite.

The concerns expressed by the Seattle protestors, the dissension among the major industrial powers, and the challenge of the industrializing countries to the international economic order have raised the issue of "international governance." How is an increasingly integrated world characterized by fractious sovereign nation-states to be managed effectively, and how can stability and fairness be ensured? Scholars have set forth a number of proposals to improve governance of the global economy, including reform and strengthening of existing international institutions and greater reliance in international decision-making on such NGOs as activist environmental groups. Although many of these proposals have merit, they have not adequately addressed the fundamental question of "governance for what?" Toward what ends and in whose interest will international governance be exercised?

Governance first and last is about the exercise of power to achieve political, social, and other objectives. Every scheme to govern the global economy must confront the question of the purpose to be served by mechanisms proposed for governing the global economy. At the end of the Cold War and with the triumph of global capitalism, the purpose of the international economy seemed resolved. Most American officials, business leaders, and professional economists were convinced that the purpose of the global economy and the ways in which it should be managed were settled. They believed that the global economy should maximize global wealth and should be governed in accordance with the policy prescriptions of neo-classical economics; that is, the rules governing the global economy should be based on market principles. Free trade, freedom of capital movements, and unrestricted access by multinational firms to markets around the globe henceforth would be the goals of international governance.

On April 15 and 16, 2000, this neo-liberal consensus was challenged on two fronts. In Washington, D.C., thousands of protestors gathered in the streets to denounce the alleged evils of global capitalism and demand that the IMF, WTO, and World Bank be made more accountable to environmental and other humanitarian concerns. However misguided many of these protestors may have been, they represented millions of Americans and others worried about the alleged negative consequences of economic globalization for wages, job security, the environment, growing inequalities, and other concerns. At the time of the Washington protests, the Group of 77, representing the world's LDCs, was meeting several hundred miles to the south in Havana to draft demands for a larger share of the world's wealth and a strengthened voice in governance of the global economy. Unlike the protestors in Washington, however, these countries did not oppose global capitalism, but rather demanded a more equitable distribution of its fruits. Thus, although both the Washington protestors and the Group of 77 demanded increased control over the global economy, their social, economic, and political purposes were largely opposed. On such issues as debt relief for poor countries, increased financial assistance to LDCs, and greater control over multinational corporations their agendas did coincide. With respect to other fundamental issues such as delegation of greater authority to the WTO over environmental matters, human rights, and labor standards, however, the protestors and the Group of 77 could not have been farther apart.

Both the Washington protestors and the Group of 77 demanded fundamental changes in the purposes pursued by the governing institutions of the global economy. Making their differing demands, they rejected an international economy based solely on the principles of neo-classical economics and market principles. In place of the exclusively economic objectives of neo-liberalism, the Group of 77 and the protestors wanted to substitute one or another of such non-market objectives as protecting the environment, safeguarding workers' rights, or redistribution of global wealth to poor countries. Once again the battle has been joined between those who desire a world governed by the market and those who want the market subordinated to some higher political authority that would pursue various social purposes. Throughout much of modern history, this battle over the ends of economic activity has been fought principally at the domestic level between the representatives of capital and those of labor. In the increasingly integrated global economy of the twenty-first century, the entire globe has become the battleground, and the types as well as the number of participants have greatly expanded to include nation-states, international organizations, and NGOs. The twenty-first century contest over the nature of the new global economic order has begun.

August 15, 2001

Notes

1. *New York Times*, February 23, 2001, C1.
2. *New York Times*, June 8, 2000, C2. The size of this debt is extraordinary. In early 2001, foreigners owned 38 percent of outstanding Treasuries and 20 percent of corporate bonds. *New York Times*, February 23, 2001, C1.
3. These matters are discussed in I. M. Destler and Peter J. Balint, *The New Politics of American Trade: Trade, Labor, and the Environment* (Washington, D.C.: Institute for International Economics, 1999).
4. Daniel C. Esty, *Greening the GATT: Trade, Environment, and the Future* (Washington, D.C.: Institute for International Economics, 1994).
5. Although this agreement was hardly perfect, it permits countries to bar import of genetically modified foods. *New York Times*, January 30, 2000, A1.
6. Economists such as Jeffrey Sachs and Paul R. Krugman have pointed out that the most important issue in many LDCs is whether there will be enough jobs.
7. Under both GATT and WTO rules, a country can impose duties on goods being dumped on the world market. Both the United States and Western Europe have grossly misused this safeguard provision for purely protectionist purposes.
8. David Woods, "The Seattle Fiasco," *Braudel Papers*, no. 24 (2000), 1.
9. The candidate of the coalition of African and Arab states was Stanley Fischer, a distinguished American economist and highly experienced IMF official. The Japanese, supported by some East Asian countries, nominated Eisuke Sakakibara, a former high official in the Ministry of Finance, colloquially known as "Mr. Yen," in part because of his strong and outspoken criticisms of American monetary policy.
10. Votes in the IMF are based on a country's financial contribution. On this basis, the United States has 17 percent of the votes, and the combined vote of the 15 European Union members is 37 percent. Thus, the United States and the European Union together control just over a majority of the votes.

* Acknowledgments *

IN THE PREPARATION of this book, I have benefited greatly from the support and assistance of many institutions and individuals. My most important debt is to the Woodrow Wilson School and the Center of International Studies of Princeton University for their financial and other support. The Abe Fellowship Program, funded principally by the Japan Foundation Center for Global Partnership, also generously supported my research. I also wish to thank the John Sloan Dickey Center for International Understanding at Dartmouth College for providing me with an intellectual home during the winter term 1998. Special thanks are due to Joanne Gowa, Robert Keohane, and Atul Kohli, who gave me excellent comments on an early version of the manuscript. Seminars sponsored by the Dickey Center, the Department of Political Science of MIT, and the Department of Political Science at the University of Vermont enabled me to receive outstanding criticisms of my ideas. Special thanks are due to Malcolm Litchfield of Princeton University Press, especially for his patience with missed deadlines and other trying experiences with the author as he shepherded this book through the Press.

* List of Abbreviations *

ADCs	advanced developed (or industrialized) countries
AFDC	Aid to Families with Dependent Children
AMF	Asian Monetary Fund
APEC	Asia-Pacific Economic Cooperation
ASEAN	Association of South East Asian Nations
BWS	Bretton Woods System
CAP	Common Agricultural Policy
EC	European Community
ECB	European Central Bank
EcoFin	European Union financial ministers
EEC	European Economic Community (Common Market)
EMI	European Monetary Institute
EMS	European Monetary System
EMU	Economic and Monetary Union
ERM	Exchange Rate Mechanism
ESCB	European System of Central Banks
EU	European Union
Euroland	members of the EMU
Euro-zone	*refer to* Euroland
FDI	foreign direct investment
FTA	Free Trade Agreement (between the United States and Canada)
G-7	Group of seven major developed economies
GATS	General Agreement on Trade in Services
GATT	General Agreement on Tariffs and Trade
GDP	Gross Domestic Product (sometimes used interchangeably with GNP)
GNP	Gross National Product (sometimes used interchangeably with GDP)
IMF	International Monetary Fund
IPC	international policy coordination
ITO	International Trade Organization
LDC	less developed country
MAI	Multilateral Agreement on Investment
Mercosur	Regional agreement among Argentina, Brazil, and other Latin American countries.
MITI	Japanese Ministry of Trade and Investment
MNC	multinational corporation
MOF	Japanese Ministry of Finance
MOSS	Market-Oriented, Sector Selective

NAE	New American Economy
NAFTA	North American Free Trade Agreement
NAIRU	Non-Accelerating Inflation Rate of Unemployment
NIEO	New International Economic Order
OCA	optimum currency area
ODA	Official Development Assistance
OECD	Organization of Economic Cooperation and Development
OEEC	Organization for European Economic Cooperation
OPEC	Organization of Petroleum Exporting Countries
R and D	research and development
RTA	regional trade agreement
SDRs	Special Drawing Rights
SEA	Single European Act
SEZ	Special Economic Zone
SII	Structural Impediments Initiative
TRIMs	Trade-Related Investment Measures
TRIPs	Trade-Related Aspects of Intellectual Property Rights
UN	United Nations
USTR	United States Trade Representative
VER	voluntary export restraint
WB	World Bank
WTO	World Trade Organization

The Challenge of
Global Capitalism

*

✳ *Introduction* ✳

THE FRAGILE GLOBAL ECONOMY

Capitalism is the most successful wealth-creating economic system that the world has ever known; no other system, as the distinguished economist Joseph Schumpeter pointed out, has benefited "the common people" as much. Capitalism, he observed, creates wealth through advancing continuously to ever higher levels of productivity and technological sophistication; this process requires that the "old" be destroyed before the "new" can take over. Technological progress, the ultimate driving force of capitalism, requires the continuous discarding of obsolete factories, economic sectors, and even human skills. The system rewards the adaptable and the efficient; it punishes the redundant and the less productive.

This "process of creative destruction," to use Schumpeter's term, produces many winners but also many losers, at least in the short term, and poses a serious threat to traditional social values, beliefs, and institutions. Moreover, the advance of capitalism is accompanied by periodic recessions and downturns that can wreak havoc in peoples' lives. Although capitalism eventually distributes wealth more equally than any other known economic system, as it does tend to reward the most efficient and productive, it tends to concentrate wealth, power, and economic activities. Threatened individuals, groups, or nations constitute an ever-present force that could overthrow or at least significantly disrupt the capitalist system.

Revolt in the international system against a global economy characterized by open markets, unrestricted capital flows, and the activities of multinational firms appears repeatedly in the guise of trade protection, closed economic blocs, and various kinds of cheating. Individual nations and powerful groups within nations that believe the world economy functions unfairly and to their disadvantage, or who wish to change the system to benefit themselves to the detriment of others, are an ever-present threat to the stability of the system.

The international capitalist system could not possibly survive without strong and wise leadership. International leadership must promote

3

international cooperation to establish and enforce rules regulating trade, foreign investment, and international monetary affairs. But it is equally important that leadership ensure at least minimal safeguards for the inevitable losers from market forces and from the process of creative destruction; those who lose must at least believe that the system functions fairly. Continuation of the market or capitalist system will remain in jeopardy unless considerations of efficiency are counterbalanced by social protection for the economically weak and training/education of those workers left behind by rapid economic and technological change.

With the 1989 end of the Cold War, many proclaimed the "triumph of global capitalism," and by the late-1990s, the American people were enjoying what *The Economist* of London called the "longest-ever . . . economic expansion." Unemployment (about 4 percent) was the lowest in almost thirty years, wages were up for most American workers, and inflation was low; this was indeed an economic achievement. The performance of the stock market was extraordinary as the Dow Jones index broke through the 10,000 mark in the spring of 1999; the "wealth effect" of the high stock market, which encouraged Americans to spend freely, draw down their personal savings, and go deeply into debt, fueled rapid economic growth. With the rest of the world in recession or other dire economic straits, many Americans believed that the United States in the 1990s had fashioned a new type of capitalist economy and had escaped forever from ills historically associated with the capitalist system.

This New American Economy (NAE), many declared, had been created by several important developments, including the freeing of markets from excessive government regulations, downsizing and restructuring of American corporations, and rapid technological advances (especially the computer, information technologies, and the Internet). Moreover, economic globalization, high rates of productivity growth, and the openness of the American economy to imports had kept prices down and dampened inflationary pressures, thereby allowing the Federal Reserve (America's central bank) to pursue expansionary economic policies. Moreover, reduction of the federal budget deficit, superior business management, and reinvigorated American entrepreneurship had made the American economy better suited than its Japanese and European competitors to take advantage of the Internet economy and the inevitable shift of the advanced economies from manufacturing to service industries. These developments had greatly increased the international competitiveness of the American economy.

Enthusiastic supporters of the NAE even proclaimed that the American economy had transcended the "boom and bust" of the business cycle that has historically plagued capitalist economies. It seemed that the economic boom could continue forever. Most academic economists, on the other hand, were skeptical of such claims and warned that the American economy was experiencing a "speculative bubble." Like the Japanese bubble of the late 1980s and similar bubbles of the past, the American bubble would also necessarily burst one day.

Rejoicing in their own good fortune, Americans failed to appreciate that the country's prosperity was highly dependent on the global economy and that, in international economic affairs as in other aspects of life, no person or country is an island. Few appeared to be aware that, although global capitalism had indeed triumphed, the larger global economy was in serious trouble. Nor were they concerned that the Clinton Administration and the Congress were doing very little about it. However, rapid U.S. economic growth throughout much of the 1990s was significantly assisted by exports to overseas markets and also by large amounts of imported capital as well as by inexpensive imports. The United States is one of the world's largest exporters, and long-term economic progress is dependent on these exports. Many American workers benefit greatly from the export economy because exports are associated with higher paying jobs. With the lowest rate of personal savings in the industrialized world, the American economy has also become very dependent on capital imports, and it prospered in the 1990s in part because foreign investors were contributing significantly to financing the American stock market and thus to economic growth.

Although the changes associated with the NAE provide part of the explanation of America's good economic fortune in the 1990s, equally important contributing factors included skillful management of the economy by the Federal Reserve under the chairmanship of Alan Greenspan and just plain good luck. And the United States benefited from highly favorable international developments. The victory over inflation and low interest rates was due in large part to the fact that the rest of the world economy was experiencing slow growth or recession

5

throughout much of the 1990s; this situation led to lower import prices, especially for petroleum, other raw materials, and consumer goods. For the same reason, the United States has been able to import huge amounts of capital on highly favorable terms; with few other places to invest their capital, both American and foreign investors inflated the American stock market or purchased Treasury bills. As Greenspan has warned, the resultant accumulation of foreign debt could cause the dollar to fall significantly and cannot continue forever.

Resumption of economic growth in Europe and Asia would lessen these favorable conditions and, in the short term, would slow U.S. economic growth, even though over the longer term a revival of global economic growth would immensely benefit American exports. Furthermore, it is not clear that the revival of productivity in the late 1990s can be sustained. During the Reagan boom of the early 1980s, a similar jump in productivity occurred; that boom dissipated by the end of the decade. The increase in productivity in the 1990s could be due to the fact that Americans have been working harder and longer during the boom years rather than be a consequence of the computer and information economy.

Throughout the 1980s and 1990s, America's trade/payments deficits reached record highs. Since the early 1980s, in fact, Americans have borrowed approximately $5 trillion from the savers of the world, especially the Japanese, to finance their consumption and investment. In the mid-1980s, the United States went from its post–World War I position as the world's largest creditor nation to become its largest debtor. If one discounts American investment overseas, the net American international debt in the late 1990s stood at approximately $1 trillion; as a consequence, a sizable portion of the federal budget must be devoted to interest payments on this huge and increasing debt. Furthermore, throughout the 1990s, Americans had emptied their personal savings accounts to fuel "seven years of good times," leaving too little for the "seven years of bad times" that many and perhaps most economists believe loom ahead; the spending spree left 20 percent of American households net debtors. And the "good times" of the 1990s left many behind as the income of the least skilled lagged.[1] Americans appeared to be unaware that one day the nation's huge accumulated debt will have to be repaid and serious adjustments in the American standard of living will be necessary.

If Japan, Western Europe, and the "emerging" markets of East Asia had also grown rapidly throughout the 1990s, world commodity prices (e.g., for oil, food, and raw materials) would have soared and increased inflationary pressures, and thus would have dampened American economic growth. However, America's unprecedented good economic fortune will one day run out, and when it does the United States must confront its low personal savings rate, deteriorating education system, and accumulated foreign debt, and it must also adjust to a rapidly changing global economy characterized by intensifying competition, exclusive regional arrangements, and an unstable international financial system. The developments transforming the global economy pose a significant challenge to the United States.

Propelled by a number of political, economic, and technological developments, the world has moved from the sharply divided international economy of the Cold War to an increasingly integrated global capitalist economy. The end of the Cold War in 1989 and the subsequent disintegration of the Soviet empire were, of course, extremely important to this change. The rapid industrialization in the 1980s and 1990s of the emerging markets of East Asia, Latin America, and elsewhere shifted global economic power and created an increasingly competitive international economy. Furthermore, the continuing technological revolution associated with the computer and the emergence of the information economy accelerated the shift of the advanced industrialized countries from manufacturing-based toward service-based economies. Enormous increases in international trade, financial flows, and the activities of multinational corporations integrated more and more economies into the global economic system in a process now familiarly known as "globalization." However, by the end of the decade these developments had also produced upheaval in both domestic and international affairs.

The global economic turmoil of the late 1990s, which began in Thailand in July 1997, reflected the growing impact of global economic forces on international economic and political affairs. Spreading quickly throughout the industrializing economies of Pacific Asia,

7

and even to Japan (already afflicted by serious economic and political troubles), this turmoil soon engulfed much of the world. By the fall of 1998, a quarter of the world economy, including that of Japan, which is the world's second-largest economy, was in recession. Evaporation of wealth in Pacific Asia and elsewhere was enormous, and commodity-exporting countries, including the United States, suffered huge losses as their export markets dried up. Although the Russian economy consti-tuted only a small portion of the international economy and its troubles were largely of its own making, disturbing economic news from Russia in the late summer of 1998 roiled international financial markets, and a large drop in the American and other national stock markets followed. The psychological impact of these developments caused worried inves-tors to withdraw from Brazil and other emerging markets.

Whereas the emerging markets had been hailed in the early 1990s as a source of huge profits for American investors, by the end of the de-cade they were considered a major source of global economic and polit-ical instability. In the 1980s, it would have been unthinkable that a financial crisis originating in a minor Southeast Asian economy could bring harm not only to the United States but also to the rest of the world. Indeed, during the Reagan and Bush Administrations (1981–1993), the United States had been celebrated as the only true super-power; President Bush (following victory in the Gulf War) proclaimed the "New World Order" of peace, prosperity, and democracy with, of course, the United States at its core. A decade later, however, serious doubts had arisen about the prospects for a prosperous and peaceful new world order based on American leadership.

At the beginning of the twenty-first century, the increasingly open global economy is threatened. Although the East Asian and global fi-nancial troubles have significantly moderated, the vulnerability of the international financial and monetary system threatens the stability of the global economy; although financial crises appear to be an inherent feature of international capitalism, only half-hearted measures have been taken to prevent future financial crises. In addition, the unity and integration of the global economy are increasingly challenged by the spread of regional economic arrangements; both the European move-ment toward greater economic and political unity and the North Amer-ican Free Trade Agreement (NAFTA) represent important shifts away from an open global economy. And, most important of all, the political foundations of the international economy have been seriously undermined since the end of the Cold War.

Even though the globe has become increasingly integrated both economically and technologically, it continues to be politically fragmented among independent, self-interested states. The forces of economic globalization—trade, financial flows, the activities of multinational corporations—have made the international economy much more interdependent. At the same time, the end of the Cold War and the decreased need for close cooperation among the United States, Western Europe, and Japan have significantly weakened the political bonds that have held the international economy together. As a consequence, the rule-based international economic system laid down at the Bretton Woods Conference (1944) has greatly eroded. Despite some important reforms, including the 1995 creation of the World Trade Organization (WTO), the rules governing trade, money, and other international economic matters are no longer adequate for a highly integrated and fragile global economy.

The problems arising from increased economic integration of national economies necessitate new rules or modification of older rules to deal with pressing economic issues and ensure the continued existence of an open and stable global economy. The international integration of financial markets, the increasing importance of multinational corporations and foreign direct investment, and the spread of regional economic blocs call for action by the major powers and the rising economies of East Asia and elsewhere. Continuing failure of the international community to address crucial international economic matters threatens the stability of the global economy. Improved governance and management have become imperative.

Atrophy of the political cooperation that characterized the post–World War II international economic order has undermined the foundations of that order. A stable and prosperous international economy (like a domestic economy) requires strong and stable political foundations to undergird the institutions and rules governing the system and to prevent problems from escalating into crises like the post-1997 financial crisis. Strong international leadership, cooperative relations among major economic powers, and a commitment by citizens to an open world are all crucial elements. From 1945 to the 1980s, strong and generally prudent American leadership, close cooperation among the United States and its major allies, and a domestic consensus in the major capitalist economies favoring free trade and an open world economy provided a firm base for the development of the integrated international economy. However, the foundations first laid down at Bretton Woods have been weakened as have the shared political interests, mutual understandings, and cooperative arrangements of the Cold War decades.

By the beginning of the twenty-first century, American leadership of the world economy had been significantly weakened by a number of developments. The faltering domestic consensus on economic affairs contributed to that decline. Whereas, during most of the Cold War, the federal government had been expected to assume an important role in management of both domestic and international economic affairs, the market became ascendant with the presidency of Ronald Reagan, and many began to believe that the market alone could govern the world. The end of the Cold War has undermined America's ability and willingness to pay the economic and other costs of world economic leadership. Throughout the Cold War, Americans believed that partisan political concerns and other divisive issues should be set aside in the interest of national unity in foreign affairs; collapse of the Soviet threat greatly weakened this belief. In the economic realm, the American domestic consensus supporting free trade was weakened by ideological and political schisms regarding economic policy and by growing fears that economic globalization was threatening American economic well-being.

In the 1990s, many constituencies in the United States protested expansion of trade and foreign investment, arguing that they harmed the American worker, the environment, and human rights. Simultaneously, more and more Americans attributed the country's economic and other problems to globalization, and accused imports and corporate investments overseas of hurting American workers, small businesses, and the overall society. Many, for example, began to believe that increased economic inequality, declining real wages, and increasing job insecurity had been caused by increased competition from Mexico, Pacific Asia, and other low-wage economies. This shift in thinking was well illustrated by the acrimonious 1997 debate over and the failure of Congress to approve "fast track" authority to facilitate new trade negotiations, and by the lengthy 1998 delay of congressional approval of an appropriation ($18 billion) for the International Monetary Fund (IMF).[2] Attacks from both the political right and left on the evils of the global economy have become symptomatic of America's retreat from international leadership.

Since the end of the Cold War, economic cooperation among the United States and its allies has eroded considerably, and American foreign and economic policy has become more unilateral and self-centered. This shift away from international cooperation began in the mid-1980s when the Reagan Administration abandoned the postwar commitment to economic multilateralism in favor of a "multitrack" trade policy that included managed trade and NAFTA; the United States became converted to economic regionalism. The Clinton Administration's aggressive economic offensive against Japan in the early 1990s underscored America's abandonment of multilateralism and of its prior emphasis on international cooperation with its Cold War allies. The Administration's "managed trade" policy toward Japan would never have been launched during the height of the Cold War.

Meanwhile, the Europeans also became much more parochial in their economic and political concerns than in the past. Their energies have been focused on intensified efforts to create a European economy and polity. They have wanted to stabilize the Continent politically, create a globally competitive European economy, and strengthen their economic and political position vis-à-vis the United States and, to a lesser extent, Japan. Led by the French-German economic alliance, the West Europeans have concentrated on achieving economic unification of the Continent and strengthening the European Union.

The Japanese have also reoriented their economic and foreign policies. Following the 1985 Plaza Agreement and the consequent substantial appreciation of the yen, the Japanese political and economic elite increased their attention to Pacific Asia, and renewed interest in the region led to efforts to fashion a regional economy tightly linked to Japan. Japanese multinational corporations, strongly backed by the Japanese government, created integrated production networks of Japanese and local firms to strengthen the competitiveness of Japanese firms in the global economy. Although this effort has been set back by the East

Asian financial crisis and Japan's own economic problems, the concerted effort to forge a Japanese-led Pacific Asian economy has continued and signifies Japan's increasing assertiveness and independent stance within the global economy.

Failure of the major capitalist powers to launch any coordinated effort to deal with the post-1997 instability in international financial markets revealed the extent to which international cooperation had receded. The weakness of American leadership was painfully evident in President Clinton's speech at the Council on Foreign Relations on September 14, 1998, and in subsequent discussions among the major economic powers (G-7) following the October 1998 annual joint meeting of the World Bank and International Monetary Fund. The centerpiece of the President's Council speech—a proposal for a global cut in interest rates—met a cool reception. The Bundesbank, more concerned with fighting inflation than with the health of the global economy, turned the President's proposal aside; Japan, with nearly zero percent interest rates already and weighed down by its own enormous troubles, appeared to do little to stimulate its economy. Although agreement to create a new loan fund in the IMF was reached by the G-7, there has thus far been inadequate progress in safeguarding international financial matters.

Many political leaders, business executives, and scholars, especially in the United States, dismiss concerns about the future of global capitalism. The world economy, they point out, has become market dominated, and free markets can successfully guide the global economy to ever higher levels of prosperity and stability. According to this argument, the failure of the former command economies and the closed economies of the less developed countries caused governments everywhere to turn toward market solutions to economic problems. Among developed countries, deregulation, privatization, and other reforms have reduced the role of the state in the economy and have led many to proclaim the triumph of international capitalism and the economic ideas on which it rests. This belief in the secure victory of liberated capitalism may turn out to be valid, but it is important to recall that the world passed this way once before in the laissez-faire era prior to the outbreak of World War I and the subsequent collapse of that highly integrated world economy. Although the threat of another major war is very small, other developments could bring down or at least seriously

12

damage the contemporary international capitalist system. As the revolt against globalization in the United States and other countries reminds us, capitalism creates its own internal enemies.

Throughout this book I shall argue that international politics significantly affects the nature and dynamics of the international economy. Although technological advance and the interplay of market forces provide sufficient causes for increasing integration of the world economy, the supportive policies of powerful states and cooperative relationships among these states constitute the necessary political foundations for a stable and unified world economy. The international rules (regimes) that govern international economic affairs cannot succeed unless they are supported by a strong political base.

Since the end of the Cold War, all the political elements that have supported an open global economy have considerably weakened. Both the ability and the willingness of the United States to lead have declined, and although the formal framework of anti-Soviet alliances has continued, the Cold War allies' political unity has eroded as the United States, Western Europe, and Japan have emphasized their own parochial national and regional priorities more than in the past. Furthermore, the domestic consensus in both the United States and Europe has been worn away by years of increased income inequalities, job insecurity in the United States, and high levels of unemployment in Western Europe. Although major structural changes driven by technological change and ill-considered national policies carry a large share of responsibility for these social and economic ills, more and more people in the United States and Europe blame globalization and competition from foreign low-wage labor. Growing concern over economic globalization and increased competition have intensified the movement toward economic regionalism and the appeal of protectionism.

A number of books proclaim that, whether we like it or not, global capitalism and economic globalization are here to stay. Unfettered markets, they argue, now drive the world and all must adjust, however painful this may be. Yet, as I argue, despite the huge benefits of free trade and other aspects of the global economy, an open and integrated global economy is neither as extensive and inexorable nor as irreversible as many assume. Global capitalism and economic globalization have rested and must continue to rest on a secure political foundation.

13

However, the underpinning of the post–World War II global economy has steadily eroded since the end of the Soviet threat. To ensure survival of the global economy, the United States and other major powers must recommit themselves to work together to rebuild its weakened political foundations.

CHAPTER ONE

The Second Great Age
of Capitalism

AMERICANS, other citizens of the industrialized world, and many peoples in other parts of the international economy have entered what the financial expert and economic commentator David D. Hale has called "the Second Great Age of Global Capitalism." The world economic and political system is experiencing its most profound transformation since emergence of the international economy in the seventeenth and eighteenth centuries. The end of the Cold War, the collapse of the Soviet Union, a stagnant yet enormously rich Japan, the reunification of Germany and its consequent return as the dominant power in Western Europe, and the rise of China and Pacific Asia are influencing almost every aspect of international affairs. Changes originating in earlier decades have also become more prominent; these developments include the technological revolution associated with the computer and the information economy and the redistribution of economic power from the industrialized West to the rapidly industrializing and crisis-riven economies of Pacific Asia. The worldwide shift to greater reliance on the market in the management of economic affairs, and what many call the "retreat of the state," are integrating national economies everywhere into a global economy of expanding trade and financial flows. However, it is the demographic revolution that will have the greatest long-term significance. The extraordinary population decline in the industrialized world and the explosive growth of population in China, India, other parts of Asia, and elsewhere in the developing world will continue to significantly alter the global distribution of economic and, of course, military power.

These developments are having important consequences for the lives of us all. There will be many winners as global capitalism refashions almost every aspect of domestic and international economic affairs. There will also be many losers, at least over the short term, as international competition intensifies and as businesses and workers lose the secure niches that they enjoyed in the past. Economic globalization presents both threats and challenges for the well-being of peoples everywhere. If individuals and societies are to adjust intelligently to the challenge of global capitalism, it is imperative that they understand the principal forces transforming international economic and political affairs.

THE TRIUMPH OF ECONOMIC LIBERALISM

The end of the Cold War in 1989 and the collapse of the Soviet Union in 1991 sparked an international debate on the nature of the "new world order." After the disintegration of the Soviet empire in Eastern Europe and the subsequent fragmentation of the Soviet Union itself, speculation on the transformation of the international system and the nature of the post–Cold War era reached flood tide. When disappearance of the Communist threat left the United States as the only true superpower, many commentators believed that the American liberal values of democracy, individualism, and free markets had triumphed and that the world was on the verge of an era of unprecedented prosperity, democracy, and peace. Less sanguine observers countered that the bipolar stability of the postwar world was being supplanted by a chaotic, multipolar world of five or more major powers, a world characterized by new forms of intense ethnic, political, and economic conflict; indeed, some even expected that the world might one day look back with nostalgia to the simpler and more certain bipolar Cold War world that the historian John Lewis Gaddis had called the "long peace."[3]

Through most of the latter half of the twentieth century, the Cold War and its alliance structures provided the framework within which the world economy evolved; now that framework has been weakened. During the Cold War, the United States and its allies generally subordinated potential economic conflicts within the alliance to the interests of political and security cooperation. Their emphasis on security interests and alliance cohesion provided the political glue that held the world economy together and facilitated compromise on important economic differences. Even though the United States did, as many European and

Japanese charged, occasionally use its political leverage to exact economic concessions from its several alliance partners, the United States also clearly emphasized its security interests and allied cooperation more than its own narrow economic interests.

With the end of the Cold War, national priorities changed and the Western allies assigned a higher priority to their own national (and frequently parochial) economic interests. A shift in American policy had already become evident during the Reagan and Bush Administrations. The new, more nationalistic emphasis was carried further in the succeeding Clinton Administration; its declaration that *economic security* had displaced the earlier concern with *military security* made the change crystal clear.[4] Proponents of "geo-economics" argued that economic conflict had displaced traditional security and political interests.[5] A change in American attitudes and priorities appeared in growing economic unilateralism and in ratification of the North American Free Trade Agreement. Another significant manifestation of this change was the pursuit in the early 1990s of an aggressive managed trade or "results-oriented" trade policy toward Japan.

The priorities of Western Europe and Japan also changed in the 1990s. Both became less willing to follow American leadership, much less tolerant of America's disregard of their economic and political interests, and more likely to emphasize their own national priorities. Reunified Germany assigned greater importance to European regional issues and less to its alliance with the United States and began to lead in creation of an economically and politically united Europe. Japan rediscovered its "Asianness" and gave growing emphasis to the development of an integrated Pacific Asian regional economy under Japanese leadership. During the 1990s, regional concerns began to take precedence over North American, trans-Atlantic, and trans-Pacific issues.

These shifts in national priorities and foreign policies have extraordinarily important ramifications for the future of the world economy. Since World War II, the principal foundations of the international economy with its free markets and trade liberalization have been America's international leadership and the willingness of Western Europe and Japan to follow America's lead. However, in the 1990s, the most prosperous and economically successful era in world history was threatened by changes. The close cooperation of previous decades had

17

weakened, and there could be serious negative consequences for world peace and prosperity. The global economic turmoil of the century's final years warns that there are serious threats to the health and stability of a liberal global economy.

The Achilles heel of the post–Cold War liberal world order is the poor public understanding of economic liberalism, of the functioning of the market system, and of how capitalism creates wealth. The acrimonious debate over the North American Free Trade Agreement (NAFTA), for example, revealed that many American citizens and even some very successful business executives failed to comprehend the rationale for trade liberalization. Economists' arguments that open markets are very beneficial and that trade protection can be very costly are frequently overwhelmed by popular misconceptions and self-serving demands for protection against "cheap" imports and "unfair" trading partners.

Economists themselves must assume part of the responsibility for public misunderstanding. Too many American economists are content to continue writing their frequently incomprehensible technical papers and to remain aloof from public discussions of crucial issues of economic policy. A notable exception to this detached attitude is found in *Globaphobia* (1998), where Gary Burtless and his colleagues use conventional economic analysis in a comprehensible manner to dispel strident and unfounded attacks on globalization.[6] Without a better understanding by the average citizen of how the market economy works, including its strengths and its weaknesses, the liberal economic order will continue in jeopardy.

ECONOMIC GLOBALIZATION

Since the early 1980s, economic issues and the global economy have become more central to international economic and political affairs than at any time since the late nineteenth century. Many commentators have noted a profound shift from a state-dominated to a market-dominated world. The market's increased importance, reflected in increased international flows of goods, capital, and services, has been encouraged by declining costs of transportation and communications, the collapse of command-type economies, and the increasing influence of a conservative economic ideology based on the policy prescriptions of economics. This resurgence of the market is really a return to the pre–World War I era of expanding globalization of markets, production, and finance.

At the turn of the century, issues arising from economic globalization confront national societies and the international community. Immediately after the end of the Cold War almost every economist, business executive, and political leader in both industrialized and industrializing countries expected that economic globalization would lead to a world characterized by open and prosperous economies, political democracy, and international cooperation. However, as the 1990s progressed, and especially in response to the post-1997 global economic turmoil, a powerful negative reaction to globalization arose in both developed and less developed countries. Rejections of globalization and its alleged negative consequences became especially strident within the United States, Western Europe, and some industrializing economies. Globalization has been blamed for everything from growing income inequality to chronic high levels of unemployment and even to the oppression of women, and critics have favored such nostrums as trade protectionism, closed regional arrangements, and severe restrictions on migration. Certainly the future of the international economic and political system will be strongly affected by the relative success or failure of the proponents and opponents of globalization.

According to the "globalization thesis," a quantum change in human affairs has taken place as the flow of large quantities of trade, investment, and technologies across national borders has expanded from a trickle to a flood. Political, economic, and social activities are becoming worldwide in scope, and interactions among states and societies on many fronts have increased. As integrative processes widen and deepen globally, some believe that markets have become, or are becoming, the most important mechanism determining both domestic and international affairs. In a highly integrated global economy, the nation-state, according to some, has become anachronistic and is in retreat. A global capitalist economy characterized by unrestricted trade, investment flows, and the international activities of multinational firms will benefit rich and poor alike.

19

Others, however, emphasize the alleged downside of economic globalization, including the increase of income inequality both among and within nations, high chronic levels of unemployment in Western Europe and elsewhere, and, most of all, the devastating consequences of unregulated financial flows. These critics charge that national societies are being integrated into a global economic system and buffeted by economic and technological forces over which they have very little control. For them, the global economic problems of the late 1990s offer proof that the costs of globalization are much greater than its benefits.

Although the term "globalization" is now used broadly, economic globalization has entailed just a few key developments in trade, finance, and foreign direct investment by multinational corporations. Since the end of World War II, *international trade* has greatly expanded and has become a much more important factor in both domestic and international economic affairs. Whereas the volume of international commerce had grown by only 0.5 percent annually between 1913 and 1948, it grew at an annual rate of 7 percent from 1948 to 1973.[7] As figure 1.1 shows, international trade has grown much more rapidly than the global economic output. Over the course of the postwar era, trade has grown from 7 percent to 21 percent of total world income. The value of world trade has increased from $57 billion in 1947 to $6 trillion in the 1990s. In addition to the great expansion of merchandise trade (goods), trade in services (banking, information, etc.) has significantly increased during recent decades. With this immense expansion of world trade, international competition has greatly increased. Although consumers and export sectors within individual nations benefit from increased openness, many businesses find themselves competing against foreign firms that have greatly improved their efficiency. During the 1990s, trade competition became even more intense as a growing number of industrializing economies shifted from an import-substitution to an export-led growth strategy. Nevertheless, the major competitors for most all American firms are other American firms.

Underlying the expansion of global trade have been a number of developments. Since World War II, trade barriers have declined significantly due to successive rounds of trade negotiations.[8] For example, over the past half century, average tariff levels of the United States and other industrialized countries on imported products have dropped

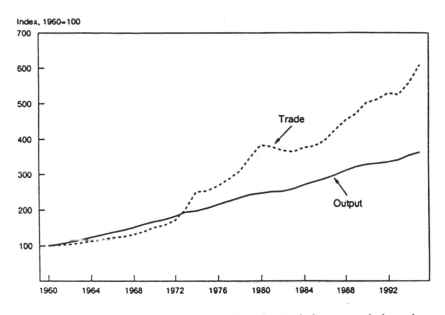

Index, 1960=100

Fig. 1.1. Growth in World Output and Trade. Trade has expanded much
faster than output, especially since the early 1970s.
Source: U.S. Council of Economic Advisors.

from about 40 percent to only 6 percent, and barriers to trade in services have also been lowered. In addition, since the late 1970s deregulation and privatization have further opened national economies to imports. Technological advances in communications and transportation have reduced costs and thus significantly encouraged trade expansion. Taking advantage of these economic and technological changes, more and more businesses have expanded their horizons to include international markets. Despite these developments, most trade takes place among the three advanced industrialized economies—the United States, Western Europe, and Japan, plus a few emerging markets in East Asia, Latin America, and elsewhere. Most of the less developed world is excluded, except as exporters of food and raw materials. It is estimated, for example, that Africa south of the Sahara accounted for only about 1 percent of total world trade in the 1990s.

Since the mid-1970s, the removal of capital controls, the creation of new financial instruments, and technological advances in communications have contributed to a much more highly integrated *international*

21

financial system. The volume of foreign exchange trading (buying and selling national currencies) in the late 1990s has been approximately $1.5 trillion per day, an eightfold increase since 1986; by contrast, the global volume of exports (goods and services) for all of 1997 was $6.6 trillion, or $25 billion per day! In addition, the amount of investment capital seeking higher returns has grown enormously; by the mid-1990s, mutual funds, pension funds, and the like totaled $20 trillion, ten times the 1980 figure. Moreover, the significance of these huge investments is greatly magnified by the fact that foreign investments are increasingly leveraged; that is, they are investments made with borrowed funds. Finally, derivatives or repackaged securities and other financial assets play an important role in international finance. Valued at $360 trillion (larger than the value of the entire global economy), they have contributed to the complexity and to the instability of international finance. It is obvious that international finance has a profound impact on the global economy.

This financial revolution has linked national economies closely to one another, significantly increased the capital available for developing countries, and, in the case of the East Asian emerging markets, accelerated economic development. However, as a large portion of these financial flows is short-term, highly volatile, and speculative, international finance has become the most vulnerable and unstable aspect of the global capitalist economy. The immense scale, velocity, and speculative nature of financial movements across national borders have made governments more vulnerable to sudden shifts in these movements. Governments can therefore easily fall prey to currency speculators, as happened in the 1992 European financial crisis (which caused Great Britain to withdraw from the Exchange Rate Mechanism), in the 1994–1995 punishing collapse of the Mexican peso, and in the devastating East Asian financial crisis in the late 1990s. Whereas for some, financial globalization exemplifies the healthy and beneficial triumph of global capitalism, for others the international financial system seems "out of control" and in need of improved regulation.

The term "globalization" came into popular usage in the second half of the 1980s in connection with the huge surge of foreign direct investment (FDI) by multinational corporations (MNCs). As shown in figure 1.2, FDI expanded significantly in the late 1980s, increasing much

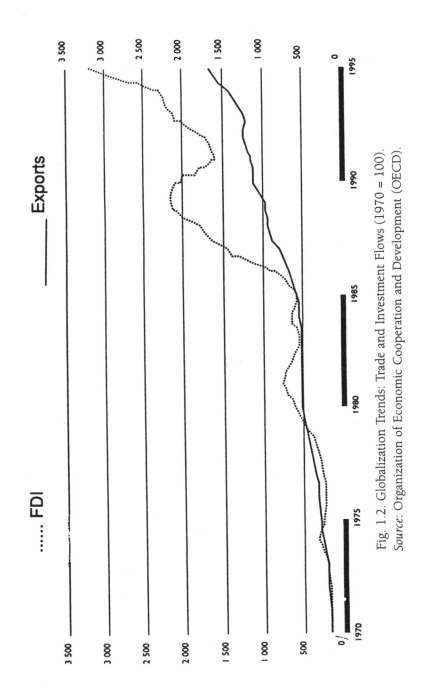

Fig. 1.2. Globalization Trends: Trade and Investment Flows (1970 = 100).
Source: Organization of Economic Cooperation and Development (OECD).

more rapidly than world trade and economic output. Throughout much of the 1990s, FDI outflows from the major industrialized countries to industrializing countries rose at approximately 15 percent annually; FDI flows among the industrialized countries themselves rose at about the same rate. In the late 1990s, the cumulative value of FDI amounts to hundreds of billions of dollars. The greatest portion of this investment has been in high-tech industries, such as those of automobiles and information technology.

These general statements, however, hide noteworthy aspects of FDI and MNC activities. Despite much talk of corporate globalization, FDI is actually highly concentrated and distributed very unevenly around the globe. Most FDI takes place in the United States, China, and Western Europe because firms are attracted to large or potentially large markets. FDI in less developed countries, with a few notable exceptions, has been modest. In addition to that in a few Latin American countries, and particularly in the Brazilian and Mexican automobile sectors, most FDI in developing countries has been placed in the emerging markets of East and Southeast Asia, particularly in China. When one speaks of corporate globalization, only a few countries are actually involved.

Despite the limited nature of corporate globalization, multinational corporations (MNCs) and FDI are very important features of the global economy. The increasing importance of MNCs has profoundly altered the structure and functioning of the global economy. These giant firms and their global strategies have become major determinants of trade flows and of the location of industries and other economic activities around the world. Most investment is in capital-intensive and technology-intensive sectors. These firms have become central in the expansion of technology flows to both industrialized and industrializing economies. As a consequence, multinational firms have become extremely important in determining the economic, political, and social welfare of many nations. Controlling much of the world's investment capital, technology, and access to global markets, such firms have become major players not only in international economic, but in political affairs as well, and this has triggered a backlash in many countries.

Economic globalization has been driven by political, economic, and technological developments. The compression of time and space by advances in communications and transportation has greatly reduced the costs of international commerce while, largely under American leadership, both the industrialized and industrializing economies have taken a number of initiatives to lower trade and investment barriers. Eight rounds of multilateral trade negotiations under the General Agreement on Tariffs and Trade (GATT), the principal forum for trade liberalization, have significantly decreased trade barriers. Since the mid-1980s, Latin American, Pacific Asian, and other developing countries have initiated important reforms to reduce their trade, financial, and other economic barriers. More and more firms have pursued global economic strategies to take advantage of these developments.

Elimination of capital controls and movement toward a global financial system along with removal of barriers to FDI have also accelerated the movement toward both global and regional integration of services and manufacturing. In both industrialized and industrializing economies, spreading pro-market thinking has strongly influenced economic policy to reduce the role of the state in the economy. The collapse of the Soviet command economy, the failure of the Third World's import-substitution strategy, and the growing belief in the United States and other industrialized economies that the welfare state has become a major obstacle to economic growth and to international competitiveness have encouraged acceptance of unrestricted markets as the solution to the economic ills of modern society. Sweeping reforms have led to deregulation, privatization, and open national economies. In the late 1990s, the debate over the costs and benefits of economic globalization became highly acrimonious.

Meanwhile, the increased openness of national economies, the enlarged number of exporters of manufactured goods, the more rapid increase in trade than in the growth of the global economic product, and the internationalization of services have greatly intensified international economic competition. Growth of the proportion of world output traded on international markets has been accompanied by a significant change in the pattern of world trade. Many less developed countries (LDCs) have shifted from exporting food and commodities to exporting manufactured goods and even services. As indicated in figure 1.3, since 1965 the developing economies' share of world trade has increased considerably. Manufactured goods have begun to provide a growing proportion of this LDC trade at the same time that the United States and

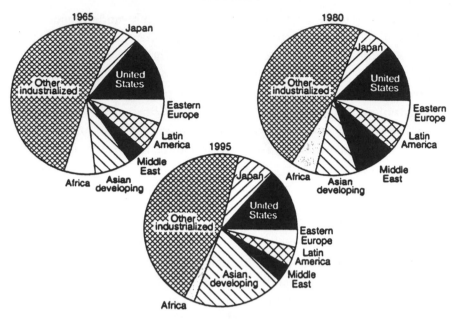

Fig. 1.3. Shares of World Trade. The share of Asian developing countries in international trade has risen greatly since 1980, increasing the overall importance of developing countries in world trade. *Note*: Eastern Europe includes the (former) USSR. *Source*: U.S. Council of Economic Advisors.

other advanced industrial economies have been shifting from manufactured exports to export of services. This restructuring of the entire global economy is economically costly and politically difficult and is producing many losers as well as winners.

Intensification of global competition in manufacturing, especially in high-tech products, has resulted in increased concern in advanced economies about international competitiveness, particularly about manufactures from the low-wage industrializing countries. The prestigious World Economic Forum reflected these concerns when it proclaimed in the mid-1990s that competition from industrializing countries was causing deindustrialization of the advanced economies. These concerns have been magnified as more and more Pacific Asian countries have sought to export their way out of economic distress; consequently, more and more groups and leaders in advanced economies worry about such competition and brand it as unfair. Some even express fear that their own living standards could be reduced to those of China. Many believe that intensified competition from the industrializing countries has, at the least, increased job insecurity, unemployment, and income inequality; growing concerns have increased pressures for trade protection and economic regionalism.

The increased openness of the world economy, emergence of new industrial powers, and the global economic slowdown have contributed to a substantial surplus productive capacity in a number of industrial sectors. A notable example is automobile manufacture, which, like possession of a national airline, has long been considered a necessary attribute of a sovereign nation as well as a source of high wages for blue-collar workers. The United States, Japan, many European countries, and some industrializing countries have large automotive industries. It is obvious that many of these firms must merge or even eventually shut down as the global supply of automobiles outruns effective demand; of the approximately eighteen major auto firms in the world, it is probable that only about seven or so will ultimately survive.

Global overcapacity in a number of economic sectors has caused some observers to declare that the world economy is suffering from a glut of manufactured goods, or what Marxists call "underconsumption"; this has led many observers to declare that global capitalism is in a systemic crisis requiring radical structural reforms.[9] Certainly, rationalization along with elimination of surplus capacity in the automobile and many other economic sectors has been made necessary by globalization. Adjustment will be painful and will result in large numbers of laid-off workers, especially low- or semi-skilled workers, who may find it difficult to find equally well paying jobs. However, as Paul Krugman has argued, a large part of the "surplus" problem is due to the exaggerated fear of inflation in such countries as Japan and Germany where central banks place a higher priority on price stability than on economic growth.[10] More expansionary economic policies would significantly reduce the surplus. Moreover, as has happened in the past, the problem of excess capacity in certain sectors will work itself out as supply is reduced to match demand. But until the problem is resolved, it will pose severe political problems for national governments and for the world economy.

Although there is general agreement on the increased importance of the market and of globalization, there is intense controversy over the role of economic factors in the determination of international economic affairs and over the likelihood of cooperation versus conflict. Oversimplifying somewhat, two schools of thought on this issue can be discerned in American and other writing. I shall call one school the "market-oriented" position because of its emphasis on free markets and its commitment to free trade and, most important, to a significant decrease in the role of the state in the economy. The other school of thought is more diverse, but, for lack of a better term, I shall call it the "revisionist" position because of its emphasis on economic conflict, trade protection, and the strong role of the state in the economy.[11]

The market-oriented position is based on the theories and policy prescriptions of economics and asserts that, whereas in the recent past the policies of powerful states and international institutions have played the dominant role in the organization and functioning of the international economy, in the twenty-first century free markets and economic forces will increasingly determine international economic affairs. The demise of communism, the increasing integration of national markets, and the failure of inward-looking economic policies of less developed countries have resulted in a global shift toward such market-oriented policies as free trade and export-led growth and to a drastic reduction of the role of the state in the economy. As the London *Economist* has observed, since the collapse of communism, there has been universal agreement that no serious alternative to free-market capitalism exists as the way to organize economic affairs.

Many also argue that the world is moving toward a politically borderless and highly interdependent global economy that will foster prosperity, international cooperation, and world peace. In this view, with the triumphal return to the free market and the laissez-faire ideals of the nineteenth century, global corporations will lead in organizing international production and maximizing global wealth. A corollary of this position is that the American economic and political system has become the model for the world. Moreover, the United States, as the only true superpower, will lead the rest of the world. Global economic policy will focus on economic multilateralism and on strengthening international rules and institutions created within the Bretton Woods system. American leadership and the reformed Bretton Woods system will facilitate continued cooperation among the dominant economic powers and thereby ensure the global economy's smooth functioning.

Revisionist critics of globalization foresee a world characterized by intense economic conflict at both the domestic and international levels. Believing that an open world economy will inevitably produce more losers than winners, revisionists argue that unleashing market and other economic forces could result in an immense struggle among individual nations, economic classes, and powerful groups. Geo-economic adherents of this position believe (paraphrasing the German strategist Karl von Clausewitz) that international economic competition, especially in manufacturing, is the pursuit of foreign policy by other means. Many assert that this global struggle for market share and technological supremacy will be embodied in competing regional blocs dominated by one or another of the three major economic powers and that the European Union under German leadership, the North American bloc under U.S. leadership, and the Asian Pacific bloc under Japanese leadership will vie for economic and political ascendancy.

This rather pessimistic position declares that the clash between communism and capitalism has been replaced by conflict among rival forms of capitalism and social systems represented in regional economic blocs. In a provocative article in 1991, for example, Samuel P. Huntington argued that, with the end of the Cold War, Japan had become a "security threat" to the United States.[12] Subsequently, in even more provocative writings, Huntington proclaimed that intracivilizational conflicts will dominate the agenda of world politics well into the twenty-first century.[13] Some commentators, reflecting on the tragic events in the former Yugoslavia and in the Soviet Union in the 1990s, argue that an age of intense ethnic and nationalistic conflict has been unleashed on the world. In a world still divided by rival national ambitions in which economic factors in effect determine the fate of nations, many conclude that international economic affairs will become increasingly filled with conflict.

TECHNOLOGY, THE INFORMATION ECONOMY, AND SERVICES

The end of the Cold War and economic globalization have coincided with a new industrial revolution. The computer and the rise of the information or Internet or knowledge economy are transforming almost every aspect of economic, political, and social affairs. Some analysts even argue that recognition by Soviet leaders that the Soviet Union was falling behind Japan and the West in such technologies was an indirect cause of their fateful decision to reform the lagging Soviet economy. Acknowledging the importance of the information economy, a number of scholars have set forth ambitious theories predicting the trajectory of social affairs in the century ahead.[14] While these theories provide some interesting insights, the long-term consequences of the computer and the information economy will be unclear for many decades to come.

Most observers believe that the information economy and computing power have been giving an impetus to the world economy similar to that produced by steam power, electric power, and oil power in the past. Since the mid-eighteenth century, as the stimulus provided by one industrial transformation has been exhausted, another technological revolution has moved the world economy to a new level. As the Industrial Revolution based on steam power lost its momentum in the last decades of the nineteenth century, steam was replaced by oil and electric power. The impetus provided by the oil age waned in the final decades of the twentieth century, and the rate of economic and productivity growth declined, especially in the United States and Western Europe. With the transition of these economies from the oil age to the information age, some argue that this recent shift has created a new economic model based on the computer, economic globalization, and corporate restructuring, and that this underlies the outstanding success of the American economy in the 1990s.

The economics profession is deeply divided about whether or not computer power represents a technological revolution on the same scale as steam, oil, and electric power. Some economists point out that it is difficult to find convincing evidence that the computer has significantly accelerated the rate of economic and productivity growth. They also argue that computing power has not transformed the overall economy on the same scale that steam or electric power transformed every aspect of economic and social affairs. Despite heavy investment in computers and associated technologies, computers and peripherals still represent a very small percentage of net nonresidential fixed capital. A growing number of other economists, however, believe that investments in computers and information technologies are beginning to have an important impact on productivity and on economic affairs in general. In support of this position, economic historian Paul David has pointed out that the long-term impact of the computer and information economy cannot be determined with any precision until well into the twenty-first century. After all, as David reminds us, it took nearly forty years, from the early 1880s to the 1920s, for the commercialization of electricity to affect economic growth and social change to a measurable degree. Resolution of this issue is also extremely hard to attain because it is very difficult to measure productivity growth, especially in the service industries that now comprise 70 percent of the American economy.

If the information economy does not result in significant increases in productivity, it is unlikely that there will be continued high and sustained increases in the rates of economic development in the advanced industrial countries. In the United States, the relatively low increases in productivity after the early 1970s resulted in stagnant wages. There has been considerable debate about whether or not a significant increase in the overall rate of American productivity growth did occur even in the 1990s. In Western Europe, a slowdown in the rate of productivity has contributed to sluggish economies. Such conditions on both sides of the Atlantic have fed the forces of trade protectionism and encouraged many to believe that the computer and the information economy are the cause of, rather than the solution to, their economic troubles. This fear has been compounded by growing concerns over competition from Pacific Asian economies with huge low-paid and disciplined workforces. Many blue- and white-collar workers in the West believe that they are caught between decreased demand for their labor because of the wide use of the computer and an increased supply of workers worldwide because of the entry of China and other East Asian economies into the world economy.

Whether or not there has been a true technological revolution based on computing power, technological changes are having a significant impact on the world economy; the following changes are particularly important:[15]

1. *Increased Rate of Technological Innovation.* There has been a flood of new scientific and technological developments in a wide number of fields such as biotechnology, microelectronics, telecommunications,

and new materials. More new knowledge has been produced over the last thirty years than in the previous five thousand. Certain factors appear to be particularly responsible for the acceleration in technological development. Significant advances in basic science and the greatly reduced cost of knowledge manipulation due to the use of computers are important contributing factors. The cost of storing and transmitting knowledge fell at the rate of about 20 percent a year for forty years; the decline in energy costs associated with the Industrial Revolution was only 50 percent during a thirty-year period. Intensified international competition among the major powers has stimulated scientific and technological innovation, and acceleration in the rate of technological change has made technology the most crucial factor in economic growth and international competitiveness.

2. *Broad Applicability of New Technologies.* Newer technologies, especially in computing and electronics, are relevant to a broad array of economic processes and other activities in many sectors of the economy. Process control, automation, and automatic data processing are revolutionizing both manufacturing and services in every industrial economy; and in all these areas, demand for low-skilled and unskilled labor has decreased.

3. *Shortened Process and Product Life Cycles.* The technological life cycles of both products and production processes have been dramatically shortened; that is, less time elapses between innovation of a new process or product, commercialization of that product, and diffusion of the technology to competitors both at home and abroad. This compression of time, in turn, has led to greater internationalization of technological developments and to such new competitive strategies as expanded strategic and technological alliances among the multinational corporations of many countries.

While technological developments obviously have implications for domestic and international economic affairs, both the nature and the importance of these implications are extremely controversial. Some critics of technology charge that rapid technological advance is having a devastating impact on the highly industrialized countries. Some "neo-Luddites" charge that the speed of contemporary technological advances will lead to massive technological unemployment and "the end of work." Most American economists, on the other hand, in response to these fears, argue that they are based on the faulty idea that if the jobs in an economy are taken over by machines, there will be fewer jobs for human beings. Economists proclaim, to the contrary, that technological progress has meant and will mean new and better jobs for everyone.

Closely associated with the rise of the information economy and a cause for fear of massive technological unemployment is the dramatic and accelerating shift from manufacturing to services (financial, software, retailing, etc.). This major transformation has been occurring as manufacturing employment has dropped and the share of services in the economy has rapidly increased; a similar change in employment took place in the late nineteenth century with the shift from an agricultural- to an industrial-based economy. Whereas the manufacturing sector accounted for 27 percent of American GNP in 1960, by 1998 its share had dropped to 15 percent of GNP. This change does not necessarily entail "deindustrialization" of the economy but rather means that the same volume of manufactured goods can be produced with a smaller and more productive workforce. The United States and Canada have taken the lead in this changeover from a manufacturing to a service economy, with nearly three-quarters of their workforces in services at the end of the century; Japan and Germany lag far behind. In the United States, the corporate "downsizing" and "reengineering" that began in the 1980s was at least in part a consequence of this momentous change.

The shift from a manufacturing to a service economy has been a wrenching experience for the United States; it is likely to be more so for Japan and Western Europe because of their economic and institutional rigidities. Although many critics in the late 1980s denounced the service economy as one of "hamburger flippers," this characterization is a distortion. Nevertheless, the ongoing switch to services has greatly increased job insecurity among many Americans, and many are losing high-paying assembly-line or middle-management positions. Such developments have been fragmenting the American workforce and will do the same in other industrialized economies. On the other hand, the rise of the service economy, propelled largely by the information revolution, has increased the demand for and raised the wage premium on education and skills while decreasing the demand for and the income of low-skilled and unskilled workers. Whether one works with or does not work with a computer has become the most important determinant of one's wages. A corollary is that the United States and the other industrialized economies are importing and will continue to import more and more manufactured goods from the low-wage industrializing economies of East Asia and elsewhere. And even though the United States has a huge trade surplus in services, its increased importing of manufactured goods has given rise to a highly emotional controversy over the impact of globalization on the welfare of American labor.

THE GLOBAL SHIFT IN ECONOMIC POWER

Also important in the transformation of the world economy has been the redistribution of world industry away from the older industrialized economies—the United States, Western Europe, and, to a lesser extent, Japan—toward Pacific Asia, Latin America, and other industrializing economies. Although these emerging markets have been in very serious economic trouble since 1997, their economic "fundamentals," especially in East Asia, are sound; they possess high savings and investment rates as well as excellent workforces and will one day recover. Although the United States and the other industrialized economies still possess a preponderant share of global wealth and industry, they have declined in relative (not absolute) terms while the industrializing economies, especially China, have gained in economic importance over the course of the postwar period. The impact of the Pacific Asian economic crisis on the larger global economy provides strong evidence of the magnitude of the change that has taken place.

In the decades immediately following World War II, political leaders and intellectuals in the less developed countries (LDCs) denounced the capitalist developed countries as "imperialist" and "exploitative." Dependency theory blamed the poverty and underdevelopment of the LDCs on the policies of the dominant capitalist economies and on multinational corporations. In an effort to break away from dependence on the developed countries, many LDCs, especially in Latin America, closed their markets to the outside world and pursued nationalist import-substitution strategies in order to become self-sufficient. Their efforts to overturn the developed countries' control of the world economy climaxed in the mid-1970s with the unsuccessful effort of an LDC coalition to establish a New International Economic Order (NIEO). By the 1980s, this effort had failed; a significant number of LDCs had become heavily burdened by huge debts, their governments were running unmanageable budget deficits, and their economies suffered from high inflation rates that discouraged productive economic activities and foreign investment.

By the early 1990s, however, the situation of a number of LDCs had again changed dramatically. The debt crisis of most of these nations had eased. Many had deemphasized the import-substitution strategy while implementing sweeping structural adjustment policies to reform and strengthen their economies. Market-oriented reforms included pursuit of sound fiscal policies, deregulation, and a drastic reduction of the role of the state in the economy. Following the example of the emerging markets of Pacific Asia, other nations began to open their economies to the outside world and to pursue export-led growth strategies. Their changing economic fortunes caused disintegration of the LDCs' former political unity into regional groupings such as the Association of South East Asian Nations (ASEAN) and alliances based on economic interests such as the Cairns group of agricultural exporters.[16] Most LDCs, however, have failed to reform and adjust to the changing global economy.

Beginning in the late 1960s, as revealed by figure 1.4, the Four Tigers of East Asia (Hong Kong, Singapore, South Korea, and Taiwan), growing by 6 percent annually, outpaced the rest of the world. Other East and Southeast Asian countries such as Malaysia, Thailand, and Indonesia also have grown rapidly. The most significant change in the international balance of economic power has been the industrialization of Pacific Asia and especially of China, which, depending upon the measurement used, has become the world's second- or third-largest economy. A number of the Pacific Asian industrializing economies have developed and are developing automobile, electronics, and other advanced industries (in such areas as steel and chemicals) that have become highly competitive in world markets.

Although there is argument about the geographic boundaries of the region, it is clear that a distinct Pacific Asian economy, including North-

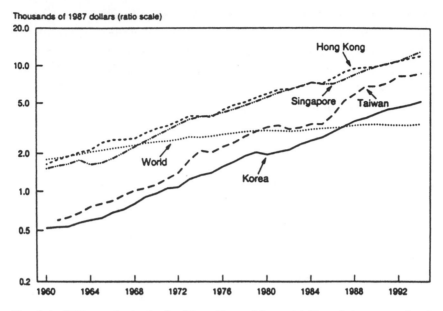

Thousands of 1987 dollars (ratio scale)

Fig. 1.4. GDP per Capita in the "Four Tigers." Since 1960, real GDP in each of the "four tigers" has grown by more than 6 percent per year.
Source: U.S. Council of Economic Advisors.

east Asia, Southeast Asia, and southern China, began to take shape in the late 1980s when this vast region became the most economically dynamic area in the world and important exporters of industrial and high-tech products. Until the 1997 financial crisis, Pacific Asia's economic success was indeed impressive. During the thirty years prior to the East Asian financial crisis, per capita income levels had increased tenfold in South Korea, fivefold in Thailand, and fourfold in Malaysia. Per capita income in Hong Kong and Singapore exceeded that of some Western industrialized countries.

In the 1980s and early 1990s, China experienced a rapid rate of economic growth and industrialization and became the most important member of the group of rapidly industrializing economies. The increasingly intertwined economies of mainland China, Hong Kong, and Taiwan (i.e., "Greater China") have become an important economic force in the region. Prior to 1850, China and India were the largest economies in the world, and at its current rate of economic growth China will most likely reoccupy that preeminent position some time in the twenty-first century. If this prediction is fulfilled, other nations in the region and around the world will have to make huge adjustments to such a shift in economic power. It is equally or more significant that Chinese military capabilities have been expanding, and that, with the declining military importance of Russia in East Asia, China has emerged as a powerful and unpredictable economic and military power. Whether or not China can continue its rapid growth and the choices it makes as it exercises its expanding economic and military power are critically important to East Asia in particular, but also to the world in general.

The relationship of Pacific Asia and the West, principally the United States and Western Europe, is an important and contentious issue facing the international community. For many Western business and political leaders, the economic rise and increasing affluence of East Asia represent an unprecedented economic opportunity. As Western businesses contemplate this huge and growing market, one is reminded of the late-nineteenth-century quip that, if every "Chinaman" lengthened his garment by one inch, the mills of Manchester (England) would boom forever. For those critical of the increasing globalization of the world, the industrialization of Pacific Asia and other developing economies threatens a "Chineseization" of Western living standards. Many Americans and Europeans believe that competition from hundreds of millions of low-wage Chinese, Indian, and Mexican workers has been forcing down American wages and causing unemployment in Western Europe. This is reminiscent of Kaiser Wilhelm's evoking of the "Yellow Peril." However, it is not inevitable that either the optimistic scenario or the dire predictions be realized.

Although most economists dismiss the fears and point out that similar shifts have taken place in the past without unduly harming more-developed economies, opponents of globalization fear that several unique and very disturbing features of the industrial rise of Pacific Asia and other developing economies have made this situation particularly threatening: (1) By historic standards, the diffusion of industry from industrialized to industrializing economies has occurred very rapidly. Moreover, not only are traditional industries migrating to the industrializing economies, but many of the advanced technologies (e.g., electronics and other technologically sophisticated industries) on which the economic fortunes of the West have become dependent are moving southward and are intensifying competition. (2) Technological advances in transportation and communication have facilitated transfer of manufacturing techniques from the industrialized to the industrializing economies. The role played by Western and Japanese multinational firms has been a major point of contention in the United States, Western Europe, and even Japan; critics charge that the global strategies of these firms have accelerated diffusion of sophisticated technologies as the firms have attempted to increase their international competitiveness by combining the cheap labor of the South with the most advanced manufacturing techniques of the North. (3) The challenge posed to the older industrialized economies by this shift in manufacturing has been aggravated by the sheer magnitude of the problem. With the end of the Cold War and the increasing integration of the world economy, literally billions of low-wage workers have suddenly entered the world labor pool. Nothing of similar magnitude has ever happened previously. These workers are even willing to forgo the costly welfare benefits and health standards that Western workers demand.

Rather than accepting the "decline of the West" and "clash of civilizations" pessimism, most American economists reject the revived "yellow peril" thesis. Indeed, in a provocative article, Paul Krugman has generally dismissed the idea that the industrial rise of Pacific Asia poses a threat to the West.[17] The economic success of these economies has been due to the rapid mobilization of capital and labor and does not represent a significant increase in national productivity levels. The failure of these economies to raise their levels of productivity significantly, he wrote, means that their economic success is a one-time event (like that of the Soviet Union following World War II). As these economies exhaust available labor and capital, their economic growth will slacken. On the other hand, Krugman concedes that China's huge labor supply should produce a high rate of economic growth for many decades.

The extraordinarily rapid industrialization of Pacific Asia and the sudden emergence of many nations as important exporters has forced the modern world economy to confront, for the fifth time, problems caused by a sizable redistribution in the international balance of economic power and competitiveness. Earlier examples were the sudden emergence of Great Britain in the early nineteenth century following the Industrial Revolution and the Napoleonic Wars; the equally sudden emergence of unified Germany, and subsequently of the United States, as major industrial export economies in the late nineteenth and early twentieth centuries; and Japan's unprecedented export expansion in the 1970s and the 1980s. With such profound shifts in economic power and international competitiveness, economic and political tension intensifies considerably; there is a search for scapegoats, and charges of "unfair trade practices" are issued. At the close of the twentieth century, the economic rise of China and other Pacific Asian economies has reproduced this familiar pattern.

THE DEMOGRAPHIC REVOLUTION

Over the long term, the most important development transforming the world economy can be described as a demographic revolution in which two separate developments are altering population distribution in the world. On the one hand, every industrialized country has experienced a decrease in population growth and is aging rapidly. Not a single nation in Western Europe is producing enough children to maintain prior rates of population growth; and while the United States with its large inflow of immigrants has enjoyed a favorable rate of population growth, even that rate has decreased. Japan will actually experience an absolute population decline early in the twenty-first century. On the other hand, the population in most of the rest of the world has been exploding. The industrializing economies, for example, are undergoing a massive demographic expansion. Between 1950 and 1998, the population of the developing world grew by 3 billion (from 1.7 billion to 4.7 billion); this population is expected to reach 6.8 billion by 2025! By that date, China is expected to have a population of about 1.5 billion, and India's population could reach 2 billion people sometime in the twenty-first century. Less dramatic but still impressive population growth will characterize other developing economies. This demographic shift will, of necessity, have a profound impact on global economic and political affairs.

Unprecedented population growth in impoverished, less developed economies constitutes a massive challenge. Problems of health, environmental degradation, and political instability will ravage many societies, and if these societies see no hope for improving their lot in a market-oriented global economy, they will surely develop the weaponry with which to destroy that economy. The international community must assist such countries to become part of the global economy and must also do what it can to raise the standard of living of billions of unfortunate peoples. Economic development of destitute countries will require huge transfers of capital and technology as well as maintenance of global markets for their exports. However, success in developing previously backward economies will also create additional challenges for the industrialized economies themselves.

Population growth leads to urbanization, and urbanization has historically been associated with large increases in an economy's total factor productivity. This means that, despite the high costs of urbanization, the productivity of an economy generally increases substantially as urban centers grow. Population decline, on the other hand, is associated with a slower rate of productivity growth; and, of course, the aging of a population entails an increasing burden of retirement and medical costs. As the rate of productivity growth determines the wealth and power of a society, one can project a profound shift during the twenty-first century in the global distribution of wealth and power away from the older to the newer industrial powers. Concerns over this shift already appear to be influencing the policies of Japan, Western Europe, and, to a lesser extent, the United States. For example, strengthening the position of the European peoples in the increasingly competitive global economy is an unvoiced goal of the movement toward a united Europe.

The Challenge of Economic Regionalism

Since the mid-1980s, the movement toward economic regionalism has become a defining feature of the global economy and has had a major impact on its shape. This "new regionalism" (to use Jagdish Bhagwati's term) differs in fundamental respects from the earlier regional movement of the 1950s and 1960s and has much greater significance for the global economy; the only survivor of the earlier regional movement is the European Economic Community, or, as it is now called, the European Union. The revived movement toward regional integration has been nearly universal, generally successful, and has increased considerably the integration of economic activities within particular regional arrangements. A substantial portion of world trade takes place within regional groupings. All major economies, with a few exceptions such as China, Japan, and Russia, are members of a regional economic bloc. This new regionalism has major implications for the global economy.

The new regionalism was initiated by the Single European Act (1986); that Act stimulated other regional efforts throughout the world, most importantly by the United States. In response to European reluctance to join the American-initiated Uruguay Round of trade negotiations, to growing concerns in the United States that Europe was turning inward, and to impatience with the slowness of GATT negotiations, the United States decided to support the North American Free Trade Agreement (NAFTA). The slow and drawn-out Uruguay Round (1986-1993) itself undoubtedly further contributed to the spread of regional trade agreements. Many nations, fearing that the Round would never succeed, joined regional arrangements, and regional trade agreements (RTAs) proliferated in the 1980s. By the late 1990s, there were approximately one hundred regional agreements, many of which had been negotiated in the 1990s. Every member of the World Trade Organization except Japan, Hong Kong, and Korea was included in one or more formal regional arrangements.

Each step toward West European integration had increased trade barriers for nonmembers and elicited an American response in the form of new multilateral trade negotiations within the GATT. The Dillon (1960–1961) and Kennedy (1963–1967) Rounds significantly lowered barriers raised by creation of the European Economic Community (Common Market), and the Tokyo Round (1973–1979) was a response to the first enlargement of the Community. When it became clear that the 1986 Single European Act would create a united and possibly closed West European market and Europeans resisted a new round of trade negotiations, the United States began to support development of the North American Free Trade Agreement (NAFTA). And in Pacific Asia, largely in response to European and North American regional developments, Japan intensified its own efforts to create a regional economy under its leadership. In Latin America, Argentina and Brazil initiated in 1991 a South American regional bloc (Mercosur).

As more and more developing countries have liberalized their economies to achieve greater efficiency and have abandoned import-substitution strategies, they too have begun to perceive the advantages of regional arrangements that would promote economies of scale for their industries and provide some balance to regionalization in Europe and North America. The expanding movement toward economic regionalism can be described as a response to what political scientists call a "security dilemma" in which each regional movement attempts to enhance its own competitive position vis-à-vis other regions.

The new regionalism has promoted regional integration of both services (finance, information-based industries, etc.) and manufacturing. Whereas previously, regionalism occurred primarily in the form of trade liberalization through customs unions or free-trade areas, regionalization in the 1990s has been accompanied by financial, manufacturing, and other forms of economic integration. Regional corporate groupings and production networks led by multinational firms have been established in Europe, North America, and Pacific Asia. Regionalism has thus had a growing impact on national, regional, and international economic affairs. Both market forces and government policies have led to regionalization of the world economy and caused some to fear that the world economy could fragment into rival blocs centered on the three dominant economies.

Although there is no single explanation of economic regionalism, both political and economic considerations have been involved in every regional movement, with their relative importance differing from region to region. Whereas the movement toward integration of Western Europe has been motivated primarily by political considerations, the motivation for North American regionalism has been more mixed, and Pacific Asian regionalism has been principally but not entirely market-driven. Attainment of political objectives, including ending French-German rivalry and creating a political entity to increase Europe's international standing, has been vitally important in European integration. Establishment of the North American free-trade area has reflected the natural integration of the three economies by market forces, but such political motives as strengthening North America's position vis-à-vis Western Europe and reducing illegal Mexican migration into the United States have also been involved. And in Pacific Asia, even though market forces have been the most important factor in the integration of the regional economies, political considerations and specific Japanese policy initiatives have played an important role as well .

Every regional arrangement represents the cooperative efforts of individual states to promote both their national and their collective economic and political objectives. Economic regionalism has been a response by nation-states to shared political problems and to a highly interdependent global economy. As the international economy has become more closely integrated, regional groupings of states have increased their cooperation to strengthen their autonomy, improve their bargaining position, and promote other political/economic objectives. Regionalization actually incorporates national concerns and ambitions rather than provides an alternative to a state-centered international system.

The major powers have incorporated economic regionalism in the strategies they employ to increase their own relative gains and to protect themselves against external threats to their economic welfare and national security while also sharing the benefits of an expanding global economy. This development reflects the belief of political and economic leaders that economic competition has become a central focus of world politics. Furthermore, international economic competition necessitates the availability of large domestic markets that enable domestic firms to achieve economies of scale. In order to survive and prosper in an uncertain and rapidly changing world, individual states and groups of states are adapting to the evolving economic, technological, and political environment as they have many times in the past. States have responded to an intensely competitive and threatening globalization by forming or extending regional economic alliances and arrangements under the leadership of one or more major economic powers.

The purpose of the Treaty on European Union, or Maastricht Treaty (1991), was to create a politically and economically unified European Union (EU) that would be the equal economically of Japan and the United States. The United States, Mexico, and Canada ratified NAFTA to create a strong North American integrated economy and perhaps eventually an entire Western Hemisphere one. In Pacific Asia, Japan has also attempted to strengthen its global position by creating a regional economy. These three movements toward regional integration and the relationships among the movements will have a profound impact on the nature and structure of the global economy.

At the opening of the twenty-first century, resolution of the tension between economic globalization and economic regionalization has become critically important to the health of the world economy. American economists have generally believed that economic globalism will eventually triumph over regionalism, and they argue that since World War II there has been an irreversible linear movement toward global interdependence. Inexorable economic and technological forces are believed to be driving the economies of the world toward ever higher levels of integration, and movements toward regional integration are viewed as building blocks in the construction of a larger and borderless global economy. This general process of economic integration and globalization has occasionally been blocked by irrational forces when parochial interests threatened by the forces of economic integration have appealed to nationalist passions and been granted protection. Nevertheless, some have argued that, in time, the inherent logic of economic efficiency will prevail, and nations will continue to move toward increased globalization. As C. Fred Bergsten has put it, although almost all countries have at one time or another attempted to resist international market pressures, such movements can succeed only in part and only for a short period.[18] Thus, try as they might, nations and regions ultimately cannot escape the inexorable forces of global unification.

Envisaging a different scenario, a minority of economists and many other observers believe that the end of the Cold War and intensification of global economic competition mean that the international economy will continue to fragment into regional economic blocs centered on the dominant economic powers. Furthermore, as regional arrangements are politically as well as economically motivated, they are likely to be influenced by protectionist pressures. Some assert, moreover, that such regional arrangements as NAFTA and the EU have the capacity to exploit their market power and implement an optimum tariff or a strategic trade policy and thus increase the benefits of trade for their own members to the disadvantage of nonmembers. In addition, the political and distributive deals that have been arranged to make a regional agreement politically possible cannot easily be undone. In the case of NAFTA, the benefits gained by American, Mexican, and Canadian automobile and auto-parts producers mean that the North American market in these sectors is unlikely to be opened to free trade anytime soon. Indeed, many observers consider a regionalized world the only realistic alternative to the dangers of economic nationalism and trade protectionism. In a world where national rivalries, oligopolistic competition, and state intervention rather than free and open markets are prevalent, global trade liberalization can proceed only so far.

A third position, with which I myself agree, argues that a dialectical process has been taking place in the world economy. There is no linear process in which the forces of global economic integration will eventually triumph over economic nationalism and economic regionalism, but the world is unlikely to fragment into regional blocs. Adherents of this position expect that economic globalism and economic regionalism will prove complementary. These seemingly contradictory developments, as one scholar has stated, actually reflect a world in which states use regional arrangements in an attempt to control what they have failed to control at either the national or multilateral levels.[19] Nation-states, as they have in the past, are again adapting to the rapidly evolving economic, technological, and political environment through various efforts to survive and prosper.

MANAGING THE GLOBAL ECONOMY

The task of managing the international economy has been made more important and more difficult by globalization and by the global economic turmoil of the late 1990s. Increasing integration of the world by powerful economic and technological forces has led more and more observers to believe that the world economy has become unstable and even out of control. An extreme yet representative statement of this concern appeared in a 1998 article in the *New York Times Magazine* by a former United States Treasury official stating that markets have become the ruling international authority; they are even more potent than military power or political influence and, arrayed against a nation, markets can cause hitherto unthinkable changes.[20] Although this article's writer, Roger C. Altman, believed that globalization could encourage the spread of democracy, he warned that a recent and frightening aspect of globalization had been revealed in the East Asian financial crisis. Although one may disagree with Altman's characterization of the good and bad consequences of globalization, one should acknowledge his stark but accurate statements that integration of the world economy has taken place much more rapidly than has development of a capacity to manage the new economic and technological forces. And, as Paul Krugman has asserted, many if not most of these troubles arise because the world economy is only partially integrated; that is, because economic integration has greatly outpaced political integration.

At the Bretton Woods Conference international rules (called "international regimes" by scholars) were established to govern international trade and monetary affairs. Although the system functioned effectively during the first decades of the postwar era, management became increasingly difficult as globalization increased integration of national economies and economic regionalism began to fragment the world economy in the 1980s. Governing the global economy became still more difficult as American leadership waned, the anti-Soviet alliance atrophied, and citizens in the industrialized countries grew increasingly concerned over the consequences for jobs and wages of the intensification of economic competition.

There have been, in fact, only two eras of effective governance of the world economy, and they have been the most prosperous eras in history. The first occurred in the several decades just prior to World War I; the outbreak of the war brought this remarkable era to a close. After the disastrous decades of the 1920s and 1930s, the second era of expanding economic prosperity immediately followed World War II. This era of very rapid economic growth (at least for the United States and Western Europe) closed with the stagflation of the 1970s and has not been reopened, despite the "good times" experienced by the United States in the 1990s. These two periods of unusual economic growth accompanied by international stability were characterized by a coincidence between the interests of the dominant power and the requirements for creating and maintaining a liberal world economy. Great Britain in the earlier era and the United States in the latter were able and willing to use their power and example to provide effective governance of the world economy. However, the circumstances surrounding the reigns of these two dominant, or hegemonic, economic powers were vastly different.

The task of governing the world economy in the decades prior to World War I was modest because the purpose of economic activity was modest. The remarkable decades from the early 1880s to 1914 were the high points of free trade and economic laissez-faire; the free market and economic globalization reached achievements that have not been equaled before or since. The British opted for trade liberalization when they repealed the Corn Laws (1846) and subsequently promoted free trade through a series of bilateral treaties. The international monetary system, based on the classical gold standard, provided price and monetary stability. As most other countries were also on the gold standard, the Bank of England was able to steer the world economy by lowering or raising interest rates. Economic growth, employment, and investment around the world rose or fell in response to decisions taken by "The Old Lady of Threadneedle Street" (the Bank of England), and immense British capital exports contributed greatly to the development and unification of the world economy. Objective economic laws beyond the reach of governments were believed to govern the market, but such views changed dramatically following the Great Depression of the 1930s and the development of Keynesian economics.

In the 1930s, powerful states and domestic interest groups (both large firms and organized labor), unwilling to leave economic matters up to the market, abandoned laissez-faire, and national governments began to play a more central role in the determination of international commerce. Although the emergence of powerful state and domestic actors called for more positive and assertive management of the world economy, none was forthcoming. The Great Depression of the 1930s, fragmentation of the world economy into rival political/economic blocs, and the outbreak of World War II prevented development of any solution until the United States asserted leadership following World War II.

With the United States as the leader, the Bretton Woods system was established, trade liberalization was promoted through the GATT, and the dollar was assigned an international role and became an important source of international monetary stability. In the 1960s and beyond, however, the quality of American leadership deteriorated. The Nixon Administration's jettisoning of the system of fixed exchange rates in 1971, the American-led movement toward New Protectionism in the mid-1970s, the significant shift of the Reagan Administration in the mid-1980s from multilateralism to a multitrack foreign economic policy, and the Clinton Administration's aggressive pursuit of geo-economics and strategic trade policy all seriously undermined the fundamental principles of the Bretton Woods system. Following the end of the Cold War, the United States and its allies began to pursue more parochial policies and to emphasize regional rather than global solutions to economic problems. Indeed, since the mid-1980s, the West Europeans have concentrated on the process of European economic and monetary unification. At the domestic level, more and more Americans, West Europeans, and others have questioned the costs of free trade, unregulated financial movements, and the freewheeling activities of multinational corporations.

These developments have raised again the issue of governing or managing the global economy, and that raises an even more fundamental question: What is the purpose of governance? During the Cold War, the fundamental purpose of the world economy was to strengthen the economies of the anti-Soviet alliance and solidify the political unity of the United States with its allies. Although the global economy, or at least those economies outside the tight Soviet bloc, was based on economic principles such as free trade and (after the mid-1970s) freedom of capital movements, these principles were set aside whenever necessary to serve the political purpose of increasing the strength of Allied economies and the cohesion of the anti-Soviet alliance. A notable example was the formation of the European Economic Community by the Treaty of Rome (1957), a violation of the principle of nondiscrimination and of at least the spirit of Article XXIV of the GATT regarding regional economic agreements. Now that regional economic arrangements have become the norm rather than the exception, it has become more important than ever to determine a new purpose for the global economy of the twenty-first century and the principles on which it should be based.

Many, if not most, American public officials, business leaders, and professional economists, as well as many commentators, believe that the issues of management and economic purpose have already been determined. The global economy, according to this position, should be guided by the policy prescriptions of economics and be based on market principles. Free trade, freedom of capital movements, and unrestricted access by multinational firms to markets around the globe henceforth should govern international economic affairs. With the triumph of the market, economic logic and the relative efficiencies of national economies will determine the distribution of economic activities and wealth (and, of course, power) around the world. Moreover, the success of the United States in the 1990s and the serious economic problems of Japan and East Asia in that same period are believed to have demonstrated the superiority of the American market-oriented economic model.

The reality of "the market triumphant" is challenged by many political leaders, powerful interest groups, and public commentators around the world. In the industrial economies, this dissent generally takes the form of opposition to globalization as a threat to employment, wages, and job security. Some individuals and groups consider that free trade and the activities of multinational firms threaten livelihoods and communities; free trade and foreign investment, they argue, are not the route to economic prosperity for workers and others disadvantaged by globalization. In many less developed and industrializing countries, as nineteenth-century critics of international capitalism proclaimed, "free trade is the policy of the strong," as are international financial movements and foreign investment by multinational firms. Although opponents to a market-governed international economy are less influential than its proponents, their numbers have increased in proportion to the increasing globalization and the growing role of international markets in determining the economic welfare of people everywhere.

As one considers the prospects for a market-governed world economy, it is important to remember that economists themselves are deeply divided over the principles that should guide the post–Cold War international market economy. There is near unanimity among economists on the virtues of free trade; indeed, as Paul Samuelson has said, the law of comparative advantage (upon which the doctrine of free trade is based) is "the most beautiful idea in economics." However, beyond the issue of trade, agreement within the economics fraternity rapidly dissipates. For example, although most economists appear to favor unfettered capital markets, a number of very distinguished economists, including Nobel Laureate James Tobin and Jagdish Bhagwati, one of the world's foremost international economists, challenge the wisdom of permitting unregulated international financial flows; finance, they argue, is too important to be left in the invisible hand of the market. There are also serious differences among economists concerning the international monetary system, economic regionalism, and economic development, as well as other important matters. Thus, there are few agreed-upon fundamental principles beyond the belief in free trade on which to base a market-determined global economy.

CONCLUSION

This book argues that, although the post–World War II international economic order no longer exists, no agreement has yet been achieved regarding a new world economic order or its rules and guiding principles. The purpose of economic activities is determined not only by the prescriptions of technical economics but also (either explicitly or implicitly) by the norms, values, and interests of the national social and political systems in which economic activities are embedded. Even though economic factors will play an important role in determining the characteristics of the global economy, the most important factors are and will be political. The characteristics are and will be determined largely by the security and political relations among the major powers, including the United States, Western Europe, Japan, China, and Russia.

Markets by themselves are neither morally nor politically neutral; they embody the values of society and the interests of powerful actors. Whereas the post–World War II economy reflected to a considerable degree the political, economic, and security interests of the United States and its allies, the nature and functioning of the twenty-first-century global economy will ultimately be determined by the power and interests of its dominant members. While it is impossible to ascertain the outcome of present and future interactions between economic and political affairs, it is quite unlikely that powerful states will leave such vital matters as the distribution of wealth, industry, and power up to the unencumbered interplay of market forces. Nor is it likely that nations will sacrifice economic autonomy, political independence, and security concerns to a maximization of the efficient functioning of the global economy. Both economic efficiency and national ambitions, particularly those of the dominant powers, will be driving forces in the global economy of the twenty-first century and will ultimately determine its economic and political purpose.

The Cold War International Economy

FOR THE FORTY years following World War II, the fierce political struggles of the Cold War and the distinctive international economy created in response to those struggles dominated international affairs. Since its beginning in the sixteenth century, the world economy has in fact passed through several phases, generally beginning and ending with political upheaval and a major war. The first period from the sixteenth to the end of the eighteenth century was labeled the "age of mercantilism." Following the end of the Napoleonic Wars in 1815, the victorious British laid the political foundations for an international market economy that led to the first great era of economic globalism. This era ended with the outbreak of World War I, and the period from the end of World War I to the end of World War II witnessed economic chaos, severe contraction of international trade, and fierce conflict among rival great powers. Then, at the Bretton Woods Conference near the end of World War II, the United States assumed leadership of efforts to revive a global world economy.

The beginning of the Cold War in the late 1940s frustrated this effort to create a truly unified international economy, as that economy divided into what Stalin called "the two systems"—the command or Communist economies of the Soviet bloc and the capitalist economies of the "free world." Under American leadership, the members of the Western alliance created an international economy based on agreed-upon rules and close cooperation. During the Cold War, for the first time in world history the dominant capitalist powers cooperated with one another as the exigencies of survival necessitated that they subordinate parochial interests to alliance unity. International economic institutions such as the World Bank and the International Monetary Fund reflected this commitment to an overriding political purpose. With the end of the Cold War, and therefore of an obvious need for close allied cooperation, the political understandings that underlay the Cold War international capitalist system began to weaken, and the continued well-being of the world economy was threatened.

The evolution of the post–World War II international economy and the Cold War were intimately joined in every particular. With the end of the Cold War, although mutual economic interest in the survival of an integrated and stable international economy still encourages nations to cooperate, conflicting national ambitions and interests increasingly threaten to undermine the cooperation on which the world economy has been grounded. Therefore, a more secure political foundation for the world economy must be constructed to replace the crumbling underpinnings of the international economy.

POST–WORLD WAR II ECONOMIC ACHIEVEMENTS

The quarter century from the end of World War II to the early 1970s was the most prosperous in human history. Following a period of reconstruction in the late 1940s and early 1950s, the rate of economic growth of the industrialized economies reached a historically unprecedented level. Western Europe grew by about 4.5 percent annually in the 1950s, and by nearly 5 percent annually in the 1960s.[21] Even more extraordinary was the case of Japan; in the 1950s and 1960s, Japan grew at the unprecedented rate of approximately 10 percent a year. The United States was laggard, growing at about 3 percent in the 1950s and about 4 percent in the 1960s. The less developed economies did not share in this spreading postwar prosperity. The Communist or command economies had isolated themselves from the larger world economy; among them, only the Soviet Union enjoyed rapid economic growth. Economic growth in the West and Japan was accompanied by, and in fact stimulated by, rapid expansion of international trade. As national economic barriers fell, international economic interdependence among the capitalist economies grew rapidly in trade, money, and investment. The Western and Japanese economies left behind the economic miseries of the 1930s and committed themselves to the recreation of an open, multilateral world economy.

Underlying the extraordinary economic growth were propitious economic and political factors. Supplementing positive supply and demand were favorable political and institutional factors. The political factors responsible for rapid economic growth and trade expansion included American international leadership and every industrial economy's commitment to develop economic policies to promote full employment. In addition, new international rules and institutions provided a stable framework within which the world economy could flourish. Favorable economic factors constituted the sufficient conditions for the extraordinary performance of the post–World War II economy; the political and institutional environment provided the necessary conditions.

In the early 1970s, however, the postwar era of rapid economic growth came to an abrupt end, and the advanced industrial economies (with the notable exception of Japan) settled into a decade-long stagflation characterized by an unprecedented combination of low rates of economic growth, high rates of unemployment, and very high rates of inflation. Although the causes of this reversal in economic fortunes are still debated, the most important cause was the dramatic slowing of the rate of productivity growth in the United States and Western Europe. Several other developments were undoubtedly also significant. It is certain that the irresponsible and highly inflationary economic policy of the United States accompanying escalation of the Vietnam War in the mid-1960s and the simultaneous expansion of social welfare programs were major contributing factors. The 1973 oil crisis also contributed greatly to these unfortunate developments. Changes in a number of policies and institutions, including environmental and other regulations that decreased economic efficiency, have also been put forth as possible causes. The 1970s setback concluded with the triumph of central bankers committed to strict anti-inflation policies and with the deep recession that ended the stagflation, but at a very high price.

FOUNDATIONS OF POSTWAR ECONOMIC SUCCESS

Several highly favorable economic factors were vital to the outstanding success of the early postwar economy. On the demand side, the war itself had created a large unsatisfied demand in the United States and other industrial economies. Western Europe and Japan not only needed to rebuild after the devastation of World War II, but wished to "catch up" with the United States as mass consumer societies; indeed, although the United States had developed a mass market for automobiles as early as the 1920s, the European and Japanese mass markets did not develop until after World War II. On the supply side, there was a huge backlog in the United States—including developments in World War II military and industrial research and development—of unexploited technologies and productive techniques. Domestic investment in these technologies provided a huge stimulus to productivity growth, and economic growth in Western Europe and Japan was accelerated by the process of technological catch-up with the United States.

Investment rates in most Western European countries and Japan (especially in the 1960s) reached extraordinary heights. Moreover, both Western Europe and Japan had large supplies of excess labor that migrated from the countryside to industrial areas in the postwar years and contributed to economic growth. Until the energy crisis of 1973, the advanced economies enjoyed very favorable terms of trade in oil and other commodities. Finally, the opening of markets and the expansion of trade further stimulated both investment and economic growth. In short, favorable demand conditions, rapid accumulation of productive factors, and high productivity growth contributed to an era of rapid economic growth.

In addition to these favorable economic conditions, the United States assumed economic and political leadership. After World War II the United States had thrown itself into the effort to create a stable and prosperous world economy. The realization that failure to create a viable world economy after World War I, along with the enormous costs of the Great Depression, had been major causes of World War II caused the United States and many other nations to decide to make the international economy work to avoid a return to the previous disastrous economic conditions. Important economic interests in the United States (industry, finance, agriculture) realized that they had a vital stake in a prosperous world economy. This shift in American thinking was manifest in the crucial role played by the United States in the creation of the Bretton Woods System embodying the belief that a rule-based international economy and international institutions to manage these rules were necessary.

A fundamental change in political thinking and emergence of a novel domestic consensus in Western Europe and in the United States supported a liberal world economy. Central to the new consensus was a distributional settlement between capital and labor in which the major economic powers pledged themselves to pursue full employment policies and to guarantee the welfare of their populations. In effect, governments attempted to convert organized labor to the idea of supporting a world economy based on free trade and to thus help solve the distributional problems that would inevitably arise as nations opened their economies to imports and international competition. Recognizing that free trade would create losers as well as winners, governments also promised to compensate the losers through full employment and social insurance policies. This general commitment took different forms in each of the advanced industrial countries. American enactment of the Full Employment Act (1946), the French system of "indicative" economic planning, and the German concept of the social market, along with the distinctive Japanese commitment to lifetime employment and export-led growth, exemplified this new commitment. New domestic political consensus in many countries supported national economic policies based on the price system and private property. At the international level, the new consensus facilitated agreement on economic policies that promoted an open world economy based on free trade.

However, we must remember that this domestic political consensus rested on certain important conditions. In the early postwar years, national economies were generally closed, and therefore governments were relatively free to pursue economic policies promoting rapid economic growth and full employment. As economies were opened after successive rounds of trade negotiations and increases in international economic flows, governmental ability to pursue expansionary economic policies became more constrained; this resulted in increasing tension between national policy autonomy and the commitment to an open world economy.

Rapid economic and productivity growth also supported the domestic consensus; the distribution issue was, in large part, solved by the expanding economic pie. However, when the rates of economic and productivity growth slackened in the 1970s, new distributional conflicts arose. Also, although rapid economic growth and expansion of the welfare state had been considered complementary and not conflicting, growth of a more conservative political ideology in the late 1970s led citizens to question the costs of the welfare state and even to assign to the welfare state responsibility for the economic woes associated with stagflation. Thus, when the favorable conditions underlying the post-war domestic consensus began to erode in the 1970s, the political foundations of an open world economy were weakened, at least in the United States and Western Europe.

BRETTON WOODS SYSTEM

The institutional framework of the postwar world economy was constructed at the Bretton Woods Conference in 1944 and reflected American and British thinking. The small number of players involved in formulating the agreement accounts in large part for the extraordinary success of the conference and is in marked contrast to subsequent efforts to agree on rules to govern the world economy. Although a number of disagreements divided the American and British negotiators, the conference succeeded in formulating unifying principles to be embodied in the institutions comprising the Bretton Woods System (BWS).

The major economic powers agreed that trade and other economic activities should be regulated by binding rules and that states were not to interfere in the determination of international economic outcomes. These rules were based on several fundamental principles, including the following: (1) commitment to trade liberalization via multilateral negotiations incorporating the principle of nondiscrimination, (2) agreement that current account transactions should be free from controls but that controls on the freedom of capital movement were permissible, and (3) agreement that exchange rates should be fixed or pegged and that, while an individual nation could modify its exchange rate, it had to consult with the IMF before making major changes. In addition to establishing guidelines and institutions for the international economy, the Bretton Woods Conference also permitted governments to pursue economic stabilization and social welfare policies; that is, individual nations would be free (within prescribed limits) to pursue economic growth and full employment. These fundamental principles and the international institutions embodying them provided the framework within which the postwar international economy flourished.

The original BWS has been repeatedly and significantly modified in response to economic and political realities. The prostrate European and Japanese economies, the "dollar shortage" experienced by those economies in the years before the Marshall Plan, and especially the exigencies of the Cold War brought about major changes in the original BWS.[22] In the interest of forging an alliance system against the Soviet Union, the United States reversed its prior positions on a number of international economic issues and maintained a decisive role in the world economy. Allied cooperation had a major impact on the original BWS and, in the late 1940s, became a major factor in the continued development of the postwar international economic order. For example, the Marshall Plan, which more than anything else transformed American–Western European relations and the postwar international economy, could never have passed the U.S. Congress if there had been no Soviet threat.

The world's foremost creditor nation, the United States, used its financial reserves, primarily through the Marshall Plan, to facilitate rebuilding the West European economies as a buffer against Soviet expansion. From 1947 to 1951, the United States dispersed to its European allies approximately 2 percent of its GNP annually; such a sizable transfer of wealth was unprecedented. In addition to providing this financial assistance, the United States, despite its historic aversion to trading blocs, encouraged West Europeans to pursue economic integration. As a precondition for receiving American assistance, governments were required to lower barriers to intra-European cooperation and to coordinate their economic plans through the Organization for European Economic Cooperation (OEEC, the forerunner of the Organization for Economic Cooperation and Development [OECD]); they were also encouraged to carry out domestic economic reforms, including adoption of America's more productive manufacturing and management techniques. The United States even tolerated European discrimination against American agricultural and manufactured exports. It also used its financial and other resources to help rebuild the Japanese economy and integrate it into the Western system. Thus, during the early years of the Cold War, the postwar international economic order and the international security order became intimately joined.

Two international regimes (rules) embodied in institutions were particularly important to the early success of the international economy. The International Monetary Fund (IMF) administered the international monetary system based on fixed but adjustable exchange rates. The General Agreement on Tariffs and Trade (GATT) was developed to manage the international trading system; responsibility for that regime was diffused among a number of nations, and as this number increased the trading regime became more and more unwieldy.

International Monetary System of Fixed Rates

The most important BWS regime was the monetary system designed by experts from a number of countries with shared views on technical issues. The system had to provide monetary reserves in sufficient amounts to enable member governments to maintain the exchange rates for their currencies at predetermined values. The IMF was designed to solve this problem by using contributions from member countries and offering reserve credits to states with international payments problems. In addition, the monetary system had to anchor its members' monetary policies to some objective standard in order to prevent global inflation or devaluation. Stabilization of a monetary system can be achieved by tying every currency to a "nonmonetary" asset (gold being the asset of choice), by coordinating national monetary policies, or by following a leader whose past policies promise that it will provide the desired degree of economic stability in the future. Although all three methods were in fact employed in the early postwar years, the monetary policies of member states were anchored by tying every currency to the dollar, which in turn was tied to gold, and the major powers also informally coordinated their economic policies.

This monetary system, which lasted until the early 1970s, was extraordinarily successful. Designed to provide both domestic policy autonomy and international monetary stability, the system in effect provided a compromise between the rigid gold standard of the late nineteenth century, under which governments had little ability to manage their own economies, and the monetary anarchy of the 1930s, when governments had too much license to engage in competitive devaluations and other destructive practices. To achieve both autonomy and stability, the system was based on the following principles: fixed or pegged exchange rates but sufficient flexibility to enable individual states to deal with extraordinary situations, including pursuit of full employment; reliable reserve credit in the event of an international payments problem; agreement among member countries to peg their currencies to gold at $35 an ounce or to the dollar; IMF approval of exchange rate adjustments in the event of a fundamental disequilibrium in a nation's balance of payments; and monetary reserves that could be made available to deficit countries. These principles governed the system quite successfully for nearly three decades.

Nevertheless, the ways in which the system actually functioned did not fulfill the intentions and expectations of its founders. A significant difference was that, although the IMF had been assigned responsibility for maintaining reserves, in practice it was the buildup of the dollar reserves held by member governments that actually achieved this goal. In this way the American dollar became the keystone of the international monetary system. Cooperation among the United States and its allies and, until 1971, the passive U.S. attitude toward the dollar's exchange rate made IMF actions unnecessary in this area. Members also followed U.S. policy preferences in the early postwar era, and they were assured that this would provide stability to the system. However, by the time of the Vietnam War in the 1960s, the United States had ceased to pursue a policy of price stability, and the acceleration of inflation caused by the war eventually led to abandonment of the fixed rate system by the Nixon Administration in August, 1971. Even so, the United States and the dollar remained central to the system.

The key role of the dollar in the international monetary system facilitated the American alliance system and the functioning of the world economy; the international role of the dollar as both a reserve and a transaction currency became a cornerstone of America's global economic and political position. Because, for political as well as for economic reasons, America's major allies and economic partners were willing to hold dollars, the international role of the dollar conferred on the United States the right of "seigniorage"; this means that the provider of the currency for an economy, in this case the international economy, enjoys certain privileges. As President Charles de DeGaulle of France bitterly complained in the 1960s, the "hegemony of the dollar" conferred "extravagant privileges" on the United States, because that country alone could simply print dollars to fight foreign wars, could buy up French and other businesses, and could go deeply into debt without fearing negative consequences.

However, a fundamental contradiction existed at the heart of this dollar-based system. While the huge outflow of American dollars to finance the rebuilding of Western Europe and Japan and the American military buildup during both the Korean and Vietnam Wars helped solve certain problems, this outflow of dollars meant that the United States would one day be unable to redeem in gold, and at the agreed price, those dollars held by private investors and foreign governments. A distinguished economist predicted that confidence in the dollar would be undermined as the American balance of payments shifted from a surplus to a deficit. This problem became acute late in the 1960s when escalation of the Vietnam War and its inflationary consequences caused deterioration in international confidence in the value of the dollar. As that confidence declined, the foundations of the Bretton Woods System of fixed rates began to erode.

Decreased confidence in the dollar also led to intensifying speculation in gold, and this was followed by attempts to find ways to recreate confidence in the system. In the late 1960s, the creation of Special Drawing Rights (SDRs) as a new reserve asset to complement the dollar was important. However, as Benjamin Cohen has convincingly argued, the actual solution attained was essentially political.[23] America's Cold War allies, fearing that a collapse of the dollar would force the United States to withdraw its forces from overseas and to retreat into political isolation, agreed to hold overvalued dollars. Also such export-oriented economies as West Germany and, at a later date, Japan wished to keep access to the lucrative American market.

Throughout the postwar era the United States always had one primary partner helping it to defend the dollar and hence the U.S. international position. In the early postwar period, the American position and support for the dollar were based on cooperation with the British; this "special relationship," begun between the First and Second World Wars, had been solidified by wartime experience. The Anglo-Saxon powers worked together to frame the BWS and reestablish the liberal international economy. By the late 1960s, however, the relative decline of the British economy forced Great Britain to pull away from its close partnership with the United States.

West Germany then replaced Great Britain as the foremost economic partner of the United States and as the major supporter of the dollar. Throughout the Vietnam War and into the 1970s, the Germans supported American hegemony by holding dollars and buying American government securities. Inflationary and other consequences of this new special relationship weakened it in the mid-1970s and eventually led to fracture in the late 1970s when the Germans refused to support President Carter's economic policies; the Germans then joined the French to sponsor the European Monetary System. Creation of this "zone of stability" in Western Europe was the first of many efforts to isolate the European economies from the wild fluctuations of the dollar.

In the 1980s, the Germans were replaced by the Japanese when, through their investments in the United States, the Japanese provided financial backing for Reagan's economic and military policies. In the 1990s, sporadic informal cooperation among American, German, and Japanese central banks supported the international role of the dollar. This cooperation continued largely due to fear of what would happen to the international economic and political system if the monetary system were to break down.

Trade Regime

The trading regime was born in conflict between the American and British negotiators at Bretton Woods. Reflecting American industrial supremacy, the goal of American negotiators was to achieve free trade and to open foreign markets. Although the British were also committed to the principle of free trade, they were extremely concerned over the "dollar shortage," possible loss of domestic economic autonomy to pursue full employment, and a number of related issues. The eventual British-American compromise agreement to create the International Trade Organization (ITO) left many trade issues unresolved.

As an interim measure, in 1948 the United States and its principal economic partners had created the General Agreement on Tariffs and

Trade (GATT). With the defeat of the ITO by the U.S. Senate in 1950, the GATT became the world's principal trade organization. The purpose of the GATT was to promote "freer and fairer" trade, primarily through negotiated reductions of formal tariffs. Although the GATT proved remarkably successful in fostering trade liberalization and providing a framework for trade discussions, its authority and the scope of its responsibilities were severely limited; it was essentially a negotiating forum rather than a true international organization, and it had no rule-making authority. Moreover, it lacked an adequate dispute-settlement mechanism, and its jurisdiction applied primarily to manufactured goods. The GATT did not have authority to deal with agriculture, services, intellectual property rights, or foreign direct investment; nor did the GATT have sufficient authority to deal with customs unions and other preferential trading arrangements. Successive American administrations and other governments became increasingly cognizant of the GATT's inherent limitations and, following the Uruguay Round, replaced it in 1995 with the World Trade Organization (WTO), whose responsibilities are much broader and which, unlike the GATT, is a full-fledged international organization rather than merely an international secretariat.

Despite the limitations of its mandate and organizational structure, however, the GATT for many years played an important role in reducing barriers to international trade. The GATT provided a rule-based regime of trade liberalization founded on the principles of nondiscrimination, unconditional reciprocity, and transparency (for example, the use of formal tariffs and the publication of trade regulations). Trade barriers were to be reduced and rules determined by multilateral negotiations among GATT members. In effect, GATT members agreed to establish regulations lowering trade barriers and then let markets determine trade patterns; member states pledged not to resort to managed or results-oriented trade that set import quotas for particular products. Under GATT, markets were opened and new rules established by international negotiations; agreements were based on compromise or unconditional reciprocity rather than on unilateral actions by the strong or by specific reciprocity. GATT's goal was an open multilateralism; that is, the agreement provided for extension of negotiated trade rules to all members of the GATT without discrimination. However, candidates for

TABLE 2.1

Trade Chronology

1948	The General Agreement on Tariffs and Trade (GATT) provisionally comes into force, and the International Trade Organization (ITO) Charter is drafted.
1950	The ITO Charter is defeated.
1955	The United States has certain agricultural policies excluded from the GATT.
1947–1961	Early rounds of trade negotiations cut tariffs by 73 percent.
1963–1967	Kennedy Round of GATT negotiations.
1973–1979	Tokyo Round of GATT negotiations.
1974	Multifiber Arrangement restricting textile imports.
1986	Launching of the Uruguay Round at Punta del Este.
1994	At Marrakesh, GATT Ministers agree on the Final Act of the Uruguay Round and agree to establish the World Trade Organization (WTO).
1995	The WTO established.

membership did have to meet certain criteria and agree to obey the rules. The founders of the GATT wanted a steady progression toward an open world economy with no return to the cycle of retaliation and counterretaliation that had characterized the 1930s.

The postwar period witnessed a number of agreements to lower tariff barriers. A significant shift in negotiations took place during the Kennedy Round (1963–1967). That Round substituted general reciprocity for the prior product-by-product (specific reciprocity) approach to tariff cuts; GATT members agreed to reduce tariffs on particular products by agreed-upon percentages and made trade-offs across economic sectors. The Round resulted in an approximate 33 percent reduction of trade barriers on manufactures and in a number of basic reforms, including regulation of "dumping" practices. In addition, preferential treatment was given to exports from LDCs.

The next major initiative to liberalize trade was the Tokyo Round (1973–1979) that, after years of bitter fighting, succeeded in being far more comprehensive than earlier efforts. It included significant tariff cuts on most industrial products, liberalization of agricultural trade, and reduction of nontariff barriers. In addition, the industrial countries pledged to pay greater attention to the demands of less developed countries (LDC) for special treatment of their exports. However, the most important task of the Tokyo Round was to fashion codes of conduct to deal with unfair trade practices. The negotiations prohibited export subsidies and eliminated some discrimination in public procurement. However, the Round did not resolve the American-European dispute over agriculture, satisfy the LDCs, or stop the noxious proliferation of nontariff barriers that occurred throughout the 1970s.

Nevertheless, trade-liberalizing agreements did enable international trade to grow rapidly. Substantial expansion of trade meant that imports penetrated more deeply and exports became a much more important aspect of domestic economies. In fact, for some EEC countries, exports reached as high as 50 percent of Gross National Product (GNP). And even the domestic markets of the United States and Japan were made much more open to imports. It is particularly significant that since then, Japanese imports have included a growing percentage of manufactured goods. Meanwhile, GATT membership greatly expanded over the years, and growing trade flows created a highly interdependent international economy despite the 1970s slowdown.

Limitations of the System

The BWS had several inherent limitations that would in time weaken the foundations of the postwar economy. Many issues and topics of potential importance had been left vague or had simply not been covered by the rules of the system. On the trade issue, the fundamental purpose of the GATT was to govern exchanges of products and commodities; at the insistence of the United States, and much to its later regret, agriculture had been excluded from GATT rules. Then, in the 1970s, services, foreign direct investment, and intellectual property rights, issues that had been quite unimportant at the time of the founding of the Bretton Woods institutions and were not included in GATT rules, became major components of international commerce.

The problems of adjustments in payments imbalances and determination of the responsibilities of deficit and/or surplus countries to correct imbalances were never satisfactorily resolved.

The role of international financial flows, which transformed the global economy in the 1970s, had been unanticipated, and no rules had been developed to govern financial matters. Finally, the increasing importance of the multinational corporation and foreign direct investment in the postwar era profoundly transformed the international economy, especially as trade and investment became tightly linked. Initially, most multinational corporations (MNCs) were American corporations that had begun a rapid overseas expansion in the late 1950s in response to creation of the European Common Market; subsequently, many firms of other industrialized and some industrializing countries also became multinationals. Indeed, many of the economic activities and economic problems that had become extremely important by the 1980s and 1990s had *not* been covered by the original GATT framework.

In addition to these inherent limitations, a number of postwar developments weakened the BWS. One important development was the U.S. use of protectionist devices; another was the relative economic decline of the United States when the growth of powerful competitors led to decreased U.S. willingness to use its economic resources and political influence to support the System. Still another development was the increasing number and heterogeneity of the participating players. By the 1970s, the BWS institutions had ceased to be private clubs of North Atlantic economies with shared interests and common ideology; the institutions indeed became organizations with highly diverse memberships. The increasing openness of domestic economies was another development with a major impact. As their economies opened, governments found it more and more difficult to pursue economic policies of full employment and social welfare, and they were frequently forced to choose between their international obligations and their domestic economic priorities.

At the time of the BWS founding, economists assumed that the domestic and international economic realms were in large part independent of one another. They believed that national economies were closed economies, and they even regarded them as empty boxes connected by trade flows and exchange rates. The GATT was given responsibility for the trade flows, and the IMF, for exchange rates. Because economists considered trade, finance, and other areas of economic activity to be separate from one another, the rules and policies dealing with each economic area were mainly considered independently of one another, and policy changes in one area were not expected to have any significant effect on others. Also, analysts regarded comparative advantage and national economic specialization as products of nature rather than as results of deliberate corporate and government policies; this latter perception would change dramatically in the 1970s with the economic rise of Japan. In the early postwar years, the rules governing international trade told nations what they *could not do* and not what they *had to do* to be fair to their trading partners. Proscriptions were directed primarily at formal and external barriers affecting international commerce and not at informal barriers or at such domestic practices as government procurement or business relationships that might discriminate against foreign firms.

Despite its limitations, the BWS succeeded in the early postwar decades because it had resolved, at least temporarily and to the satisfaction of the major economic powers, the fundamental problems of the world economy. The *distribution* problem was settled at both the domestic and international levels. At the domestic level, the postwar consensus within the major capitalist economies resolved the distribution issue between capital and labor; at the international level, the United States was so economically superior to all other countries that it did not worry about controlling the distribution of the gains from trade and other economic outcomes between itself and its trading partners. Until the late 1960s, the issue of *national autonomy* really did not arise among the major powers because they were political allies and largely closed economies; although the LDCs were very much concerned about their economic and political dependence on the United States and other industrial economies, they really could do nothing about it. As for *international regimes,* they functioned effectively both because the United States pursued fiscally responsible economic policies and because the issues with which they dealt were relatively simple.

In the 1970s, however, the inherent limitations of these regimes and profound changes in the world economy resulted in the unraveling of all of the early postwar solutions to problems in the global economy. By

67

the 1980s, almost every major feature of the Bretton Woods System had changed, was changing, or was being challenged. With increased interdependence among national economies, differences in the ways that nations regulated and conducted business inside their own borders became more important and indeed a major source of economic friction. International financial flows, foreign direct investment, and services had multiplied and had become more intertwined both internally and externally so that policy coordination among nations had become imperative but also more difficult to achieve. These developments created serious challenges for the effective management of the international economy.

Bretton Woods System Undermined

Several developments in the 1970s challenged the BWS. Although the roots of these developments can be found in the 1960s and even earlier, their effects became obvious during the 1970s. The end of the system of fixed exchange rates, the oil crisis of 1973, and, most important of all, the slowdown of American productivity growth gave rise to the Great Stagflation, and this influenced decisively the health and functioning of the world economy.

Great Stagflation (1973–1979)

In the early 1970s, the world economy had to deal with the high inflation of the late 1960s, the postwar era of rapid economic growth ended, and a decade-long era of economic turmoil began. Escalation of the Vietnam War and the simultaneous launching of the Great Society Program by the Johnson Administration (1963–1969) had caused acceleration in the global rate of inflation. The American Administration, attempting to hide the financial cost of the Vietnam War from its citizens, refused to increase taxes and chose instead to pay for its warfare and welfare policies through inflationary macroeconomic policies. The succeeding Nixon Administration (1969–1974) compounded the problem of inflation. In addition, the Federal Reserve threw caution to the winds by significantly stimulating the economy, a move labeled by critics as a blatant attempt to reelect Nixon in 1972. Subsequent intensification of speculative attacks on the overvalued dollar and ballooning of the American trade deficit resulted in the decision on August 15, 1971, to force a devaluation of the dollar. In 1973, the first oil crisis plunged the world into the Great Stagflation; that unprecedented combination of hyperinflation, low economic growth, and high unemployment in the United States, Western Europe, and other countries forced profound changes on the world economy.

End of Fixed Exchange Rates

The postwar system of fixed exchange rates became a casualty of inflation and of the increasing mobility of capital; the greater amount of capital movement had permitted investors (and speculators) to move their assets from one country to another in anticipation of a currency revaluation. As the currency of one country or another came under attack and revaluation was forced, maintenance of the system of fixed rates had become more and more difficult. In the late 1960s, attacks on the dollar had mounted as both inflation and America's balance of payments difficulties undermined confidence. Responding to speculative attacks, the United States and its allies launched joint initiatives to shore up the dollar. However, none of the efforts was successful; high inflation continued to undermine not only the dollar but also the overall trading position of the United States. By the early 1970s, American officials concluded that a substantial devaluation was needed. However, the United States could not devalue the dollar by itself because, if it did so unilaterally, its trading partners would immediately follow suit to preserve their export positions. The Nixon Administration, therefore, believed that it had to take decisive action to force a devaluation on its trading partners. In effect, the Administration decided to destroy the postwar system of fixed rates rather than carry out domestic deflationary measures required if United States were to fulfill its commitments under the BWS.

Death of the system of fixed rates led eventually to the end of the Bretton Woods monetary system. The United States announced that it was closing the gold window and would no longer redeem dollars for gold. Simultaneously, in order to force other countries to appreciate their currencies, the Administration imposed a 10 percent surcharge on imports into the American economy and announced that the surcharge would be removed only after a satisfactory devaluation of the dollar had been achieved. Following bitter denunciations, especially by West Europeans, of this unilateral American action and intense negotiations, the dollar was indeed substantially devalued by the Smithsonian Agreement of December 1971, when other countries agreed to appreciate their currencies. The international monetary system was thus changed, at least de facto, from one based on fixed exchange rates to one based on flexible rates.

Efforts by an international committee to develop a new system of stable but adjustable exchange rates failed because of overwhelming problems caused by increased capital mobility and by fundamental differences between the United States and Western Europe over any new system. After this failure to agree, industrial countries at the Jamaica Conference (1976) accorded de jure recognition to a *nonsystem* of flexible rates. Although some scholars object to such a characterization, I believe that the term "nonsystem" is appropriate because the international monetary system had no agreed-upon rules to guide decisions on such problems or on whether deficit or surplus countries should have the primary responsibility to make policy adjustments.

The Bretton Woods rule-based international monetary system was replaced by a shaky political agreement reached by the dominant economic powers and managed by their central bankers. What later became known as the "reference range" system was based on the cooperative, and sometimes not so cooperative, efforts of the major economic powers to stabilize currency values and international monetary affairs. As time went by, however, this cooperative mechanism became increasingly unsatisfactory and led to many proposals to reform the nonsystem. Partially because of European frustration with American macroeconomic policies, the effort to stabilize European monetary affairs resulted in the decision of the European Council in 1978 to accept the French-German proposal for the creation of the European Monetary System (EMS) and the accompanying Exchange Rate Mechanism (ERM).

Oil Crisis of 1973

The other major event that contributed to the end of the postwar era of rapid economic growth was the 1973 oil crisis. In response to the Yom Kippur War, Arab members of the Organization of Petroleum Exporting Countries (OPEC) initiated an oil boycott and thus forced a substantial increase in the world price of oil that then led to deterioration of those favorable terms of trade that had contributed to the postwar prosperity of the developed and many developing economies. That successful boycott also resulted in a shift of control over the global petroleum market from the United States and American multinationals to the OPEC oil producers, resulting in a significant decrease in American influence over global economics and politics. Whereas the United States had previously used its control over the oil supply as an instrument of its foreign policy, this source of leverage was no longer available. Transfer of wealth and power to OPEC had a major impact.

The huge increase in the price of oil, and therefore of other forms of energy and many other products, produced simultaneously recessionary and inflationary pressures. The price rise had a *deflationary* effect because it withdrew a substantial amount of purchasing power from the world economy; the effect was similar to what would happen if a government suddenly taxed away a large portion of a nation's money supply. The other and opposed impact of the price rise was *inflationary*, because oil is so important as a raw material in the cost of transportation and in almost every other aspect of the modern industrial economy that the increase in the price of oil raised prices of almost all goods and commodities throughout the world. The differing reactions of the United States, Western Europe, and Japan to these challenges had profound consequences for the world economy in the 1970s and beyond.

The United States reacted primarily to the *deflationary effects* of the price rise; throughout the 1970s it attempted unsuccessfully to stimulate its economy and pull itself out of the recession. To avoid domestic inflationary consequences, Americans pressured their European and Japanese allies to stimulate their economies and thus increase American exports. Europeans responded primarily to the *inflationary effects* of the price rise and reined in their economies; this resulted in "Eurosclerosis." The Japanese implemented a series of important economic reforms and corporate restructuring that greatly increased the efficiency of their industry and transformed their economy into a highly efficient export machine; this laid the base for trade conflict with its partners. Much of the succeeding history of the world economy has focused on the conflicts that originated in the differing adjustment strategies employed by the three most powerful economies following the 1973 oil crisis.

Slowdown in Productivity Growth

Ever since the industrial changes in the latter decades of the nineteenth and early decades of the twentieth centuries, the United States has been blessed with an extraordinarily high rate of productivity growth as measured by the output per worker. This high rate explains America's ever-rising standard of living and the general American belief that each succeeding generation would be more economically successful than the preceding. From 1889 to 1937, American productivity grew at an average of 1.9 percent annually. This growth rate accelerated to over 3 percent between 1937 and 1973. Beginning in the early 1970s, however, the rate declined sharply; having outpaced the rest of the world for decades, the U.S. rate of productivity growth fell to a disturbingly low rate of less than 1 percent. Although the United States continued to have higher worker productivity than almost all other advanced economies, the decline in its productivity growth rate was a significant factor in the decreased growth rate of the overall economy. This decline weakened the economic preeminence of the United States and slowed improvement in the standard of living. In the 1980s, these developments contributed to growing fears of economic decline and deindustrialization, fed protectionist forces in the American economy, and thus undermined the American leadership that had been so vital to the strength of the BWS.

DECLINE OF THE BRETTON WOODS SYSTEM

By the end of the 1970s, serious deficiencies in the Bretton Woods System had become obvious. Among the developments that weakened the System were the "financial revolution," the limited nature of international policy coordination, the movement toward European regionalism, New Protectionism, the conservative counterrevolution in economics, and the triumph of the central bankers. The subsequent history of the world economy tells the tale of attempts to strengthen the international economic order.

Financial Revolution

The shift from a system of fixed to flexible exchange rates, which began with the 1971 cutting of the link between gold and the dollar, generated an intense debate in the economics profession. The majority of economists, certainly the majority of American economists, expected that this shift would be beneficial for the world economy. They believed that the combination of fixed rates and increasing economic interdependence through trade, investment, and monetary flows had placed severe constraints on national economic policy and thereby had decreased the ability of individual governments to pursue macroeconomic policies promoting full employment. Economists, therefore, believed that a system of flexible rates was needed to delink national economies from one another and thus permit each government to pursue those economic policies best suited to its own national circumstances.

A minority of economists, however, strongly disagreed with this optimistic assessment and was very concerned about the potentially inflationary and destabilizing consequences of delinking the international monetary system from the anchor of gold or some other commodity. If the system were not anchored to an objective standard, the value of money and the stability of prices, they reasoned, would henceforth rest entirely on the discretion of individual governments. Believing that governments were not to be trusted to pursue stable economic policies, they worried that governments would behave so irresponsibly that inflation and monetary instability would soon disrupt the world economy. The majority of economists remained convinced that such fears were unfounded.

However, the unanticipated "financial revolution" of the mid-1970s and its consequences proved the optimistic majority of economists wrong. Growth of the Eurodollar market (dollar accounts in European banks) and overseas expansion of American banks in the 1960s had led

73

to the emergence of an international financial market. Then in the 1970s, development of the new international financial system accelerated with deregulation of domestic financial systems, removal of capital controls in a number of countries, and the greatly increased size and velocity of global financial flows. This increase in financial flows had been made possible by modern communications and new financial techniques and instruments. It was, however, the huge OPEC monetary surplus following the oil crisis and the need to recycle those funds that proved most important in the development of the international financial market. Before the end of the 1970s, the sheer scale and speed of international financial flows had expanded enormously and truly transformed the international economic system.

The integration of global financial markets has had a significant impact on domestic as well as international economics through the increase in the monetary and financial interdependence of national economies. Financial market integration means that the macroeconomic policies of one country have a significant impact on the economic welfare of other countries. For example, if country A raises its interest rates to decrease domestic inflationary pressures, those higher rates will attract capital from other countries with lower interest rates, and the resulting increase in country A's money supply then contributes to the inflationary pressures that higher interest rates were intended to counter. Simultaneously, economic activity is reduced in the economies experiencing capital outflow. In this way, the integration of national financial markets actually reduced macroeconomic policy autonomy. Despite the shift to flexible exchange rates, domestic and international economic spheres became more closely linked to one another because of financial market integration.

Another unanticipated consequence has been that international financial flows have become an important determinant of exchange rates, at least in the short term. This has greatly increased exchange rate volatility, especially between the dollar and such other major currencies as the yen and the mark. By the end of the 1970s, international financial flows dwarfed trade flows by a ratio of about 25 to 1; the size of the flows also contributed greatly to volatility. The principal mechanism producing these fluctuations in exchange rates is the tendency of exchange rates to "overshoot" in response to financial flows. This has made it difficult for markets to move smoothly from one equilibrium exchange rate to the next and for economists and government officials to know what the equilibrium exchange rate should be.

Since fixed rates were eliminated, economists and public officials have debated heatedly whether or not exchange rate volatility has produced negative consequences for the real economy through its impact on trade flows, business activity, and economic growth. This situation may have contributed to the shift toward the New Protectionism that took place in the mid-1970s. This seeming interaction of exchange rate volatility and trade protectionism has led many economists to believe that the world should return to a system of fixed rates.

Freeing financial markets also facilitated reorganization and transformation of international business. The unification of national financial markets encouraged creation of a single, globally integrated market for corporation ownership and corporate takeover activities, as exemplified in the late-1990s merger of Chrysler and Daimler-Benz. The huge increase in acquisitions and alliances by multinational corporations in the 1970s and the 1980s resulted from these developments. (In Japan, government regulations and the system of corporate groupings, or *keiretsu*, have made foreign takeovers very difficult.)

These changes in trade, finance, and other areas of the economy have contributed to a substantial increase in international interdependence, and that has had a profound impact on domestic economic policy. Economic interdependence has considerably reduced the capacity to pursue full-employment policies, and this in turn has undermined the domestic consensus in support of an open world economy. Increased interdependence also has integrated once-isolated policy issues such as trade flows and exchange rate determination, thus immensely complicating the task of managing the world economy and raising important questions about the adequacy of the rules governing international economic affairs. Each of the original Bretton Woods institutions was responsible for an exclusive sphere of economic activity; therefore, as those once isolated spheres became more and more interconnected, it became increasingly difficult for those institutions to manage their respective spheres of economic activity. Many efforts to reform the institutions have been made, particularly those that resulted in creation of the World Trade Organization. The immense difficulties faced by efforts to achieve policy coordination across such issue areas as trade, monetary matters, and investment undoubtedly have encouraged pursuit of regional solutions to these novel problems.

International Policy Coordination

Following the 1973 OPEC price revolution, the idea of international policy coordination or cooperation became popular with most economists, other scholars, and public officials; to economists, this term means "synchronized change" of national policies. While there had been some informal policy coordination at an earlier date, more formal efforts to achieve such coordination were undertaken as the economic problems of the interdependent world economy compounded. The economic rationale for international economic cooperation is straightforward. In an increasingly integrated world economy, the actions and policies of one government inevitably have an impact on the economic well-being of other countries.

The large monetary imbalances caused by the oil crisis in 1973 led the major economic powers or Group of Seven (G-7) to begin formal coordination of their macroeconomic and other economic policies. The first of these American-led efforts—the Rambouillet Summit (1975)—dealt with international monetary issues; on the whole, this and other early coordination efforts were quite successful and probably reduced protectionist pressures. Subsequent to the Rambouillet Summit, however, the nature of international policy coordination changed from a cooperative effort of the G-7 to an American unilateral effort to change the policies of its allies to meet America's economic interests. The agendas of the London Summit (1977) and especially the Bonn Summit (1978) focused on American efforts to get Germany and Japan to pursue expansionary economic policies. Although a number of scholars believe that these summits and international policy coordination contributed significantly to resolution of the problems posed by the tension between an increasingly integrated global economy and a fragmented global political system, the record does not support this conclusion.

The high, and also the low, point of the first round of international policy coordination was reached at the 1978 Bonn Summit. The world economy had been suffering the consequences of stagflation, and the

Carter Administration, experiencing domestic pressure to pursue an expansionary macroeconomic policy, could not by itself stimulate its economy because of the threat of inflationary consequences. The Administration, therefore, wanted a joint reflation by the three major economies to pull the United States and the rest of the world out of recession. Throughout the mid-1970s, the West Germans strongly rejected this so-called "locomotive" strategy, arguing that such a measure would not work and would actually have additional inflationary consequences. Nevertheless, in response to American pressures, the West Germans and the Japanese finally agreed to stimulate their economies. Also, at German insistence, the United States, as a quid pro quo, agreed to undertake a serious effort at energy conservation, an agreement which the United States never fulfilled.

The expansionary economic policies of the Germans and Japanese unfortunately coincided with (or perhaps actually caused) another oil crisis in 1978–1979, and that resulted in another large surge of inflation. This experience gave international policy coordination a bad name in Germany. Thenceforth, the Germans resisted—sometimes politely and sometimes acidly—all American importuning to coordinate national economic policies. The Germans questioned the need for any intergovernmental cooperation, at least in the area of macroeconomic policy, and believed that each government had sole responsibility for managing its own economic affairs. This German position was reinforced by the increasing influence of conservative ideology and the growing conviction in the United States and Western Europe that countries should "get their own house in order"; that is, they should let markets work so that governments would not need to coordinate their economic policies. Not surprisingly, subsequent attempts to coordinate national policies became less ambitious than they had been in the past.

Movement toward European Regionalism

At the beginning of the twentieth century, the European powers dominated international affairs, and the several European empires stood astride continents. Europe was the unchallenged center of the world economy; its foreign trade and overseas investments united and drove the rest of the international economy. In science and technology,

Europe also led the rest of the world. Czarist Russia was indolent, and in Asia the once-great Chinese empire had crumbled and become prey to foreign imperialists. Although Japan and the United States were rapidly gaining as industrial and technological powers, Europe was preeminent in almost every aspect of modern industry, technology, and scientific affairs.

After two devastating world wars and the Great Depression of the 1930s, Europe found itself considerably reduced in power and influence. One by one, European powers had lost their overseas empires, and this had required huge economic and political adjustments. As the division between the American and Soviet superpowers deepened, Europeans found that they had become the focus of American and Soviet rivalry for global supremacy. By the end of the Cold War the United States had surpassed Europe in economic, technological, and scientific affairs. The Soviet Union for a time became the world's second-largest economy, but in the 1970s it was displaced by Japan. By the mid-1980s, China and East Asia were growing at an incredible pace, and, prior to the 1997 East Asian financial crisis, these Asian economies were expected to eclipse Western Europe early in the twenty-first century.

Despite its diminished global power, post–World War II Western Europe's internal transformation is a great success story. The intense and unforgiving rivalry of France and Germany, which twice during the twentieth century plunged Western Europe into internecine warfare, has largely dissipated, and these two formerly hostile powers have become partners in creating a united Europe. Despite the continuing reluctance of the United Kingdom—which for centuries had stood aloof from the Continent except for its interventions to thwart the efforts of Louis XIV, Napoleon, and Hitler to control all of Europe, and which had long opposed a unified Europe—even the United Kingdom's progress toward acceptance of a united Europe has been remarkable. The achievements of the movement toward European political and economic unification can only be described as extraordinary. Yet, the task that lies ahead to forge a more completely unified European economic and political entity remains formidable.

Western Europe enjoyed rapid economic growth in the late 1950s and in the 1960s. At the heart of its economic success were the process of technological and productivity catch-up vis-à-vis the United States and the transformation of the West European economies into urbanized mass consumer societies. On the demand side, European states had emerged from the Second World War committed to macroeconomic policies of economic expansion. On the supply side, the massive shift of surplus labor from rural to urban sectors and the huge transfers of capital associated with the Marshall Plan and with American investment in Europe accelerated the rate of economic growth. This extraordinary growth period came to a sudden end with the oil crisis of 1973. In response to the inflationary consequences of the severalfold increase in the price of petroleum, the rate of economic growth of the West European economies declined precipitously. "Europessimism" or "Eurosclerosis" blanketed the Continent. During the final quarter of the century, West European economic stagnation motivated nations to follow the course of economic and political unification.

Nevertheless, the primary purpose of European unification has been the reconciliation of France and Germany and, thereby, prevention of another great war in Europe. The United States supported European integration to create a bulwark against the Soviet threat. Reestablishment of Europe's position in the world as an economic and political power has been an additional and very important motive for the Europeans themselves. While the goals of integration have been both political and economic, the primary means employed to achieve the goals have been economic. Through successive steps—the European Coal and Steel Community (1952), the European Economic Community (1957), and the European Union (1993)—the West Europeans have moved toward comprehensive political and economic objectives.

The Treaty of Rome (1957) that led to creation of the European Economic Community (EEC), or Common Market, was a crucial step toward unification.[24] Although the Rome Treaty made no reference to political unity, it laid the foundations for later efforts as it created the major institutions that would eventually provide the political leadership of the Community: the European Council representing the member countries; the Commission, which is the Community's principal executive organization; and the European Parliament and European Court of Justice. However, the Rome Treaty defined the purposes of the Community in modest terms and confined them primarily to economic matters; namely, erection of a common external tariff. Subsequently, the EEC, in response to French pressure, implemented the Common Agricultural Policy (CAP). In time, the Commission began to assume responsibility for representing the Community in GATT trade negotiations.

Two decades later, Europeans took a further important step toward economic and political unity. At the initiative of French President Valéry Giscard d'Estaing and West German Chancellor Helmut Schmidt, the European Economic Community in 1978 agreed to establish the European Monetary System (EMS) and the associated Exchange Rate Mechanism (ERM) and thus created a system of relatively fixed exchange rates among the West European currencies. A major purpose of the EMS was to isolate Western Europe from the disruptive effects of erratic American macroeconomic policies and the fluctuations of the dollar that followed abandonment of the BWS's regime of fixed rates. The serious economic troubles of the 1970s had converted most European governments, at least in principle, to the virtues of balanced budgets and strong anti-inflationary policies. By tying their currencies to one another, Europeans intended to stabilize their monetary affairs through use of relatively fixed exchange rates. Other European countries agreed to peg their currency rates to the West German mark, and under the EMS, the West German Bundesbank, with its unwavering commitment to price stability, in effect became the central bank for the EEC.

New Protectionism

Despite, or perhaps because of, the success of the GATT in lowering tariff barriers, a negative reaction to trade liberalization began to develop as early as the 1950s; this opposition accelerated in the 1970s. As formal tariff barriers were lowered, informal nontariff barriers were raised, especially on steel, shoes, and textiles. New protectionist devices were created to protect threatened economic sectors; these novel measures included local-content rules, extensive abuse of the antidumping and other provisions of the GATT, and governmental pressuring of exporters to accept "voluntary export restraints" (VERs). Differing from the formal tariff barriers that had been eliminated by GATT negotiations, the new barriers, appearing first in the 1970s, set quantitative limits on imports.

In the United States, retreat from trade liberalization and the movement toward the New Protectionism began with greatly increased imports and rising fears over the decline of American industrial superiority. The most notorious example of the New Protectionism was the international Multi-Fiber Arrangement (1973) that placed restrictions on textile and apparel imports from developing countries and thus violated the GATT principle of nondiscrimination. The New Protectionism gained momentum throughout the 1970s due to a number of economic setbacks—fluctuating exchange rates, the effects of the oil crisis, and the onset of stagflation; the increasing technological sophistication of Japanese exports was also an important factor. Steel and automobiles became Japan's principal exports, and this greatly alarmed American competitors. In fact the New Protectionism was in large part directed against Japan. Whereas the protectionist device preferred by the United States was voluntary export restraints, West Europeans perfected ways to abuse the antidumping provision of the GATT, as well as ways to use local-content rules. The West Europeans wanted protectionist techniques that would allow them to discriminate against the Japanese in ways that did not offend the United States.

The New Protectionism was so named because it had important characteristics differentiating it from older forms of trade protection. Many aspects were informal and lacked transparency; that is, the protectionist devices were hidden and hard to recognize. Protectionism sometimes took the form of administrative decisions ostensibly intended to safeguard health or safety. It also involved a greater emphasis on bilateral trade negotiations. Whereas the GATT regime was based on explicit rules, multilateralism, and elimination of formal trade barriers, the New Protectionism involved a substantial increase in informal trade barriers, unilateralism, and administrative discretion. In the United States, the spirit of this shift toward unilateralism was expressed in the Trade Act of 1974, especially in its Section 301 that authorized the United States Trade Representative (USTR) to take punitive action against countries the United States found to be "unfair" traders. That Act embodied a major shift from a commitment to trade liberalization toward protectionism and bilateralism. In practice, Section 301 was

81

frequently used effectively to force America's trading partners to accept VERs (Voluntary Export Restraints).

The rise and spread of the New Protectionism resulted in part from an important shift in the patterns of world trade. In the early postwar era most trade had been either interindustry trade between developed and less developed countries or intraindustry trade across the Atlantic Ocean. Interindustry trade means trade between countries that takes place in different economic sectors; for example, the export of manufactured goods by the developed countries to the less developed in exchange for the export of commodities (food and raw materials) by the less developed countries to the developed. Intraindustry trade refers to the exchange of goods in the same industrial sectors, such as the export of motor vehicles by the United States and Western Europe to one another. In the early postwar years, intraindustry trade patterns moderated economic conflict. For example, intraindustry trade among the advanced industrial economies of the North Atlantic meant that increased imports did not threaten the survival of particular industrial sectors. But when these overall trade patterns began to change in the 1970s, trade friction intensified.

Underlying the New Protectionism was the emergence of Japan and subsequently of the emerging markets of Pacific Asia and their dramatic impact on world trading patterns. Unlike that of other advanced industrial countries, Japanese trade has been largely interindustry trade. Japanese exports, which greatly expanded in the 1970s, have consisted almost totally of industrial goods (with a substantial fraction going to other industrial countries); Japanese imports have been largely commodities (food, energy, raw materials) from the United States and from developing and other countries. Explanations of this unique Japanese trading pattern are highly controversial and will be discussed later. Whatever the causes of this trading pattern, American and European governments charged that Japan had intentionally kept its market closed to their manufactured exports. Moreover, U.S. revisionists charged that Japan's adversarial economic strategy had been intended to destroy, one by one, the high-technology industries of its trading partners. In the 1980s, the shift by the industrializing economies of Pacific Asian countries from commodity exports to manufactured exports greatly intensified the trade conflict between East and West.

Conservative Counterrevolution in Economic Theory and Political Ideology

In the late 1970s, there were important changes in public officials and in economic and political ideology. Monetarism became the dominant macroeconomic theory to explain the overall performance of the economy, and this shattered the postwar consensus of economics. Monetarism undermined the previously accepted concept that demand could be managed by government policies in order to achieve full employment. At the microeconomic level, the doctrine of structural adjustment provided the basis for emergence of a conservative political ideology advocating deregulation of the economy, a substantial reduction of the welfare state, and downsizing of the government. In addition to these ideological developments, President Carter's appointment in 1979 of Paul Volcker as chairman of the Federal Reserve had a profound impact on American economic policy and the international economy.

Monetarism's successful overthrow of prior orthodoxy was, to a large degree, the achievement of economists Milton Friedman and Edmund Phelps. The monetarist argument rested on the quantity theory of money and the concept of a "natural" rate of unemployment. According to the quantity theory, inflation is primarily a monetary phenomenon caused by the creation of excessive money by central banks. The natural rate hypothesis implies that every economy has an inherent rate of unemployment; this rate may go up or down by a few percentage points, depending on circumstances, but it will always be there as an upper limit on economic activity. Monetarists argue that, therefore, governmental efforts to decrease unemployment below this natural rate will result only in higher inflation. Disagreeing with the belief of other economists that they had learned how to fine-tune the economy, monetarists prescribed that the Federal Reserve should establish a firm rule of steady, noninflationary growth of the money supply and then retire from the scene. Government intervention in the economy, which had entailed huge welfare programs, high taxes, and extensive regulation, was believed to have distorted the market, decreased incentives to save, invest, and work, and thus to have undermined the productiveness of the economy. The solution to these debilitating problems, according to Friedman and other conservative economists, was to severely restrict the role of government.

The doctrine of "structural adjustment" also became an important component of the conservative counterrevolution. Whereas monetarism identified inflation as the fundamental economic problem of modern societies and advocated constraints on macroeconomic policies, advocates of structural adjustment argued that reforms at the microeconomic level were also necessary if industrial economies were to regain substantially higher rates of productivity and economic growth. Proponents of structural adjustment argued that excessive taxation, overregulation of the economy, and other government interventions distorted private economic incentives and thus retarded economic growth. In effect, they argued that the welfare state had been responsible for the economic troubles of the 1970s. Therefore, drastic restriction of government intervention in the economy was essential to the health of the industrial economies. Some proposals for deregulation and privatization were implemented in both the United States and Western Europe. These reforms resulted in considerable harmonization of economic policies and structures among the Western economies and thus laid the foundations for both global and regional integration. When Margaret Thatcher came to power as Prime Minister in the United Kingdom and Ronald Reagan as President in the United States, these conservative ideas became political orthodoxy, profoundly reshaped the economic and political landscape, and began to dominate the global economic agenda.

LDC Debt Crisis

The mid-1970s were favorable times for many developing countries and for some socialist economies in Eastern Europe. Emergence of the huge international capital market and stagflation in the industrial economies provided an important opportunity for developing economies because they could borrow directly from American, European, and Japanese commercial banks that were eager to make them huge loans. This "sovereign borrowing," that is, borrowing by governments from international banks to finance state-led projects and import-substitution strategies (development of industries to serve the domestic market), meant that these countries were able to escape dependence on "imperialistic" U.S. multinational corporations and the conditions placed on funds borrowed from the IMF and the World Bank. Although many believed that this was a risky strategy for both banks and borrowers, their cautionary words were thrown to the winds; as Citibank's Walter Wriston put it, "Countries do not go bankrupt." Moreover, the hyperinflation of the 1970s meant that real interest rates were very low or even negative. Under those circumstances, the banks were more than willing to loan, and it would have been foolish for countries not to borrow.

In 1979, these circumstances favorable to LDC borrowers changed dramatically following the appointment of Volcker as chairman of the Federal Reserve. To rid the world of hyperinflation and restore economic growth, Volcker and his colleagues at the Fed believed that draconian measures were required. The resulting Federal Reserve decision to increase interest rates plunged the world into a severe recession in which less developed country (LDC) borrowers found themselves with huge debts, rising real interest rates, and decreased foreign earnings with which to service their debts. The heavy indebtedness of many LDCs in Africa, Latin America, and elsewhere threw these countries back into dependence upon the World Bank and the International Monetay Fund. To receive assistance from the IMF and the World Bank, the debtors had to agree to a stringent program of structural adjustment. The terms for granting assistance were that debtor nations had to abandon state interventionism and the strategy of import substitution and adopt market-oriented economic policies that pervaded the thinking of the leaders of the Fund and the Bank. These reforms paved the way for greater LDC success, especially in Latin America, in the 1980s and 1990s until the financial crisis of the late 1990s dealt them another severe blow. For the poorest LDCs, this international debt has continued to weigh heavily; this led to the June 1999 decision of the major powers to recommend that the debt be written off.

Triumph of the Central Bankers

The monetarist counterrevolution had a powerful political and economic impact because it provided a convincing rationale for the desire of German, American, and other central bankers to wrest control over the economy from "irresponsible" politicians and thus to safeguard national economies from the evils of runaway inflation. Profound distaste for inflation was particularly strong in West Germany because of its disastrous experience with hyperinflation in the early 1920s. Throughout the 1970s, successive American Administrations had employed traditional techniques (fiscal deficits and expansion of the money supply) to lift the American economy out of stagflation. This effort required the cooperation of America's economic partners, especially the West Germans, who had to be willing to absorb the outflow of dollars resulting from American economic expansion. The Germans, however, grew more and more reluctant to cooperate and complained bitterly that the United States was exporting inflation. By the end of the 1970s, the Germans had become completely frustrated with American inflationary policies and reportedly informed Volcker that they were planning to create a European Monetary System to protect themselves and Western Europe from erratic and inflationary American economic policies.

Although Volcker himself was not a strict monetarist, he agreed with German financial authorities that the root cause of the problems of the world economy was high inflation generated in large part by excessive American money creation. His own conservative convictions and the threat posed by the European Monetary System to the international position of the dollar led Volcker and his colleagues at the Federal Reserve to adopt the monetarist emphasis on limiting the money supply and thus to make inflation fighting the principal goal of American macroeconomic policy. In the fall of 1979, the Federal Reserve drastically tightened monetary policy to wipe inflation out of the American and world economies. This courageous action ended stagflation, but it also plunged the world into a severe recession that produced dire consequences, especially for the heavily indebted developing and communist countries. The triumph of the central bankers meant that price stability had higher priority than did eradication of unemployment.

Conclusion

The profound recession of the late 1970s, the 1979–1980 Iranian hostage debacle in which the United States was clearly unable to deal effectively with terrorism in the Middle East, and the inept handling of the second oil crisis by the Carter Administration led to the landslide election in 1980 of Ronald Reagan as President and also to a profound counterrevolution in American economic policies. Reagan's policy innovations were in part a rejection of past policies, but they also constituted the first concerted attempt by an American Administration to address the relative economic decline of the United States and to begin adjustment of the American economy to the economic, technological, and other developments then transforming the world economy. As the 1980s progressed, other industrial powers and a growing number of developing economies also began to adjust their policies to the changing realities of economic and political affairs.

The Insecure Trading System

ONE OF THE MAJOR paradoxes of international trade is that, even though it greatly benefits societies in general and consumers in particular, trade liberalization is constantly being threatened by protectionism. Like many Americans I drive a Japanese car, listen to music on a radio or CD player made in East Asia, and watch television on a set also made in East Asia. Also, like many Americans, I do not want to give up these benefits of free trade. Because trade competition forces American manufacturers to improve their products and keep prices low for consumers, and because many of the best jobs in the United States are located in America's huge export sector, most Americans also receive indirect benefits from international trade. Nevertheless, Americans complain bitterly and demand protection when "unfair" imports threaten their own particular livelihoods. Although protectionist tendencies are always present, this tendency balloons when times are difficult and/or the trade deficit balloons.

In the 1980s and 1990s, free trade has come under increasing attack. This development, foreshadowed by New Protectionism in the 1970s, has been due to growing concerns about America's huge trade/payments deficits and the threat of "deindustrialization" perceived in the 1980s, the formulation of new trade theories supporting trade protection, and the growing importance of trade issues not covered by the GATT. Despite creation of the World Trade Organization in 1995 and other reforms, the problems of the international trading system have not yet been resolved, and the perennial debate continues between the proponents of trade liberalization and those who favor trade protection.

Tension between Trade Liberalization and Trade Protectionism

Every economist agrees that free trade is superior to all forms of trade protection. In fact, economists consider free trade the best policy for a country even if all other countries were to practice trade protection, arguing that, in such a case, the economy that remained open would still gain more from cheaper imports than it would lose in denied exports. Nevertheless, trade protection has never totally disappeared, and indeed, during the past two centuries, restrictions on trade have been a persistent and pervasive feature of the world economy. Historically, protectionism has been more prevalent than has free trade. Although nations want to take advantage of the benefits of free trade, they are frequently unwilling to open their own markets and to permit market forces to determine the international distribution of gains from trade. Although the argument favoring free trade remains powerful, the doctrine of trade protection continuously resurfaces in new guises. In fact, there has never really been "free" trade with either no or few barriers. For this reason, the term "trade liberalization" (the movement toward really free trade) is more appropriate than the term "free trade."

The first era of relatively free trade began with the repeal of Britain's Corn Laws (1846) and the removal of British restrictions on grain imports. This and other initiatives were important moves toward liberalization in the last half of the nineteenth century. However, during the final decades of that century, the tide began to turn and trade protection grew steadily. During the period between World War I and World War II, international trade contracted greatly. Then, for three decades following World War II, the world experienced another era of trade liberalization and expansion. Largely as a consequence of eight successive rounds of GATT trade negotiations that began shortly after the war, international trade grew even more rapidly than did national economies; this trade in effect integrated national economies more closely with one another. Then in the mid-1970s, global stagflation and other developments caused New Protectionism to surface in one country after another, slowing trade expansion. In the 1990s, completion of the

Uruguay Round of trade negotiations (1993) resulted in the creation in 1995 of the World Trade Organization (WTO), and this renewed hopes for continuing trade liberalization. However, simultaneously, new hurdles had been raised in the form of managed trade, economic regionalism, and fears of globalization. Thus, the tension between trade liberalization and trade protection continued, and the future of the "free trade" system remains in question.

At the opening of the twenty-first century, trade liberalization is threatened by intellectual, economic, and political developments. The theoretical or intellectual arguments for trade liberalization have been undermined in several ways, including the shift from "comparative" to "competitive" advantage as the basis of trade, the formulation of the "new" (strategic) trade theory, and integration of trade with foreign direct investment by multinational firms. Increasing penetration of trade into domestic economies has forced recognition of complex issues as definitions of "fair" and legitimate economic behavior have been devised, because what is fair in one society may be considered unfair in another. Furthermore, there is increasing political opposition to trade liberalization from many concerned about worker welfare, the environment, and human rights. Although the Uruguay Round and the WTO have attempted to deal with these issues, there are substantial problems still confronting the trading system. Clearly, management of trade in a highly integrated global economy composed of independent and competitive nation-states has become a formidable challenge.

TRADE LIBERALIZATION AND ITS CRITICS

Throughout modern history the proponents and opponents of trade liberalization have been engaged in an intense continuous debate. While the specific issues in the debate have changed, the basic arguments of the two sides have remained remarkably stable. In their essential aspects, they take the following positions: The *proponents* of trade liberalization base their case on the fundamental principles of the market system first formulated almost two hundred years ago. Economists Adam Smith and David Ricardo argued that removing the impediments to the free movement of goods would permit national specialization and optimal utilization of the world's scarce factors of production. This, in turn, would permit patterns of international trade to be determined by the principle of comparative advantage; that is, by prices. Operation of the principle of comparative advantage ensures that a country will ultimately achieve greater economic efficiency and welfare through participation in foreign trade than through trade protection. Underlying this commitment to free trade is the belief that the purpose of economic activity is to benefit the consumer and maximize global wealth. Free trade maximizes consumer choice and facilitates efficient use of the world's scarce resources. From this perspective, the primary purpose of exports is to pay for imports, rather than to enhance the wealth of producers or the power of the state.

Proponents of trade liberalization argue that the costs incurred by efforts to protect domestic businesses are very high, indeed much higher than most people realize. Capitalism is driven by competition, and a country risks falling behind economically if it shuts itself off from trade competition. Except in those instances of successful "infant industry" protection, the principal consequence of protectionist measures is to transfer income from consumers and unprotected sectors to capital and labor in protected sectors. The costs to the overall economy can be and usually are very high. Indeed, a 1994 study by Gary Hufbauer and Kim Elliot, published in the context of the bitter controversy over ratification of the North American Free Trade Agreement (NAFTA), found that trade protection was very costly to the American economy; the effort to preserve jobs through trade barriers cost, on average, $170,000 per job saved, and the cost per job was $500,000 or more in a number of industries.[25] Although the cost of protection is frequently defended on the ground that it gives the protected industry time to become competitive once again, available evidence lends little support to this rationale.

Nevertheless, economists acknowledge that protection of *infant* industries can be a valid reason for temporary trade protection. An infant industry is one that, if protected from international competition, will become sufficiently strong and competitive to enable it to survive when protection is eventually removed. A major problem with infant industry protection, however, is that there is no way to determine whether or not a particular infant industry, if protected, could eventually achieve a competitive position in world markets. In fact, only a trial-and-error process can determine the long-term competitiveness of the protected industry. An additional problem is that protectionist policies too frequently become permanent and are often used to protect *senile* industries. The Japanese have proved that infant industry protection can work. Indeed, most successes attributed to industrial policy and strategic trade policy are really examples of successful infant industry protection.

Opponents of free trade have included eighteenth-century mercantilists, nineteenth-century economic nationalists, and contemporary critics of economic globalization; over the years, the rationale for trade protection has changed in important ways. Mercantilists in the seventeenth and eighteenth centuries wanted a trade surplus primarily because they identified such a surplus with military power. Following the Industrial Revolution in the late eighteenth century, industrialization became the primary focus of economic nationalists, who considered manufacturing of great value to the nation because of its association with military power and national autonomy. As Alexander Hamilton, the mercantilist theorist of American economic development, wrote in a 1791 defense of protecting American manufacturers, "Not only the wealth but the independence and security of a country appear to be materially connected to the prosperity of manufactures." At the beginning of the twenty-first century, some modern-day technonationalists emphasize the importance of protecting and supporting high-tech industries associated with an advanced industrial economy, and others regard trade and globalization as threats to the domestic welfare (jobs, wages, etc.), the environment, and human rights.

Pressures for trade protection have never gone away, and these pressures have been especially strong and usually successful during economic slowdowns. Approval of protectionist measures is due in part to public misunderstanding of what trade does and does not do for an economy. However, a more important reason for protectionism's success is that the political process tends to favor special interests that desire protection. Whereas those groups know their interests and are usually well organized and well funded, consumers frequently do not know their interests and are seldom well organized or well funded. Also, a number of trade developments since World War II have added support to protectionist causes.

The rhetoric and attitude of American protectionists and even public opinion have shifted in a direction disturbing to proponents of trade liberalization. The American public and officials have always spoken of making trade "concessions" to foreigners despite the fact that trade liberalization also benefits the United States; under most circumstances, trade is not a zero-sum game. In the 1980s, skepticism regarding trade liberalization was reinforced by concerns that unfair trade had put Americans out of work; American policy began to emphasize ways to make the unfair traders behave properly. In the 1990s, this attitude changed in a troubling direction as more and more Americans began to question the very idea of trade liberalization. Reflecting this new attitude, the Clinton Administration became loath to advance a new multilateral round of trade negotiations. The failure to win "fast track" trade-negotiating authority had been a chastening experience.

Although this debate will probably never be resolved, several general points regarding trade and its consequences should be clarified. While trade does increase a nation's wealth, it also creates losers. As losers feel the pain more acutely than winners feel the gain, both ethical and political reasons make it necessary that national policy assist or compensate workers and others harmed by trade liberalization. Contrary to oft-expressed opinions in public debates, trade neither increases nor decreases overall employment in an economy; the level of employment is determined by macroeconomic (fiscal and monetary) policies. On the other hand, trade does increase national efficiency and high-paying jobs by restructuring national economies; competition shuts down industries that are losing comparative advantage and thus releases resources (capital and labor) to be used by more efficient and competitive industries. A nation's overall trade balance is determined principally by the difference between its savings and its investments; a nation's trade deficit (surplus), for example, is due mainly to a low (high) savings rate and not to the unfair behavior of another country, a point highly relevant to discussions of the persistent American trade deficit with Japan. On the other hand, the type of goods that a country exports can be influenced by such national policies as successful infant industry protection and support for education and for research and development (R&D).

POSTWAR DEVELOPMENTS IN INTERNATIONAL TRADE

Since its formulation in the 1930s by Eli Heckscher and Bertil Ohlin, conventional trade theory (sometimes called the factor endowments model and referred to as the H-O theory) has been accepted by economists as the standard explanation of international trade.[26] This theory postulates that a country will specialize in the production and export of those products in which it has a comparative cost advantage over other countries. It is based on the assumption that there are constant returns to scale (i.e., that an increase in production does not reduce costs), that every production technology is universally available, and, by implication, that a country's comparative advantage and trade pattern are determined solely by their factor endowments such as capital, labor, and natural resources. The theory of comparative advantage, like every theory, greatly oversimplifies the real world.

The problem with this theory is that actual trading patterns differ considerably from those it predicts. A notable example is intraindustry trade between countries with similar factor endowments; for example, the United States and Western Europe are major trading partners even though they have very similar factor endowments. Over the years, economists' efforts to explain this and other anomalies have significantly modified the concept of comparative advantage. Now, trade patterns are regarded as resulting from such factors as historical accidents and government policies as well as from natural endowments. Moreover, standard trade theory itself has been modified and expanded to include such factors as the importance of human capital (skilled labor), "learning-by-doing," technological innovation, and economies of scale (which means that the average cost of production decreases with increased output). These revisions have so transformed the H-O model that some economists now argue that the theory of international trade is not much more than an eclectic enumeration of the many factors that determine comparative advantage and trade flows.

Integration of International Trade and Foreign Investment

The increasingly important role of the multinational corporation (MNC) in the global economy has greatly affected the trading system. A substantial proportion of world trade now takes place as *intrafirm* transfers at prices set by the firms and as part of a global corporate strategy; the resulting trade patterns frequently do not conform at all to conventional trade theory based on traditional concepts of comparative advantage. Moreover, the amount of trade resulting from the activities of multinational corporations has grown considerably; one estimate is that in the early 1990s, one-half of total American and Japanese trade was between foreign-owned firms and their home countries.[27] This type of managed trade has become an important feature of the international economy. Indeed, internationalization of manufacturing is one of the fundamental features of the international economy at the beginning of the new century. Obviously, this situation too frequently motivates governments to support their own MNCs against foreign competitors.

From Comparative to Competitive Advantage

Another important intellectual development that has undermined the conventional theory of international trade has been the shift from "comparative" to what can be called "competitive" advantage. Trade is frequently due to arbitrary specialization, historical accident, and technological developments.[28] This new thinking recognizes that technological change has grown in importance in determining trade patterns. And it is also important to realize that the technology underlying competitive advantage and determining trade patterns is frequently deliberately created through corporate and government policies.

An important study that demonstrates the shift from comparative to competitive advantage was done by Michael Porter of Harvard University's Business School.[29] His central finding was that the characteristics of a national economy affect the environment of domestic firms in ways that either facilitate or obstruct the development of competitive advantage in certain industries. According to Porter, several aspects of a national economy are of particular significance: the national culture and its effect on the purpose of economic activities, the status of capital and

95

labor, existence of sufficient demand, the health of supporting industries, and the industrial structure of the economy. Porter has demonstrated that these factors determine domestic competitive conditions
that, in turn, influence the international competitiveness of particular
sectors of the economy.

Substituting the term "competitive advantage" for the traditional emphasis on "comparative advantage," Porter provides strong support for
the idea that advantage in international trade, at least in industries, can
be and in fact is created by deliberate corporate and governmental decisions and policy choices rather than being a static gift from Mother
Nature. While individual firms are ultimately responsible for creating
or failing to create competitive advantage, governments can play an
important and even decisive role to promote their own national firms in
international markets.

A nation with a head start in a particular technology tends to
strengthen its position over time, and a technology-deficient nation,
especially a small one, may find it impossible to ever catch up. This is
because productivity and competitiveness increase with cumulative experience (an idea called "path dependence" by economists) and are
largely determined by the initial pattern of specialization; for example,
I am writing these lines using an Apple Macintosh computer, which is
technologically superior, or at least equal, to Wintel (Windows software
and Intel chips) computers; however, marketing errors by Apple permitted Wintel computers to gain such a substantial portion of the market that Apple has been unable to catch up. The importance of a head
start in the innovation and marketing of high-tech products has greatly
intensified competition in that area.[30]

Strategic Trade Theory

The conventional theory of international trade with its unqualified support for trade liberalization has been challenged by development of the
"new trade theory," more commonly known as "strategic trade theory."
The essence of the new theory is that a firm, assisted by its home government, can design a strategy that will enable it to compete effectively
in an oligopolistic industry; that is, an industry such as the commercial
aircraft industry where only a very few viable firms are possible. This

theory leads to the conclusion that national governments can and should assist their own national firms to compete successfully in oligopolistic markets. The universal drive for technological superiority has greatly increased the receptivity of governments to economic policies implied by the new theory.

The new theory is particularly applicable to such high-tech-sector products as automobiles, computers, and pharmaceuticals, where economies of scale and "learning-by-doing" are of particular importance. In industries where unit costs fall as output increases, the firm with a head start can increase its efficiency and lower its prices to drive competing firms out of the market. Thus, economies of scale in such industries will lead the market to support only one or just a few large firms; that is, that industry will become oligopolistic, and the market will eventually be dominated by a limited number of firms. This means that the behavior of one firm will make a difference and will alter the decisions of other firms. Where imperfect or oligopolistic competition exists, monopoly rents or abnormally high profits exist. Such rents or superprofits can be captured by a very small number of firms or even by one firm. Individual firms, then, may well pursue strategies to increase their profits or economic rents. In a truly competitive (or nonoligopolistic) market, the new theory would not apply. For example, an individual dairy farmer competing against thousands of others is subject to the laws of supply and demand and cannot change the market prices paid for his products.

On the other hand, competing oligopolistic firms such as automobile and airplane manufacturers can and do consciously choose a course of action that anticipates the behavior of their competitors. If successful, this enables them to capture a much larger share of the market than would be possible with perfect competition. Oligopolistic firms can and do follow strategies in which they adjust their own prices and output in order to alter the prices and output of competitor firms. Two of the most important strategies used to increase a firm's long-term domination of an oligopolistic market are dumping (selling below cost to drive out competitors in that product area) and preemption of a market (through huge investments in productive capacity to deter others from entering the market). Such competitive strategies can be and are pursued by many oligopolistic firms.

In oligopolistic competition, strategic trade theory assigns a crucial role to the firm's home government. Assuming that governments can greatly assist national firms, a government may protect a domestic firm against foreign competitors, or it could provide a firm with subsidies to lower its costs and increase its competitive advantage in domestic and foreign markets. The United States government has helped Boeing with generous defense contracts, and the British/French governments have helped Airbus through direct subsidies. Many of the supported sectors are "dual technologies" very important to both military weaponry and economic competitiveness. The importance of these industries and of a head start encourages firms and home governments to attempt to enter such markets ahead of potential competitors through a first-strike strategy; cumulative processes ("he who has gets") and path dependence will over time strengthen their market position. Both commercial and security reasons lead many nations to take actions to ensure as strong a capability as possible in such technologies.

Strategic trade theory has become a highly controversial subject within the economics profession. Some critics argue that it is a clever, flawed, and pernicious idea that gives aid and comfort to trade protectionists. Other opponents agree with this assessment, but also make the point that the theory itself adds nothing really new to earlier discredited arguments for trade protection. Responding to the denunciations by leading mainstream economists, some of its earliest and strongest proponents have moderated their initial enthusiasm. For most economists, strategic trade theory has become an intellectual game that has little or no relevance to the real world of trade policy. Despite the criticisms and recantations, however, strategic trade theory has had an important impact on government policy and, according to some, has been a factor in the slowdown in the growth of world trade.

Most economists reject the assumption underlying strategic trade theory that some industries or economic activities are more important than others and believe, instead, that *all* industries are created equal and that no economic sector is intrinsically more valuable than any other. The rate of productivity growth of an economic sector is considered the only real measure of its value and of its contribution to the nation's long-term economic welfare. A nation should, therefore, specialize in those sectors in which high rates of productivity growth exist and where it has a comparative advantage. This sentiment was expressed in an oft-repeated statement attributed to Michael Boskin, Chair of the Council of Economic Advisors in the Bush Administration: that "chips are chips," and that it is unimportant whether an economy produces one type of chip or another. If a nation has a comparative advantage in potato chips but not computer chips, then it should export the former and import the latter. Moreover, even if some economic activities may be intrinsically more valuable than others, critics of strategic trade policy argue that governments are incapable of picking "winners" and that any effort to do so would eventually be captured by special interests. Favoring one sector, the critics charge, would of necessity divert scarce resources and harm other sectors that might be even more valuable to the economy over the long term. Furthermore, critics charge that subsidies and trade protection will lead to foreign retaliation, and then everyone would lose.

What can be concluded about strategic trade theory and the industrial policy for which it has provided intellectual support? On the one hand, economists find it very difficult to assess whether or not government intervention in oligopolistic markets actually works and benefits a particular national firm. Yet, the argument that, under appropriate circumstances, government assistance for a firm can have important technological payoffs or spillovers for the rest of the economy is supported by ample evidence. Even though empirical evidence for the success of industrial policy is admittedly mixed, government support for infant industries in particular sectors has frequently been very successful in creating technologies that spill over into the rest of the economy; what better example than the American government's support for the innovation and development of the Internet?! Certainly governments around the world believe that support for high-tech industries produces great benefits over the long term. Most importantly, there is strong evidence that government support for research and development greatly benefits the entire economy.

The Uruguay Round and the World Trade Organization

By the early 1980s, the Bretton Woods trade regime was no longer adequate to deal with the highly integrated world economy and its oligopolistic competition, scale economies, and rapidly changing comparative advantage. In addition, the New Protectionism of the 1970s had resulted in erection of numerous nontariff barriers in such forms as quotas and government subsidies. Moreover, the character of trade itself was changing and had outgrown the rules and the trading regime. Trade had become closely entwined with the global activities of multinational firms, and trade in both services and manufactures was rapidly expanding. In the 1980s, the new regionalism, especially acceleration of the movement toward European integration, became recognized as a threat to the multilateral trading system. And significantly, the United States had begun pressuring its European and other trading partners for a new round of trade negotiations to strengthen the multilateral trading system. Eventually, this American pressure overcame European and other resistance, and the Uruguay Round of trade negotiations was launched at Punta del Este in 1986; following intense negotiations, the Round was concluded in 1993, and the Agreement was signed in April 1994.

The Uruguay Round Agreement, which took effect on January 1, 1995, reduced rich countries' tariffs on manufactured goods to an average of only a few percent and created the World Trade Organization (WTO). Not only were formal tariffs on merchandise goods reduced to a very low level, but the Round also reduced or eliminated many import quotas and subsidies. Textile quotas, for example, were to be removed over a ten-year period. The Agreement's twenty-nine separate accords also extended GATT rules to such new economic sectors as agriculture, services, intellectual property rights, and foreign investment. Some have estimated that implementation of the Agreement will add approximately $750 billion to world merchandise trade by around the year 2005. While many economists and public officials praised the agreement, others emphasized how much more needed to be done to achieve an open world economy. It is obviously impossible to summarize the entire Agreement, so I emphasize here only a few of the Round's major achievements.

The most significant accomplishment of the Uruguay Round was its creation of the WTO, an important step toward completion of the framework of international institutions originally proposed at Bretton Woods fifty years earlier. Although the WTO replaced the GATT and incorporated many of its rules and practices, the legal mandate and institutional structure of the WTO were designed to enable it to play a much more important role than GATT had played in the governance of international commerce. The WTO, for example, has more extensive and binding rules than the GATT. Moreover, the WTO will, in effect, possess the primary responsibility for facilitating international economic cooperation in trade liberalization and for filling in the many details omitted in the 22,000-page and 385-pound document. The Agreement establishing the WTO expands and entrenches the GATT principle that trade should be governed by multilateral rules rather than by unilateral actions or bilateral negotiations.

Although the WTO was not given the extent of rule-making authority desired by some, it does have much more authority than the GATT. It is important that the GATT dispute settlement mechanism was incorporated in the WTO and that it was reformed and greatly strengthened by elimination of such basic flaws as long delays in the proceedings of the dispute panels, disputants' ability to block proceedings, and the frequent failure of members to implement decisions. The Agreement also established a new appellate body to oversee the work of the dispute panels. The institutional structure of the trade regime also changed significantly. Whereas the GATT had been a trade accord supported by a secretariat, the WTO is a membership organization that provides greater legal coherence among its wide-ranging rights and obligations and establishes a permanent forum for negotiations. Biennial ministerial meetings are expected to increase political guidance to the institution. The Uruguay Round also created a trade-policy review mechanism to monitor member countries' actions. With more than 130 members, however, one may wonder how such a huge organization can manage these responsibilities.

The agreement to establish the WTO represents a trade-off between the interests of the highly industrialized countries and those of the industrializing economies. Whereas the former obtained greater protection of their intellectual property rights and access to the markets of the industrializing economies for their service and manufacturing industries, the latter acquired increased and more secure access to the markets of the former, especially for their manufactured exports. At one time the developing economies were very suspicious of GATT as an instrument of Western domination and promoter of dependence, but when they became exporters of manufactured goods, they began to look to the GATT and its successor to defend their interests. While the industrialized democracies (the United States, Western Europe, and Japan) and the world's leading Third World exporters (e.g., India, Brazil, Malaysia, Pakistan, Singapore, Indonesia, South Korea, and China) will all certainly benefit from the Agreement, estimates suggest that the Asian emerging markets will be the greatest beneficiaries. On the other hand, the vast majority of the nations outside the WTO, the poorest of the less developed economies, could experience major losses due to the WTO trading regime.

One of the most important achievements of the Round was creation of the "built-in" agenda for the future activities of the WTO. The built-in commitments include the implementation of Uruguay Round agreements, WTO leadership in completion of many unresolved issues, and new initiatives toward further trade liberalization. Items for further negotiation include policies on government procurement and on trade in agriculture and services. Another matter that will require continued negotiation is implementation of the textile and clothing agreement. Several issues that deserve further attention are:

1. *Intellectual Property Rights.* Although the Trade-Related Aspects of Intellectual Property Rights (TRIPs) agreement was a major step forward, protection of these rights and related issues continue to be a source of intense controversy, especially between developed and developing countries.

2. *Services.* The General Agreement on Trade in Services (GATS), included in the Round, provides the basic framework for liberalization of trade in services, trade that now accounts for over 60 percent of the world gross product. Although sectoral agreements were reached on information technology products (1996), telecommunications services (1997), and financial services (1997), many important issues involved in liberalizing trade in services are still unresolved.

3. *Agriculture.* The Uruguay Round achieved a number of important successes in the agricultural sector: inclusion of agricultural trade in the WTO framework, a shift from nontransparent nontariff barriers to transparent tariff barriers, and curbing (but not eliminating) of export

subsidies and codification of domestic agricultural programs. Nevertheless, there are still huge obstacles to achievement of free trade in agriculture. For example, export subsidies were actually legitimated and the
farm programs of the major industrial powers were left generally un-
touched. However, there is an extremely important agricultural problem still unresolved, and that is the conflict between the United States
and the European Union.

4. *Foreign Direct Investment.* Despite agreement on Trade-Related Investment Measures (TRIMs), a satisfactory agreement on a code cover-
ing FDI is far off.

The ways in which these important remaining issues are resolved will
have a huge impact on the trading system, and it is certain that many
years of intense negotiations lie ahead. As trade expert John Jackson has
said of the Uruguay Round Agreement, the "devil is in the details."[31]

HIDDEN BARRIERS AND THE NEW TRADE AGENDA

In addition to the many issues on the built-in agenda, trade negotiations
in the decades ahead will have to deal with the problems of both formal
and hidden trade barriers and what is called the "New Trade Agenda."
Although trade barriers have dropped significantly over the past half
century, they continue to be major obstacles to the free flow of goods
and services. A considerable portion of argricultural trade and of trade
in sevices is still subject to real barriers, and tariffs in some LDCs remain
as high as 30 percent. Trade flows are still largely determined by political boundaries. How else does one explain the fact that trade between
Chicago and New York is five to ten times the trade across the 49th
parallel! As formal, transparent, and measurable tariffs have declined to
almost zero, the important remaining trade barriers are such domestic
obstacles as technical standards, administrative discretion, and the like.

Trade negotiators will have to deal with the seemingly intractable political problems associated with the New Trade Agenda. The New Trade
Agenda arises mainly from the fact that trade flows, having reached
deeply into domestic affairs, have upset powerful domestic interests.

These politically sensitive trade problems include several interconnected social and environmental issues. Many trade experts and public officials perceive a need for an international competition/antitrust policy that would clarify "fair" and "unfair" economic behavior. Economic regionalism also provides new challenges for the new trade agenda.

Labor Standards and Environmental Protection

These issues have become very important and highly controversial. Their significance cannot be denied, but the controversy surrounding them centers primarily on whether or not these highly sensitive issues should be grouped together with trade issues. On the one hand, powerful groups, especially in the United States and Western Europe, believe strongly that these matters should be incorporated into the international trade regime. On the other hand, many economists, public officials, and business groups are equally fervently opposed to complicating matters by integrating these issues into international negotiations over trade liberalization. The stalemate generated by these seemingly uncompromisable positions accounts for the defeat of President Clinton's 1997 request for fast-track authorization to expedite trade negotiations.

The emerging conflict between policies to promote environmental protection and those supporting trade liberalization is of great and urgent significance.[32] This problem is particularly complicated because, while many advocates of environmental protection have pressured their respective governments, especially the American government, to use trade measures to promote environmental objectives, many other environmentalists oppose trade liberalization as a threat to national or international environmental standards. American environmentalists were particularly infuriated by a 1991 GATT ruling against the U.S. ban on the importation of tuna, a ban intended to discourage the usage of methods that were killing dolphins; they were subsequently and equally incensed in 1998 when the WTO declared illegal an American law protecting sea turtles. Such experiences have actually led trade protectionists and environmentalists to ally themselves with one another to oppose trade liberalization. This happened in the debate over the North American Free Trade Agreement; many other examples could be mentioned. Together, many groups of environmentalists have become formidable opponents of further trade liberalization. Needless to say, most economists strongly object to this intermingling of trade liberalization and environmental protection. On the other hand, the Clinton Administration, largely for domestic political reasons, has become responsive to such concerns.

While proponents of trade liberalization may be sympathetic to the importance of protecting the environment, they are concerned that environmental regulations would be used for purposes of trade protection; they also worry that trade measures designed to protect the environment would shift trade negotiations from products to production methods. This could extend the trade regime even more deeply into domestic matters and thus create resistance to trade rules as unwarranted intrusions on national sovereignty. Yet, environmentalists are rightly concerned that trade negotiators and the trade regime do place commercial interests over environmental goals. Moreover, neglect of environmental considerations in trade discussions could lead to harmonization of environmental standards through dilution of those standards. As both trade liberalization and environmental protection are desirable objectives, future trade negotiations must balance the two goals.

Conflict over labor standards has also become a major impediment to trade liberalization, especially in the United States. Most economists reject the idea that labor standards should be incorporated into trade negotiations and argue that the proper venue for such discussions is the International Labor Organization. They are concerned that labor standards could provide a rationale for protectionist measures against low-wage economies. The issue of labor standards has been raised by organized labor and by human rights advocates and their allies in industrialized countries. These proponents of incorporating into trade agreements clauses dealing with such matters as "fair" labor practices, prohibition of child labor, human rights, and promotion of democracy have been especially strong in France and the United States. The issues of workers' rights and of social dumping, that is, competing unfairly by denying basic rights and decent conditions to workers, are legitimate concerns. China, in particular, has been charged with denying fundamental human rights to its workers. Nevertheless, most Western economists are very dubious about making workers' rights a part of the trade regime, as this would unduly complicate trade negotiations. They also fear that labor standards could too easily be employed as protectionist devices.

The developing countries themselves have strongly denounced efforts to impose Western standards, alleging that the standards are used by protectionist interests and as devices to reduce the comparative advantage of their economies based on low-wage labor and provision of only minimum welfare benefits. Although many advocates of workers' rights are indeed protectionist, many others are sincerely concerned over the poor treatment of workers, and particularly over child labor, in many developing countries. It will be very difficult indeed to reconcile those who support and those who oppose incorporation of workers' rights into the trade regime.

International Competition Policy

Development of international rules governing competition policy is an important issue confronting the world economy. The purpose of international competition policy (called antitrust policy by Americans) is to set the terms for the globalization of business competition, a task made increasingly necessary by growing interdependence of national economies. While globalization has increased competition, it has also led to increased anticompetitive behavior. Efforts to cartelize market sectors, the growing numbers of transnational mergers and acquisitions, and exclusion of foreign firms from domestic markets attest to the seriousness of the problem. Moreover, the increasing integration of national economies with very different antitrust and other regulatory traditions, as well as the increasing importance of economies of scale, oligopolistic competition, and strategic interactions in international competition, have brought to the fore the fundamental question of what "fair competition" means with respect to government policies regulating business activities.

National differences in competition policy (governing mergers, dealing with trusts, etc.) and business regulations have, in effect, become important barriers to trade and foreign investment. Compared to Japan, for example, the United States has very strict regulations governing the concentration of corporate power, government support for business, and restrictive business practices. Under such circumstances, it is necessary to question how much harmonization among different national regulations is required to achieve a "level playing field" and thereby create a situation in which no one believes that a competitor has an unfair advantage. One of the issues to be resolved is the increasing use of the antidumping provision of the GATT as a protectionist device.

While almost every country has regulations governing domestic cartels, merger activities, and unfair business practices, countries differ considerably on matters such as the transparency of internal corporate affairs and tolerance for the concentration of corporate power. Examples include the German system of universal banks and their corporate allies, a relationship that is largely opaque to outsiders; another example is Japanese restrictions on the American practice of "hostile" or unwanted takeovers. Such ingrained differences among national systems of political economy frequently cause great difficulties for firms trying to export goods to a foreign market and/or to invest in other economies. Restrictions on inward foreign direct investment in other countries have become very important because of the increasing linkage between trade and foreign investment and increased internationalization of business activities. Therefore, harmonization of competition policy has become a major issue in international trade negotiations.

The GATT and the WTO have dealt principally with "border" (or external) barriers to trade. Differences in national economic policies, corporate structures, and private business practices were not considered very important in the early post–World War II era characterized by low levels of integration among national economies. However, with increased interdependence and the integration of trade with FDI, these differences in national economies have become considerably more significant in determining international competitiveness and trade patterns.

There has been a great increase in attention to government policies and characteristics of national economies that affect trade patterns, particularly with Japan and other Pacific Asian economies. Many American and European critics believe that Japan has long pursued a strategic trade policy. The Japanese system of "industrial groupings" (*keiretsu*), critics charge, discriminates against non-Japanese firms and constitutes a major barrier to imports into the Japanese market. In the late 1980s, the United States demanded that Japan modify features of its competition laws that Americans considered objectionable; these features included toleration of collusive behavior among firms and regulations restricting distribution channels. Dealing with these types of trade and investment barriers is made particularly difficult because they frequently have been erected primarily to achieve domestic social purposes. Japan, for example, has protected "mom and pop" stores against competition from large Japanese firms as well as from foreign firms in order to preserve neighborhoods. While the intent of that policy was not protectionist, it did discriminate against imports.

Two basic approaches to greater harmonization of competition policy have been proposed. One solution, favored by the European Union (EU), would be to establish an international code and rules governing this policy. A general agreement on competition policies could be incorporated into the trade regime and supervised by the WTO. Another approach, favored by the United States, is international cooperation in the enforcement of either national or regional competition laws. Both approaches would be exceedingly difficult to implement because competition policies, long considered domestic matters, are intimately joined to a particular society's attitude toward the market and economic matters. Moreover, it is frequently difficult to determine whether a particular policy is intended to promote domestic welfare or is a deliberate attempt to keep out foreign competitors. International cooperation is undoubtedly the more feasible approach. However, as the 1997 conflict between the United States and the European Union over the Boeing–McDonnell-Douglas merger suggests, cooperation will be difficult in the absence of agreed-upon legal and economic principles. If the United States and the European Union cannot agree on what is fair, what nations can?!

In the increasingly integrated and globalized economy, some way to regulate competition policy must be devised to overcome fundamental differences over fair business practices and regulatory competition, both of which threaten the unity of the global economy. Yet, inability to agree on international rules or to increase international cooperation in this area has contributed to the development of both managed trade and regional arrangements. Competition policy is now frequently determined at the level of such regional economic agreements as the EU or NAFTA, and every regional agreement contains its own definition of "fair competition." An integrated global economy and regionalized competition policies could be difficult to reconcile.

Challenge of Economic Regionalism

Regionalization is a very important challenge to the WTO trade regime. During the 1980s and 1990s, regional pacts expanded until they covered much of world trade. With a few notable exceptions, most WTO members are also members of a regional trading arrangement. The rapid spread, increasing scope, and changing nature of the regional arrangements have raised questions about the compatibility of regional arrangements with an international trading regime based on trade liberalization. During the first decades of the postwar period, such regional arrangements as the European Common Market generally reinforced economic multilateralism. Any resultant trade diversion or discrimination against nonmembers was more than offset at that time by trade creation and expansion caused by the more rapid economic growth resulting from regional integration.

There are several reasons why proliferation of regional trading arrangements in the 1980s and 1990s has raised concerns. The major concern is that regional trading blocs tend to discriminate against nonmembers; this certainly applies to the European Union and the North American Free Trade Agreement. Also, new trading and customs rules increase costs and thus impede trade. For example, free trade areas such as NAFTA invariably employ industry-specific "rules of origin" to restrict imports. Furthermore, evidence suggests that one important motive for regional arrangements is to enable groupings of states to attract foreign investment by MNCs. This last factor helps explain the rapidity with which regional arrangements have been spreading around the globe.

The WTO should ensure the compatibility of regional arrangements with continuing multilateral trade. Rules governing regional trading blocs should increase the likelihood that trade creation will outweigh trade diversion, but that will not be easy. At the opening of the new century, WTO rules have not been particularly effective in dealing with the protectionist tendencies of regional arrangements. New rules should be formulated to deal with the intensifying competition for FDI, with governmental violations of the principle of nondiscrimination and with other situations that create incentives for regional arrangements.

The International Trade Organization (ITO) had been assigned a mandate to regulate competition policy. It is rather ironic that the United States, now irate with Japan's and other countries' competition policies, defeated the ITO in 1950 precisely because it would have dealt with unfair business practices. With no international agreement on competition policy, efforts to achieve harmonization have focused on the regional level. While establishment of a new organization patterned on the original ITO might make good economic sense, there would be formidable political hurdles to be overcome in any such effort.

This quick review of current trade issues demonstrates the appropriateness of a prominant economist's comment that the Uruguay Round is yesterday's agreement and that it dealt mainly with the issues of the past and not those of the future.

Managing the Trading System

Creation of the WTO was a major achievement, and its accomplishments thus far have been impressive in resolving trade disputes and other matters. Yet, given its mandate, the structure and resources of the WTO leave much to be desired. Although it is indeed a major advance over the GATT, the WTO suffers from serious resource constraints both in funding and in personnel. Although the Uruguay Round conferred substantial responsibilities on the WTO, member governments have not committed sufficient financial and other resources to enable the organization to carry out its responsibilities. Furthermore, its structure is extraordinarily unwieldy.

The GATT (like the World Bank and the International Monetary Fund) was governed by a small executive council whose membership included all the major trading economies. Decisions were made on the basis of a system of weighted votes that placed control over these organizations in the hands of the United States and other dominant industrialized economies who held similar views of the world economy and were allied politically with the United States, so that the United States was able to exercise a significant leadership role. The WTO, on the other hand, is directed by a council composed of *all* members of the organization, a governance structure demanded by the smaller economic powers, especially the less developed economies, and similar to the structure implicit in earlier LDC efforts to create a New International Economic Order. However, this unwieldy structure has caused the major economic powers, or the Quad (the United States, Western Europe, Japan, and Canada), to resort to ad hoc extralegal processes outside the WTO. One must presume that the governance mechanisms of the WTO could become still more ineffective and inefficient with admission of Russia and/or China to the organization.

Uruguay Round signatories instructed the WTO to cooperate with the IMF, the World Bank, and other international organizations to ensure that they all would follow consistent and mutually supportive policies. The signatories assumed that the WTO would provide an institutional framework for dealing with complex issues that involved linkages among trade, monetary, and other novel features of a highly interdependent world economy. But, given the resources and governing structure of the WTO (and also, alas, the entrenched positions of the IMF and World Bank), this effort is unlikely to succeed. In addition, the huge number of trade issues on the table and the large number of players mean that the WTO is already facing an immense challenge to assemble a package for a new round of trade negotiations large enough to permit nations to make trade-offs among sectors and issues. If the WTO fails in this task, the fundamental concept of general reciprocity will be further undermined, and the tendency toward specific reciprocity and managed trade will intensify.

The increase in the responsibilities of the WTO has caused many American and other observers to fear that the WTO's mandate violates the national sovereignty of its members. The Dole (named after then Senator Robert Dole) Amendment to American ratification of the Uruguay Round, for example, specifically reserved for the United States the right to withdraw from the WTO if it infringed on American sovereignty, a right that every nation already possessed. American critics (on both the right and left of the political spectrum) have worried that the WTO could compel the United States to change such laws as those dealing with business activities or the environment. Another concern has been that the WTO's system of simple majority voting could lead to rewriting trade laws to the disadvantage of the major economic powers.

Obviously, there are no easy answers to these concerns. Decisions of the WTO have already conflicted with American environmental law. However, WTO decisions must be accepted by a member state before they can be applied to that state. Furthermore, there is no way to compel a state, especially a powerful one like the United States, to comply with WTO decisions. Officially, if the United States were found liable for an infringement of the trade regime, a plaintiff could demand compensation or retaliation against the United States. However, U.S. power has ensured that such things seldom happen. One can expect, therefore, that (as under the GATT) the normal practice will continue and WTO regulations will tend to be based on consensus. Moreover, although a decision by majority vote is possible, the procedures of the organization are structured in such a way that the big powers can block any significant decision with which they disagree. Therefore, it is more likely that the WTO will be ineffective than that it will threaten the national sovereignty of the United States or any other country.

CONCLUSION

The achievements of the trading system during the past half century have been remarkable. The many rounds of trade negotiations since the early 1960s have reduced tariffs in industrialized countries to less than 6 percent on average (one-tenth of what they were in the 1940s); quotas have been reduced and subsidies, restricted. Industrializing economies have also begun to reduce their own trade barriers significantly. The WTO dispute mechanism has worked moderately well thus far, but has experienced a stalemate in the frequent clashes between the United States and the European Union. The number of GATT/WTO members has increased from twenty-three to one hundred thirty-two in the late 1990s, with about thirty additional states wishing to join. This increase reflects the global shift since the 1980s to more market-oriented economic policies, but it also greatly complicates negotiations. Moreover, as trade liberalization and globalization penetrate more and more deeply into domestic economies, they conflict more frequently with powerful local interests and popular beliefs. In the late 1990s, these forces won a considerable victory in defeating President Clinton's request for fast-track authorization, legislation that would have enabled him to expedite trade negotiations. This episode should remind us that the clash between the forces of globalization and those of trade protection continues to threaten the global trading system.

CHAPTER FOUR

The Unstable Monetary System

A STABLE AND well-functioning international monetary system is in everyone's interest, even though most people are unaware of the ways in which the international monetary system affects their daily lives and economic well-being. It is only when they travel abroad that different currencies and the changing value of money are likely to impinge directly on their lives. Yet, currencies and their value pervade every aspect of the global economy and significantly affect the welfare of individuals everywhere. In the 1980s, Americans went on a spending spree because the high value of the dollar decreased the cost of foreign-made goods. American exporters, however, suffered greatly from the high dollar and demanded trade protection. The prolonged economic expansion of the 1990s can be explained in large part by the strong dollar and weak foreign currencies. If and when the dollar were to depreciate considerably, most Americans would suffer even though their export industries would benefit. When the value of the dollar fluctuates, as it frequently does, millions of Americans are affected whether they realize it or not. And if the international monetary system were to collapse as it did in the 1930s, calamity would result.

The international monetary system is closely tied to the international finance system. Flows of international capital and foreign investment are conducted in money, so that changes in exchange rates or the value of currencies inevitably change the value of a foreign investment or a tourist's traveler's checks. If one buys marks to invest in Germany and the value of the mark suddenly falls, the value of the investment is that much less. I once lost hundreds of dollars while flying across the Pacific because the yen in my pocket greatly depreciated during my flight; this was my first lesson in international finance. It is also possible that changes in international capital flows can change currency values. Huge inflows of foreign capital can cause a currency to appreciate (or rise in value) as happened to the dollar in the mid-1980s and much of the 1990s. Like the international monetary system, the international financial system is very vulnerable and can cause international economic turmoil like that in the late 1990s. Monetary instability and financial disturbances can have a disruptive impact on individual lives and on the global economy.

Before discussing the international monetary system, the system of international finance, and the global financial crisis of the late 1990s, I note that the distinction between money and finance can be misleading and that, as many nations have relinquished control over international capital movements, the international monetary and international finance systems have had an increased impact on one another. Significant fluctuations in currency values have affected finance, and the integration of financial markets around the world has had a negative impact on the functioning of the international monetary regime.

Since the breakdown of the system of fixed exchange rates, there has been no stable and satisfactory international monetary system. Making improvements involves complex and important technical issues, and solutions devised to resolve these technical matters have important political ramifications. The issue of a fixed versus a flexible exchange rate system and the associated problem of governing the international monetary system are at the heart of these matters. The prospects for a stable and integrated international monetary system will remain clouded until, and unless, these matters can be resolved,.

TECHNICAL AND POLITICAL ISSUES EMBEDDED IN THE INTERNATIONAL MONETARY SYSTEM

The subject of international money is highly technical and even esoteric. The formal models and mathematical techniques required to deal with monetary and financial matters are beyond the technical competence of most noneconomists and even beyond many economists; yet the international monetary system is of intense concern and importance to national governments and private economic interests. The mechanisms responsible for the system's efficient functioning—adjustment, liquidity creation, and confidence-building measures—produce a differential impact on the national interests of various countries and also on the interests of powerful groups within domestic economies. Technical mechanisms are seldom politically neutral; they affect the economic welfare, political autonomy, and even the international prestige of individual states; they also have an impact on the interests of capital, labor, and other domestic groups. Every state wants an efficient and well-functioning international monetary system. However, individual states and powerful domestic groups may disagree strongly on such matters as currency values and the precise mechanisms to be employed to solve technical problems.

A well-functioning system requires strong leadership by a nation or group of nations with an interest in maintaining the system. The leader must assume the initiative in solving highly technical problems as well as providing and managing the key currency used for maintaining reserves, carrying out economic transactions, and providing liquidity. Furthermore, the leader must be the "lender of last resort" and, from time to time, must provide financial assistance to countries experiencing severe financial problems. Although this leadership role could, in theory, be provided by two or more nations, or even by an international organization, leadership has historically been provided by a dominant economic and military power, such as Great Britain in the late nineteenth century and the United States following World War II. Not surprisingly, the rules governing the international monetary system have in general reflected the interests of these leading economic powers.

The Belgian economist Paul DeGrauwe has pointed out that economists differ fundamentally with one another over almost every aspect of international monetary affairs, from determination of currency values to the virtues of fixed versus floating rates; this makes explication of economists' views on this matter quite challenging.[33] Particularly since the early 1970s, the area of international monetary affairs has been the focus of very intense controversy among economists. Although professional books and journals have been filled with proposals to reform the monetary regime, few proposals have been implemented, and the monetary system's inherent problems and contradictions remain unresolved. Economists' theories about the varied and complex aspects of the international monetary regime have usually followed rather than preceded events that they attempt to explain. Indeed, many theories regarding monetary affairs have been merely ex post facto explanations of important developments that economists had failed to predict. Theoretical and policy differences among experts make solution of the problems difficult.

The Adjustment Problem

An international monetary regime must determine the method by which national economies will restore equilibrium (i.e., reduce a deficit or a surplus) in their international accounts (balance of payments). The essence of the adjustment problem is that every adjustment policy results in economic costs; furthermore, some methods of adjustment are considerably more costly than others for individual economies and for the overall world economy. An efficient international monetary system should minimize such costs.

A country with an imbalance in its international payments may pursue such short-term expedients as drawing down its national reserves (a deficit country) or adding to its national reserves (a surplus country). However, a deficit country cannot continue drawing down its reserves forever, and eventually the debtor country must take measures that eliminate the cause of the imbalance. On the other hand, a surplus country, like the United States for much of the twentieth century and Japan at the end of the century, can continue to add to its reserves for a very long time, a practice that irritates trading partners. Both deficit and surplus countries employ additional methods to overcome a payments imbalance. One such method is to change the exchange rate by devaluing (a deficit country) or appreciating (a surplus country) the currency. Another method is to make changes in macroeconomic policy; that is, to shift to deflationary (deficit country) or expansionary (surplus country) economic policies.

Some currencies will inevitably get out of line. Many nations live beyond their means and pursue inflationary policies; others, like Japan during most of the second half of the twentieth century, desire a continuous payments surplus and thus choose to live below their means (a deflationary policy). Such national differences in inflation/deflation rates will cause currency values to change; some method acceptable to all must be available to bring currencies back into equilibrium. And, of course, for every deficit country, there must be one or more surplus countries. While either the deficit or surplus country (or both) could make adjustments, under the Bretton Woods System it was generally assumed that the burden of adjustment rested with the deficit country. However, the deficit country can and frequently does take actions to impose the costs of adjustment on the surplus country. For example, the United States has attempted, with some modest success, to impose the burden of adjustment on Japan through elimination of the American-Japanese trade/payments imbalance.

Adjustment, for a deficit country, means that it must reduce its standard of living; that is, achieve a long-term reduction in national income and/or reduce employment levels. The rules governing the international monetary system will determine the approved methods of making such an adjustment. However, regardless of the choices available, transition from "high living" to "living within one's means" must necessarily impose a real cost on the deficit country, and the precise manner in which adjustment occurs will also impose costs on other countries; for example, the post-1997 deflationary consequences of the East Asian financial crisis harmed many American exporters. It is clear that all countries would like to shift as many adjustment costs as possible to others and away from themselves. Working out the distribution of the costs of adjustment among deficit and surplus nations is the essence of solving the adjustment problem.

For a deficit country living beyond its means, both currency devaluation and/or deflation of the economy are painful because the former entails a drop in national income and the latter, a rise in unemployment. For a surplus country, currency appreciation is painful for its export industries while beneficial to its importers and consumers; on the other hand, macroeconomic stimulus of the economy carries the risk of inflation. How much better it would be, therefore, to transfer the adjustment costs to one's trading partners! As mentioned above, a case in point is the long simmering economic clash between the deficit United States and the surplus Japan. Beginning in the 1980s, the United States resisted deflationary policies that would reduce its trade deficit but would also mean a decline in the American standard of living. Meanwhile, Japan resisted appreciation of the yen because that would harm its export industries. Japanese agreement at the Plaza Conference (September 1985) to appreciate the yen was achieved only after intense

American pressures. Since solution of the adjustment problem impinges on the interests of states and of powerful interests within states, adjustment mechanisms do and will reflect the interests of powerful states and groups.

The Liquidity Problem

An efficient international monetary system must also provide international liquidity. Participating countries must have financial reserves sufficient to meet balance of payments deficits caused by such economic shocks to the system as the sudden increase in the price of petroleum in 1973 or by persistent use of such unwise policies as an inflationary macroeconomic policy or maintenance of an overvalued currency. Reserves are important because they enable a deficit country to finance, at least for a short period, a payments disequilibrium and to increase the time and options available to the country as it seeks a longer-term solution to its deficit problem. A country can also use reserves to delay a possibly costly devaluation of its currency. A nation's reserves (like any other form of money) are also a store of value; they may include gold, convertible foreign currencies, or deposits with the International Monetary Fund.

While provision of optimal international liquidity facilitates the world economy's functioning, neither underprovision nor overprovision is desirable. Underprovision may be recessionary and overprovision, inflationary. During the last decades of the nineteenth century under the gold standard, there was underprovision of reserves, and while the gold standard was a very stable system, this system frequently resulted in high levels of unemployment and depressed wages. On the other hand, during the early post–World War II era of the dollar standard, overprovision of reserves by the United States meant a high level of inflation that eventually led to the breakdown of the Bretton Woods monetary system of fixed rates. With economists and governments disagreeing about the rules that should govern international reserves, the rule of the strong has generally prevailed, and the dominant power(s) have had a significant impact, at least over the short term, on maintaining the level of international liquidity to accord with their own economic and political interests.

Seigniorage, that is, the economic benefits accruing to the country supplying the primary international currency, is an important aspect of liquidity creation. Not only is national prestige enhanced when a nation's currency is selected as the most important currency, but seigniorage can also be a major source of increased income to the nation, particularly to its banking system. In addition, seigniorage can increase the economic and political autonomy of the country because that country is freed, at least for a time, from balance of payments constraints. On the other hand, seigniorage has associated costs; for example, the nation with the right of seigniorage usually has to pay interest to other countries holding assets denominated in its currency. To maintain seigniorage also means that a country must avoid actions that undermine confidence in the value of its currency. Moreover, the country supplying the key currency may find it difficult to devalue its currency, as happened to the United States in the early 1970s.

Gains in national income and in national autonomy or freedom of action are important benefits of seigniorage. The banking system of a country supplying an international currency enjoys both economies of scale and other cost advantages over its competitors simply because the greater part of international reserves and transactions are held in its national currency. Under the gold standard in the late nineteenth century, sterling was the key currency, and London financial institutions enjoyed high profits as the center of the international monetary system. Following World War I, London and sterling were challenged by New York and the dollar, and the profits from seigniorage began to flow to the United States and its banking system. Today it remains to be seen whether or not the euro of the European Union and a European city or cities will eventually take over financial and monetary leadership.

Seigniorage also confers on the key-currency country greater freedom from economic restraints and hence more autonomy than other countries enjoy. Throughout the Cold War, the capacity of the United States to fight foreign wars, maintain troops abroad, and finance its foreign policy was largely dependent on the willingness of its allies to hold American dollars and dollar-denominated assets. Even after the Cold War, for years the role of the dollar as the world's key currency permitted the United States to live far beyond its means and thus to become the world's foremost debtor nation. Other countries, by holding dollars, actually gave the United States interest-free loans. As the American debt has been denominated in dollars, this debt burden could be inflated away, and devaluation of the dollar in the 1990s did indeed reduce the debt owed by the United States while simultaneously imposing heavy costs on Japanese and other lenders. Nevertheless, as long as there is no acceptable alternative and dollar holders maintain confidence in the dollar, the United States will continue to enjoy the privileges of seigniorage.

The Confidence Problem

A stable international monetary system is also dependent on solution of the confidence (credibility) problem, and the supplier of the key currency must make certain that other countries have confidence that the reserve-currency country will not pursue inflationary policies leading to devaluation of their own reserves. If they lose confidence, other countries will shift the composition of their reserves. A shift can also occur because of changes in the interest rate paid on assets denominated in a currency, changes in exchange risk, or inflationary concerns. A reserve-currency country must pay an attractive interest rate on assets denominated in its currency, and it must also take confidence-building measures to convince private and public holders of its currency that its currency will continue to be convertible into other sound assets and will not lose value because of inflation or changes in exchange rates. These confidence-building measures can be quite costly.

DEVISING AN INTERNATIONAL MONETARY SYSTEM

Although an efficient international monetary system benefits every country, serious political and economic difficulties can impede the creation or improvement of a monetary system. Every solution to the technical problems discussed above produces important distributive consequences that affect differently both various nations and powerful domestic constituencies; because some may lose more or benefit less than others from a monetary arrangement, strong reactions can be evoked. During the early postwar years, both the United States and its trading partners were upset over the asymmetries of the dollar-based system. Many Europeans objected to the economic and political privileges bestowed on the United States, and the United States, as the reserve-currency country, increasingly fretted over its inability to reduce its trade deficit by devaluing the dollar. Eventually, President Nixon in August 1971 "solved" U.S. concerns about asymmetry by forcing appreciation of other currencies.

Differing subjective judgments among public officials and disagreements among economists about the appropriate applicable economic model or theory also complicate development or modification of a monetary system. Intellectual and theoretical disagreements exist among economists and public officials about many possible solutions to the technical issues embedded in a monetary system. Economists, for example, even disagree about the economic model to apply to determination of exchange rates, and trade-offs exist among desirable but mutually exclusive goals. A choice, primarily political, must be made.

At the heart of the difficulties in finding solutions to exchange-rate instability is the fact that national economies have very different rates of inflation or price instability. Whereas some governments place a high value on price stability, others prefer to pursue expansionary and frequently inflationary policies to reduce unemployment or stimulate economic growth. Germany and Japan, having given priority to price stability throughout the postwar era, have followed strong anti-inflationary policies while the United States, at least until the late 1970s, pursued mild to highly inflationary policies.

The difficulties of devising a stable and politically acceptable international monetary system are further compounded by the inevitable trade-off among the desirable goals of an international monetary/financial system: that is, fixed exchange rates, national independence in macroeconomic policy, and capital mobility (these three are referred to by economists as a "trilemma" or as the "irreconcilable trinity"). Nations may want stable exchange rates to reduce economic uncertainty and also want discretionary monetary policy to promote economic growth and steer their economies between recession and inflation. In addition, governments may want freedom of capital movements to facilitate the conduct of trade, foreign investment, and other international business activities.

Unfortunately, an international monetary system can incorporate at most two, but not all three, of the desirable but irreconcilable goals. For example, a system of fixed exchange rates such as the Bretton Woods System, with some latitude for independent macroeconomic policies, is incompatible with freedom of capital movement because capital flows could undermine both fixed exchange rates and independent macroeconomic policies. A system with fixed exchange rates and independent macroeconomic policies promotes economic stability and enables a government to deal simultaneously with domestic unemployment. However, such a system sacrifices freedom of capital movement, one of the most important goals of international capitalism.

Different countries and domestic interest groups prefer to emphasize different goals. The United States, for example, prefers independent monetary policy and freedom of capital movements, and deemphasizes stable exchange rates; the members of the European Community (EC), on the other hand, prefer relatively fixed rates. Some countries, notably Malaysia and China, place a high value on macroeconomic independence at this time and have imposed controls on capital movements. Specific economic interests also differ in their preferences. Whereas export businesses have a strong interest in the exchange rate, domestic-oriented businesses place a higher priority on national policy autonomy. Investors prefer freedom of capital movements whereas labor tends to be opposed to such movement unless it leads to inward investment. As national situations and interests differ, there is no one solution to the trilemma that would be satisfactory for all.

The tension or trade-off between international monetary stability and domestic economic autonomy has existed for a very long time, and a number of "solutions" have been devised to deal with that tension. Many economic conservatives argue that the first major effort to resolve the problem was the most successful; this was the creation of the Classical Gold Standard under British leadership in the latter decades of the nineteenth century. Under this system of "golden fetters" (to use the title of Barry Eichengreen's important book on the subject), there was indeed international monetary stability, but governments had little control over their own economies and the domestic economy frequently suffered.[34] The collapse of the gold standard at the outbreak of World War I resulted in a situation in which governments had too much license regarding their economic policy; the 1930s and 1940s were an era of economic anarchy, competitive devaluations and "beggar thy neighbor" policies that lasted until the Bretton Woods System was created at the end of World War II. This system, based on fixed exchange rates and supervised by the International Monetary Fund, continued until officially terminated in the mid-1970s. The subsequent volatility and unpredictability of exchange rates produced by the more recent "nonsystem" have led to many proposals to reform the international monetary regime.

Reform of International Monetary Affairs

Since the breakdown of fixed exchange rates in the 1970s, there has been a nonsystem of flexible exchange rates. The term "nonsystem" refers to the fact that international monetary affairs are not governed by any rules or understandings regarding such things as exchange rate adjustment or liquidity creation. The "system" may, at best, be characterized as a "reference range" system, so named because the central banks of the three dominant monetary powers—the United States, Germany, and Japan—have cooperated (and sometimes have not cooperated) to keep their exchange rates aligned or to change them in an orderly fashion.

The reference range system represents the triumph of the central bankers over national governments. Stability of the international monetary system has rested mainly on informal cooperation among the American Federal Reserve, the German Bundesbank, and the Bank of Japan, which have intervened in currency markets to protect the integrity of the system, prevent financial instability, and stabilize exchange rates. (After January 1, 1999, the Bundesbank was replaced by the European Central Bank.) Through secret agreements and sporadic intervention in the market, these central banks have attempted to maintain monetary stability. After the disturbing experience of hyperflation in the 1970s, interbank cooperation has been employed to suppress inflationary tendencies. However, many critics, especially on the political left, have denounced this "international alliance of conservative bankers" as the cause of high unemployment and even of the global economic crisis of the late 1990s.

While many economists and others believe that this system of informal cooperation among central bankers is the best possible solution to the problems of the international monetary system, others believe that the present nonsystem is threatened by several problems: erratic currency fluctuations, especially between the dollar and the yen; huge imbalances between surplus countries (Japan, Taiwan) and deficit countries (the United States); and frequent Japanese and U.S. attempts to manipulate currency values in order to increase the international competitiveness of their industries or to achieve some other economic objective. Economists and officials who worry about these problems believe that a fundamental reform of the international monetary system is urgently needed.

Proponents of international monetary reform focus on one or another of the goals called the "irreconcilable trinity." For example, whereas Milton Friedman's proposal for a system based on flexible exchange rates would facilitate freedom of capital movement, others prefer a return to the nineteenth-century gold standard that stresses fixed rates. Both completely flexible and rigidly fixed rates, however, are believed too drastic by most economists and public officials. Many consider Friedman's proposal unacceptable because it would leave exchange rates entirely up to the vicissitudes of the market, while a return to the gold standard would be deflationary and would strip governments of any ability to respond to market shocks. Most economists believe that it is necessary either to return to a system of more or less stable (but not fixed) exchange rates or to make floating flexible rates more workable. In reality, any reforms would probably entail a compromise between these goals.

Arguments for More Stable Exchange Rates

The advocates of a return to more stable exchange rates assert that the experiment with flexible (floating) rates has failed. They argue that flexible rates have resulted in excessive currency and price volatility, destabilizing international capital flows and inflationary economic policies. Excessive exchange rate volatility increases uncertainty and risk in both international trade and foreign investment and thus impedes international economic integration. Some experts also argue that volatility of currency values has decreased the effectiveness of the price mechanism and of the principle of comparative advantage as tools in international trade and foreign investment decision-making.

Within a period as short as one or two years, erratic swings in the three major currencies have occurred in which their values have varied by as much as 30 to 40 percent. The resulting uncertainty in relative prices has made it almost impossible to calculate relative costs and comparative advantage, calculations needed to provide the basis for a market economy to function efficiently. Some have concluded that floating rates impose high costs in economic growth and in the efficient allocation of economic resources. And they argue that unstable exchange rates have at least contributed to trade protectionism. Fixed rates, on the other hand, are believed by these individuals to provide international discipline over inflationary monetary policy, reduce the uncertainty that interferes with trade and investment, and thereby facilitate competition based on comparative advantage and efficient capital flows.

Proponents of more stable exchange rates are fully aware that economic and political developments have made a return to the type of pegged-rate system laid down at Bretton Woods impossible. For example, the huge and speculative international movements of capital due to the deregulation of capital markets make maintenance of a system based on fixed rates much more difficult. Instead, these individuals advocate a compromise between greater international stability and provision of some policy flexibility for governments in responding to economic shocks and other developments. Various schemes based on the idea of a contingent exchange-rate target have been put forth; they have such labels as "pegged but adjustable exchange rates," "crawling peg," "managed floating," "adjustable peg," and "exchange rate target zones."

Arguments for Flexible Exchange Rates

In the opinion of some experts, a system of flexible exchange rates provides the least costly means for economies to adjust to external shocks like the 1973 rise in oil prices. Proponents of this position argue that when a government faces a balance of payments disequilibrium, it is far better to devalue its currency than to deflate its economy or to resort to capital controls. In the event of a change in relative prices, the value of a currency should be free to change so that other more important values or "real" variables such as wages and employment need not have to change. Indeed, if there had been fixed rates during the 1973 oil crisis, countries would have had to adjust to the price rise either through severe deflation or capital controls.

Advocates of floating rates argue that they are inherently desirable because the value of a currency acts as a balancing mechanism for the rest of the economy, and because flexible rates protect and cushion an economy from disturbances originating in the international economy. While there may be some problems of uncertainty and inflation associated with flexible rates, reliance on fixed rates to avoid such problems makes adjustment both more costly and more difficult. Many argue, moreover, that the costs of floating rates have been greatly exaggerated and point out that the problem of monetary uncertainty can be reduced by private firms' "hedging" in the foreign exchange market.

Monetary expert Barry Eichengreen argues persuasively that the conditions for a system of fixed rates no longer exist.[35] A stable and efficient monetary system that achieves currency stability and also maintains the ability of governments to adjust exchange rates to meet economic shocks must be flexible and robust enough to contain market pressures. Because the monetary system must be flexible enough to cope with external shocks, governments must be able to make policy changes and other adjustments in response to changes in relative prices. The system must also be robust enough to convince the market (especially currency speculators) that governments intend to defend pegged rates in all but the most extreme circumstances. Furthermore, establishment of rules governing monetary policy must make existing rates more credible. Should speculators decide, nonetheless, to challenge governmental commitment to existing rates, the system must have the capacity to contain market pressures, especially speculative capital flows. The principal instruments available to central banks to counter market pressures are managed interest rates, imposition of capital controls, and joint intervention in the market by central banks to defend currencies under serious attack.

Although past systems of fixed rates, such as the gold standard of the late nineteenth century and the Bretton Woods System of the early postwar era, met these requirements and did contain market forces, Eichengreen argues that future fixed-rate systems will not be able to do so because of changed circumstances. One change is the institutionalized structure of labor markets associated with the welfare state, a development that seriously restricts the fluidity with which prices and wages can adjust to economic shocks and thus increases the importance of adjusting exchange rates to changes in relative prices. Another important change is the increasingly politicized environment in which domestic monetary policy must be formulated; politicization of macroeconomic policy in almost every democratic country has eroded the dependability or credibility of government policies and the commitment to pursue noninflationary monetary policy. Few governments can be relied on to maintain robust or steadfast monetary policy over the long term. The most important change is the greatly increased mobility of capital movements around the world, encouraged by deregulation of capital markets, technological developments, and new financial instruments, all of which have also greatly limited governmental ability to contain market pressures.

In these changed conditions, Eichengreen believes that the international monetary system has just two options available. One is a "regime" based on flexible rates in which a country intervenes to manage the value of its currency; however, the new conditions would not permit a country to target and maintain a specific rate. In the late 1990s, more and more countries have in fact permitted their currencies to float. The other choice is for a group of countries to create a single currency, as the European Union has done. The balance of power in international monetary affairs, Eichengreen suggests, has shifted so far away from individual nation-states and central bankers toward currency traders and international financial speculators that individual states can no longer resist market forces; furthermore, international cooperation will not work over the long term. Thus, he concludes that regional monetary unity may be essential to counterbalance global market forces.

Managing the International Monetary System

Public officials, central bankers, and economists continue to search for a compromise that will achieve both currency stability and policy flexibility, despite the seemingly irrefutable logic of Eichengreen and other economists that the only choices are either floating rates or regional monetary unity. Economics literature is in fact replete with mechanisms proposed to strengthen governance of international monetary affairs; the proposals range from creation of a world central bank and single world currency to strengthened international coordination of economic policies. Proliferation of such schemes reveals the large differences among economists on these matters and the intractable nature of the politics associated with international monetary affairs. Although many more alternatives have been set forth, this section will discuss only monetary hegemony, an international monetary authority, and international policy coordination. Consideration of these proposals provides insight into the profound problems involved in stabilizing the global monetary system.

Monetary Hegemony

During the past century, monetary hegemony of one country over the international economy has been associated with monetary stability, trade liberalization, and rapid economic growth. Therefore, some individuals advocate a return to strong leadership by one country as the most desirable solution to the problem of monetary instability, and the United States would be the most likely candidate for this role. The Japanese are certainly unable and/or unwilling to assume such a responsibility, and although the European Union's euro will undoubtedly play an increasingly important role in the global economy, it is not likely, at least for some time, to assume the role that the dollar has played over the past half-century.

However, it appears unlikely that American hegemony in monetary affairs could be reestablished. The dollar must compete against other currencies and will undoubtedly face intensifying competition from the euro. The relative decline of the American economy and the fluctuating value of the dollar also make renewal of unchallenged American monetary preeminence unlikely. The United States accounted for about 50 percent of world GDP during the early postwar era of unquestioned dollar hegemony; in the 1990s, the United States has accounted for only about 25 percent. Moreover, the ups and downs of the dollar have been very costly to Japanese and to other purchasers of dollar-denominated assets. The United States continues to live well beyond its means;

its growing net international debt of approximately \$1 trillion has weakened confidence in the dollar as a reserve currency. The "hegemony of the dollar" is clearly over, and from now on the dollar must share the stage with the euro and the yen.

An International Monetary Authority

A number of economists and others have proposed that an international monetary authority be created to govern the system. None of the proponents of this idea has been more forceful than John Williamson of the Washington-based Institute of International Economics; he has proposed that authority over international monetary affairs be given to an executive council lodged in the IMF.[36] This council, representing the international community, would function according to agreed rules and would have responsibility for keeping the exchange rates of states within certain parameters. Whereas the current reference-range system has been based on central bank secrecy and joint intervention, under Williamson's scheme countries would preannounce bands within which their exchange rates could vary, and each nation would specify a central rate with a 10 percent margin up and down. Governments would commit themselves publicly to such target zones for their currencies and, supervised by the special executive council established in the IMF, would defend the rates through interest-rate policies and, when necessary, central bank intervention. Although governments would try to keep their nominal exchange rate within the band, if necessary and before the limits were reached, the exchange rate could be realigned with executive council guidance. Moreover, if faced with a speculative attack, a country could suspend its commitment to the target zone. Such a compromise system, Williamson believes, would retain some flexibility, yet would be more stable than managed floating rates.

Williamson's proposal has drawn considerable attention and criticism from fellow economists.[37] There are a number of issues that must be resolved: (1) How would the proposed executive council determine the equilibrium exchange rate of individual currencies when there is profound disagreement among economists on how to determine such a rate? (2) How would the council counter powerful market forces created by the enormous monetary and financial assets in private hands that could be used for financial speculation? (3) How would the council convince reluctant governments to give up one of their most important instruments of economic policy, namely, control over the value of their currencies? In the opinion of many economists, an international monetary authority, such as the one proposed by Williamson, is unlikely to be able to solve the problems of the international monetary nonsystem.

International Policy Coordination

International policy coordination (IPC) among the major economic powers has been suggested frequently as a solution to the problems of international monetary affairs. IPC is a process whereby individual countries change their economic policies in a mutually beneficial manner.[38] The Bretton Woods Commission issued a fiftieth-anniversary report, entitled *Bretton Woods: Looking to the Future* (July 1994), and this contained a proposal that IPC should be increased. The Commission made a number of specific recommendations for reform of the IMF and World Bank to enable these institutions to accommodate to the enormous changes of the last half-century.[39] One important recommendation was that the IMF, in cooperation with the major economic powers, should work toward a new system of flexible exchange rate bands. This cooperative effort would require that the leading industrial economies forge a new agreement on equilibrium values for their currencies. However, reflecting political reality, the new system would function on the basis of national self-discipline, international policy cooperation, and joint intervention in the currency markets. The IMF would assume primary responsibility for strengthening macroeconomic policies, furthering macroeconomic convergence among the major economies, and establishing a formal system of policy coordination.

However, past experience with IPC does not promise future success. In the mid-1970s, the United States and its major economic partners did successfully cooperate in recycling the OPEC surplus. However, a later cooperative effort to steer the international economy fell apart at the Bonn Summit (1978) where, after much American pressure, West Germany and Japan reluctantly agreed to pursue expansionary economic policies. The resulting high inflation convinced both Germany and Japan that IPC had been too costly. After a hiatus of nearly a decade, a second round of policy coordination took place in the mid-1980s, again at the insistence of the United States. The high point of this effort was the Plaza Agreement (September 1985) that forced the Japanese to substantially appreciate the yen, thus making Japanese exports much more expensive.

Although the technical problems associated with IPC are formidable, the political problems of coordinating the economic policies of sovereign states are even more challenging; differences that have impeded policy coordination include domestic political/institutional arrangements, national views about economic policy, and, of course, the problem of ensuring that governments carry out their commitments. Most importantly, national governments and central banks are extremely reluctant to surrender policy autonomy. A strong state-centric mentality pervades the economic thinking of almost every government. Central bankers, for example, believe that their primary responsibility is to their own economy, so that their interest rate and other policies should promote the welfare of their citizens and not some international objective.

As Toyoo Gyohten, an experienced participant in international monetary diplomacy and a perspicacious observer of these matters, has commented, the prospects for a return to a more formal system of international policy coordination are very poor.[40] The formal coordination that characterized the early years of the Bretton Woods System, Gyohten points out, required a strong and willing hegemon; the world in the last decade of the twentieth century, as Gyohten also notes, lacks such a leader. The United States no longer appears to have the will or the ability to lead that it possessed earlier. It is equally significant that America's economic partners have become less willing to follow than in the past. Nor are the major economic powers willing to sacrifice domestic objectives such as economic growth and price stability for the sake of a formal mechanism of policy cooperation. Gyohten concludes with the somber assessment that an institutionalized solution to the problems of the international monetary regime is impossible, because market forces have become too powerful and states too unwilling to make the sacrifices necessary to achieve a coordinated solution to the problems of international monetary affairs. Although Gyohten—a diplomat to the core—has not himself emphasized this point, even informal policy coordination cannot possibly succeed unless the United States becomes more willing to heed the concerns and pay greater attention to the interests of its economic partners, especially the Europeans and the Japanese.

If there is no coordinated solution to international monetary anarchy, there will be a danger that the smaller economic powers will tie their currencies to the currencies of their most important trading partner. This development could lead to creation of currency blocs based on the euro, the dollar, and possibly the yen; such potentially competitive blocs could fragment the international monetary system and greatly complicate the management of the global economy.

Conclusion

As Gyohten has pointed out in another context, a stable and efficient international monetary system must rest on a secure political foundation. In the early postwar era, such a foundation was provided by the United States and interallied cooperation; unfortunately, this secure foundation no longer exists. Moreover, political disagreements among the major economic powers mean that emergence of a system based on firm rules and institutionalized policy coordination is unlikely. The only possible solution, as Gyohten has suggested, is a balance among the three dominant currencies (the dollar, the euro, and the yen), reinforced by what he calls a "crisis management mechanism"; the relevance of his admonition has been significantly heightened by subsequent developments in international financial matters.

CHAPTER FIVE

Global Financial Vulnerability

THE GLOBAL financial turmoil of the late 1990s was the latest episode in a series of financial "manias, panics, and crashes" (to use the title of Charles Kindleberger's book) that have shaken international capitalism over the last three hundred years.[41] Beginning in East Asia and subsequently spreading to much of the globe, the troubles of the global financial system brought misery and hard times to millions of people. Initially, Americans and citizens of other industrialized economies considered themselves safe from the dire effects of the East Asian crisis. In little more than a year, however, the crisis spread, and its effects were increasingly felt by Americans and others. Thousands of American and other investors lost millions of dollars as stock markets dropped around the world and many financial institutions collapsed. American farmers who had invested heavily to increase production suddenly found that their former markets in East Asia and elsewhere had vanished. Boeing aircraft and many high-tech industries also lost lucrative export markets. The costs have been enormous. Yet, the major economic powers are deeply divided with respect to reforms that might prevent similar financial earthquakes in the future.

The 1990s financial troubles resemble their predecessors in many ways. As in the "tulip mania" (1637) in Holland and the South Sea Bubble (which burst in 1720) in England and other "get-rich-quick" schemes, the greed of international investors led them to make very risky speculative investments in the emerging markets of East Asia. Then when the investment boom showed signs of collapsing, investors fled in panic and left behind shattered lives, lost fortunes, and economic chaos. However, there were important differences between earlier episodes and the 1990s crisis. Whereas the earlier crises were restricted to particular markets or regions of the world, the immense scale and velocity of international financial flows and the equal swiftness of information flows today have resulted in a situation where, with the push of a button, billions of dollars can be shifted from one country to another, and the whole globe can quickly be drawn into the maelstrom.

As a consequence of the global financial turmoil of the late 1990s, the economics profession and many governments have become increasingly concerned about, and deeply divided over, international finance and the regulation of international capital/investment flows. Many American economists, and certainly the Clinton Administration, believe that international financial flows perform a crucially important role; they also believe that such flows should be free of government regulation. Most believe that the financial system should ensure that capital will move from economies with surplus savings to those where investment opportunities exceed local savings, and that capital should be free to move toward those places and activities where it would be used most effectively; thus, efficient utilization of the world's scarce capital resources would be achieved.

To this end, markets and not governments or international organizations would govern the international financial system. In addition, at least since the Reagan Administration, the United States government has strongly believed that American financial interests would greatly benefit from freedom of capital movements and has made concerted efforts to open foreign economies to those investments. The Clinton Administration, led by Treasury Secretary Robert Rubin and Deputy Secretary Lawrence Summers, enthusiastically carried this effort further. The Administration adopted a strategy of using economics to foster foreign policy objectives and made a world open to unrestricted American capital movements a key objective of that strategy. This emphasis on use of open markets to promote democracy was based on the influential and controversial doctrine of the "democratic peace" that, as President Clinton stated, "democracies rarely wage war on one another."[42]

However, the East Asian financial crisis caused many other Americans and many governments and citizens of other countries to become increasingly concerned about the frequently devastating impact of international financial movements. A significant and growing number of prominent economists in the United States and elsewhere have challenged the value of unrestricted international capital flows. They have argued that it has been amply demonstrated that international trade benefits the global economy, but that the benefits of freedom of capital movements have not been adequately demonstrated. The costs to the international economy of frequent financial crises, on the other hand, have become painfully obvious. Indeed, as Kindleberger has shown, international financial history records recurring speculative manias, panics, and crises. Therefore, many conclude that international financial matters should not be left entirely up to the free play of market forces, but that some rules or mechanisms to regulate international capital movements should be in place.

The East Asian financial crisis of the late 1990s and the global financial turmoil to which it contributed elevated the issue of international finance to the top of the agenda of problems confronting the global economy. Many experts and governments consider these economic upheavals as the most serious threat to the international economy since the end of World War II and the Great Depression of the 1930s. Yet, as the twenty-first century opens, economists who once declared that they had learned how to fine-tune the economy failed to predict the crisis, disagreed fundamentally regarding its underlying causes, and bitterly debated the best means to resolve the crisis. Furthermore, economists and public officials do not agree on the measures or reforms needed to prevent future financial crises. With such disarray among professional economists themselves, few guidelines exist to help one understand turmoil in global financial markets and what should be done about it.

This chapter discusses the inherent vulnerability of the international financial system and the global financial/economic crisis of the late 1990s. The difficulties faced by such an analysis are complicated by the fact that writings by economists on the dynamics of financial crises are sparse. Obviously, conclusions drawn from any analysis of international finance must be highly tentative. As these words are written in 1999, the East Asian financial crisis and the turmoil of global finance have yet to complete their course, and many unexpected yet significant developments could still occur.

Dynamics of Financial Crises

Recurrent financial crises lead one to question the rationality of markets and to ask how rational actors can become caught up over and over again in the investment booms or manias that almost invariably result in financial panics and crises. Or, to put the matter another way, if economic actors are rational, as they are assumed to be by economists, how can one account for the frequent utter irrationality of financial markets? Although a number of distinguished economists have developed theories to explain currency crises, equally distinguished economists have denied that there really is any problem. Prior to 1997 some economists had even argued that economic and institutional changes had made serious financial crises impossible, but that, if crises were to occur, they would be caused by unique historical circumstances and would certainly not be caused by the inherent workings of the capitalist system. Given these attitudes in the profession, it is not surprising that so few economists anticipated the East Asian or global financial turmoil.

The generally dismissive attitude of professional economists to the danger and destabilizing consequences of international financial crises has been challenged by Hyman Minsky, a maverick economist hardly at the forefront of the discipline. In a series of articles spanning a number of years, Minsky set forth what he called "the financial instability" theory of financial crises.[43] According to his theory, financial crises are an inherent and inevitable feature of the capitalist system, and they follow a discernible and predictable course. The events leading up to a financial crisis begin with what he calls a "displacement," or an external shock to the economy; this external shock, which must be large and pervasive, can take such different forms as the start of a war, a bumper or failed crop, or innovation and diffusion of an important new technology. If large and pervasive enough, the external/exogenous shock increases the profit opportunities in at least one important economic sector while simultaneously reducing economic opportunities in other areas. In response to a shift in profit opportunities, a number of businesses with adequate financial resources or lines of credit rush into the new area and abandon existing areas. If the new opportunities turn out to be sufficiently profitable, an investment boom or mania begins.

A key aspect of an investment boom is that it is fed by a rapid and substantial expansion of bank credit, which in turn greatly expands the total money supply. However, as Minsky points out, bank credit is notoriously unstable. An investment boom is also fueled by personal and business funds as well as by bank credit. This, too, expands to finance the speculative boom and thereby adds further to the money supply and expansionary activity. In time, the urge to speculate drives up the price of the sought-after goods or financial assets. The price rise in turn creates new profit opportunities and draws more investors into the market. This self-reinforcing, or cumulative, process causes both profits and investments to rise rapidly. During this "euphoria" stage, to use Minsky's apt word, speculation on price increases becomes yet another important factor driving up the market. More and more investors, lusting after the rewards of rising prices and profits, forsake normal considerations of rational investment behavior and invest in what by its very nature is a highly risky market. This irrational development is the "mania" or "bubble" phase of the boom. As the mania phase accelerates, prices and the velocity of speculative monies increase.

At some point along this path of speculation, a few insiders, believing that the market has reached its peak, begin to convert their inflated assets into money or "quality" investments. As more and more speculators realize that the "game" is about over and begin to sell their assets, the race to get out of risky and overvalued assets quickens and eventually turns into a stampede toward quality and safety. The specific event or market signal that triggers the rout and eventually causes a financial panic may be a bank failure, a corporate bankruptcy, or any number of untoward events. As investors rush out of the market, prices fall, bankruptcies increase, and the speculative "bubble" eventually bursts, causing prices to collapse. Panic follows as investors desperately seek to save what they can. Banks frequently cease lending, and this causes a "credit crunch"; a recession or even a depression may follow. Eventually, the panic ceases through one means or another, the economy recovers, and the market returns to an equilibrium, having paid an enormous cost.

The economics profession, with a few notable exceptions, rejects Minsky's model of financial crises. One reason is that economists believe a general model is impossible, because every financial crisis is either unique or of a particular type for which a more specific model is required; they consider every financial crisis to be a historical accident not amenable to general theorizing. Another criticism is that "things are different today"; these critics argue that although Minsky's model may have been valid in the past, a number of fundamental structural changes in the nature of capitalism (the rise of the corporation, modern banking, and faster communications) have undermined a theory based on credit instability. A further criticism is that Minsky's model of financial crises assumes that such crises are generated by uncertainty, speculation, and instability—and economists assume rationality and brush away such awkward aspects of economic behavior.

Nobel Laureate Milton Friedman, for example, has even proclaimed that, because economic actors are at all times rational, speculation cannot occur in a market economy. In fact, he argues that what most of us call "speculation" is the effort of investors to protect themselves from the irrational actions of governments. For Minsky, on the other hand, irrationality ("euphoria") and financial crises are an inherent feature of modern capitalism. In Kindleberger's formulation, even if one were to assume the rationality of the individual investor, the historical record demonstrates over and over that even markets themselves sometimes behave in irrational ways and that "mob psychology" provides the best explanation of financial manias. Although individuals may be rational, financial speculation is a herd phenomenon in which the seemingly rational action of many individuals leads to irrational outcomes.

Although Kindleberger is reluctant to declare that financial crises are an inherent feature of domestic capitalism, he asserts that they are an inherent feature of international capitalism. He argues that Minsky's model is applicable to the realm of international finance where one finds the essential features of an international financial crisis that were set forth by Minsky. Risky speculation, monetary (credit) expansion, a rise in the price of the sought-after assets, a sudden and unexpected sharp fall in the price of the assets, and a rush into money or quality investments are endemic in the international pursuit of high profits by international investors. The East Asian financial crisis and the subsequent global financial turmoil have closely followed Minsky's model. Speculative investment in emerging markets by highly leveraged "hedge" funds fueled the mania and investment bubble until the collapse of the Thai baht on July 2, 1997, signaled the end of the East Asian miracle. Somewhat over a year later, in mid-August 1998, devaluation of the Russian ruble and other bad news from Russia triggered global financial turmoil.

INTERNATIONAL FINANCE SINCE WORLD WAR II

At the close of World War II, the United States and other governments feared that unrestricted international financial movements would be destabilizing to the international economy, as they had been in the

1930s, and this shared apprehension led to strict controls over capital flows in the early postwar years. The Bretton Woods System was designed to prevent a return to the financial anarchy of the Great Depression. Its founders were concerned that large international capital flows would undermine a system of stable exchange rates and restrict domestic economic policy. Imposition of capital controls did contribute to the stability and smooth functioning of the postwar system of fixed exchange rates. But this situation changed in the 1960s and 1970s as international capital flows grew dramatically; the succeeding "financial revolution" had a significant effect on the international as well as domestic economies.

One can date the beginnings of a truly global financial system from the mid-1970s when Saudia Arabia and other oil exporters, rich from the 1973 oil price rise, invested their immense surplus funds in the Eurodollar market. With the industrial world experiencing stagflation, international banks recycled a substantial amount of Eurodollar capital to less developed countries in Latin America and communist countries in Eastern Europe. Although many economists and public officials were worried by investments in such risky economies, they were assured by Citibank President Walter Wriston that nations "don't go bankrupt." Unfortunately, Wriston was wrong, and this investment boom ended with a financial crisis in the late 1970s and early 1980s from which a number of debtor countries have yet to recover. Subsequently, the deregulation of domestic financial markets, innovations in financial instruments (such as derivatives), and advances in communications led to a significant increase in the level of integration of national financial systems around the world.

The international financial market has become a prominent feature of the global economy. The volume of foreign exchange trading in the late 1990s has been approximately $1.5 trillion per day, an eightfold increase since 1986; by contrast, the global volume of exports (goods and services) for all of 1997 was only $6.6 trillion, or $25 billion per day! In addition, the amount of investment capital seeking higher returns has grown enormously; by the mid-1990s, mutual funds, pension funds, and the like totaled $20 trillion, ten times the 1980 amount. Moreover, the significance of these huge investments is greatly magnified by the fact that foreign investments are increasingly leveraged; that is, investments are made with borrowed funds. Finally, derivatives (repackaged securities and other financial assets) play an important role in international finance. International financial transactions, valued in 1997 at $360 trillion, which is far larger than the worth of the entire global economy, have contributed to financial complexity and, many believe, to international financial instability.

Prior to the East Asian crisis, the postwar international economy experienced a number of financial crises, and three of them were especially important. The first was caused by the debt problems of many less developed countries in the late 1970s and early 1980s. The second was the 1992-1993 collapse of the Exchange Rate Mechanism (ERM) that forced Great Britain to withdraw from the effort to create a common European currency. The third was the 1994-1995 crisis of the Mexican peso. Worried that the crisis would spread from Mexico throughout Latin America, the Clinton Administration used American funds and pressured the IMF to use its funds to end the crisis. The political fallout was severe. Many critics, especially those on the political left, complained that the Administration had used American taxpayers' money without congressional authorization to rescue American bankers from their own greed. Milton Friedman and other conservatives, on the other hand, charged that the Administration had laid the foundations for future crises by encouraging investors and governments to believe that, if they were to get into trouble, the United States and the IMF would bail them out. These attacks made the Clinton Administration wary of involving itself in the East Asian financial crisis.

These earlier crises were concentrated in particular regions, were not threatening to the larger international economy, and were managed relatively easily, at least when compared with the East Asian financial crisis. The East Asian crisis has been vastly different. This end-of-the-century crisis began in the most economically robust region of the world, its consequences have been truly devastating for that region, and the crisis has spilled over into the larger global economy. It is possible to say that the crisis resulted, at least in part, from the globalization and transformed nature of modern finance; that is, from the absolute scale of international financial movements, especially speculative and short-term investment flows, the increased velocity of these movements across national boundaries, and their global scope. This crisis has led many to believe that international financial movements must be made subject to some governance mechanism.

EAST ASIAN FINANCIAL CRISIS

In the summer of 1997, the economies of Pacific Asia suffered a devastating blow from a severe financial shock; subsequently, a much more general economic crisis brought the East Asian "miracle" to an abrupt halt. Economies that only four years earlier had been hailed by the World Bank as exemplars of "pragmatic orthodoxy" and as being "remarkably successful in creating and sustaining macroeconomic stability" experienced the worst economic collapse of any countries since the 1930s and were declared to be victims of their own irresponsible ways! It had been unthinkable that a financial crisis of this magnitude could occur, given modern economic knowledge. In fact no one had predicted the crisis.

In retrospect, however, a crisis of some sort appears to have been inevitable after all the things that could and did go wrong in the months just prior to the crisis. In the lanaguage of social science, the East Asian financial cisis was overdetermined. If one cause had not plunged the East Asian economies into crisis, a half-dozen others might have done so. As these lines are written, both the crisis itself and its consequences are still unfolding. Some countries, especially Korea, appear to be recovering, but in mid-1999 Indonesia and others have not yet begun to recover. Because it may take some years for the full social and political effects of this economic disaster to be recognized and understood, this discussion will deal only with the early stages of the crisis and with useful lessons that may be discerned at such an early point in what will obviously be a long-drawn-out drama.

Regional Causes

Like most historical developments, the precise causes of the East Asian financial crisis are a matter of dispute.[44] Was it, for example, because Japan in April 1997, over strong American protests, raised its sales tax from 3 to 5 percent and thus slowed economic growth and drastically curtailed imports from the region? Or was it because of the 1994 substantial devaluation of China's currency? Or, as many believe, was it the rumor that Japan intended to raise interest rates and thus drain capital from the rest of East Asia? Experts disagree. Yet, three developments

TABLE 5.1

Chronology of the East Asian Financial Crisis and Its Spread

July 1997   Thailand, under strong pressures from international speculators, re-
verses its policy of tying the baht to the dollar and lets it float. This action,
signaling the serious troubles of the Southeast Asian economies, triggers
the crisis. The contagion begins to spread throughout the region. Malaysia's Prime Minister Mahathir Mohamad blames "rogue speculators."

August 1997   The International Monetary Fund (IMF) approves a $17 billion
loan to Thailand. Mahathir calls George Soros a "moron."

October 1997   The Hong Kong stock market (*Hang Seng*) falls 25 percent in four
days and a few days later falls another 5.4 percent, precipitating a large fall
in the American stock market and other stock markets. The IMF offers a
$42 billion rescue plan to Indonesia.

November 1997   The crisis spreads to Brazil, and the South Korean won col-
lapses. In Japan, Yamaichi Securities fails, signaling serious trouble in the
Japanese economy. Clinton calls the crisis "a few glitches in the road."

December 1997   The IMF approves a $58 billion loan, the largest-ever rescue
package, to save the rapidly deteriorating South Korean economy.

January 1998   The IMF and Indonesia sign an agreement on economic reform as
Indonesia sinks into deepening crisis.

April 1998   The Japanese economy displays increasing signs of serious trouble.
Yet another IMF-Indonesian agreement on economic reform. The IMF
comes under increasing attack in the U.S. Congress for its performance in
Asia.

May 1998   The political crisis in Indonesia degenerates further with student riots
and more bad economic news. President Suharto resigns. Russia's troubles
become increasingly apparent.

August 1998   The devaluation of the ruble and other negative economic news
from Russia causes market panic around the globe, including a sharp drop
in the American stock market. The Brazilian real comes under attack.

October 1998   The IMF, with strong American backing, gives Brazil a huge assistance package of over $40 billion accompanied by the requirement that
Brazil carry out a significant overhaul of its economy.

January 1999   The failure of Brazil to take significant steps to reform its economy
leads to a 35 percent devaluation of the Brazilian real and to investor flight.

appear to have been important in causing the crisis. First, as early as 1996, the emerging economies of Southeast Asia began to experience a significant slowdown in their merchandise exports, and this raised serious doubts among investors about the continuing economic success of the region. The United States had engineered a significant appreciation of the dollar in 1995, and currencies in the region, pegged to the dollar, also appreciated and thus decreased the region's international competitiveness. Increased Chinese competition with Southeast Asia for foreign direct investment and for export markets contributed to growing concerns over the economic prospects of the region. In addition, there was a perception that comparative advantage was shifting away from Southeast Asia to China because of the latter's relatively lower wages. Third, and more speculatively, overcapacity and declining demand in a number of economic sectors and intensifying competition for export markets in memory chips, steel, and automobiles raised long-term worries about the export-led growth strategy of the economies in the region. These regionwide developments set the stage for the domestic factors to trigger the crisis.

Domestic Causes

The domestic causes of the crisis originated in the investor boom of the 1990s, which was driven by the euphoria of foreign investors who poured billions of dollars into the Southeast Asian emerging markets and also by local investors who made risky investments in real estate, equities, and other assets of poor quality. The banking and financial systems of these economies were poorly supervised and subject to "cronyism" and other questionable practices. Overextension of credit, especially in dubious activities, made these economies highly vulnerable to the shift in credit availability that took place beginning in the summer of 1997. Declining exports and efforts to defend overvalued currencies through high interest rates caused inflated property values to fall and led to a large number of nonperforming bank loans. Moreover, in Thailand and Indonesia, vulnerability was increased because a large portion of the debt was in instruments with short-term maturities and/ or denominated in foreign currencies. The liquidity and overvalued currency problems of the Southeast Asian economies invited speculative attacks on local currencies, increased the consequences of currency appreciation, and greatly limited the ability of governments to manage the crisis. Against this general background, a crisis was precipitated in Thailand and spread quickly throughout the region.

Precipitation and Spread

Prior to the financial crisis, Thailand, like other economies in Southeast Asia, had benefited greatly by borrowing dollars and other foreign currencies and converting them into baht to speculate in local real estate, securities, and other baht-denominated assets. A basic assumption underlying this risky investment behavior was that, because the baht was pegged to the dollar, it would not lose its value. Anticipating strong economic growth and believing that their investments were secure, foreign banks, hedge funds, and other financial institutions were only too delighted to flood Thailand and other emerging markets with money. However, as early as the final weeks of 1996, foreign investors had become concerned over Thailand's ability to repay its huge accumulating foreign debt and had begun to move their money out of the country. In February 1997, both Thai and foreign investors, worried that selling baht-denominated assets would soon undermine the baht's value, rushed to convert their holdings into dollars. As early as the spring of 1997, Japan urged joint action to prevent a crisis, but the Clinton Administration, fearing a negative domestic reaction, failed to act.

To counter the dangers and maintain the value of the baht, the Thai central bank used its dollar reserves to purchase baht and also raised interest rates. The increase in the interest rate reduced demand for real estate and other assets, and this caused a significant drop in prices. All these developments compounded the crisis. More investors were alerted to additional serious problems in the Thai economy, including a trade deficit and a weak banking system burdened by huge debts. As more investors rushed to abandon the baht for dollars, the Thai central bank ran out of dollar reserves. Faced with a serious liquidity crisis, Thailand was no longer able to hold back the tide and, on July 2, 1997, Thailand's central bank stopped defending the baht's peg to the dollar. The baht lost 16 percent of its value, and this plunged Thailand into a serious recession.

The substantial devaluation of the baht and Thailand's economic troubles triggered a panic in neighboring economies with similar problems. Like Thailand, the economies of Malaysia, Indonesia, and others were afflicted by heavy foreign borrowing and banking systems weakened by large numbers of unpaid or nonperforming loans. As in Thailand, investors throughout the region rushed to convert local currencies into dollars. In late August the IMF offered an emergency loan to Thailand (somewhat over $17 billion) to shore up the baht in exchange for promises that Thailand would raise interest rates, restrain government spending, and close troubled banks. The Clinton Administration was very slow in recognizing the serious nature of the unfolding crisis; indeed, as late as the November 1997 Asia-Pacific Economic Cooperation (APEC) Summit in Vancouver, the President dismissed the crisis as "a few small glitches in the road." This abandonment by the Clinton Administration caused the Thai government, a close friend of the United States, to feel deep resentment.

Political leaders and others in the region also originally dismissed the seriousness of the developing crisis. One local commentator observed that the financial and currency troubles were a mere "hiccup" and did not merit concern, while an economist declared that "we're at the bottom" and that "an era of greater stability" was dawning. A decade of hubris, economic success, and celebration of Asia's unique and superior values had built a powerful psychological barrier to recognition that the East Asian miracle was over. When reality finally did break through and humiliation replaced hubris, a search for foreign scapegoats, led by Malaysian Prime Minister Mahathir Mohamad, began. At various moments, he proclaimed that Southeast Asia was the victim of an international "Jewish" conspiracy, of a "new form of Western imperialism," and/or of the villainy of George Soros and other financial speculators. As the crisis spread throughout Southeast and East Asia, the search for scapegoats turned into alarm. And as one domino after another fell throughout the region, realization of the seriousness of the crisis took hold.

One of the first dominoes to fall, and fall very hard, was Indonesia when its own speculative "bubble" burst early in the fall of 1997 plunging the country into a severe recession. The rupiah collapsed and fell approximately 80 percent against the dollar. The stock market also fell, and the country, unable to repay its huge debt, became insolvent. Despite the devastating crisis, President Suharto strongly resisted the reforms that the IMF required in exchange for financial assistance. As he understood only too well, such reforms would seriously harm the interests of his family and political allies. Sparring ensued between the IMF and the United States on one side and the Suharto government on the other, as the IMF and the United States sought to get the Suharto government to reform its economy and eliminate its "crony capitalism." By late October, the IMF and the United States offered Indonesia a $42 billion loan in exchange for promised reforms. After months of dithering, the Suharto government, at the insistence of the IMF, significantly reduced food and other subsidies and raised gasoline prices in May of 1998. Following serious rioting in which many Christians and ethnic Chinese were killed and intervention by the military, President Suharto resigned later in the month and was replaced by a government committed, at least verbally, to economic and political reform.

Hong Kong had borrowed heavily to finance its rapid rate of economic growth and was also threatened by investor panic. The city's currency board, at a high cost to the economy, did successfully defend the Hong Kong dollar against frightened investors and speculators. However, this effort was very costly to Hong Kong's huge foreign reserves. The Hong Kong central bank, like Thailand's, raised interest rates and produced disastrous results. The drop of stock prices on the Hong Kong stock market (*Hang Seng*) by 24 percent in four days sent shock waves around the world. Spreading recognition of the very serious nature of East Asia's troubles threw panic into investors everywhere. On October 27, 1997, the tenth anniversary of the 1987 crash of the American stock market, the Dow Jones plunged 554 points (somewhat more than 7 percent), the largest one-day loss ever. Similar declines took place in Western Europe, Brazil, and elsewhere. Investors were panicking and abandoning the emerging markets.

In November, attention shifted to South Korea, which was the second major economic and industrial power in the region and ranked as the eleventh-largest economy in the Organization for Economic Cooperation and Development (OECD), the club of industrialized countries and their closest friends. While renowned for its success as an exporter, Korea had also become a major importer of products from the

147

United States, Japan, and other countries. Serious trouble in Korea could mean even more serious trouble for the region and especially for Japan. Even before the currency crisis had begun, the Korean economy had shown signs of trouble. Korea had violated one of the cardinal principles of international finance: that a country should never rely excessively on short-term loans denominated in foreign currencies, because such loans put the economy in a highly vulnerable position if interest rates should rise or the currency, depreciate.

Several of Korea's largest conglomerates (*chaebol*) had gotten into serious trouble due to heavy overborrowing and had entered bankruptcy even before the crisis struck. Korean banks had raised foreign capital and passed it on to the conglomerates in Korean won. The subsequent devaluation of the won created a severe liquidity crisis as the banks were no longer able to service their short-term debts of approximately $100 billion denominated in the dollar, yen, and other foreign currencies. In response to these problems, investors began to flee the won for the dollar and other strong currencies. On November 1, 1997, the Korean central bank had vowed that it would "never, never, never" let the won fall below 1000 won to the dollar; despite this brave proclamation, on November 17, the central bank stopped defending the won. The subsequent collapse of the won, the ensuing failure of banks and of financial institutions, the precipitous drop of the stock market, the large numbers of corporate bankruptcies, and the near default of the government itself revealed that Korea was in desperate straits. As a consequence, the humiliated Korean government, like other East Asian economies before it, appealed to the IMF for financial assistance; in time, help was forthcoming, although at a heavy economic and political price.

The initial IMF/U.S. response to Korea's battered economy was aloofness. As Korea's troubles, like those of others, had arisen in the private sector, the Clinton Administration did not want to be viewed as rescuing foreign bankers from the consequences of their own greed and foolishness. However, the possibility or even probability that the Korean economy would collapse finally jolted the United States into action. While considerations of maintaining security on the divided Korean peninsula undoubtedly played an important role in this reversal of American policy, the most important consideration was the fear that

Korea's default on its huge international debts would trigger a much larger international crisis. Collapse of the Korean economy could also have brought down the weakened Japanese economy, and that in turn could have produced disastrous consequences for the United States and the rest of the world.

In response to these dangers in Korea, the United States in mid-December 1997 engineered the largest-ever IMF rescue package ($58 billion) and pressured the newly elected government of Kim Dae Jung to accept it. More IMF loans and other forms of international assistance, such as easing the servicing and repayment of loans to foreign bankers, followed. Although the rescue effort provided assistance to many American and other foreign investors, many Koreans were seriously hurt, and the country was required to make a number of costly and deeply resented concessions, such as opening its banking system to foreign (mainly American) investors and also closing many banks and businesses that employed tens of thousands of workers. As such actions directly violated an implicit national social contract that the government would not let any major enterprise fail, these developments had highly corrosive political consequences for Korean society and attitudes toward the United States. In addition, IMF demands for economic austerity and structural reforms were regarded by organized labor as a threat to its economic well-being and were deeply resented by Korean nationalists.

As the financial crisis spread northward along the East Asian coast, the greatest fear was that the domino or contagion effects of the crisis would eventually engulf Japan itself. The Japanese economy was already in recession and heavily burdened by the government's failure to deal effectively with the serious financial consequences of the collapse in the early 1990s of its "bubble" economy. The Japanese banking and financial system was in shambles and especially vulnerable because of the large number of nonperforming loans held by Japanese banks. The spreading financial crisis posed a serious threat, because Japanese banks had made substantial loans to the economies of Southeast Asia; mounting troubles in South Korea were especially worrisome because of its extremely close links to Japan. In addition, the substantial decline in the growth rates of the economies in the region would inevitably decrease the large Japanese export surplus with the region and would slow growth in Japan's depressed economy even further. After the 1985 appreciation of the yen (*endaka*), Asia had replaced the United States as Japan's principal export market. Economies in the region were already threatened by a vicious cycle of slowing growth, failing banks, and contracting credit that could lead to a profound slump. If Japan also were overwhelmed by the crisis, the results for the region and for the whole world could easily have been disastrous.

CONFLICTING EXPLANATIONS

The East Asian economic crisis has given rise to an acrimonious debate over its causes among economists, public officials, and other commentators. The explanations of the crisis are important because the different interpretations have significant implications for the economies and for the longer-term issue of how the international community should deal with the threat of financial crises. One explanation argues that the crisis was mainly a financial crisis, and that that type of crisis could occur in the most sound economy. Another explanation, popular in the IMF and the U.S. Treasury, attributes the crisis to the irresponsible economic and political practices of the economies themselves. The more wide-ranging explanation places much of the blame for Asia's troubles on the U.S. Treasury and on American financial interests.

A Typical Financial Crisis

This interpretation of the East Asian crisis, most closely identified with Harvard economist Jeffrey Sachs, is that the crisis was a modernized and high-tech version of a traditional financial crisis whose negative consequences were greatly exacerbated by IMF policy blunders. In this interpretation, both domestic and international investors had made highly speculative investments, in such things as real estate and equities, in the then-booming economies, and subsequently, for various reasons, had panicked and rushed to salvage their threatened investments. Eventually, the panic became a self-reinforcing financial crisis.

Like Minsky's theory of financial crises, this explanation emphasizes the local banking system. The banks in these economies were borrowing short-term funds (denominated in dollars and/or perhaps yen) from external sources and loaning them long-term to local investors. The mismatch between short-term dollar/yen liabilities and insufficient long-term assets made these financial systems, which had inadequate liquidity of their own, highly vulnerable. When the crisis commenced and investors began to withdraw their money, the economies had to choose between undesirable alternatives; they had to either raise interest rates to defend local currencies and thereby bankrupt many local firms or allow the currency to plunge and increase the debt burden of local firms. Both options were tried at one time or another, and each caused immense damage to local firms and the overall economy.

The financial crisis explanation assumes that the East Asian economies were fundamentally sound. As Minsky pointed out, a financial crisis does not necessarily mean that any major aspects of the financially stricken economy are in any sense improper. The United States has suffered a number of financial crises such as the Savings and Loan fiasco of the late 1980s. Other economists still assert, to the contrary, that the East Asian economies were indeed quite unsound. For example, some make the point that if these economies had been in good shape, and there had been only a financial crisis, the crisis would not have been so severe, and the afflicted economy would have recovered much earlier than has proved to be the case. Such a position is taken by proponents of the "crony capitalism" explanation.

The Vice of "Crony Capitalism"

The East Asian financial crisis has been seized by many American economists, political conservatives, and public officials to discredit the state-led East Asian model of economic development and to support their belief in the superiority of such Western economic principles as free markets and minimal state intervention in the economy. A large chorus of American commentators who have deeply resented Asian leaders' claims that "Asian values" had proved superior to decadent Western values have taken comfort in the crisis. Many in the United States have asserted that the serious setback to East Asia and the simultaneous success of the American economy proves, once and for all, the failure of the Japanese "developmental state" model and the superiority of the Western economic system based on free markets, individual initiative, and minimal state interference. At the heart of this interpretation is the belief that the developmental state (labeled "crony capitalism" by its detractors) was deeply flawed and the basic cause of the crisis.

According to this interpretation, the East Asian developmental state contained the "seeds of its own destruction." Those characteristics of the Asian model that are credited with the extraordinary success of these economies in promoting rapid industrialization were the very ones that led to the financial crisis and subsequent economic disaster. Proponents of the superiority of the developmental state had argued that the intimacy among government, banks, and industry was a strength of the East Asian economies because it facilitated the allocation of scarce financial resources to the most-valued industrial sectors. Critics, on the other hand, charged that these close ties were a corrupt feature of Asia's "crony capitalism." The financial crisis, they proclaimed, wreaked such havoc on these economies and resulted in a serious economic/political crisis precisely because these economies had made themselves very vulnerable.

The underlying cause of the severity of the financial crisis and of the ensuing economic/political crisis, this position alleges, was the problem of "moral hazard" due to the widespread, improper, and frequently corrupt lending practices of local banks and the poorly regulated financial systems of these economies.[45] A large number of the loans had gone to individuals and institutions with important political connections, such as Thai finance companies, the Suharto family and its allies, and Korean *chaebol*-affiliated banks that investors perceived as backed by government guarantees in the event of financial troubles. This situation created an incentive for excessive risk taking in speculative real estate ventures and highly leveraged, ambitious corporate expansion; risk increased considerably in the 1990s as foreign capital flowed into these economies. The inflated financial markets of these economies became a huge bubble that finally had to burst. The bubble collapsed as creditors—realizing that governments would have to spend billions of dollars to bail out troubled institutions—abandoned these economies and compounded their financial problems. The resulting bankrupt institutions, declining currency values, and collapsing asset prices plunged these economies into a severe depression. According to this position, the East Asian financial/economic crisis was due to inherent features of the state-led economies.

Victims of the "Wall Street–Treasury Complex"

This position, identified mainly with Columbia University economist Jagdish Bhagwati and Asian scholar Robert Wade, argues that the policies of the U.S. Treasury, designed to promote American financial interests worldwide, bear the primary responsibility for the East Asian financial crisis.[46] This position is shared by many East Asian leaders, who believe that they were the innocent victims of economic globalization and greedy capitalist speculators. Some prominent economists maintain that flooding the emerging markets with short-term loans was indeed the primary cause for the crisis. This irresponsible investor behavior was, in turn, due to the perverse and herdlike behavior of international banks, financial institutions, and hedge funds.

Believing that investor euphoria had led to overinvestment in these economies, Wade explained that institutional money managers around the world had known that they would be punished if they failed to get involved in potentially lucrative business opportunities (in this case, the fast-growing emerging markets of East Asia) in which other investors were getting deeply involved. They also knew that if the investment turned sour and they, along with other investors, had to get out, they would not be blamed for their losses because everyone else would also be losing. Moreover, in their enthusiasm, investors ignored such obvious signs of impending trouble as the immense increase in short-term liabilities assumed by East Asian borrowers. In such a fashion, the huge investments in the region, which were well above rational profit expectations, were driven by the irrational euphoria of international investors. Disagreeing with this interpretation, Treasury Secretary Rubin has absolved international investors from any responsibility for the crisis.

The financial crisis was actually precipitated, according to Bhagwati and Wade, by the premature liberalization of financial markets and capital accounts (freedom of capital movements) that was forced upon these economies by what Bhagwati calls the "Wall Street–Treasury Complex." According to this thesis, the U.S. Treasury, strongly influenced by American financial interests (banks, hedge funds, etc.), used its immense political clout to force these economies to open for American investment, including acquisition by American firms of local banks and financial institutions. A shared free-market ideology that has prevailed since Reagan and the demise of communism, powerful economic interests, and close personal ties (cronyism), according to Bhagwati, played a role in this American-directed effort to open the economies to international finance. Many note, for example, that Treasury Secretary Rubin is a former Wall Street currency trader. The IMF was not only subject to strong American influences, but its own institutional ambitions would be well served by becoming the manager of the international financial system and hence the key player in the global economy.

The opening of local financial markets to international investors did indeed prove to be a disaster as, in effect, these countries became victims of speculative international capital flows. Whereas, in 1996, total private capital flows to the Southeast Asian economies reached $93 billion, in 1997 the flow reversed direction and $12 billion flowed out. Few countries could survive such a situation.

As explained by Robert Wade, the extraordinary economic success of these states had been due in large part to close ties among government, local banks, and industry. These intimate relationships, which he calls "alliance capitalism," and critics label "crony capitalism" facilitated channeling bank capital into promising industries and thus promoted rapid industrialization. At the same time, national governments severely restricted both foreign direct and portfolio investments by international firms and thus insulated their economies from disruptive external influences. Although this system resulted in huge liability/asset ratios in the larger enterprises such as the South Korean *chaebol*, the system worked very effectively and was stable as long as those governments controlled domestic financial markets and the capital account, a situation that changed dramatically in the 1990s.

Throughout the 1990s, largely in response to intensifying pressures from the United States and the IMF as well as from local business interests, East Asian countries other than Japan opened their markets to foreign banks and firms. The United States, for example, offered to support Korean membership in the OECD if Korea agreed to open its economy to American banks and investors. The process of financial liberalization, according to this explanation, significantly reduced government control over the economy. Unfortunately, the international community, which had pushed for openness, failed to push for regulation of the financial sector, and the governments were too inexperienced to appreciate the dangers of an unregulated financial market. Governments in the region maintained relatively fixed exchange rates; however, freedom of capital movements and fixed rates proved to be a dangerous combination. Fixed rates encouraged capital inflow because investors believed that the governments would not devalue the currency and jeopardize its value. However, this situation did cause exchange rates to rise and, as early as 1995 and 1996, resulted in decreased national competitiveness, which then led to a decline in export growth and overall deterioration of the current account balance. As Wade argues, unusually rapid financial liberalization in Asia in combination with unsupervised banks and fixed exchange rates undermined the existing system of bank-industry cooperation and exposed weak debt structures to powerful shocks. Wade goes on to note that China and India did not open their financial markets, and they thereby escaped damage.

According to this interpretation, the pullout and flight of investors into liquidity and investments of better quality, like the earlier huge inflows, was an irrational response and an overreaction to a "gestalt shift." At one moment international investors saw the East Asian "miracle," and at the next moment they saw "crony capitalism." This dramatic shift in perception precipitated the financial crisis. Capital flight destroyed local fortunes and plunged these economies into the serious economic troubles that threatened to rip apart their social fabric. Whereas the "crony capitalism" and financial crisis explanations were based on assumptions of investor rationality, this last explanation argues that, even though individual investors may have behaved rationally, the individual behaviors resulted in a collective irrationality. Shades of Minsky!

IMF and Its Critics

Responsibility for breaking the vicious cycle in which the East Asian economies found themselves was assumed primarily by the International Monetary Fund and strongly backed by the United States. The primary task of the IMF was to stem capital flight and restore investor confidence in the financial systems of the region. This was an enormous challenge because of the scale of the problem and the extremely high costs of bailing out the banks and other financial institutions throughout the region. By one estimate, the nonperforming loans of Southeast Asian banks reached about $73 billion in 1997, a figure that then represented over 13 percent of Southeast Asia's GNP. The IMF's rescue effort was strongly backed and influenced by the United States. Rubin and Summers, who took great pride in saving Mexico in 1995, prescribed the same harsh medicine for the troubled economies in the region: spending cuts, high interest rates, and appreciated currencies. The IMF sought to restore confidence in the banking systems by leading the effort to assemble huge financial rescue packages for individual countries.

The IMF also took on the difficult and long-term mission of encouraging or, more accurately, pressuring recipients of IMF assistance to reform their economies and to eliminate the underlying causes of the crisis. To receive financial assistance, recipient governments were required to implement a number of policy changes and structural reforms. As unsound banking practices were considered by the IMF and the U.S. Treasury to have been the principal cause of the crisis, policy and structural changes were mandated to solve the problems of the banking and financial sector. These reforms included consolidation of many small banks into fewer and stronger banks, improvement of accounting and disclosure practices to increase transparency and responsibility, cutting links between bankers and local politicians, and opening local banking systems to buyouts and competition from outsiders. Moreover, more drastic and controversial reforms were required throughout the overall economy. Draconian reforms that included elimination of food subsidies, reduction of government expenditures, and maintenance of strong currencies to attract international investors resulted in a serious clash between the IMF and its U.S. supporter and the local governments.

Implementation of IMF-mandated reforms in Korea, Indonesia, and elsewhere has been very costly in economic, political, and social terms. The economic cost of repairing the banking system alone has been tens of billions of dollars. Powerful economic and political interests have been, or will be, harmed by reformed financial systems that significantly reduce cronyism and favoritism. Closing or consolidation of in-solvent banks and enterprises has resulted in huge layoffs and intense labor unrest and social conflict. A region that had enjoyed a rapid rate of economic growth and a greatly improved standard of living in the 1990s has had to accept a prolonged and indeterminant period of eco-nomic austerity; social strife has inevitably followed.

Moreover, the reforms demanded by the IMF and the United States, designed to transform these economies into the American economic model of markets freed from government intervention, collided with social values and with important aspects of the development strategies of these economies. Many leaders and opinion makers in the region believe that the primary motive of the United States was to undermine the successful economic strategies of these societies and open them to American investment. For example, the U.S. demand that these coun-tries open their economies to FDI ran directly counter to a development strategy that had kept the financial and other sectors of these economies closed to foreign investors. Many in the area place much of the blame for the dire situation in which these countries found themselves on the IMF and the United States. The deep and pervasive resentments against the American-backed IMF demands for financial reform will surely mean serious long-term political problems between the IMF and the United States and governments throughout the region.

The central role of the IMF in the rescue of East Asia has led to intense criticisms of the institution not only in the region but also in the United States, Western Europe, and Japan. Because these criticisms have been diffuse and wide-ranging, it is difficult to summarize them. The following criticisms of the IMF and of the Clinton Administration (or, more precisely, of Treasury Secretary Rubin and Deputy Secretary Summers) are particularly noteworthy:

1. Economists like Jeffrey Sachs believe that the crisis was primarily financial rather than due to faulty fundamentals, and experts on the region like Robert Wade, who blames the "Wall Street–Treasury com-plex," argue that the IMF diagnosed the nature of the crisis incorrectly and prescribed the wrong medicine. The IMF, they charge, failed to take into account such specific features of the crisis as the fact that these economies were suffering from a collapse of demand rather than from

the excessive demand and runaway inflation that had typified the 1994–1995 Mexican/Latin American crisis.

These critics assert that the misdiagnosis led the IMF to apply its standard rescue formula of setting high interest rates to reassure investors along with an appreciated currency to ease repayment of debt. These measures proved totally unsuited to the nature of the crisis. In contrast to earlier economic crises of developing economies, these economies had been pursuing responsible macroeconomic policies (e.g., no high budget deficits and only low rates of inflation), and they therefore were not in need of the IMF's harsh austerity and structural adjustment policies; it was reckless, these critics believe, for the IMF to prescribe a dose of austerity and to expect restructuring to take place during a severe economic crisis. Moreover, as the crisis was in the private banking sector, the IMF, as the lender of last resort, should have pumped substantial funds into the banking system to stop the panic and should not have imposed such measures as demands for high interest rates, closing of troubled banks, and reduction of government spending. These critics allege that the IMF's punishing demands on recipient countries were totally inappropriate and greatly aggravated the crisis. Finally, many critics believe that if the IMF, backed by the United States, had intervened immediately in Thailand's liquidity crisis in July 1997, spread of the crisis throughout East Asia could have been prevented. Fund officials have reluctantly acknowledged the validity of many of these criticisms.

2. Many Americans on both the political left and political right who have long held profound suspicions of the IMF have disputed the Clinton Administration's use of American taxpayers' money, especially without proper congressional authorization, to rescue private firms and banks from their own folly and corruption. Critics on the left ask why the United States should provide support for countries pursuing unfair trade policies that are putting Americans out of work. Moreover, the IMF, critics charge, is too elitist, secretive, and, in the opinion of conservatives, has an antimarket mentality. Former Secretary of State George Schultz, Milton Friedman, and other prominent Americans argue that the IMF's rescue effort was wrong because it encouraged moral hazard and risky investments. Such critics argue that the IMF

should be abolished outright or (as many members of Congress believe) should at least be drastically reformed and made subject to greater congressional oversight. Thus, critics on the left and on the right reject completely the judgments of both the Treasury and Federal Reserve Chairman Alan Greenspan that the rescue was necessary to prevent a global economic crisis and that it was in America's economic interest.

3. Many non-American observers have taken note of the fact that the IMF's program of structural adjustment included specific items that the United States had long demanded of Asian governments, and that the latter had long rejected. For example, recipients of IMF assistance were required to open their banking systems to foreign investors, most of whom were Americans and who were then able to buy local banks at cheap prices. The United States, these critics have charged, took advantage of the crisis to force open the economies in the region and to make them susceptible to domination by American financial interests.

4. For a number of critics, the policies and reforms demanded of governments seeking assistance demonstrate the insensitivity and, even worse, the arrogance of IMF and American officials and economists dealing with the crisis. These officials, according to critics, made little effort to understand local social and political conditions when they prescribed their economic medicine. For example, forcing Indonesia to eliminate food subsidies failed to take into account the importance of these subsidies in the lives of tens of millions of ordinary people and resulted in terrible hardships; and some even believe that the resulting anger was responsible for the killing of many Indonesians. Although these critics note that the IMF subsequently gave greater attention to the social and political consequences of its rescue packages and eased the demands it placed on recipients, the damage had already been done. As a result of these failures in political judgment, both the IMF and the United States made themselves targets of a political backlash in the region.

In response to these harsh criticisms, American officials and some economists have defended the IMF's intervention and actions in the crisis. American officials considered IMF intervention necessary because of the economic threat to Japan and the security threat to South

Korea from North Korea. A collapse of the Japanese economy, they feared, could have triggered a major global economic crisis, and South Korea's troubles could have lead to North Korean adventurism. These officials believe that the IMF and American assessment of the fundamental flaws in these economies was correct, and that any solution to the crisis would require strong remedial actions. High interest rates and currencies were required to restore investor confidence and buy time in which to carry out longer-term reforms. The argument that the IMF could have acted as lender of last resort is said to be unrealistic; such a task would have required financial resources well beyond those available to the IMF. Moreover, the IMF did not and does not have the amount of political support required for such an extensive role.

Lessons of the Crisis

The subject of international finance remains a matter of intense controversy among economists, public officials, and national governments. Whereas there is consensus among economists on the virtues of trade liberalization, no comparable agreement exists with respect to capital flows and whether or not they should be regulated. It is worth noting, for example, that six of America's most distinguished economists—Jagdish Bhagwati, Stanley Fischer, Milton Friedman, Paul Krugman, Jeffrey Sachs, and Joseph Stiglitz—have disagreed with one another vehemently, and not always in a friendly spirit, over the East Asian financial crisis and the policies that should be pursued to prevent future crises. Despite these serious disagreements, several conclusions may be drawn from the foregoing analyses of the East Asian crisis.

The East Asian economic crisis has made credible to many people the charge that economic globalization has significantly increased international economic instability and has been harmful to domestic societies. It is certainly undeniable that the economic plight of East Asia attests to the fact that international financial markets can wreak havoc on domestic economies. However, imprudent domestic economic policies were as important as global economic forces in making these economies highly vulnerable to sudden shifts in financial flows. Many of the allegedly negative effects of economic globalization are actually due either to poor economic management (the 1992 British crisis, the 1994–1995 crisis of the Mexican peso, and the 1997 East/Southeast Asian financial crisis) or to developments that have nothing whatsoever to do with economic globalization. Moreover, the victims in these situations have generally been small states. The United States, for example, has run a trade/payments deficit for approximately three decades without unleashing any dire consequences! While large states with large markets and resources may be able to defy economic forces for a long time, such a privilege is rarely accorded to small states, especially small states pursuing reckless policies.

For these reasons, it is quite erroneous to place the blame for the crisis solely on the forces of economic globalization and wicked Western speculators, as East Asian leaders and peoples do. Although international speculators and premature liberalization certainly played an important role in the crisis, every one of the afflicted economies had serious deficiencies and was highly vulnerable to a sudden shift in economic fortunes. These flaws greatly exacerbated the seriousness of what otherwise might have been a severe but limited financial crisis. Yet we should not overlook the fact that these economies did suffer from over-investment by international financial interests and from the abrupt withdrawal of these funds. This experience suggests that something is seriously amiss in the international financial system. Attention should be given to whether or not regulations should be established to govern international finance.

The fact that there is no mechanism to govern international finance is surely one of the most extraordinary features of the world economy at the opening of the twenty-first century. Although the world economy experienced three major financial crises in the 1990s—the 1992–1993 crisis of the ERM, the 1994–1995 Mexican/Latin American financial crisis, and the East Asian financial crisis beginning in 1997—efforts to create effective regulations governing international capital flows and financial matters have progressed very little, if at all. A number of scholars, including Charles Kindleberger, Susan Strange, and James Tobin have noted that the international financial system is the weakest link in the chain of the international economy and that it should be governed more effectively. Financial markets, these scholars have argued, cannot police themselves; they are too subject to irrational manias and crises.

Although it is true that financial markets will eventually return to an equilibrium, financial crises impose an unacceptably heavy cost on innocent bystanders and the larger world economy. For this reason, scholars such as Kindleberger, Strange, and Tobin advocate establishment of international regulations or a formal regime to govern financial markets. For example, Tobin and others have proposed an international tax to discourage financial speculation, especially in short-term investments. Others, such as George Soros, go further and argue that creation of an international central bank and true lender of last resort should be at the heart of a mechanism to govern international finance; that is, an international authority should be created to function as central banks do domestically. Then, when a government finds itself in trouble, the international bank would step in to rescue it. It is not necessary to say that the prospects of establishing such an international central bank are quite remote, at least under prevailing political conditions!

Conclusion

Even as the East Asian financial crisis unfolded, governments ignored Minsky's and Kindleberger's arguments that international financial crises would remain unavoidable, at least until and unless international capital movements were regulated. After all, Washington believed that errant economies, and not international finance itself, had been totally responsible. However, the indifferent attitude toward the dangers of international capital movements changed abruptly in late summer 1998. In August, the Russian devaluation of the ruble and other serious financial troubles triggered a sharp decline in the American and other stock markets. Capital flight and the threat of currency collapse engulfed Brazil and other countries. The world was plunged into the worst economic crisis since the Great Depression. With America's own economic interests at stake, the Clinton Administration was galvanized to create a "new international financial architecture."

CHAPTER SIX

Age of the Multinational

MULTINATIONAL corporations have an overwhelming presence in the global economy. Most American economists, public officials, and ordinary citizens appear to approve of the important role of such firms. However, many Americans of all political persuasions believe that these giant firms pose a serious threat to the social and economic well-being of American workers, small businesses, and local communities. Some allege that "runaway" plants are putting Americans out of work, lowering wages, and destroying previously healthy communities. The multinational corporations (MNCs) themselves attempt to convince Americans and citizens of other home countries that MNCs actually increase exports, jobs, and wages. Recipients of foreign direct investment have a very ambiguous attitude toward the activities of MNCs. On the one hand, they realize that foreign direct investment (FDI) brings capital and valuable technology into the country. On the other hand, they fear becoming dominated and exploited by these powerful firms. No one denies that MNCs have become an essential feature of the global economy, and all acknowledge that efforts to put this genie "back into the bottle" will not succeed. Therefore, international regulations are needed to ensure that both firms and governments behave in ways beneficial to the global economy.

ERA OF THE MULTINATIONAL FIRM

Multinational corporations are internationalizing both services and production. Opinions differ greatly about the significance of this development for domestic and international economic and political affairs. Some observers believe that MNCs, having broken free from the narrow confines of national economies, have become truly "global corporations" and are positive forces for the economic development and prosperity of all societies. Some even argue that the establishment of the MNC represents the triumph of economics over politics and is a major step toward rational management of the global economy. Others, however, believe that these giant firms, in combination with international finance, epitomize global capitalism at its worst, and that they have become laws unto themselves, exploiting the whole world to enhance the corporate "bottom line." A third view is that an MNC is really not a global corporation at all but simply a firm of a particular nationality that has organized its production, distribution, and other activities across national borders. Proponents of this view argue that an MNC's behavior is determined primarily by the economic policies, economic structures, and political interests of their home society. Although MNCs as a group are neither good nor bad, international rules are required to govern the relationships of MNCs and national governments. Although there is some truth in each of these positions, I believe this chapter will demonstrate that the latter view is more nearly accurate than are the others.

There are several rather technical definitions of a multinational firm, but I refer simply to a firm of a particular nationality with partially or wholly owned subsidiaries within two or more national economies. Such firms expand overseas primarily through foreign direct investment (FDI). The purpose of FDI by firms (as distinguished from portfolio investment in bonds and equities) is to achieve partial or complete control over marketing, production, or other activities in another economy; investment may be in services, manufacturing, or commodity production. FDI may entail either purchase of existing economic activities or the building of new facilities (the latter being called "greenfield" investment). Overseas expansion is frequently accompanied by intercorporate alliances with firms of another nationality. FDI is used as part of a corporation's overall strategy to establish a permanent position in another economy.

MNCs have greatly accelerated the integration of the global economy. The 1950s and 1960s were characterized by a huge expansion in international trade, accompanying the revival of economic growth and lowering of import barriers. At that time, international competitiveness was measured by the penetration of imports into national economies and by the international market shares achieved by individual countries. Next, during the late 1960s and into the 1970s, FDI by multinational corporations increased dramatically. During this phase, dominated by the overseas expansion of American firms, investment in foreign production facilities became an increasingly important form of industrial expansion. American corporations built generally autonomous replicas of themselves overseas (horizontal investment), and international competitiveness was measured by the proportion of global sales attributable to production abroad.

The true internationalization phase beginning in the mid-1980s was characterized by a significant shift from an American-dominated era of FDI to a more pluralistic and far more complex system of international corporate activities; many nations greatly increased their foreign investments, and the United States became the world's foremost host economy as well as home economy. At the same time that cross-national investments significantly increased integration of national economies, the nature of investment itself also changed. Rather than the earlier predominance of investment in raw materials and, subsequently, of investment in manufacturing, investment in services around the globe grew largely because of the information revolution and increasing linkages between services and manufacturing. MNCs, technological advances, and economic liberalization (deregulation and privatization) have transformed the world of international business.

During the internationalization of services and production in the 1980s and 1990s, corporations from every advanced industrial country and some from a number of developing countries expanded into other countries. This change from an American-dominated to a pluralistic system of FDI was accompanied by an important shift in corporate strategies. In the early postwar period, American MNCs had generally pursued a horizontal investment strategy in which they had established relatively self-sufficient subsidiaries in such overseas markets as Western Europe. This type of foreign investment tends to reduce trade in that the investing firm usually obtains component parts from local suppliers rather than from its home economy. As years passed, however, multinational corporations of all nationalities moved from horizontal investment to a strategy of "vertical" investment and extensive global "outsourcing" in which production processes around the world were integrated and rationalized. International outsourcing means that components produced in one location are assembled in other economies

165

and eventually exported throughout the world economy, including into the firm's home economy. The loci of production, assembly, and marketing of the firm's products are determined by its global corporate strategy. These corporate strategies, in turn, are highly affected by the characteristics of the host economy, existing trade barriers, and the desire to minimize taxation. Corporate strategies have had a significant influence on the geographic distribution of services and industry throughout the world economy.

Firms from many nations have dramatically increased their overseas investments since the 1980s. European firms, Japanese firms, and the firms of such industrializing countries as Taiwan and South Korea have become major players and have invested heavily in other economies. The total number of firms of all nationalities investing abroad has increased substantially, while the number of economic sectors in which firms invest abroad has also grown dramatically; such service industries as insurance, banking, and retailing have received increasing amounts of FDI, and this has been especially significant for American business. The nature of international business has been revolutionized by the nature and extent of these changes. As the well-known Japanese business consultant Kenichi Ohmae has observed, this greatly increased worldwide expansionism has resulted from firms having realized that they must establish a strong presence in what he calls the Triad (North America, the European Union, and Japan) in order to become and remain internationally competitive.[47]

Despite an initially strong resistance to investing overseas, Japanese corporate strategy has changed dramatically. Japanese FDI expanded rapidly following the yen's significant appreciation after 1985, and Japan has now become one of the most important overseas investors. Although the overall Japanese stock of FDI still lags far behind that of the United States and Western Europe, Japanese investment has risen rapidly and will undoubtedly catch up eventually with American and European levels. The great preponderance of Japanese FDI has gone to the United States, Western Europe (especially Great Britain), and—until the East Asian financial crisis—Pacific Asia, especially southern China.

Japanese firms have traditionally preferred to produce at home and export their products to foreign markets. However, the threat of foreign trade barriers, rising wage rates, and production costs in Japan itself as well as the substantial appreciation of the yen have forced Japanese firms to increase their investment and manufacturing overseas. Construction of "export platforms" in the low-wage countries of Southeast Asia has been an important feature of their overseas investment strategy. Initially, Japanese FDI was intended to facilitate the exportation of finished goods and component parts to the American, Western European, and other foreign markets. Subsequently, however, the Japanese built regionally integrated production networks in those areas.

Technological change has provided the basis for these changes in the role of the MNC in the global economy. Revolutionary advances in communications and transportation, such as the Internet and teleconferencing have made it technically possible for businesses to organize and manage global industrial and distribution systems. These technological advances have greatly reduced the costs of globalizing both service and manufacturing industries. Other factors have also been important. The deregulation of financial markets and of other services in many countries has facilitated FDI. Comparative advantage in some aspects of manufacturing has shifted to low-wage industrializing economies. These changes have permitted multinational firms to choose their sources of supply and manufacturing sites on the basis of competitive advantage and other considerations. While some nations, especially Japan, have wanted to leap trade barriers and to reduce growing trade friction, trade protection has been less important in the growth of FDI than some have assumed.

Changes in production methods and industrial organization have provided another important determinant of the internationalization of business. The American era of horizontal FDI was based on what some scholars call "Fordism"—the manufacturing system of mass production of standardized products, strict division of labor, and single-site manufacturing—but this system of industrial production has become less competitive. The continuing shift from mass production to "lean and flexible" manufacturing means that a firm must incorporate technological sophistication, maximum flexibility, customized products, and extensive networks of suppliers if it is to compete internationally. And consequently, corporations more and more frequently interact on a global scale through a wide range of external corporate alliances, for example, joint ventures, subcontracting, licensing, and interfirm agreements. Multinational firms have gone beyond exporting and building foreign facilities through FDI to establishing intricate international alliances and networks of research, production, and marketing.

While the conventional theory of international trade assumed that comparative advantage is determined by an economy's factor endowments or factors of production, now it is recognized that a firm must frequently look to other economies to gain advantage in production, marketing, and research. That which a particular economy is able to contribute to the global strategies of multinational corporations has become important in defining its comparative advantage. Therefore, the importance of natural resources and unskilled labor as sources of comparative advantage and determinants of industrial location has decreased in many industries. Because of de-emphasis on natural resources, unskilled labor, and factor endowments, there has been a tendency to relocate production closer to the ultimate consumer, a development that supports the increasing regionalization of services and production in Western Europe, North America, and elsewhere.

The dramatic increase of intercorporate alliances of all kinds and descriptions across national borders has become another notable feature of the global economy. International competition has increasingly taken the form of competition between industrial complexes composed of major corporations, their overseas subsidiaries, and some foreign allies. This means that a firm's competitive position may depend on the type and scope of relationships it has been able to establish with other firms. Their corporate allies, in turn, depend on the firm's financial and technological resources as well as its market position both at home and overseas. One important reason for alliances is to enable a firm to gain access to a particular market. Transnational corporate alliances have become very important in determining the distribution of market share among firms and the geographic location of global industry. While the increasing importance of corporate alliances can be witnessed in all industries, these alliances are especially important in high-tech sectors characterized by costly research and development activities, large economies of scale, and high risk; these are sectors such as aerospace, electronics, and automobiles. The rapid pace of technological change, the huge costs involved in technological innovation, and protectionist regional arrangements mean that even the largest firms need foreign partners with whom to share technology and other resources as well as to gain access to protected markets.

Statistics tell the story of what happened during the 1980s and 1990s. Between 1985 and 1990, FDI grew at an average rate of 30 percent a year, an amount four times the growth of world output and three times the growth rate of trade. FDI has in fact become a major determinant of trade patterns as the annual flow of FDI has doubled from 1992 to nearly $350 billion in the late 1990s. Intrafirm trade—that is, trade between subsidiaries of the same firm—now provides a major portion of world trade. In 1994, intrafirm trade—transactions between U.S. parent firms and their overseas subsidiaries—accounted for one third of U.S. exports and two fifths of U.S. imported goods. About one-half of the trade between Japan and the United States is actually intrafirm trade. This intrafirm trade takes place at transfer prices set by the firms themselves and within a global corporate strategy that does not necessarily conform to conventional trade theory based on traditional concepts of comparative advantage. Evidence suggests that these trends will continue and could even accelerate.

These gross statistics, however, hide noteworthy aspects of FDI and of the activities of MNCs. Despite much talk of corporate globalization, FDI is actually highly concentrated and is distributed very unevenly around the world. As figure 6.1 shows, FDI in developing countries has grown rapidly; however, most FDI is in the United States and Europe, and only a small percentage of U.S. foreign direct investment has gone to developing countries. This concentration of FDI is due to the simple fact that the United States and Europe are the world's largest markets. Nevertheless, throughout most of the 1990s, FDI in less developed countries (LDCs) has been growing at about 15 percent annually. However, FDI in LDCs has been highly uneven and concentrated in a small number of countries, including a few Latin American countries, especially Brazil and Mexico, and the emerging markets of East and Southeast Asia. The largest LDC recipient of FDI has been China, which ranks second only to the United States as a host economy; between 1991 and 1995, inward FDI in the United States amounted to $198.5 billion; in China, $114.3 billion; and in Mexico, only $32 billion. The emerging markets were attractive, at least prior to the 1997 financial crisis, due to

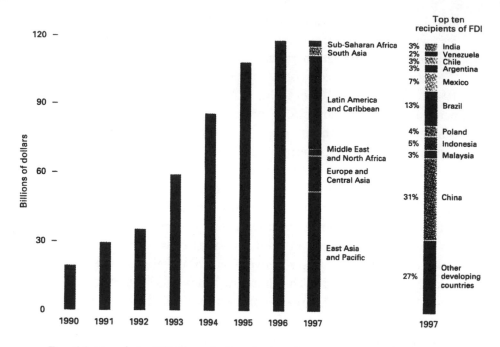

Fig. 6.1. Trends in FDI Flows in Developing Countries. FDI in developing countries rose severalfold from 1990 through 1997—but remained concentrated in a few markets. *Source*: Organization of Economic Cooperation and Development (OECD).

their rapid economic growth, their market-oriented policies, and their cheap labor. One should note, however, that the least developed countries in Africa and elsewhere have received a pitifully small percentage of the total amount invested in the developing world. Need it be said that these skewed statistics do not fit the image of globalization!

According to DeAnne Julius, one of the world's most knowledgeable experts on the MNC, the huge expansion of FDI, intercorporate alliances, and intrafirm trade throughout the 1980s and 1990s reached a level at which "a qualitatively different set of linkages" among advanced economies was created.[48] Some have estimated, for example, that there were more than 20,000 corporate alliances formed in 1996–1998. The growing importance of FDI and intercorporate cooperation means that the world economy has reached a "takeoff" point comparable to that wrought by the great expansion of international trade in the late 1940s and the subsequent emergence of the highly interdependent international economy. The growth in FDI and in the activities of multinational corporations has linked nations much more closely together, and this has further affected the global economy.

Economic and Political Significance of the MNC

The growing importance of the MNC in the global economy has become a matter of intense controversy. Proponents of the MNCs consider them beneficial for industrialized and industrializing economies alike. They believe that MNCs increase the efficient and productive use of the world's resources and thus increase the world's wealth and economic welfare. Critics of the MNCs, on the other hand, charge that these giant corporations are undermining democracy, harming national societies, and even constituting a new form of capitalist imperialism. Many critics allege that these firms, answerable only to themselves, are integrating societies around the world into an amorphous mass in which individuals lose control over their own lives and become subjugated to the exploitative activities of these firms. The world, these critics charge, is coming under the sway of a ruthless capitalist imperialism where the bottom line is the only concern.

Both positions are exaggerations of the role of the MNCs in the global economy. Although some MNCs are guilty and do exploit and do damage to the world, as an institution the MNC is beneficial to peoples everywhere. However, while the MNC is an important factor in international economic affairs, nation-states continue to be the predominant actors. Domestic economies remain the central feature of the global economy at the same time that multinational firms and their investment activities have an undeniable impact on the location of economic activities around the world, international trade patterns, and national rates of economic and production growth.

The MNC is a major source of capital, technology, and market access for almost every country (including some of the most advanced economies). The activities of MNCs have a great impact on the global distribution of wealth and economic activity among national economies. Despite, or rather because of, the benefits of FDI, MNCs do have a considerable amount of economic and political power, and their activities are rightly of concern to every society. As economists themselves point out, FDI frequently has important distributive effects on domestic economies and particularly on the division of income between capital and labor.

MNCs and Host Economies

Although the MNC is criticized severely, attitudes expressed in the 1990s have been much more positive than in earlier decades. In the late 1960s Jean-Jacques Servan-Schreiber's *The American Challenge* (*Le Défi Américain*, 1968) reflected the fears of Gaullist France that American firms were taking over the French and other West European economies. Dependency theory, which swept the Third World in the 1970s, accused American multinationals of being imperialist predators that exploited developing countries. The firms were charged with causing the underdevelopment of the world's economic periphery, and some MNC subsidiaries were nationalized and severe restraints were placed on FDI. Negative views within host economies have become more moderate. Whereas in the 1960s and 1970s the global expansion of MNCs was debated seriously, by the mid-1990s national policy emphasized the desirability of attracting inward FDI.

The dissipation of earlier hostile attitudes has been caused by a number of developments, including the huge increase in FDI by firms of varying nationalities, cross-investment among national economies, and the increasing integration between trade and FDI. Although many LDCs have continued to impose constraints on inward FDI, they now appreciate its generally beneficial aspects. It has been, in fact, particularly illuminating to observe the efforts of Brazil's President Henrique Cardozo to attract American investment to his country; not long ago Cardozo, one of the leading innovators of dependency theory, denounced American MNCs as instruments of American imperialism. Cardozo and many other national leaders throughout the industrializing countries have belatedly realized that MNCs are an excellent source of both the capital and the technology required for economic development.

Although the government of almost every industrializing economy continues to impose some restrictions on inward FDI and resists unrestricted access by MNCs to its economy, only a few continue to maintain the high barriers of the past. Most are well aware that if a developing country cannot attract FDI, it will be very difficult to acquire the financial, technological, and international market access needed for economic development. A developing economy outside the alliances and the production networks spun by multinational firms is at a considerable disadvantage, particularly because a substantial fraction of world trade consists of intrafirm transfers from one subsidiary of a company to another. An important corollary of this development is that if a country does not have MNCs of its own, it risks being slighted in the game of international commerce. Although established businesses in a host country do worry about competition from foreign MNCs, the increased importance of FDI for economic growth and international competitiveness has led to greatly intensified competition among national economies to receive FDI.

Most governments wish to improve their ability to attract and maximize the benefits of FDI in their economy. Indeed, many political leaders in industrializing and formerly socialist ("transitional") economies fear that they will not be able to develop strong, productive economies without the benefits associated with inward investments by multinational firms. These concerns are frequently justified, because most less developed and transitional countries are either unattractive to foreign investors or do not have the bargaining leverage necessary to extract maximum benefits from foreign corporations. Consequently, FDI, especially on the most favorable terms, has been bypassing many countries in the world and has been concentrated in China and two countries in Latin America (Brazil and Mexico).

A bargaining relationship exists between the MNC and the host government in which each side seeks to extract maximum concessions from the other. Negotiations between MNCs and developing countries have followed the pattern of what is called the "obsolescing bargain pattern." The firm is in the stronger position prior to an investment and at that time can extract maximum concessions from the economy in which it is considering investing. However, once the investment is actually in place, bargaining power shifts toward the host economy. The obsolescing bargain pattern was most relevant when FDI was concentrated in resource extraction, and it has become less relevant now that FDI is concentrated in manufacturing. A manufacturing firm usually retains much greater freedom of action than does a resource-extracting firm. Nevertheless, continuous bargaining remains characteristic of the relationship between firms and host governments. The firm seeks to acquire from the host economy as many concessions as possible, such as favorable tax treatment and trade protection, and the host country attempts to impose "performance requirements" on the firm. MNCs, for example, may be required to export a certain percentage of their output, to place nationals in high executive positions, and/or to share technology. One of the most important and vexing requirements imposed by host governments is "local content" in which the investing firm is required to purchase or produce locally a certain percentage of the component parts or intermediate goods used in its products. Almost every host country seeks to maximize the percentage of products obtained locally by MNCs.

Despite the advantages of FDI, many less developed countries continue to fear the loss of national autonomy either through an alliance between domestic and foreign business interests or through intervention by the home government of the MNC. One should be aware, however, that in almost every confrontation, the host government wins; and host governments have learned how to exploit MNCs for their own purposes. On the other hand, it is true that there have been a number of outrageous episodes such as the overthrow of Allende in Chile and Mossadegh in Iran in which the American government was involved through support of American firms; it remains unclear, however, whether American intervention was motivated by the desire to protect the interests of American investors in Iran or Chile or to prevent a suspected communist takeover of the country. Nevertheless, whatever has happened in the past, fears over the loss of national autonomy due to FDI have significantly declined, but not disappeared; yet weak countries are quite correct to be concerned about domination by large foreign MNCs.

The increasing importance of FDI as a source of capital and technology for economic development has led host economies to weigh carefully the costs and benefits of FDI. As economists point out, the gains to the host economy from inward FDI are very similar to those from opening the economy to international trade. These benefits include the gains from economic specialization, increasing ability to reach optimum production/organization size by selling in a larger market, and increased competition (i.e., reducing monopoly power and lowering consumer prices by subjecting domestic firms to competition from more efficient firms in their industry).

FDI can create externalities, spin-offs, or spillovers that confer benefits on the host economy over and above the strictly economic benefits of trade. This helps explain policies intended to encourage inward FDI, including erecting or increasing trade barriers so as to motivate firms to avoid such barriers through inward FDI. Among the externalities gained through inward FDI are worker training and technology transfers from multinational firms to the host economy. It is frequently pointed out, for example, that the American and British economies have greatly benefited from the high levels of Japanese investment in their economies; this FDI has encouraged firms in both countries to adopt Japanese "lean production" techniques and to increase product quality. Japanese FDI has also been a major factor in the industrialization of China and Southeast Asia.

Despite its many benefits, critics charge that FDI also causes problems for host economies. Some critics charge, for example, that the entry of foreign MNCs into an economy creates unfair competition for local firms because the foreign firms are supported by their home governments through subsidies and industrial policies. These concerns, frequently directed at Japanese firms, have led some other countries to place restrictions on Japanese investment; European limits on Japanese automobile production facilities provide an example of this. A more complex complaint against FDI is based on the theory of strategic trade, which really should be called the "theory of strategic trade and investment" because of the close linkage of trade and investment. Some potential host governments restrict inward FDI in important industrial sectors because they believe that FDI creates barriers to the entry of local firms into an industry; such reasoning has been a factor in Japan's highly restrictive policy against FDI into its own economy. In addition to the direct economic costs to the host economy, there may also be indirect economic costs. Rather than having positive externalities or spin-offs, critics believe that FDI is less beneficial to the host economy than is investment by local firms; the argument is made, for example, that local firms displaced by FDI would have been more likely to conduct their research and development activities at home rather than abroad. Finally, FDI is said to have certain important noneconomic costs related to such matters as national security and culture.

An objective assessment of the costs and benefits of FDI for host economies is impossible since there is no effective way to quantify the direct and the indirect economic costs and benefits. Although economic theory tells us that receiving FDI has the same economic effects as trade, this begs the point because it is also very difficult to measure the overall direct impact of trade on an economy. With respect to FDI's indirect impact, although there is pervasive anecdotal evidence for the existence and importance of technological and other spin-offs, there is no satisfactory method to measure these indirect effects. Nor is there conclusive evidence that local and foreign firms within an economy behave sufficiently differently from one another to permit an evaluation of their overall impact on the economy. The tendency for firms to locate their research and development (R and D) activities in their home country is an area in which the different impact of local and of foreign firms appears quite clear.

When applied to the advanced industrialized countries, the debate over the costs and benefits of FDI to the host economy is even less conclusive. Since these countries are usually both home and host economies, it is difficult to separate the costs and benefits for the home country from those for the host country. For example, because American and West European firms have access to both domestic and international capital markets, one can never be sure whether inward FDI in these economies is a substitute for or an addition to local investment. Because LDCs, on the other hand, usually lack sufficient local capital to meet their needs and international borrowing is frequently difficult for them, FDI is undoubtedly of much greater economic importance.

Despite the generally positive attitude of host countries toward FDI, governments are right to be circumspect in dealing with MNCs. MNCs represent an enormous concentration of economic—and by implication, political—power. The strategies of these firms are an important determinant of the location of industries and services in the international economy; they can benefit or harm an economy and are frequently denounced as imperial powers that exploit the rest of the world for narrow corporate advantage. Environmentalists charge often that MNCs are largely responsible for the deterioration of the natural environment. National elites continue to worry about foreign domination of their economies, especially foreign ownership of the most rapidly growing high-tech sectors. Unless the country possesses such bargaining chips as substantial financial and technological capabilities or control over access to a wealthy market, it will be at a considerable disadvantage in its dealings with foreign firms. Indeed, one motive for economic regionalism is to strengthen host governments in their dealings with foreign firms.

Although fear that FDI will harm an economy or reduce national autonomy has generally been confined to less developed countries (LDCs), some advanced developed countries (ADCs) have also expressed this concern. ADCs worry that FDI will lead to foreign control of high-tech sectors important to national security or of strategic importance for the overall performance and competitiveness of the economy. A closely related concern is that the subsidiaries of foreign firms behave differently from domestic firms and do not contribute as much to the overall welfare of the economy. In the mid-1980s, such fears were prominent in the United States due to a surge in Japanese FDI; this led to proposals that the Japanese takeover of vital sectors of the American economy should be stopped. Looking back from the perspective of the 1990s, the fears that the Japanese were gaining control over the commanding heights of the American economy were unfounded. Furthermore, studies have shown that, on the whole, the subsidiaries of foreign firms and American firms behave similarly even though there are some important differences in such areas as procurement and research and development. Foreign firms tend to import component parts from their parent companies and to use long-established suppliers; they also tend to carry out their most important R and D at home. Despite concerns over these and other matters, ADCs (with some notable exceptions, such as France) have left investment matters up to the market.

Although most believe that laissez-faire is the best policy toward FDI, some economists and public officials believe that laissez-faire should not apply when the relevant industry is highly concentrated and characterized by oligopolistic competition, especially if that industrial sector is important to national security. In those strategically important industries characterized by large economies of scale and/or dynamic gains from "learning-by-doing," governments frequently do not and probably *should* not leave matters entirely up to the market. Under such conditions, and following the implications of "strategic trade and investment theory," government action can sometimes be justified. Government interventionism may be required if a national firm is to protect itself and one day be able to join the small circle of global producers supplying products in the aerospace, computer, and other high-tech industries. However, many economists doubt the ability of governments to identify such strategic sectors and warn that industrial and strategic trade policies can easily be protectionist devices. Lastly, even though no country, not even the United States, can be self-sufficient in every important industry, it is highly unlikely that governments will voluntarily leave the location of strategic industries up to the market and the strategies of MNCs.

MNCs and Home Governments

In the 1960s, many Americans became very concerned that the huge outflow of FDI from the United States was having a detrimental impact on the American economy. They worried that the corporate tendency to produce abroad rather than to export from the American economy would lead to "deindustrialization" of the economy. These concerns were exaggerated and have abated, but they certainly have not disappeared; organized labor and other critics of globalization remain very worried. Since the United States itself has become the principal host to FDI from other industrial economies and has gained enormously from this investment, many groups in the United States have a positive attitude toward FDI. Simultaneously, many Japanese and Europeans have begun to worry about runaway plants and weakening of their industrial base as their own MNCs have significantly increased their FDI due to high labor costs and appreciated currencies.

In the 1990s, debates over ratification of the Uruguay Round of trade negotiations and the North American Free Trade Agreement raised once again the issue of the costs and benefits of FDI by American MNCs. In an attack led principally by Ross Perot and supported strongly by organized labor, MNCs were accused of "exporting" jobs to such low-wage economies as Mexico and of being indifferent to the interests of American workers and local communities. Moreover, charges were made that an MNC threat to locate abroad forced both workers and the government to make overly generous concessions to those corporations. Proponents of MNCs, on the other hand, argued that FDI actually increased American exports because foreign subsidiaries imported American components and other products. In addition, they argued that to be competitive in global markets, a firm must invest abroad to lower costs and gain access to foreign markets. They also pointed out that outward FDI generates exports to foreign subsidiaries from plants in the United States.

The issue of whether FDI harms or helps the home economy is of great importance, but it is extremely difficult to resolve. For example, if an American firm decided not to invest abroad, it would not necessarily make the same investment at home nor necessarily increase its exports from American plants. The firm's behavior depends on many considerations such as whether or not the United States retains a comparative advantage in the industry. As in so many aspects of economic analysis, what happens is dependent on the specific situation. However, as figure 6.2 reveals, it is worth noting that most FDI by American firms goes to other developed countries. This fact weakens critics' charges that U.S. MNCs are transferring jobs to low-wage LDCs.

A major problem for home governments has been host government imposition of "performance requirements" on MNCs. These requirements, which must be fulfilled before an MNC is permitted to invest, have included sharing technological know-how, establishment of export quotas, and incorporation of local components in the product. If an MNC agrees to such demands, that may be costly to the home economy in terms of lost technological advantages or exports from the home economy. In the late 1980s, the local content issue was at the heart of the dispute between the Clinton Administration and the Japanese government over managed trade in automobiles and auto parts. Issues like this will become more numerous with the increased globalization of industrial production. The desire of host governments to

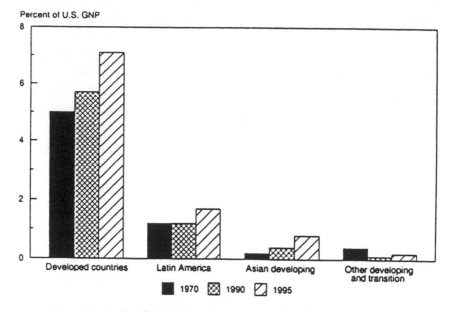

Percent of U.S. GNP

Fig. 6.2. Stock of U.S. Direct Investment Abroad. Investment of
U.S. companies in developing countries is still well below the stock of
U.S. investment in other industrialized countries, but it has increased
rapidly in the 1990s. *Source*: U.S. Council of Economic Advisors.

impose performance requirements on MNCs is one reason that industrializing countries have resisted proposals for international rules cover-
ing FDI.

In the 1990s, the performance requirements issue led to a bitter controversy over American investment in China. The rapid growth and
potentially immense size of the Chinese economy has made China a
magnet for FDI. American, Japanese, and other MNCs have been involved in an intense competition to establish themselves firmly in the
Chinese market. The attractiveness of investing in their market has not
been lost on Chinese officials, and they have frequently imposed very
costly performance requirements on potential investors. American critics fear that firms, eager to gain a foothold in the Chinese market, could
give and in fact have given the Chinese access to vital American technology, especially dual-use technology; that is, technology with military as
well as economic significance. For example, China refused to purchase
aircraft from Boeing unless Boeing agreed to produce aircraft in China;

this coproduction agreement obviously increased Chinese capabilities in aircraft design and manufacturing. Although Boeing and other American firms deny that they are giving away vital secrets to the Chinese or anyone else, critics charge that American firms are selling out U.S. commercial and security interests to gain corporate profits.

Nevertheless, economists' research generally supports the proposition that outward FDI is beneficial to the home economy and should not be prevented by government policy. It is clear, however, that the growing role of FDI in the global economy has affected the balance of power among economic interests within and across societies; the increased mobility of business has clearly weakened the bargaining position of organized labor. American businesses frequently threaten to move to Mexico or elsewhere unless labor accedes to management demands. This shift in the balance of power between capital and labor has undoubtedly been a significant factor in the increasingly protectionist stance assumed by organized labor in the United States and other industrialized countries. In addition, the threat to produce abroad and the growing importance of intercorporate alliances may have weakened, at least to some extent, the position of home country governments vis-à-vis MNCs. Nevertheless, in the struggle for power between the nation-state and the multinational corporation, the preponderance of power still rests with the nation-state.

Regionalization of Foreign Investment

The regionalization of services and production has been occurring even more rapidly than has global integration, and this will continue as a counterbalance to globalization. Since ratification of the North American Free Trade Agreement, more and more American firms have been utilizing Mexico rather than East Asia for outsourcing of component production and assembly, and production of "American" automobiles has become increasingly regionalized in North America. Similarly, Japanese firms prefer East Asian subcontractors and import a large share of their manufactured imports from that region. Western Europe, especially Germany, for both economic and political reasons, has taken increasing advantage of the skilled, low-wage labor in Eastern Europe. In effect, the major economic powers are concentrating FDI in their own backyards.

This trend toward the regionalization of investment, services, and production can be explained in several ways. New methods of production and management such as "lean production" and flexible manufacturing encourage regionalization; both techniques require highly trained and motivated workforces that can be more fully utilized with less risk at the regional than at the global level. Indeed, the need to move to low-wage areas has been greatly reduced as the share of unskilled labor in production has fallen dramatically since the 1970s. Regional concentration of production also facilitates scale economies in both production and distribution. Another consideration is that regional production networks enable firms to be closer to their principal customers; this factor will become even more important as regional markets continue to develop in Western Europe and North America. Cultural affinities may also play a part in this trend. Furthermore, regionalization of production can insulate economies throughout the region from trade wars and currency fluctuations. For these and other reasons, the movement toward regionalization of production will continue within North America, Pacific Asia, and Western Europe and is likely to strengthen in Latin America and elsewhere.

The increased importance of regionalization in the world economy raises some disturbing possibilities. For one, the trend toward regionalization could lead to weakening of the post–World War II move toward trade liberalization. While the MNCs of the major economic powers continue to pursue global strategies and to invest in one another's economies (with the exception caused by Japan's relatively low level of inward FDI), they are also concentrating their own FDI in neighboring countries. As economist Charles Oman has pointed out, creation of regional production and sourcing networks, rather than global ones, has become a notable trend.[49] If the movement toward globalization should be slowed by increased regionalization of services and production, the open global economy could suffer a setback; and this situation would have serious negative consequences for countries that were not members of a regional arrangement. And, in 1999, the great majority of less developed economies lie outside the emerging regional blocs.

New Rules for FDI and the MNC

In light of the increased significance of the MNC in every facet of the global economy—trade, finance, and technology transfer—the absence of international rules to govern FDI is remarkable. No rules exist comparable to those affecting international trade and monetary affairs. There are national, bilateral, regional, and multinational agreements on MNCs and FDI, but no overall comprehensive agreement. Although the Uruguay Round took a number of steps toward establishment of such rules, these efforts were minor compared to the magnitude of the issue. Many economists believe that an investment regime is unnecessary because markets will discipline errant states and firms. Perhaps! But this is asking too much of markets. The evidence suggests, to the contrary, that an international agreement governing MNCs and FDI is desirable. It would "lock in" the trend toward liberalization of national policies affecting FDI, eliminate distortions caused by governmental "beggar thy neighbor" policies, and reduce the conflicts among states and multinational firms.

As set forth by Canadian trade negotiator Sylvia Ostry, an international investment regime would have to have several characteristics, such as the right of establishment, national treatment, and nondiscrimination.[50] The "right of establishment" means that firms of every nationality have the right to invest anywhere in the world. The principle of "national treatment" requires that national governments must treat the subsidiaries of foreign firms as if they were domestic firms. In addition, countries should not discriminate against the firms of particular countries; this provision necessitates that national policies governing inward FDI should have transparency. An investment regime would also have to deal with the fact that every country restricts or limits investment in certain economic sectors, such as finance, culture, and national security; one task of an investment regime would be to determine what types of national restrictions are legitimate and what should be prohibited. Although these objectives are reasonable, the political obstacles to incorporating them into an international investment regime are formidable.

183

Several important initiatives to enact a universal code or international regime governing MNCs and FDI have been attempted. The Uruguay Round of trade negotiations took some steps in this direction, including the agreement on Trade-Related Investment Measures (TRIMs), General Agreement on Trade in Services (GATS), and agreement on Trade-Related Aspects of Intellectual Property Rights (TRIPs), but these reforms did not go nearly far enough. Another important step toward an investment regime was taken in the United Nations Code of Conduct on Transnational Corporations, which grew out of the Nestles' infant-formula case; however, this code applies only to firms and not to governments. Both the UN and the OECD have considered the issue of regulating FDI.

The most important initiative to create an investment regime has been the Multilateral Agreement on Investment (MAI), originally proposed in September 1995 by the Clinton Administration. The purpose of this initiative, in the words of the 1998 Economic Report of the President to the Congress, is to set "high standards for the liberalization of [domestic] investment regimes and investment protection . . . with effective dispute settlement procedures." In effect, the proposal was designed to protect MNCs from nationalization, corruption, and political instability; it would forbid host-country discrimination against foreign MNCs. According to its framers, the Agreement would not only protect American firms but would facilitate much greater FDI in developing economies.

The MAI has engendered powerful opposition. The choice of the OECD as the venue for the negotiations was a serious mistake because the OECD is a rich-country club and many LDCs were excluded from the discussions; why would LDCs accept an agreement that they had no part in formulating and that protected the interests of MNCs? Even many OECD countries objected to rules that would harm their own interests; France and Canada, for instance, wanted cultural affairs (broadcasting, films, etc.) excluded and the United States wanted restrictions on the sale of farm lands. The EU did not want interference with some of its policies. Labor and environmentalists objected that MAI would give MNCs license to disregard workers' interests and pollute the environment. Many critics charged that no protection was provided against the evils committed by MNCs. Even official American enthusiasm cooled when people realized that the MAI dispute mechanism could be used against the United States and its MNCs. Needless to say, the prospects for the MAI and an international investment regime are poor.

FDI impinges directly on national economies and can infringe on national values and economic independence. For this reason, states, especially LDCs, are reluctant to surrender jurisdiction in these matters to an international body. They fear domination by the huge corporations of the United States and other industrialized economies. Moreover, the very fact that MNCs operate across two or more national jurisdictions makes the task of framing an international regime extraordinarily difficult. An investment regime would have to address such sensitive issues as taxation of foreign investment, transfer pricing (the prices charged by one subsidiary to another), and governmental use of financial and other questionable inducements to attract foreign investment. A particularly vexing problem for America's trading partners is the extraterritorial application of American law, not just to the foreign affiliates of American firms but also to those of foreign corporations; for example, the Helms-Burton Act, which punishes foreign firms that deal with Cuba, is an especially infamous example of this American effort to impose its laws and policies on other countries. Whereas LDCs and other smaller states want protection against the concentration of power represented by the MNC, corporations want guarantees against capricious actions by states; distrust is rampant on both sides.

Strategic Behavior and Competition Policy

It is likely that strategic behavior intended to deter unwanted behavior by a competitor will continue to limit FDI. In some industries, such things as the importance of economies of scale, imperfect competition, and "learning by doing" make it very difficult for new competitors to enter the market. One way for domestic firms to enter such markets has been for their government to enact policies that, in effect, keep foreigners out. Japan and other Asian governments have restricted FDI in certain sectors, at least until their own firms have become strong enough to withstand the competition of established foreign firms. Available evidence strongly suggests that Japan, other Asian economies, and most developing economies have, in fact, continued to pursue national economic strategies that prevent foreign firms from investing in those industrial sectors judged by the government to be of national importance. The same countries also resist an international investment code, because they fear that it would lead to outside interference in their economic development and industrial policies.

The arguments raised by economists against utilization of strategic behavior to limit FDI are identical to those raised in opposition to strategic behavior in the area of international trade. Economists assert that technical problems and the lack of information make it impossible for governments to determine accurately which industries to promote and/or how to promote them. They point out that, moreover, even if governments could "pick winners," only a few industrial sectors would be appropriate for strategic behavior. And, finally, many economists argue that the attempt by one government to pursue such a strategy would lead to retaliation by other governments and thus contribute to a situation in which everyone would lose. Although these arguments have some merit, they are certainly not conclusive. There is evidence that indicates, for example, that Japan and some other countries have pursued a strategic investment policy with considerable success. Also, while the number of industries selected for government support may be small, they tend to be high-tech industries and, therefore, of crucial importance to every government. And, in a situation characterized by strategic interaction—that is, by retaliation and counterretaliation—the more powerful and daring players are likely to be the winners. For these reasons, one can not rule out the possibility that a number of countries will continue to employ strategic investment policies

Nevertheless, the opponents of strategic behavior are undoubtedly correct that harmonization of competition and antitrust or merger policies would reduce the temptation for nations to engage in strategic behavior. Instead of blocking FDI or resorting to strategic behavior, a host government would still be able to employ antitrust and related policies to prevent foreign firms from obtaining a monopoly position within its economy. It must be admitted, however, that there are huge obstacles to employing antitrust regulations. Furthermore, certain countries— Japan, for instance—really do not want a significant foreign presence in their economies; fortunately, this attitude has begun to change. Also, whether or not Japan wants inward FDI, Japan's and some other countries' lack of an effective competition policy would appear to rule out use of antitrust regulations. And, as has already been noted, the problem of reconciling fundamentally different national approaches to competition and merger policy is particularly complex.

Significant differences among national economies' competition and merger policies could be resolved through international agreement on universal rules governing fair competition and corporate mergers. Indeed, the European Union has taken steps toward enactment of a European competition policy and has tried to involve the WTO in these matters. However, an international code governing mergers and competition policy is very difficult to achieve because these policies lie completely outside the present jurisdiction of the WTO and/or other international institutions. Furthermore, the troubled history of past efforts to expand the jurisdiction of these institutions into the domestic policy realm discourages further efforts. The limited success of the efforts of the European Union to prevent the merger of Boeing and McDonnell-Douglas and the strong negative response in the United States to those efforts reveal the sensitivity of this issue.

Attempts to achieve a coordinated international solution to national differences in competition policy have been faced with such difficulties that one is led to the unsatisfactory conclusion that individual states will continue to attempt to apply their own national competition policy laws and, at times, will attempt to extend them across national boundaries. Examples of controversial extraterritorial application of national laws have already appeared. All in all, there is little reason for optimism that agreement on competition and merger policies could be achieved soon.

Employment Creation, Technology Transfer, and Local Content

Other problems have resulted from the efforts of individual states and groups of states to manipulate FDI to maximize benefits to their own economies of increased employment and technology transfer. Some states have abused the "antidumping" provisions of the GATT, performance requirements, and local content rules. In order to force a firm to increase its investment, governments have threatened to take antidumping actions against that firm; European governments and even the European Commission have employed this tactic to force Japanese, South Korean, and other firms to make desired investments in the European Union. Performance requirements and local content rules have also been used to force an investing firm to increase the value of local components or intermediate goods incorporated in its products. This tactic is frequently directed against so-called "screwdriver" plants; that is, foreign firms' local subsidiaries that assemble products designed and produced elsewhere.

While antidumping, performance requirements, and local content rules have been used by many countries, the EEC has been especially active in its attempts to use these devices to increase the employment and technological spin-offs from inward FDI. Although economists criticize excessive use of these protectionist-type devices because they cause economic distortions, such use is unlikely to disappear in the near future. During the professed laissez-faire Reagan Administration, fears of deindustrialization and of Japanese takeover of strategically important sectors of the economy led to enactment of a number of laws governing inward FDI.

Asymmetrical Access to National Economies

An international investment regime would also have to resolve the problem of asymmetrical, differential, or reciprocal access to national markets, an issue made highly contentious by the increasing linkage between trade and investment. Foreign firms can easily establish subsidiaries in the United States, but American and other foreign firms are frequently denied access to Japan and other countries; as figure 6.3 shows, Japan is the outlier among the three major economies. This problem, technically labeled "the right of establishment," is of particular significance in heavily regulated service sectors such as banking and telecommunications. Dealing with such areas, the Uruguay Round of trade negotiations passed trade-related investment measures (TRIMs), and this eventually lead to a number of important reforms. Subsequently, American-sponsored agreements on financial services and telecommunications extended the effort to open foreign economies.

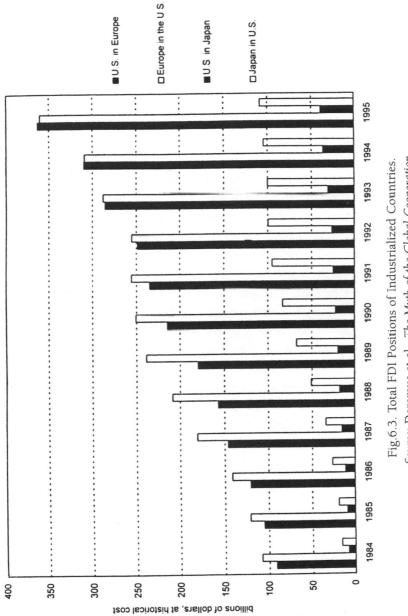

Fig. 6.3. Total FDI Positions of Industrialized Countries.
Source: Doremus et al., The Myth of the Global Cooperation.

However, some ADCs and most developing economies have strongly resisted reforms, and the results have not satisfied the United States.

Another area of concern has to do with corporate takeovers and mergers, activities that constitute a major means for foreign firms to gain access to new markets. National regulations that severely constrain mergers and acquisitions, and the structure and practices of private business (the structures of stockholding, business ethics, cultural norms) that prevent corporate takeovers and mergers, also constitute obstacles to achieving market access through FDI. Japan, for example, has strict rules against "hostile" or unwanted takeovers of firms. In the United States, unless the proposed takeover severely restricts competition and violates American antitrust law, the attitude is that even "hostile" takeovers benefit the economy.

Although barriers to FDI are found in every country, the most frequently cited culprits have been Japan and South Korea. When compared to other industrial economies, Japan has a relatively low level of foreign investment. Similarly, among the rapidly industrializing economies, South Korea has restricted inward foreign investment and, despite the Asian economic crisis, even in 1999 continues to resist opening its economy to FDI. Both government regulations and the corporate structure of these economies have contributed to this anomalous situation. Although formal restrictions on investment and acquisition of domestic firms by foreigners have declined worldwide in the 1980s and 1990s, the system of industrial groupings (the Japanese *keiretsu* and the Korean *chaebol*) have in effect prevented foreign firms from establishing a strong presence in their economies. One of the requirements imposed on South Korea by the IMF and the United States for it to receive assistance following the 1997 financial crisis was that it open its economy to foreign direct investment.

GLOBAL OR REGIONAL INVESTMENT RULES?

The presumption of the economics profession that FDI (like international trade) is beneficial for the world economy leads to the proposition that governments should not interfere in the investment activities of multinational corporations. Economists' policy prescriptions regarding FDI arise from this general presumption and propose that national policy should be neutral regarding trade or foreign investment; whether a firm chooses to reach foreign markets through exporting its products or producing abroad should be left up to the firm itself. Also, the principle of national treatment should be followed closely; that is, governments should treat domestic and foreign firms alike and should not discriminate against the foreign firms. In addition, there should be universal access; governments should restrict neither the access for the exports of foreign firms to their economies nor the right to establish a subsidiary. In other words, corporate strategies and market factors alone should determine international investment patterns.

As I have already pointed out, the prospects for a global investment regime based on universal and neutral principles are poor. The technical issues that would have to be resolved for such principles to be applied—that is, regulation of transfer pricing or of taxation across national jurisdictions—are formidable. However, these technical matters are less important than the political obstacles that must be surmounted. Two political issues stand out. There is a serious conflict between home countries and host economies (many of which are developing countries) over such issues as national autonomy and distribution of the benefits of FDI; whether a firm invests at home or abroad may not necessarily constitute a zero-sum situation, but governments frequently behave as if this were the case. Another problem arises because an international investment regime would have to intrude significantly into domestic economic and political affairs in such areas as competition and merger policy. The industrializing countries are especially sensitive to proposals that would restrict their control over inward FDI. In a world composed of national economies with very different economic structures and ideas regarding the definition of fair or legitimate economic policy or behavior, creation of an international investment regime is a daunting task.

If an effective global investment regime cannot be established, it is likely that a number of regional investment regimes will be developed. The prospects for such regionally based regimes are enhanced by cultural and institutional similarities among economies within a region and by the growing regionalization of foreign investment. In fact, regional investment regimes were already appearing at the end of the twentieth century. The European Union has been fashioning rules governing competition policy and related subjects, and the North American Free Trade Agreement included an elaborate body of rules and regulations regarding FDI. Whether these regional regimes constitute a step toward a global regime based on principles of neutrality or whether they prove to be protectionist devices that will be utilized against outside investors is not yet clear. If regional regimes are strengthened and no global regime is developed, the current tendency toward regionalization of services and international production will be reinforced.

Conclusion

There is little doubt that MNCs provide immense benefits to consumers and to economies around the world. Even such severe critics as William Greider and George Soros might agree that American consumers have gained from Japanese and Western European competition with Detroit, and that developing economies have progressed more rapidly due to access to the capital and technology associated with FDI. Nevertheless, MNCs do constitute concentrations of immense economic power and, like all large and powerful social institutions (including government bureaucracies and even nonprofit organizations), MNCs can behave in corrupt, arrogant, and socially irresponsible ways. Where power exists, it can be abused. Competition among firms helps reduce undesirable behavior, and national antitrust policies can restrain certain types of questionable activities. While an international regime could prove beneficial, there is no ready and permanent solution to the problems generated by concentrations of wealth and power in economic, social, and political affairs, so constant vigilance is required to prevent abuses.

CHAPTER SEVEN

European Regional Integration

THE MOVEMENT toward economic regionalism that accelerated in the late 1980s threatens the survival of an open and integrated global economy. Regionalization has already diluted the postwar effort to use multilateral negotiations to create a world freed from import and other economic barriers, and it is likely to have a significant impact on the distribution of global wealth and on the welfare of people everywhere. European regional integration, for example, could entail maintaining or even raising barriers to restrict the access of American and other exporters to the European market. And the North American Free Trade Agreement (NAFTA) discriminates against exporters into the North American market and thus raises prices for American consumers. The early movement toward regional integration in Latin America (Mercosur) also threatens to be highly discriminatory. The problems posed by economic regionalism are serious.

The concerted effort to create a unified Europe has been by far the most important regionalization movement. The success or failure of the European Union (EU), established in 1993, will have profound consequences for the nature and functioning of the international economy.[51] An open EU would greatly benefit American and other non-European exporters, but a closed EU would cause considerable harm. Moreover, the new common European currency (the euro) could have negative consequences for both the dollar and the yen, and creation of the EU has stimulated other regional integration efforts, including those in North America and Pacific Asia.

MOVEMENT TOWARD EUROPEAN INTEGRATION

The primary purpose of the postwar movement toward European unity has been political, but the principal means utilized have been economic. Economic goals such as a more efficient and competitive European economy have, of course, been important; however, these economic goals have been secondary to political concerns and could never have propelled the extraordinarily high level of European economic and political integration since the end of World War II. Economic integration alone has never led to political integration; there is no logic of economic interdependence that necessitates political integration. Historically, political integration has preceded economic integration.

It is noteworthy that the three North American economies—the United States, Canada, and Mexico, especially the latter two—are far more integrated in terms of trade, financial, and foreign direct investment than are the economies of Western Europe. Although intra-European trade has greatly increased, the European financial market continues to be highly fragmented and there is much less transnational European corporate integration than North American. Yet, despite the very high level of North American economic integration, there is no pressure for political unity, and it is highly doubtful that North American political unity will ever result from the North American Free Trade Agreement.

Since the European movement was launched in the 1950s, both the political objective and the economic tactics have changed considerably. In the early postwar years, the desire to rid Europe of the French-German rivalry that had been a source of conflict for generations became the driving force for regional integration. The effort began with the agreement to create the European Coal and Steel Community in 1951; its political purpose, according to the Treaty of Paris, was "to substitute for ageold rivalries the merger of their essential [economic] interests." Another important initiative was taken in the Treaty of Rome (1957), which led to the establishment of the European Economic Community (EEC/Common Market) composed of France, the Federal Republic of Germany, Italy, Belgium, Luxembourg, and the Netherlands. In the 1960s, West Europeans began to consider the possibility of achieving monetary unity. Establishment in 1979 of the European Monetary System (EMS) was an important early initiative toward monetary unity. The purpose of EMS was to stabilize monetary affairs in Western Europe and protect Europe from the wild swings in the value of the dollar. Little additional progress in regionalization occurred until signing of the Single European Act (SEA) in 1986; that specified the

TABLE 7.1
Chronology of European Integration

1951	The Treaty of Paris establishes the Coal and Steel Community.
1957	The Treaty of Rome establishes the European Economic Community (EEC, or Common Market), composed of the six original member nations (Belgium, France, the German Federal Republic, Italy, Luxembourg, and the Netherlands).
1962	The European Commission sets the goal of monetary unity.
1966	The Luxembourg Compromise establishes primacy of "vital national interest" claims as a limitation on EEC powers.
1967	Integration of European institutions to form the European Community (EC), thus replacing the EEC.
1969	The Hague Summit calls for economic and monetary union, stronger institutions, and greater political cooperation.
1970	The Werner Plan proposes European monetary unity.
1973	Denmark, Ireland, and the United Kingdom join the EC, raising the six members to nine.
1979	The beginning of the European Monetary System (EMS), including the Exchange Rate Mechanism (ERM) of loosely fixed rates.
1981	Greece joins the EC, raising the nine members to ten.
1985	(June) The European Commission publishes a White Paper proposing completion of the internal or single market.
1985	(December) Commission White Paper proposals are encapsulated into the Single European Act.
1986	Portugal and Spain join the EC, raising the ten members to twelve.
1987	(July) The Single European Act enters into force.
1989	End of the Cold War.
1989	(April) Publication of the Delors Plan for creating the European Economic and Monetary Union (EMU), including a single currency and the European Central Bank.
1989	(June) The Madrid Summit sets July 1, 1990, as the beginning of stage one of the EMU.
1990	German reunification.
1991	(December) The Maastricht Summit approves the Treaty on European Union (Maastricht Treaty), agrees to create a single currency (euro), and sets a three-stage timetable to achieve the EMU.
1992	(June) The Danes reject the Maastricht Treaty.

continues on next page

TABLE 7.1 *(cont.)*

1992	(September) The French approve the Maastricht Treaty by a narrow margin and England drops out of the ERM.
1993	(May) The Danes approve the Maastricht Treaty in a second referendum.
1993	(September) The United Kingdom opts out of the EMU.
1993	(November) The Maastricht Treaty comes into force, creating the European Union (EU).
1994	(January) Beginning of the second stage of the EMU.
1995	(January) Austria, Finland, and Sweden join the EU, raising the twelve members to fifteen.
1995	(December) The Madrid Summit confirms January 1,1999, as the beginning of stage three, the final move toward the euro and the EMU.
1996	(December) The Dublin Summit agrees on the Stability and Growth Pact.
1999	(January) Beginning of the third and final stage toward EMU.
2002	The euro is fully enthroned as Euroland's currency.

goal of creating a unified European market by 1992. Since the SEA, the movement toward European unity has accelerated.

At the core of the effort to integrate Western Europe has been the ambitious attempt to create Euroland (or, as the French prefer, "Euro-zone"). The concerted effort to weld together by peaceful means so many sovereign states into a unified economic and political structure constitutes a mammoth political experiment. There are no historical precedents to provide insights into the process of peaceful economic and political integration on such a scale. If ultimately successful, Euro-land (composed of eleven countries within the larger European Union) will be a powerful presence in the global economy. In 1999, the population of the Euroland eleven was about 290 million; there were 270 million Americans and 125 million Japanese. In 1997, Euroland's GNP of $6 trillion was smaller than America's $8 trillion economy but larger than Japan's $4 trillion economy. Because of its central importance for the movement toward greater European unity, this chapter will concentrate on the process of Euro-zone creation and especially on the crucial role of the German-French alliance in the integration effort.

ACCELERATION OF EUROPEAN UNIFICATION

In the mid-1980s, the movement toward greater European unity regained energy. European leaders' realization that Western Europe was losing influence in world affairs led them to revitalize the European idea. Concerned that the Americans and Russians were discussing with one another issues relevant to Western Europe without consulting West European governments, leaders also worried that Europe was falling behind both Japan and the United States economically. Whereas the United States and Japan were enjoying rapid rates of economic growth, Western Europe continued to suffer from the stagflation and Eurosclerosis of the 1970s. In these circumstances, European political and business leaders pressed for a decisive response to the troubling developments.

The European Commission White Paper, *Completing the Internal Market*, published in 1985, advocated completion of the internal market. Strongly motivated by fears of declining European competitiveness in the high-tech industries most relevant to both international competitiveness and national security, the White Paper advocated that by the end of 1992 all barriers to the free movement of capital, goods, services, and people within the European Community should be removed. The White Paper's proposals, incorporated in the Single European Act (1986), became the basis for the creation of a huge single West European market and Economic and Monetary Union (EMU). Leaders believed that the dynamism of such a market would revitalize the European economy and enable Europe to develop large MNCs that could compete effectively with their American and Japanese rivals.

The movement toward European unification took a decisive turn in the early 1990s. The end of the Cold War in 1989, collapse of the Soviet threat, and especially the 1990 reunification of Germany caused West European leaders to transform dramatically the purpose, logic, and timetable of integration. Germany's sudden reunification stimulated French and German political leaders to accelerate unification and to create a European *federal* political system in order to lock the reunited Germany firmly into a larger European institutional structure. German

Chancellor Helmut Kohl, strongly supported by French President François Mitterrand, moved to integrate Germany as rapidly as possible into a centralized institutional structure and thereby prevent reemergence of German nationalism. A speeded-up timetable for political and economic unity was accepted at the hastily convened Maastricht Summit (December 1991) and embodied in the Treaty on European Union (or simply Maastricht Treaty). As Kohl said of the treaty, "We want a treaty that makes clear that economic union, currency union, and political union are irreversible."

Establishment of the European Union in November 1993 reoriented the European movement. Prior to that time, the goal had been "greater political unity," and the timetable had been based on slow but steady progress toward that implicit but imprecise goal; the basic assumption was that slowly evolving successful economic union would facilitate political cooperation and greater political integration. The Maastricht Treaty transformed the nature of the movement when it reshaped the long-term goal and accelerated development of a centralized federal Europe through construction of the necessary economic and monetary foundations. Responding in part to the tragic events in the former Yugoslavia and Eastern Europe, leaders enlarged the political purpose of the movement to include the economic, political, and social stabilization of the entire continent.

Centrality of the French-German Alliance

The alliance between Germany and France has been crucial in propelling the movement toward European unity, especially since the 1978 agreement to establish the European Monetary System (EMS)/Exchange Rate Mechanism (ERM). These two dominant players desired a greater European presence on the world scene and were concerned about the long-term dangers of a fragmented European economic and political system, and they believed that the foundations of peace and stability would be strengthened by the single market, European economic and monetary unity, and a more centralized European political system. Both France and Germany expected to benefit economically from a unified European economy. As Western Europe's foremost industrial power, Germany would be the principal beneficiary of the single market and, in particular, of enlargement of the European Union to include Eastern Europe. Since the fall of the Berlin Wall, expanding German trade with and investment in the former Soviet bloc economies had made those countries part of a German economic sphere. Although France would also gain economically from the single market, it was more concerned about gaining some measure of control over a reunited and powerful Germany.

Ultimately, a trade-off between political and economic interests has provided an essential base for the French-German alliance. Germany has desired European political unity to confirm the country's return to democratic Europe and to guarantee a peaceful, nonnationalistic Germany. In addition, Chancellor Helmut Kohl and other German leaders, long concerned about Germany's location on the front line between a stable Western Europe and an unstable Eastern Europe (including Russia and the Balkans), wanted a common European economic, foreign, and security policy to stabilize Europe and to provide military and political security. As Chancellor Kohl sternly warned his fellow Europeans, European unity had become a matter of "war and peace in the twenty-first century."

France, the economically weaker of the pair, had long wanted security against the inevitable resurgence of German economic power. To achieve this goal, French policy was to share control over European financial and monetary affairs with Germany; this meant both "Europeanizing" the German central bank (Bundesbank), which under ERM had become the de facto European central bank, and giving a greater voice to France in management of the European economy. Germany wanted some control over French foreign policy, and France wanted some control over German economic policy. Some have said that the French got the euro (which Germany originally opposed) in exchange for its support of German reunification. Despite this victory in the economic sphere, however, French policy has been ambiguous about political unification because France fears loss of national sovereignty and political flexibility.

Despite the overriding importance of their shared economic and political objectives, Germany and France have been deeply divided on several crucial matters. Whereas Germany, at least initially, preferred a centralized federal political system in which it would obviously be the dominant force, France favored a "Europe des patries" that would permit nations to have greater freedom of action. Another fundamental difference arose from the clash between Germany's traditional commitment to minimal intervention by the state in the economy and France's favoring of an interventionist state that would assume responsibility for managing the economy. The two countries have also disagreed on the issue of enlargement; that is, incorporation of Eastern Europe into the European Union (EU). For political and economic reasons, Germany has placed a high priority on this objective; France has had serious reservations. Incorporating these countries into the EU could harm French agricultural interests and strengthen German influence in the EU. Thus, while Germany and France share a strong commitment to greater European unification, their political and economic differences have greatly complicated implementation of the Maastricht Treaty.

Maastricht Treaty

The Maastricht Treaty (Treaty on European Union), signed in December 1991, resulted from a French-German initiative to create an economically and politically integrated Western Europe. The centerpiece of the Treaty was the establishment of the Economic and Monetary Union (EMU), which would move beyond the coordination of exchange rates that the ERM had established; EMU's explicit goal was to create a common European currency (the euro) and a European central bank and thus provide the prerequisites for completion of an integrated European market. Completion of the internal market requires removal of the many formal and informal barriers that impede the free movement of goods, services, people, and capital among members of the European Union. However, the ultimate objective of the Maastricht Treaty was establishment of a European federal political system with a centralized institutional framework and a common foreign and security policy. This federalist scheme was eventually abandoned due to intense political objections from member countries and the German *Länder* (state goverments). The principle of subsidiarity, which asserts that policies should be decided at the lowest effective governmental level, became the central working principle governing the EU.

The movement toward European unity has been committed to achieving unity in three areas: economic and monetary affairs, foreign and security affairs, and social policy. Although there are basic differences among member countries on these goals, they are accepted, at least in principle, by the majority of EU members. There are different decision-making procedures and differing roles for member governments in these different substantive areas. The integration process was planned to begin with the least politically sensitive issues and progress step by step to more sensitive areas.

The *first goal* of a united Europe has been European monetary and economic union through creation of a common European currency and central bank. The European Commission, located in Brussels and composed of European civil servants, was given the responsibility for this task. Dealing with the least politically sensitive issues, the Commission's major role has been to initiate policies to achieve the single market and to forge economic unity. However, final decisions about a single currency and a European central bank remained with the Council of Ministers representing member governments. Council decisions are based on a complex system of majority voting that varies, depending on the importance of the issue, and that sometimes accords the vote of smaller members disproportionate weight. Indeed, the Luxembourg Compromise (1966) had provided that a member state could veto any action that it regarded as a threat to its "vital interests," but it had wisely left undefined the nature of a "vital interest." Some members have chosen not to participate in monetary unity. Great Britain and several other EU members, for example, had not yet joined the EMU at the time of this writing.

The *second objective* has been to achieve unity in the much more politically sensitive areas of foreign policy and security affairs. Responsibility in these areas rests primarily with the Council of Ministers. While the goal of the Maastricht Treaty was very ambitious regarding establishment of a common foreign and security policy for the Union, there has been little or no progress in this area because of serious conflicts of interest among the major European powers. However, in June 1999, the air war against Serbia led the members of the European Union to agree to create a military arm that would have the capability of "autonomous action" and thus free Europe from overdependence on the United States. Many observers were skeptical that the EU members would be willing either to pay the high costs of this effort or to make the necessary changes in their own national military establishments.

The *third objective* is concerned with particular substantive areas of domestic policy that impinge on the lives of ordinary people and that are frequently riven by ideological differences. Two such areas are migration and "social policy." Migration into Western Europe from both Eastern Europe and the lands bordering the Mediterranean has become a highly explosive issue in every West European country. The term "social policy" encompasses the welfare state and policies toward organized labor and is characterized by a deep ideological division between Social Democrats and Conservatives. Under the Conservatives, Great Britain chose not to participate in the area of social policy; the Labour Government of Tony Blair moderated this attitude, but both Conservatives and Labour have reserved the right to control migration. The extraordinarily sensitive nature of these substantive areas has lead to their management by loose cooperation and/or informal agreement among some member states rather than by formal policy decisions of the whole EU membership.

Although considerable progress has been made toward the achievement of monetary and economic unity, progress has been very slow with respect to the other two objectives.

Monetary Unity

The effort to achieve the Economic and Monetary Union (EMU) has been central to the movement toward greater European unification. After the Maastricht Treaty, the struggle to create a single European currency (the euro) and a European Central Bank (ECB) dominated both European political affairs and the domestic politics of member states. The emphasis on the EMU arose from several sources. Both France and Germany, whose leaders assumed that economic unity would naturally follow from monetary unity, regarded it as the cornerstone of a united Europe and the necessary first step toward greater economic and political integration. Moreover, members of the EU believed that monetary "deepening" had to take place before there was an economic "widening" or enlargement of the Union to include some or all of the formerly communist countries of Eastern Europe.

On a purely economic level, most European leaders believe that a common currency will constitute a bulwark against inflation and currency manipulation and will also prevent member countries from utilizing competitive devaluations to gain trade advantages. On a psychological level, many have believed that once monetary unity was achieved, everything else would fall naturally into place and Europe would be able to deal with such serious common economic problems as low economic growth and chronic high unemployment. For these and similar political, economic, and psychological reasons, European leaders have expected that the success or failure of monetary unity would shape European integration.

Agreement on EMU

The formal inauguration of the movement toward European monetary unification occurred in June 1989 at the Madrid Summit of the European Council when the Council adopted the Delors Plan or Report for European Economic and Monetary Union. Two years later the central ideas of the Delors Plan, with certain modifications, were embodied in the Maastricht Treaty (1991). While the Treaty committed the members of the planned European Union to achieve economic and monetary unity, it also enlarged the purpose of EMU from completion of the single market to promotion of economic and political unification of Western Europe.

The proposals of the Delors Report, subsequently modified by and incorporated in the Maastricht Treaty, foresaw the achievement of monetary unity in three stages:

1. The first stage, which began on January 1, 1990, eliminated capital controls, introduced the framework of comprehensive surveillance and coordination of member country economic policies, and intensified monetary coordination. During this first stage, all the EC currencies would be joined through the European Monetary System (EMS) fixed-rate mechanism. The financial crisis in the fall of 1992 that forced

Great Britain to withdraw from the Exchange Rate Mechanism (ERM) crippled these plans.

2. The second stage, which began in January 1994, continued the transition to EMU by introducing strict limits on national budget deficits. A European Monetary Institute (EMI) was created to manage the EMS, to coordinate the monetary policies of member states, and to prepare the way for attainment of a single monetary policy in the third stage. Currency realignment was considerably restricted. Guided by the EMI, each government had to tailor its economic policies to meet strict "convergence criteria" in economic performance; the most important criterion was that a government's budget deficit could not exceed 3 percent of its GNP. Toward the end of stage two, the European Central Bank (ECB) and the European System of Central Banks (ESCB) were created to assume management of the EMS and to begin formulation of a common monetary policy. In the spring of 1998, by virtue of much "creative accounting," eleven members of the EU were declared to have met the convergence criteria and were therefore eligible to advance to stage three.

3. The third stage began January 1, 1999. Exchange rates for Eurozone members were locked, and the ECB assumed full responsibility for European monetary policy. During this stage, the euro will gradually replace all national currencies, official reserves will be shifted to the ECB, and the ECB will manage the Community's exchange rate policy. Last, although individual states will retain responsibility for fiscal policy (taxes and government spending), the Council of Ministers will be responsible for enforcing EMU fiscal rules to ensure that individual governments pursue anti-inflationary policies. By early in the twenty-first century, the process of monetary integration will have created a single currency and a politically independent European Central Bank controlling a common monetary policy.

Costs and Benefits of the Euro

The debate among economists, public officials, and members of the business community over the costs and benefits of a single currency has been intense. The considerable uncertainty surrounding the future of the EMU has prevented resolution of such important questions as who will determine monetary policy and to what extent fiscal policy will be left to member states or be centralized at the EU level. It will be many years before these and other equally important questions can be answered, but the central question facing Western Europe can be addressed even if it cannot be answered precisely: that is, what is the trade-off between the presumed benefits and costs of a common currency?

PROPONENTS

Continental European economists and public officials have reached a near consensus that economic and political gains will outweigh any loss of national macroeconomic independence. The most authoritative statement of this position has come from the Commission of the European Community itself.[52] According to the Commission's report, *One Market, One Money* (October 1990), and other analyses, a single currency is expected to produce the following benefits: (1) Elimination of foreign exchange transactions within the single market will reduce transaction costs then (1990) estimated at $30 billion a year. (2) A single currency will reduce the uncertainty of exchange rates and thereby lead to gains in efficiency for trade and capital movements. (3) A single currency will provide monetary stability, stabilize prices, and hence constitute a strong defense against inflation. (4) A single currency will strengthen the EU's negotiating position vis-à-vis the United States and also will make the EU a better economic partner. (5) A single currency will provide a prerequisite for eventual fiscal federalism. (6) A single currency will eliminate the risk of competitive devaluations. (7) A single currency will increase transparency in economic transactions and thus encourage a decline in prices. (8) The euro will speed economic integration and economic growth through increasing competition and higher productivity. (9) The euro and the single market will encourage corporate restructuring and the creation of large European firms with the resources and economies of scale to compete against American and Japanese giants. (10) EMU will accelerate the process of political integration.

Proponents have argued that, at the macroeconomic level, a single market requires a single currency to ensure monetary stability.

Although macroeconomic policy coordination or a system of fixed rates among the member countries of the EU (such as the ERM) could provide solutions to monetary instability, Europeans decided that the establishment of a single currency and a central bank was the only practical solution. A system of fixed rates was considered potentially unstable because it lacked an adequate mechanism to unify EU members' decision making on monetary policy. Also, fixed rates would be difficult to maintain without capital controls. However, there was a price to be paid for the EMU. To reach an integrated regional economy, the member governments had to recognize that not all the desired objectives (fixed exchange rates, freedom of capital movements, and national autonomy in monetary policy) could be attained simultaneously. Because this "trinity" was "irreconcilable," EU members chose protection against both inflation and exchange-rate instability but surrendered the possibility of maintaining independent monetary policies. Some critics believe that the price of this decision will prove too costly.

American economist Peter Kenen, an astute analyst of the subject, believes that by the mid-1980s the European Union had reached a point where it could not stand still; it had to retreat to greater exchange-rate flexibility or advance to full-fledged monetary union. A return to floating rates would make it very difficult to maintain free trade within the EU since, for example, floating rates could undermine the Common Agricultural Policy (CAP) that has been one of the most important and sensitive political foundations of the movement toward European unity. Moreover, a common currency prevents members from engaging in currency manipulation to increase their international competitiveness (the problem of competitive devaluations). A single currency overcomes the problems of commitment and defection that weakened the ERM during its early years when many devaluations took place. Euro-Zone members should now be confident that others would neither cheat nor pursue inflationary and other irresponsible policies.

Most important, monetary unity became the symbol of Western Europe's willingness to set aside national differences in the interest of political unity. If the first step of monetary union could not be achieved, how would it be possible to take even more difficult steps toward economic and political union? As former West German Chancellor Helmut Schmidt warned, failure to achieve monetary union would have caused the EU to revert to a mere customs union and would have split the group into antagonistic parts. In effect, the overriding purpose of monetary unity was to support the political objective of greater European unity.

CRITICS

The critics of the EMU, including many American and British economists, argue that the benefits of a single currency have been greatly exaggerated and the costs, significantly underappreciated. These critics point out, for example, that such supposedly "negative" effects of multiple currencies as transaction costs and the impact of exchange-rate risk on trade and investment are minimal. They also argue that the considerable efforts of member countries to meet the convergence criteria have contributed to Europe's high rates of unemployment and caused political havoc in France, Italy, and even Germany itself. Europe already suffered from high unemployment caused by such other factors as labor market rigidities; efforts to meet the convergence criteria have seriously aggravated the problem. By one estimate, in the late 1990s about 12 percent of the EU's workforce was unemployed, and there were much higher percentage rates in some countries. In the opinion of many American critics, the West Europeans should focus their attention on reforming and deregulating their economies to deal with unemployment and other pressing issues. Moreover, critics contend that a single currency is not essential either to achieve a single market or even gain greater political unity. If the international economy gets along moderately well with many currencies, why should not the European economy do well also?

American economists' principal criticism of a common currency has been based on the argument that the European Union does not constitute an optimum currency area (OCA). The theory of an OCA, formulated by Robert Mundell (1961) and Peter Kenen (1969), asserts that two or more countries constitute an optimum currency area only when setting the nominal exchange rate between their currencies does not impose real costs on their economies.[53] More specifically, an OCA exists when one or two conditions prevail. If prices and wages in both countries are perfectly flexible—that is, if prices and wages in both countries rise and fall together in response to a change in economic conditions—then, if country A were to reduce its prices and wages, country B would respond in such a way that the real exchange rate between the two countries would not change. Or, if labor and capital were perfectly mobile between the two countries, then a change in demand away from the exports of country A toward the exports of country B would be offset by the migration of labor and capital from country A to country B. Because Euroland is not an optimal currency area the members' vulnerability to economic shocks is increased and their ability to deal with such shocks is decreased.

EMU critics are correct that the European Union is not an optimal currency area; indeed, it lacks both of the necessary preconditions. Prices and wages in the member countries are insufficiently flexible, and, since wages do not drop when unemployment increases, wages are quite inflexible. Nor do labor and capital move freely from country to country within the Union in response to changes in demand. On the contrary, despite talk of an integrated European labor market, labor within the EU is highly immobile and is likely to remain so well into the twenty-first century.

Now that the members of Euroland have a single currency, an economic shock to a particular region—a sudden and drastic change in demand or supply that would plunge a particular region into a recession—could easily have a devastating economic and political impact not only on the immediate area but possibly on the EU as a whole. The 1973 oil price rise was a supply shock and the costs of German reunification, a demand shock.

Because Euro-zone members are not allowed to use independent monetary policies to pull themselves out of a shock-induced recession, they would normally utilize such a fiscal policy as tax cuts or public works to stimulate demand. The EU itself could have a fiscal policy to distribute financial resources to a depressed area to stimulate demand. However, the role of fiscal policy in Euroland has not yet been determined. Although it is unclear whether or not member states will retain some fiscal powers, the Stability Pact demanded by Germany and discussed below suggests that members' fiscal powers will be greatly restricted. The extent to which the EU would be empowered to take actions to benefit an affected region is also unclear. The problem of moral hazard and the fear that the stronger economies would have to bail out the weaker ones make it doubtful that a federal authority will make a fiscal response to members in trouble. In that case, the affected region probably would suffer declining wages, higher unemployment, and disturbing political developments.

With national fiscal responses unlikely, adjustment to a demand shock would be a slow and painful process; unemployment would surely rise. Therefore, critics of a single currency fear that such a shock would lead to a prolonged and painful recession in the affected region. Weak peripheral members, such as Greece, Spain, or southern Italy, would be particularly vulnerable to such an eventuality. Having given up the option of an expansionary monetary policy, a government could be helpless to respond to a drop in demand and would have to stand aside until market forces caused wages to fall to the point where the supply and demand for labor returned to an equilibrium. It is highly unlikely that citizens will accept the exercise of such patience in the interest of greater European unity.

Yet, as the fundamental purpose of a single European currency is political rather than economic, these economic considerations have carried little weight. The fact that the EU is not an optimum currency area (OCA) may raise the costs of a single currency, but it does not necessarily mean that the project will or should be abandoned. The economic arguments for and against a single currency miss the point. Both the microeconomic gains and the macroeconomic losses have been greatly exaggerated, and the question of whether or not the EU is an OCA carries little weight in the debate over the EMU. Every independent state or political entity wants its own currency whether or not it makes good economic sense. Although there are economic reasons for this, the principal reason is that having one's own currency is a symbol of national sovereignty, and one of the first acts of a newly independent power is to create its own currency. This explains why a majority of the members of the European Union believe that if the EU is to assert itself as an independent power, it too must have its own currency.

French-German Conflict over EMU

The key to understanding the debates and conflicts over implementation of the Maastricht Treaty is found in the clash between Germany and France over the governance and policies of the proposed European Central Bank. Although Germany and France have been the principal supporters of the EMU, they have also had sharply opposed views on almost every important issue. Germany and other strong currency countries (the Benelux countries) desired an independent European central bank whose primary purpose would be to keep inflation under control. But France wanted a European central bank over which it would have substantial influence and one—unlike the Bundesbank-dominated EMS—that would give priority to economic growth and job creation rather than to fighting inflation. Another and longer-term difference between the two countries is that the Germans wanted a strong euro as a bulwark against inflation while the French wanted a weak euro vis-à-vis the yen and dollar in order to increase France's trade competitiveness. As Kenen has commented, the shift from the EMS to the EMU could be interpreted as an effort by France and some other members to Europeanize the management board of the Bundesbank. The history of the effort to achieve European monetary unity has been in large part a tale of the conflict between the divergent national interests of Germany and France.

For many years, a deep schism within German society underlay German policy toward European monetary unity and the European Union more generally. The German federal government under Chancellor Helmut Kohl, strongly motivated by the desire to integrate Germany into a denationalized Europe, became the principal proponent of a single European currency. At the same time, however, the German states (*Länder*), the German central bank (Bundesbank), and the German people had strong reservations. The *Länder* were reluctant to cede their control over many policy areas, and the Bundesbank and German people were equally reluctant to abandon the mark for the euro. The German public considered the strong mark a symbol of Germany's outstanding postwar economic success and its revival as a great power. This public attitude produced overwhelming support for the position of the Bundesbank in the formulation of German policy toward European monetary integration.

The Bundesbank, concerned over loss of its political independence and worried that a central European bank over which it could not exercise control would pursue reckless inflationary economic policies, pressured the German federal government to ensure that fighting inflation would be the principal objective of a central European bank. To this end, the Bundesbank lobbied for enforcement of strict convergence criteria to prevent countries from joining the EMU unless their economic performance had reached the level achieved by Germany itself. The Bundesbank reluctantly supported the EMU as a means to discipline the more irresponsible and inflation-prone members of the Union, and the views of the Bundesbank have had a profound impact on German policies toward the EMU.

The issue of convergence criteria was central to the most important controversy between France and Germany. The Maastricht Treaty set forth several measures of economic performance that an EU member had to satisfy to join the EMU. However, the crucial requirement that a government's budget deficit had to be lower than 3 percent of GNP proved very difficult. For example, to meet this goal, governments had to scale back their welfare expenditures. Some observers, in fact, have suggested that the Maastricht convergence criteria were intended to force West European governments to cut back their welfare programs under the political cover of meeting EMU requirements. It is unarguable that Bundesbank pressures led the German government to insist on this criterion for entry into the EMU, and that this strict requirement resulted in a considerable amount of "creative accounting" and "cooking the books" to enable many countries, including Germany itself, to meet the limit on government budget deficits.

In 1995, there was a major clash between France and Germany when Germany proposed a post-EMU Stability Pact that would require EMU members either to keep budget deficits below the 3 percent deficit limit or face sanctions, including steep fines. This extraordinary proposal was intended to reassure the German people that neither Italy nor some other errant member of Euroland would relapse to its former irresponsible fiscal ways after it had been admitted to the EMU. Implementation of the stability pact, accepted after much wrangling at the Dublin Summit (December 1996), greatly decreased the possibility of independent fiscal policies and, with the establishment of the single currency, significantly limited independent national macroeconomic policies.

EU members' efforts to meet the convergence criteria imposed a high economic cost and, as critics had warned, led to political discontent. In June 1997, the deep resentment throughout Western Europe over decreased economic growth and high unemployment erupted in France and threatened to derail French actions to meet the convergence criteria. In response, Conservative French President Jacques Chirac called for a general election to prepare the ground for the major spending cuts and other economic sacrifices required to meet the public deficit limit. However, the election produced a landslide victory for the Socialists, whose views on EMU had changed from positive to negative after the death of the previous president François Mitterand. Although the newly elected Socialist prime minister Lionel Jospin proclaimed that France would adhere to the EMU timetable, he assured the French people that his government would not impose further burdens by increasing revenues or decreasing expenditures to reduce the budget deficit. To the contrary, he promised a program of job creation and wage increases.

Another major clash between Germany and France under the Socialists occurred at the Amsterdam Summit (June 1997), at which the participants had been expected to sign an ambitious new treaty to reform the EU's governance structure and prepare the way for EU enlargement. The Treaty of Amsterdam did open the way for formal negotiations between the EU and its prospective eastern members, but in almost every other particular, the Summit was a serious setback for the movement toward greater unity. The Summit was riven by intense battles among EU members. Germany vehemently rejected French demands for an "economic government" to supervise the ECB, for the Stability Pact to be weakened, and for establishment of an ambitious public-works program of job creation. It is equally noteworthy that the French-German proposal that the EU create its own defense capability was defeated by a British-led coalition, and that efforts to strengthen EU foreign policy also suffered a setback.

There were only modest efforts at Amsterdam to deal with social issues, due to Germany's strong insistence that decisions on many of these politically sensitive issues be approved by unanimous votes. This Amsterdam Summit failed to reach agreement on the crucial issues of voting rights and institutional reform, issues that must be resolved before the EU is enlarged. In several important areas, members led by Great Britain and Germany strongly asserted their right to weaken prior commitments. At the Amsterdam Summit, then, there was a significant reassertion of the national sovereignty of member states.

Although progress toward EMU has been extraordinarily successful, many pitfalls and questions lie ahead that could prevent its ultimate success. For example, what will be the role of fiscal policy in the EU? And who will control it? Will the European Central Bank pursue a strict antiinflation policy or, as many Social Democrats and Socialists desire, an aggressive pro-growth policy? What will the relationship of Euro-land be with other EU members? Will EMU be blamed for high unemployment and other EU economic problems? This list could be easily extended to include institutional and other matters. It is significant that the ultimate fate of the Euro-zone remains uncertain, and that achievement of a favorable outcome will require an enormous amount of political goodwill.

GOVERNANCE OF THE EU

The problem of governance is the most fundamental issue that the West Europeans must resolve to achieve greater economic and political unity. The process of regional economic and political unification, like national unification, requires vigorous political leadership. The European Union (EU) will have to strip away internal barriers to economic activities much as the territorial European nation-states in the early modern period had to use their power and authority to remove internal barriers inherited from feudalism that stood in the way of a national economy. Today's vested interests and declining industries must go the way of the ancient guilds. It will be necessary to make extensive reforms of labor and business practices comparable to those that paved the way for the transition from guilds and craft industries to the modern factory and mass-production systems. Because changes of such magnitude will confront deeply entrenched resistance, effective leadership will be required. If Western Europe is to regain international competitiveness and to achieve vigorous economic growth, it can no longer accept compromises based on the least common denominator acceptable to the various nations.

The tasks of leadership at the regional level are similar to those at the global level: to promote economic—and, in Western Europe, political—integration, to provide certain public goods (such as a stable currency), to prevent free riding (such as competitive devaluations), and to overcome resistance through compensation (the "cohesion" fund). Successful European unification requires a political leader or leaders who can manage an integrated European economy, and, at the policy level, such tasks as formulation of macroeconomic policy. Yet, it is unclear whether or not the members of the EU will agree on the purposes of monetary policy or on the role of fiscal policy at either the national or the federal level. The only country that could exercise strong leadership is Germany, but at this writing Germany is part of the problem rather than a leader in formulating a solution.

The creation of an effective political and institutional framework for the European Union must surmount immense hurdles. The fundamental differences among the three major European powers over the appropriate model for the Union suggest the difficulties faced by efforts to build an effective governance structure.

The Maastricht model was based on a federalist structure and assumed steady evolution toward political and economic unity. Initially, Germany favored this strong federalist structure; the British, Danes, and French rejected it or were lukewarm. However, in part because of strong opposition from the German *Länder* (states), even Germany retreated from this concept and began to emphasize the decision-making principle of subsidiarity.

Another possible model is a loose arrangement of functional groupings around each of the EU's objectives, an arrangement that would permit each member to choose to participate in EU activities as it suited its particular interests. For example, Great Britain wants to be part of the single market, but it does not want (at least not yet) to be a member of the EMU or to subscribe to the Social Charter. This model, which has been called a Europe of "variable geometry" or "Europe à la carte," is anathema to both the Germans and the French.

There is also a possibility of a European entity based on the core French-German alliance (joined by other strong-currency countries) and a periphery composed of a series of concentric circles. This model is usually referred to as a "multispeed Europe." These concentric circles would range outward from countries with close ties to the core to those with only loose ties. This model, favored by the Germans and the French and strongly opposed by the British, is the one most likely to be realized.

A number of tracts by academics and others argue that Europeans have been fashioning a radically new type of political system. Some argue that the EU constitutes a novel political entity based on "pooled sovereignty." Perhaps! However, progress among the members of the EU in pooling the principal attributes of national sovereignty—the rights of taxation, of coinage, and of self-defense (foreign and security policy)—has been slow or even nonexistent. Despite the beginning of stage three of monetary unity on January 1, 1999, the prospects for a single currency and a unified monetary system early in the twenty-first century are still problematic, and the prospects for a European system of taxation and defense are extremely dim. How can one have a governance structure that does not have the power to tax, has few resources of its own, and has no foreign or security policy? A new European economic and political order is surely coming into existence, but its nature is far from clear.

"Democratic Deficit"

Europeans must create a democratic and accountable polity to remove what has been called the "democratic deficit." Thus far, the movement toward greater European economic and political unification has been an elite movement composed of national public leaders, business leaders, and EU civil servants. Public opinion throughout the European Community, on the other hand, has been either hostile or at least unprepared for the increasingly ambitious steps being taken toward a unified European political and economic structure. Indeed, the Maastricht Treaty, even though it was signed by all fifteen members of the EU, soon met opposition in the ratification process in Denmark, France, and Great Britain. Even in Germany there has been strong citizen resistance to the idea of giving up the mark in favor of the euro. Despite creation of the EU and talk of a new "European" mentality, political consciousness in Europe at this writing remains largely national—German, French, and so forth. The hard political facts of separate national identities have continued to clash with the intense efforts of the European political elite to implement the extraordinarily ambitious Maastricht Treaty.

The peoples of Western Europe do not have any direct influence over the major decision-making institutions of the EU—the Council and the Commission—and those institutions have no accountability to EU citizens. Despite its success in forcing the Commission members to re-sign in 1999, the directly elected European Union's Parliament in Strasbourg has only limited powers. Because of this "democratic deficit," the peoples of Western Europe have little sense of identity with the Union and lack loyalty to its institutions; the Germans, French, British, and others continue to identify with and be loyal to their respective nation-states. Without a committed European citizenry, it may be very difficult for the EU to weather the serious economic and political problems that lie ahead. Until this problem is resolved and a true European polity is achieved, both the political unity within the European Union and the institutions of the Union will remain extremely vulnerable.

Monetary Unity and Economic Governance

There is reason to doubt that monetary and economic unity can survive without greater political unity. Indeed, in their haste to achieve monetary unity, Europeans have reversed the historic relationship between monetary and political unity. No less a Brussels bureaucrat than former Chief Commissioner Jacques Delors has proclaimed that the EMU could not work without a "European economic government." Yet the French, who were for a long period the foremost advocates of an economic government to exercise control over the policies of the European Central Bank, have simultaneously strongly resisted a political government. It is very doubtful that the EMU will work without a centralized authority of some kind. Indeed, Great Britain rejected the EMU in part because it feared that a centralized European political system would necessarily have to accompany monetary and economic unity.

The history of both regional and international monetary affairs indicates that monetary and economic unity cannot proceed far without a strong political foundation. Political leaders must ensure that member countries maintain the credibility of their commitments and do not cheat. A secure political underpinning of European monetary integration and solution of the credibility problem could be achieved either through close cooperation of the major European powers or by the exercise of strong leadership by one or another of the major powers. Thus far, the three major powers have failed to achieve such a cooperative relationship. Although the Germans and the French have cooperated in the sense that the Germans (at considerable expense to themselves) supported the threatened franc, the British refused to cooperate in the 1992 financial crisis when they decided not to defend sterling because of the potentially high cost to the British economy. Furthermore, fundamental differences between Germany and France have limited their cooperation, and Germany has thus remained the sole power that could possibly perform the tasks required for greater European economic and political unity.

In December 1997, the French proposed establishment of an Economic Policy Forum, or Euro Club, to oversee the European monetary system. They intended such an organization to coordinate economic policy among the Euro-zone members of the Union prior to meetings of the EU financial ministers (EcoFin), a group that serves as the EU's principal decision-making body in the area of economic policy. The French hoped that this Euro Club would increase their leverage over the monetary and other economic policies of the ECB. The British, on the other hand, feared that the Euro Club would downgrade EcoFin, strip the British of any influence over EU's economic policies, and even possibly drive a wedge between Euroland members and nonmembers. Between these protagonists were the Germans who, while they favored the idea that a Euro Club would facilitate cooperation and create a common identity among Euro-zone countries, strongly opposed any attempt to restrict the policy independence of the ECB. In the spring of 1998 this conflict was resolved, at least temporarily, by a compromise permitting the finance ministers of countries participating in the Euro Club to meet to discuss matters relevant to the euro while Ecofin remained the final decision-making body for such economic policies as taxation and labor-market policy. It is likely, however, that the Germans, French, and British will continue their own and frequently conflicting efforts to influence the economic policies of the European Central Bank.

Until and unless the governance issue is resolved, the governing structure of the European Union will continue, as it has been described by the *Financial Times* (London) columnist Samuel Brittan, as a hybrid operating through a system of loose cooperation among national governments in politically sensitive areas and tempered by some supranational authority vested in the European Commission. Brittan has also observed that the supreme decision-making body, the Council of Ministers, meets only once a month and works according to very complicated decision-making procedures. The authority of the Parliament has been slowly expanding through codecision with the Council, but until the late 1990s its authority was based primarily on its ability to block legislation. How far the Union will be able to move beyond these ineffective arrangements toward its proclaimed ultimate goal of political unification remains to be seen.

GLOBAL IMPLICATIONS

The rest of the world has paid close attention to the movement toward European integration. The EU and Euroland could have a formidable presence in world affairs. The United States, Japan, and other economies have been very concerned over the possibility of a "Fortress Europe" that would restrict access to the single market. Many Americans have been worried about the impact of the euro on the dollar. European trade policy and the international role of the euro are of considerable importance to the global economy. Although there are many unknowns as this is written in 1999 that will affect both issues, a tentative assessment can be made.

For the Trading System

The question of whether or not the EU will be open to trade and investment from nonmember countries has grown in importance as European integration has both deepened and widened during the final years of the twentieth century. Indeed, the nature of the world economy in the beginning decades of the third millennium will be greatly affected by developments in this area. Despite Europe's serious economic problems with its high level of unemployment and its backwardness in many manufacturing sectors, the policies of a united European economy will affect every other country in important ways. An open Europe that did not discriminate against non-European goods and services would give a significant boost to the forces of economic globalization; a more closed Europe that erected trade and investment barriers and/or gave trade preferences only to specific external countries, such as those in Africa, Eastern Europe, or the Middle East, would stimulate trade protectionism and economic regionalism around the world. Although removal of internal barriers and transfer of decision-making authority over important aspects of economic policy to Brussels could prepare the way for eventual removal of all economic barriers on the Continent, West Europeans might well regard the unified internal market as the private preserve of their own business interests and as a means to strengthen Europe in its relationships with external powers.

Economists differ among themselves over the extent to which the Common Market discriminates against nonmembers; most would certainly agree that the Common Agricultural Policy does discriminate against nonmembers. It is difficult to determine, however, the impact on nonmembers of the EU's barriers to trade in the areas of services and manufactures. This is because the pattern of European trade may be due to geographical propinquity rather than discrimination against nonmembers. In an extensive analysis of the subject, economist Jeffrey Frankel sought to resolve this matter and concluded that, as the European Common Market has enlarged, the external tariff has had a moderate but increasingly negative impact on imports from nonmembers.[54] Other economists, however, believe that the EU conciously discriminates. No concensus exists among economists on the impact of the EU on the trading system.

Whatever the trade consequences of the EU thus far, the long-term prospects for an open Europe are not promising. Despite efforts to reform the Common Agricultural Policy, it is doubtful that the European market will be thrown open any time soon; this issue is particularly important to the United States. And the fact that the EU has been expanding its economic sphere of influence raises additional problems for nonmembers. The European plan (Agenda 2000) to admit a number of East European nations to the EU could become a step to a more closed European bloc. The EU already has special economic pacts with former European colonies in Africa and has established bilateral trading arrangements with other countries, such as Turkey. Furthermore, it is negotiating trade agreements with many other regions, including countries bordering the Mediterranean, Mercosur and East Asia. It is unlikely that this emerging hub-and-spoke system of economic linkages will become a stepping-stone to a more open world economy.

Resolution of a number of the issues confronting Europeans in the late 1990s could have a major impact on trade policy. The fate of the European welfare system, for example, is extremely important. Although the crisis of the European welfare state is due primarily to domestic causes, increased trade competition has exacerbated its problems, and economic openness and globalization have received much of the blame. Many European industries view themselves as caught between the high-tech firms of the American and the Japanese economies on one side and the low-wage producers of East Asia and other rapidly industrializing economies on the other. An open European economy would increase the impact of these problems and have serious implications for the welfare state. Although the generous, or overly generous, social welfare programs of continental Europe have been a major factor in maintaining social peace since the end of World War II, accompanying welfare costs have risen dramatically throughout the period and are expected to rise even more precipitously due to the aging of the population. These welfare programs and the domestic consensus that they have mirrored and supported were important factors in converting Europeans to accept trade liberalization at the end of the war; weakening of the programs could easily trigger a protectionist reaction.

Unless the European welfare state is reformed, its high costs will make opening the single market to non-European competitors extremely difficult, especially given the high level of unemployment throughout Western Europe. Many Europeans believe that their governments will eventually have to choose either to reduce significantly the costs of the welfare state and its burdens on industry or protect high-cost European industry from foreign competition. The problems associated with the European welfare state and with high unemployment are being greatly aggravated by economic integration. Inevitably, the highly fragmented industrial structure of Western Europe will have to experience a painful process of consolidation, rationalization, and "downsizing" similar to that experienced by American industry in the 1980s and 1990s. The West European automobile market, for example, cannot possibly support the large number of firms that have survived into the 1990s only with the help of large state subsidies or protected national markets. In automobile manufacture and other sectors, mergers and buyouts have already increased and are transforming the European industrial landscape. And as industries are rationalized, the burden on European welfare programs will necessarily increase.

Rationalization and restructuring of economic activities within Western Europe could pose another serious challenge for an open Europe. The elimination of political boundaries will inevitably lead to a considerable relocation and reorganization of economic activities within the single market. The most noteworthy example is the European automobile industry, with its considerable overcapacity and technological lag as compared with their American and especially their Japanese rivals. Indeed, one major motive for the single market is to forge a European industrial structure that will produce economies of scale, especially in high-tech industries. European industry will have to become more highly concentrated. Moreover, the EU will have a strong incentive to increase Europe's international competitiveness through protecting firms and enabling them to achieve economies of scale. However, the eventual location of these concentrations of industry is unclear. On the one hand, concentration of demand and other factors might attract economic activities to the core economies of northern Europe. On the other, lower labor and other costs might attract industry to the peripheral regions of southern Europe. Whatever the outcome of this potentially massive restructuring process, dislocation will occur in certain regions, and European adjustment policies, required to decrease or at least retard the impact on those who are harmed, will certainly also stimulate protectionist pressures.

The issue of a closed or an open Europe is also closely linked to the "enlargement" issue. The former communist countries of central and eastern Europe, especially Poland, the Czech Republic, and Hungary, are rapidly being integrated into the EU, principally through German FDI. These countries and their relatively highly skilled but low-wage labor force were very attractive to German industry after its loss of international competitiveness due to elevated labor costs and the burdens of German reunification. A substantial portion of the increased output from Eastern Europe is already exported to Western Europe. It is also extremely significant that West Europeans have demanded and received preferential treatment for their own exports to Eastern Europe. Extension of the Common Agricultural Policy to Eastern Europe would probably further increase protectionism throughout Europe in the agricultural sector.

The EU's unresolved and serious economic problems have led many knowledgeable observers to predict that the EU will be more closed than open in its commercial and other economic policies. EU nations will be very tempted, some believe, to solve their welfare, restructuring, and other problems by retreating behind trade barriers and perhaps even investment barriers as well. In theory, of course, Europeans could design the single market and their economic policies in ways that would lessen the impact of integration by compensating losers without sacrificing the interests of outsiders. Tax, competition, and other policies could be used to guarantee satisfaction of the interests of both members and nonmembers. Indeed, the European Union already has the interestingly named "cohesion fund" that transfers substantial resources to the southern periphery. Nevertheless, it is undeniable that there are formidable political obstacles to be overcome to safeguard the interests of both nonmembers and members, and that the economic costs of working to achieve that goal will be extremely high. It is possible and even likely that the effort to achieve European economic unification will sacrifice the interests of nonmembers in order to achieve internal cohesion. At the least, a Europe devoting its energies to economic and political unification is unlikely to assume the lead in promoting multilateral trade initiatives. Nevertheless, Sir Leon Brittan, the EU's leading trade official, has advocated both a Transatlantic Trade Agreement and a Millennium Round of WTO negotiations. Unfortunately, to date the Clinton Administration has made no concerted effort to pursue this possibility.

For the Monetary System

The implications of the euro for the dollar and the international economy more generally have been the objects of considerable interest and disagreement among public officials, economists, and political pundits on both sides of the Atlantic and in other parts of the globe. The most important questions are whether or not the euro will displace the dollar as the world's principal currency, what the consequences for the United States would be if that happened, and how the euro will affect the functioning and management of the international monetary and economic system. The large number of economic and political unknowns surrounding the euro make it impossible to provide any conclusive answers to these and other relevant questions. Nevertheless, these issues are of such moment for the future of the global economy that they must be addressed even if only tentatively.

EURO VS. DOLLAR: DISPLACEMENT OR COMPETITION?

Somewhere between 40 and 60 percent of international financial transactions are in dollars. The dollar has also been the world's principal reserve currency; in 1996, the dollar accounted for approximately two thirds of the world's foreign exchange reserves. Today, the question of whether or not the euro will replace the international role of the dollar as a transaction and reserve currency is extremely important, particularly for the United States and its financial community.

It is almost an act of faith in Western Europe that the size of Euroland means that the euro will significantly replace the dollar as the world's principal international currency. In early 1999, the position taken by the Clinton Administration (that is, by Treasury's Robert Rubin and Lawrence Summer) and most American economists, on the other hand, has been that the euro is highly unlikely to displace the dollar.[55] Moreover, if this shift from the dollar to the euro were to occur, it would happen very slowly over a lengthy period, thus giving the United States sufficient time to make the necessary adjustments, such as eliminating its huge trade/payments deficit. According to Summers, the continuing international role of the dollar will depend more on the strength of the American economy than on anything else. In addition, the importance of the dollar to international financial markets will be determined primarily by the international competitiveness of the American financial system. Moreover, the euro will replace the dollar in international financial transactions only if the EU creates an integrated and efficient financial market. Many doubt that this will happen for some time. Thus, American officials and economists tend to discount the possibility that the international reign of the dollar will be undermined by the euro.

POSSIBLE ECONOMIC CONSEQUENCES

Assuming that the euro were to displace the dollar, public officials, economists, and commentators in the United States and Western Europe have debated the consequences of such a shift. Displacement of the dollar by the euro would certainly affect the interests of many Americans and West Europeans, but the economic and political consequences of such a development would not necessarily be important. Yet, as noted earlier, many Europeans believe that such a change would entail a major shift in the international balance of economic and political power. Some Americans share this opinion and regard overthrow of the dollar with great misgivings. A number of frightening scenarios have been set forth depicting the United States without an all-powerful dollar as a potential victim of the manipulations of monetary affairs by West Europeans. These depictions of a powerful Europe and a weakened United States are certainly considerably exaggerated.

If the euro were to replace the dollar as the world's key currency, there would be important implications for both private American financial interests and the federal government. The success of the euro could have a negative impact on American banks and financial institutions. A large volume of transactions in a particular currency leads to economies of scale and lower transaction costs. The larger the volume of currency transactions in a particular country's currency, the greater the profits and competitiveness enjoyed by the banks and financial institutions of that country. If the euro were to replace the dollar as a reserve or transaction currency, the benefits of scale and lower transaction costs would be transferred from American to European financial interests. By one estimate, the portfolio switch from the dollar to the euro could be as large as $1 trillion. A threat that the euro would displace the dollar could trigger a serious conflict between the European Union and the United States. If a struggle between the dollar and the euro were to erupt in a similar way to the earlier struggle in the 1920s and 1930s between the dollar and sterling, such a transatlantic conflict would carry considerable political costs.

The international role of the dollar has conferred a number of concrete economic and political benefits on the United States that it would forfeit if the dollar were to lose its status as the world's key currency. The international demand for dollars has meant that the United States has been able to finance its huge and continuing trade/payments deficit since the early 1980s at a minimal cost. In effect, the United States government has been able to assume that other countries would automatically finance the huge American international payments deficit because others, needing dollars to conduct their international business, did not demand high interest rates. Moreover, the United States has been able to borrow in its own currency and thus avoid exchange-rate risks. Most of the dollars in circulation are overseas in the hands of non-Americans; this so-called "dollar overhang" of about $265 billion is the equivalent of an interest-free loan to the United States estimated to be worth about $13 billion in saved interest payments. Furthermore, American prestige is enhanced by the international role of the dollar. However, most American officials and economists believe that loss of the dollar's special status would not significantly harm the United States. Indeed, the political gains from creation of a strong united Europe would achieve a major goal of U.S. policy throughout the postwar period.

LIKELY POLITICAL CONSEQUENCES

Many West European leaders believe that the euro will greatly strengthen their political position vis-à-vis the United States in international negotiations; many Americans fear that the euro will have negative consequences for American security and the international standing of the United States. Both conjectures are likely to be proved wrong. Although a united Europe will be a more powerful actor on the world scene than it is at present, the euro by itself will not greatly change the power balance between the United States and Western Europe. The euro could decrease the nearly automatic financing of the American balance-of-payments deficit and limit the considerable financial freedom the United States has had in pursuit of its economic and foreign policies. Such a loss would probably not be significant. However, the impact of the euro on the yen and Japan could be quite important. The euro could undercut Japan's ambition to have the yen play a much larger role as an international currency. In a global economy composed of three major currencies, the Japanese fear that the yen could be the "odd man out." This concern has stimulated Japan to propose a global "currency triumvirate" of the dollar, the euro, and the yen, to be managed by the three major economic powers.

Conclusion

Regardless of the rhetoric of "one Europe," Western Europe at the opening of the twenty-first century continues to be characterized by individual nation-states and rival nationalities attentive mainly to their own economic and political interests. Despite the impressive goals achieved by postwar efforts to create European political and economic unity, individual European nations remain unwilling to sacrifice economic autonomy and political independence to a truly unified European economy and a European polity capable of speaking with one voice in international affairs. While three decades of generally successful efforts to create a united Europe should not be belittled, "Europe" continues to be primarily a geographic expression. Yet, a more united Europe of some kind is surely emerging; nations have gone too far to go backward, and powerful interests favor going forward. Nevertheless, many years and perhaps decades will be required to determine how far integration will proceed, the direction in which it will move, and the effects it will have on both Europe and the rest of the world.

Although there is good cause to have reservations about the ultimate prospects for European integration, it is undeniable that the economic importance of Western Europe in the world economy has been restored since it reached its nadir in the early postwar period. Greater economic unity has resulted from the single market and the overall movement toward continental unity. In 1945, European economies were not only shattered, but were oriented toward their overseas colonies. By the 1980s, they were participating as a unified entity in the GATT and elsewhere, with European Community membership having grown from its original six to fifteen. Whether or not the projected further enlargement of the EU actually takes place, Central and Eastern Europe are becoming increasingly integrated with the EU through various formal agreements and market forces. The "old world" in its new regionalized guise will certainly be an important player in the future world economy.

CHAPTER EIGHT

American Economic Strategy

IN THE MID-1980s, American policy toward the international economy changed in important ways. Since the end of World War II, the United States had supported the cause of an open and integrated international economy. Motivated by both economic and political reasons, American leaders believed that an open world was in the interest of the United States; they also believed that an integrated international economy (excluding, of course, the Soviet bloc) would strengthen allied unity. Beginning with the Reagan Administration (1981–1989), the United States undertook a much more parochial and nationalistic foreign economic policy that entailed a change from a multilateral trade policy to a multitrack policy. In earlier years, following the multilateral policy, the United States had made an unqualified commitment to an open and nondiscriminatory trading system, to be achieved through multilateral negotiations in the General Agreement on Tariffs and Trade (GATT). With the multitrack approach, a variety of policies (unilateral, regional, and multilateral) have been utilized to achieve the nation's economic and political objectives. This historic shift occurred because of growing concerns over American industrial decline, the trade deficit with Japan that had mounted throughout the 1980s, and the "deepening" regionalization in Western Europe. However, an erosion of public support for trade liberalization and the detrimental consequences of President Reagan's economic counterrevolution were also very important in this radical shift in American economic policy.

REAGAN'S ECONOMIC COUNTERREVOLUTION

Believing that he had a mandate to reenergize the American economy, Ronald Reagan assumed the presidency of the United States in January 1981. The new President diagnosed the causes of America's economic problems as the large size of the federal government, an excessively high level of taxation, and an overburdening welfare state that had weakened both private initiative and the free market. Reagan and other economic conservatives believed that the heavy hand of the federal government was destroying the incentive to work, save, and invest. The solution to these problems, they asserted, was to reduce the size of the federal government, drastically lower taxes, and let markets work. Under the banner of a novel economic theory—"supply-side" economics—which promised more growth with less government, the Reagan Administration, supported by a Democratic Congress, cut American federal income taxes significantly in 1981.

Unfortunately, the President and Congress failed to simultaneously reduce the overall expenditures of the government, and they even substantially increased military expenditures. This combination of a large tax cut with a continuing high level of federal expenditures produced a massive stimulus to the American economy and also to much of the world economy. From the fall of 1982 to the collapse of the stock market in October 1987, the American and other economies enjoyed the boom of the "Reagan economic miracle." It soon became evident, however, that the dramatic shift in American fiscal policy had created a burdensome legacy of "twin deficits" (budget and trade deficits) that would continue to distort the American and the world economies in the 1980s and 1990s.

Anticipating the huge federal budget deficit and the consequent need to finance the resulting debt, American and global financial markets reacted strongly. American interest rates rose dramatically, and this resulted in a large capital inflow. Foreign investors' demands for dollars raised the value of the dollar, and with its substantial appreciation, American exports dropped precipitously while American imports rose sharply. As revealed by figure 8.1, the U.S. trade and international payments balance deteriorated alarmingly, and by the mid-1980s the annual trade deficit reached the then unbelievable figure of approximately $170 billion; the American trade deficit with Japan was a substantial portion of its overall deficit, thus exacerbating economic friction with that country. The United States, needing to borrow heavily from abroad to finance its budget deficit, initially borrowed primarily from Japan. In the mid-1980s this heavy foreign borrowing transformed the United

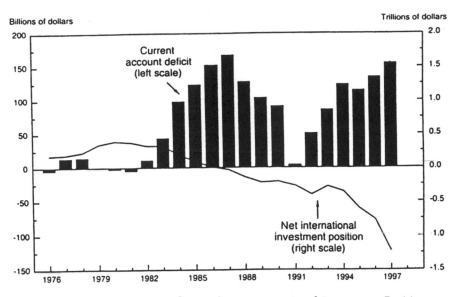

Fig.8.1. Current Account Deficit and Net International Investment Position. As the United States started to run large current account deficits in the early 1980s, the net investment position declined. *Note*: Net investment position at current cost. *Source*: U.S. Council of Economic Advisors.

States from the world's largest creditor nation to its outstanding debtor nation. During this same period, Japan supplanted the United States as the world's foremost creditor nation and also displaced West Germany as America's most important economic partner.

These developments were of enormous economic benefit to American consumers, the U.S. financial community, and those other countries exporting to the United States, especially West Germany, Japan, and the emerging markets of East Asia. However, the high value of the dollar proved disastrous for large sections of American industry. While other economies prospered as they shifted to an aggressive strategy of export-led growth, American industry lost markets in the United States itself and also around the world. As the nation's trade deficit persisted, more and more Americans began to become concerned over loss of market share, "deindustrialization" of the economy, and loss of jobs. Although the Reagan counterrevolution and the triumph of the supply-siders had indeed resulted in a systematic effort to deal with the problem of America's relative economic decline, many believe that the Administration's reckless fiscal policies not only actually accelerated that decline but also gave rise to powerful protectionist forces.

SHIFT TO AN ACTIVIST EXCHANGE RATE POLICY

Initially, the Reagan Administration was indifferent to rising concerns about the overvalued and volatile dollar. The high dollar, Americans were told, was a sign of economic strength. Complaints from foreign governments that erratic dollar fluctuations were causing havoc in overseas markets were summarily dismissed. As Under Secretary of the Treasury Beryl Sprinkel said, "It may be our dollar, but it is their problem." This policy of "benign neglect," however, changed radically in the mid-1980s with the mounting trade deficit and intensified protectionist sentiments in the Congress. In response to these developments, the Reagan Administration began to put pressure on America's trading partners to appreciate their currencies in order to decrease their trade surplus with the United States. During the second Reagan Administration, Secretary of the Treasury Baker shifted American foreign economic policy in order to reduce the trade deficit. The principal target of renewed American efforts to achieve "international policy coordination" was again Japan, whose trade and payments surpluses with the United States and the rest of the world were enormous.

As the dollar had approximately doubled in value against the Japanese yen and other currencies between 1980 and 1985, the Reagan Administration wanted a substantial appreciation of those foreign currencies, especially the yen. American pressures on its trading partners led to the Plaza Conference (September 22, 1985), at which the United States in effect forced the Japanese to carry out a substantial and painful appreciation of the yen. Although by the time of the Conference, the value of the dollar had already declined considerably from its highest point, the United States wanted to push it down even further. In exchange for Japanese commitment to appreciate the yen, the United States agreed to reduce its huge federal budget deficit. The subsequent appreciation of the yen (*endaka*) by approximately 30 percent had a profound impact on the Japanese economy and economic policy. The

Ministry of Finance began to pursue a loose monetary policy and increased the money supply to counter the contracting effects of appreciation; the result was Japan's "bubble economy" and the financial crisis of the early 1990s, a crisis from which the Japanese economy had not yet recovered by early 1999. *Endaka* also meant a considerable decrease in the competitiveness of Japanese industry, and this in turn resulted in a major reorientation of Japanese foreign economic policy toward Pacific Asia. Yet, appreciation of the yen did not have the desired effect on the American trade deficit, in part because the United States did not fulfill its commitment to eliminate the huge federal budget deficit.

The Plaza Agreement failed to end the bickering over exchange rates among the major economic powers. By early 1987, the dollar had dropped considerably from its high point in 1985. Some U.S. officials wanted it to fall even further to benefit American exports, while Japan and other major exporters wanted to stabilize its value. To resolve differences over monetary issues, the major economic powers convened an international conference at the Louvre in Paris in February 1987 to determine a range of exchange-rate values acceptable to all. At that conference, the powers agreed to stabilize the dollar within unpublished target zones (unpublished in order to discourage currency speculation) and to promote monetary stability. This effort required substantial dollar purchases by the German and Japanese central banks, and this produced negative consequences for both economies. Once again, however, the major economies failed to implement supportive macroeconomic policies that might have resolved their monetary difficulties. The United States did not reduce its budget deficit sufficiently, and West Germany and Japan did not adequately stimulate their economies.

By October of that same year the Louvre Agreement had begun to break down. Secretary Baker, wanting coordinated action to stabilize exchange rates, publicly criticized the Bundesbank for a small increase in interest rates and declared that the German action was contrary to the Louvre Accord. The Bundesbank deeply resented Baker's criticism and, in effect, told the American Secretary of the Treasury to "go to hell." This obvious failure of policy cooperation roiled the markets and was the precipitating factor in the October 1987 stock market crash. After this fiasco, financial officials became more cautious in their statements about exchange rates. In early 1991, the central banks of the major economies quietly began to coordinate their market interventions in order to restrict exchange-rate fluctuations and to keep currencies within an agreed-upon band. Thus was born the reference range international monetary regime.

FROM MULTILATERAL TO MULTITRACK

On September 23, 1985, the day after the Plaza Agreement, President Reagan criticized the "unfair" trading practices of other countries and announced a major shift in American trade policy. Like the Plaza Agreement, the purpose of this change was to reduce the American trade imbalance and thereby neutralize growing demands in the Congress for trade protection. The late 1970s and early 1980s had witnessed a surge of protectionist measures, the most important of which was the 1981 imposition of "voluntary export restraints" on Japanese automobile exports to the United States. Whereas these protectionist reactions to imports did not significantly affect America's overall commitment to multilateral trade liberalization, the new trade policy of the Reagan Administration did signal a major shift in America's dedication to a liberal trade regime. This new trade policy, which would be pursued more vigorously by the Bush Administration (1989–1993) and still more aggressively by the Clinton Administration, has been given a number of labels: aggressive unilateralism, GATT-plus, results-oriented, and managed trade. The term "multitrack" is more appropriate than the others because the policy shifted away from America's strong postwar commitment to an economic policy based exclusively on the principles of multilateralism and nondiscrimination (admittedly with frequent backsliding) to an intentional combination of multilateral, unilateral, and regional trade initiatives. These initiatives have been employed either to protect American markets or to increase access by American firms to foreign markets, especially in Japan and other East Asian nations.

Several motives lay behind this important and largely unanticipated shift from a multilateral to a multitrack trade policy. Despite Reagan Administration reassurances that everything was fine, pressures for trade protection had continued to gather force in the Congress and within important Republican constituencies as America's huge annual trade deficits persisted. The Administration reluctantly recognized that it could no longer ignore rising protectionist pressures. In addition, both the public and the Administration had become intensely concerned about deindustrialization and resentful that Japan seemed to be playing by different rules and perhaps even seeking to destroy one American high-tech industry after another. Japan, revisionists argued, was pursuing what business consultant Peter Drucker characterized as "adversarial" trade policies, in that it exported manufactured goods but did not import them from non-Japanese producers. As more and more critics of the Administration argued, deindustrialization of the American economy and erosion of American technological preeminence had to be stopped.

The multitrack trade policy has had several important components. One component has been a continuing, although considerably reduced, commitment to the multilateral trading regime, a commitment made manifest in the Reagan Administration's strong effort to launch a new round of GATT trade negotiations despite the opposition of the European Community. The resulting Uruguay Round, which required eight years of extremely tough negotiations to complete, reduced trade barriers and established the World Trade Organization (WTO). Another component of this trade strategy, variously labeled "aggressive unilateralism," managed trade, and "results-oriented trade," attempted to force other countries, especially Japan, to open their markets to American goods and FDI. Still another component was a historic shift toward North American continentalism, first in the form of the U.S.-Canada Free Trade Agreement and, subsequently, in the North American Free Trade Agreement (NAFTA).

Results-Oriented or Managed Trade Policy

Abandonment of America's postwar unqualified commitment to multilateralism and adoption of a commitment to a policy of results-oriented or managed trade was the most controversial component in the new multitrack trade policy. Japan, because of its huge trade surplus and its allegedly unfair behavior, was the principal target of this policy shift. For many years, the United States had made unilateral efforts to restrict

Japanese imports into the United States; the new policy complemented this protectionist effort as the United States increased pressure on Japan to open its markets to American imports. In the past the United States had forced Japan to accept voluntary export restraints (VERs); now the results-oriented trade policy could be characterized as voluntary import expansion. Although American-Japanese trade in the 1980s accounted for only a small percentage of total world trade, the bitter and continuing trade conflicts between the two largest economies threatened to disrupt the entire world economy and did place an indelible mark on the economic policies of both countries. The American shift to a multitrack trade policy and the "Asianization" of Japanese economic policy were both, at least in part, consequences of the economic clash between the two countries.

The first important step to open the Japanese market was the Market-Oriented, Sector Selective (MOSS) talks, begun in the mid-1980s. The United States implicitly threatened to increase trade barriers against Japanese exports unless Japan agreed to open several closed sectors of its economy to American business; this included telecommunications, microelectronics, medical equipment and pharmaceuticals, and forestry products. The most important issue in the negotiations was semiconductors (computer memory chips). Until the mid-1980s, when Japanese chip makers displaced American dominance in memory chips, the United States had possessed a substantial world lead in the manufacture of semiconductors. American chip makers charged that the Japanese were selling below production costs (dumping) and had a protected home market; furious over their loss of market share, producers began to pressure the government for "improved access" to the Japanese market. Many Americans believed that increased dependence on foreign producers of memory chips would constitute a security threat to the United States. This unfounded concern was supported by Shintaro Ishihara's book *The Japan That Can Say No* (1991), which in effect threatened to cease the export of chips to the United States.

Eventually, the United States prevailed over Japanese resistance and the Semiconductor Agreement was signed in the early autumn 1986; the agreement was to run for five years. Contrary to the GATT and to prior postwar American trade policy, the Agreement effectively cartelized the world market for a particular product. The European Community, furious over such a bilateral carving up of the market and the discriminatory nature of the Agreement, strongly opposed the United States on the issue, and a GATT panel eventually ruled against the United States. Also, by raising the price of chips, the Agreement harmed both American consumers and computer makers. Among the bizarre features of this complex negotiation was an American demand that the Japanese government, despite its strong opposition, agree to a market-sharing arrangement (which was, of course, illegal under GATT rules). In a "secret" side letter, the Japanese agreed that a 20 percent share of their market was a reasonable "target" for American industry. This concession was promptly leaked by the Reagan Administration. Whereas the Japanese considered the 20 percent goal a "reasonable target," the United States regarded it as a mandatory target. This difference became a source of still more intense American-Japanese hostility.

Although the Japanese subsequently claimed that they had met the quantitative target for the American share of the Japanese chip market, the United States disagreed, and in 1987, under the terms of Section 301 of the 1974 Trade Act, imposed punitive duties of $300 million on the Japanese. In 1991, the Agreement was renegotiated and the 20 percent target retained. Most American economists, critical of the Semiconductor Agreement as an example of "aggressive unilateralism," denounced the whole idea of managed trade. On the other hand, Laura Tyson, who served as the first chair of President Clinton's Council of Economic Advisors, defended the Agreement much to the dismay of many fellow economists. As Tyson wrote in her book *Who's Bashing Whom?* (1992), the pact was "a qualified success" because it stabilized America's share of the world market and may have laid the groundwork for the resurgence of Silicon Valley. Thus began the controversy among American economists over the U.S. movement toward managed trade.

In 1988, the United States had taken another major step in the direction of managed trade. In Section 301 of the 1974 Trade Act, Congress had authorized the United States Trade Representative (USTR) to take punitive actions (especially antidumping actions and imposition of countervailing duties) against any countries found to be unfair traders. In practice, Section 301 was most frequently used to force America's trading partners to accept VERs to avoid American retaliation. The Omnibus Trade and Competition Act (1988) extended the application of Section 301 to a much larger number of allegedly unfair traders. This modification, later known as "Super 301," instructed the USTR to publish an annual list of unfair traders and to negotiate, with the countries involved, ways to eliminate the offending behavior. If a country charged with unfair trading behavior failed to comply with American demands, the USTR would be permitted to take retaliatory measures against the offender's imports into the United States. When the USTR dutifully found many countries to be guilty, a number of smaller countries capitulated before publication of the list; the egregious sins of the EEC in such areas as agricultural policy, on the other hand, were conveniently overlooked. Although Japan, Brazil, and India were all eventually singled out as unfair traders, it was obvious that the principal target of Super 301 was Japan.

The next important effort was the 1989 Structural Impediments Initiative (SII). Like the MOSS talks, the purpose of SII was to "identify and solve structural problems in both countries that stand as impediments to trade and balance of payments adjustment." At least in principle, SII was an improvement over MOSS because the imperfections of both countries were to be examined. The SII also widened the scope of the negotiations as it dealt explicitly with domestic economic issues. Indeed, the savings rates of both Japan and the United States were placed on the table for discussion. In practice, however, the SII talks proved to be another attempt by the United States to change Japanese economic policies and even Japanese private business practices. Japan naturally regarded American demands as improper and misplaced. In their view, the source of the trade/payments imbalance between the two countries lay in American macroeconomic policy and in the exceedingly low U.S. savings rate. The Bush Administration was reluctant to acknowledge these points and even more reluctant to raise taxes or eliminate popular domestic programs. In other words, the United States laid the blame for the American-Japanese trade conflict solely on Japanese policies and structural features of the Japanese economy; the Japanese were obviously unwilling to accept this interpretation of the problem. After long and acrimonious negotiations, the talks produced minimal results.

By the late 1980s, the American economy was in a recession. The supply-side economic policies of the Reagan Administration not only had devastated the American trade balance but had also failed to raise the rate of national savings and domestic investment. Indeed, both the rates of savings and domestic investment had declined, and the national debt had reached unprecedented heights. Meanwhile, the Japanese national savings rate remained at approximately 20 percent of GNP, and some have even estimated that it became as high as 30 percent. The decrease in American savings was partially balanced by increased foreign borrowing; by the end of the Reagan years, American debt to other countries had increased from approximately $1 trillion to $4 trillion. As these lines are written, the foreign debt of the United States is continuing to rise.

The relative economic decline of the United States from the foremost creditor to the foremost debtor nation and concerns over deindustrialization became major political concerns. These worries were crystallized by Paul Kennedy's best-selling book, *The Rise and Decline of the Great Powers* (1987). That book, arguing that the United States had commenced an inevitable decline (like imperial Spain in the seventeenth century and Great Britain in the early twentieth century), was fortuitously published at the time of the October 1987 stock market crash. Even though the book failed to discuss such underlying problems as the decline in productivity growth and the significant drop in national savings, it had an enormous impact on American thinking. More and more Americans realized that Reaganomics was not succeeding. As Japanese imports increased and American workers lost their jobs, they knew that something was quite wrong with the economy.

President Reagan's successor, George Bush, made only sporadic efforts to deal with the troubled legacy of what he had once described as Reagan's supply-side "voodoo" economics. Betraying his campaign promise not to raise taxes, he reached a tax increase/spending reduction agreement with the Democratic Congress and thus began gradual elimination of the federal budget deficit. This was a necessary and courageous move, but it was also a significant factor in Bush's defeat in 1992 by William Clinton. Basking in his victory over Saddam Hussein, President Bush ignored the troubles of the economy and scoffed at what he called the "vision thing." Clinton (who campaigned on promises to lower taxes, reduce the budget deficit, and get the economy moving again) claimed that he did have a vision for American economic renewal, and his campaign quip "It's the economy, stupid!" carried the day for the Arkansas governor. Like Reagan, Clinton entered office with a grand strategy and the proclaimed objective of achieving a national consensus that would move the country toward reform and rejuvenation.

The Uruguay Round and World Trade Organization (WTO)

In the early 1980s when the Reagan Administration launched what is now known as the Uruguay Round of GATT negotiations, American support for free trade had been undermined by the country's huge trade deficit and by intensified Japanese and East Asian trade competition. The Administration was interested in using the Uruguay Round to forge a new domestic coalition favoring further trade liberalization. The agenda, set to a large degree by the United States, was intended to appeal to American agriculture, to the expanding U.S. service industries, particularly in the financial community, and to those high-tech and other sectors concerned about protecting intellectual property rights; on the whole, these areas had not previously been covered by the GATT. Their inclusion in the American proposal for the new negotiations reflected the shift in the U.S. economy (and in that of other industrialized nations) from a traditional manufacturing-based economy to a high-tech and service-based economy. The scope of the Round was extraordinarily ambitious; in addition to lowering trade barriers, it was expected to formulate new rules to govern such issues as export subsidies, dispute settlement procedures, and trade in textiles. And indeed, during eight years of intense and frequently acrimonious negotiations, the Uruguay Round did resolve a number of trade issues and also created the WTO.

The United States initiated the Uruguay Round negotiations despite strong opposition from the Europeans and from many LDCs. Europeans were defensive of their agricultural policies, and their attention was concentrated on the economic and political unification of the European Community. The LDCs were very suspicious because services, foreign direct investment, and intellectual property rights were to be included on the agenda. However, both the Europeans and the LDCs, fearing that the United States would retreat into protectionism, reluctantly decided to follow the American lead. They hoped that an improved multilateral dispute-settlement mechanism and other reforms would reduce the growing American tendency toward trade unilateralism. The United States did have moderate support from Japan and the Cairns group of agricultural exporters, all of whom expected to benefit from the negotiations.

After considerable vacillation, the Clinton Administration decided to support ratification of the Final Act of the Uruguay Round signed by 109 nations in Marrakesh, Morocco, on April 15, 1994. This important agreement, which came into force on January 1, 1995, created the World Trade Organization (WTO) that incorporated and expanded the GATT trade regime. As John Jackson (one of the world's leading experts on trade law) has commented, the Uruguay Round negotiations had undoubtedly been the most extensive ever carried out by any international organization. (The Agreement was immense; it contained 22,000 pages and weighed 385 pounds!) Although the Agreement failed to reach many of the objectives the United States had desired, it was an impressive achievement.

North American Free Trade Agreement

The 1994 creation of the North American Free Trade Agreement (NAFTA), comprising the United States, Canada, and Mexico, was another manifestation of the U.S. move away from multilateralism to a multitrack foreign economic policy. The United States supported NAFTA, at least initially, to increase its bargaining leverage vis-à-vis the European Union; later, North American regionalism became an end in itself. NAFTA also entailed a reversal of Canada's and Mexico's historic policies of maintaining distance from their giant (and not always congenial) neighbor. Although these radical changes grew from economic roots, political factors were important in the decisions of all three countries.

The first move toward North American regionalism had been the 1988 United States–Canada Free Trade Agreement (FTA). During the postwar period, powerful market forces had transformed the American and Canadian economies and intensified their economic linkages. Increasing transborder trade and investment became particularly important in the Canadian economy. The FTA emerged from the resultant reorientation of Canada's historic economic policy and its political stance toward its large southern neighbor. From the late nineteenth century onward, Canada had pursued a "National Policy" whose explicit purpose was to build an independent Canadian industrial base and national economy behind high tariff walls, a policy that did not produce all the intended results. Instead, the Canadian tariff actually encouraged American firms to invest heavily in Canada and to build a branch-plant economy to serve the small Canadian market; indeed, over 80 percent of FDI in Canada has been American. The most notable example is the automobile sector, which became closely integrated across the border after the 1965 United States–Canadian Automobile Pact.

Beginning with the auto pact and the linking of the American and Canadian dollars in the 1980s, economic integration of the two economies accelerated rapidly. Canadian FDI in the American economy grew significantly. By 1985, over 70 percent of Canada's exports went to the United States, and over 70 percent of its imports came from the United States. Furthermore, nearly 50 percent of these exports and imports have involved intrafirm transfers by American and Canadian multinational corporations. Thus, both trade and FDI have linked the American and Canadian economies closely together.

The United States wanted the Free Trade Agreement (FTA) in part to stem the surge in U.S. protectionism caused by America's burgeoning trade deficit. It also wanted to strengthen the emerging free-trade coalition of service industries, high-tech firms, and multinational corporations, as well as to increase pressure on other countries, especially in Western Europe, to begin the Uruguay Round of trade negotiations. The FTA (in conjunction with an American trade agreement with Israel and the subsequent upgrading of APEC by the Clinton Administration) constituted "strategic threats" or warnings to others that the United States possessed options other than the Uruguay Round. This threat appeared to have succeeded when that Round commenced in September 1986 and was successfully negotiated.

The United States–Canada Free Trade Agreement included a number of important ingredients that would accelerate the forces for the economic integration of the two economies. In addition to lowering overall tariffs and resolving investment-related issues, it contained important new procedures for resolving economic disputes. These moves toward greater market interdependence were significant but limited, and the Agreement failed to deal adequately with the heavily protected areas of steel, textiles, and agriculture. At Canada's insistence, the Agreement excluded cultural matters as well. Nevertheless, this agreement greatly expanded integration of services and industrial production on a North American regional basis and paved the way for NAFTA.

The Canadian decision to initiate discussions on NAFTA was part of a general change in economic ideology that included retrenchment of the welfare state and reduction of the high tariffs and other restrictions on foreign (i.e., American) direct investment. Having become a major industrial power in its own right, Canada became confident enough to join a regional arrangement. It had also become very concerned over the rise in protectionist sentiment in the United States and over the European Community's decision to accelerate creation of a single market. Moreover, Canadians wanted a quasi-judicial dispute settlement procedure established that would protect Canadian producers against the increasingly politicized and arbitrary decisions of American trade officials. Canadians also hoped to increase their competitiveness by gaining secure access to the huge American market and thereby providing Canadian firms with economies of scale.

Although some critics have argued that the North American Free Trade Agreement (NAFTA) originated in an American effort to dominate and economically conquer its neighbors, it was Mexico that initiated the negotiations that produced NAFTA. For economic and political reasons of their own, the United States and Canada responded favorably to the Mexican initiative. The negotiations, begun in 1991 and completed by a treaty signed in 1993, constituted a historic development. North American continentalism ranks well behind the movement toward European economic and political unification in its scope and ambition, yet NAFTA's significance for the three countries involved, and potentially for the larger world economy, is nevertheless considerable. Most important, NAFTA signaled reversal of America's strong opposition to economic regionalism.

The Mexican decision to propose NAFTA involved many of the same motives that had led to the earlier U.S.-Canadian Agreement. The American and Mexican economies had also become closely linked through trade and American investment in Mexico. At the time of the Agreement, 70 percent of Mexico's trade was with the United States, and over 60 percent of the FDI in Mexico came from American firms. In fact, American and other MNCs had constructed a huge industrial zone (*maquiladora*) for component production and assembly along the Mexican side of the Rio Grande.

Much more was at stake for Mexico. Led by American-trained economists and technocrats, Mexico in the 1980s had undertaken an ambitious program of economic and political reforms. These market-oriented reforms, like similar reforms in other Latin American countries, had been stimulated by LDC debt crises in the early 1980s and the realization that an import-substitution strategy had failed. Joining NAFTA, Mexican leaders believed, would "lock in" their liberalization reforms and convince foreign investors that the Mexican government would not backtrack on its commitments to deregulate and to open the Mexican economy to trade and foreign investment. Moreover, like Canada, Mexico had previously suffered from American protectionism and desired some guarantee that such behavior would cease. Also like Canada, Mexico feared negative consequences from the unification of the European Union and its enlargement to include the economies of Eastern Europe. The NAFTA, on the other hand, would give Mexican-based firms privileged access to the American market and would also encourage Japanese and other multinational firms to invest in Mexico.

The American decision to participate in the NAFTA negotiations was strongly influenced by political motives, including the need to resolve the issue of illegal Mexican immigration into the United States. Stated crudely, the United States was motivated by a very simple calculus: it had to accept either an ever-increasing flow of illegal Mexican immigrants or a greater number of manufactured goods from Mexico. Choosing the latter meant that the United States would help accelerate the industrialization of the poor and overpopulated Mexican economy.

Many believed that, in addition, a stable and prosperous Mexico would become a better partner in the battle against drugs. These political motives were substantially reinforced by domestic regional economic and political interests, notably in Texas, and by the growing interest of many American businesses in greater access not only to the traditionally closed but growing Mexican market but also to Mexico's huge supply of inexpensive labor.

Domestic interest groups in all three countries played important roles in formulating the Agreement. Many recognized that NAFTA (like all regional trade agreements) would have significant distributional consequences for economic interests in all the economies and would create losers as well as winners. One important conflict centered on the "rules of origin"; the textile and automobile industrial sectors became greatly involved in the political struggle over those rules. Because NAFTA would not establish any common external tariff similar to that of the European Common Market, it was particularly important to devise rules to govern importation of goods from nonmember countries into the North American market; considerable controversy centered on the nature of these rules. While the American automobile industry very much wanted to open the Mexican market to its own products, it did not want Mexico to become an export platform for Japanese or Korean producers. Mexico, on the other hand, wanted to protect its local auto parts industry and also to encourage foreign investment by Japanese and other multinationals. Canadian producers worried that overly restrictive rules of origin would harm them. The American Big Three achieved many of their objectives, and Mexican and Canadian interests received some safeguards.

CONFLICT OVER NAFTA RATIFICATION

NAFTA generated an intense and bitter debate both in Mexico and the United States. Although this debate focused on the terms of the Agreement itself, there were powerful reactions in both countries to market liberalization and to economic globalization in general. Mexicans opposed to NAFTA objected to the dangers of unbridled capitalism and the increased likelihood that American imperialism would threaten Mexican independence. American opponents, led by Ross Perot, feared that the agreement would inevitably lead to the "Mexicanization" of the

American standard of living. In this battle, Perot was joined by a surprising coalition between organized labor and environmental organizations, both of which were concerned about the consequences of integrating one of the most economically advanced and democratic countries in the world with a low-wage, underdeveloped, and, in their opinion, nondemocratic country. Perot predicted that the Agreement would create a huge "sucking sound" as American firms moved their production south of the border to take advantage of Mexico's cheap labor and lax environmental standards; this would then result in the loss of hundreds of thousands of American jobs and a precipitous drop in wages. NAFTA's American detractors never quite explained how Mexico, an economy whose GNP in 1993 was less than 5 percent of the American GNP and whose exports to the United States were very small, could cause such havoc in the American economy.

The Clinton Administration initially vacillated in its responses to these hostile criticisms of the Treaty, but eventually supported the Treaty and claimed that the Agreement would create hundreds of thousands of new jobs for Americans. The Agreement, said one Administration spokesperson, would create "jobs, jobs, jobs." The Administration attempted to mollify critics by forcing Mexico to accept two side-accords to the Treaty that dealt with labor standards and environmental protection, but attacks on NAFTA continued. Persistent opposition from American labor, environmentalists, and others has been due not only to lax enforcement of the side agreements on labor and environmental standards, but also to concerns about the larger issue of economic globalization and its allegedly negative consequences for jobs, wages, and the environment. NAFTA's opponents believe that globalization works to the disadvantage of American workers because it increases importing of products and exporting of jobs.

EFFECTS OF NAFTA

The primary purpose of the Treaty was to liberalize trade and facilitate foreign direct investment throughout the North American continent. The Agreement contained provisions for a ten-year phaseout of most trade barriers on industrial goods; the relevant sectors included automobiles, auto parts, and textiles. Barriers on most agricultural goods were to be eliminated over a fifteen-year period. As Mexico at the beginning of the negotiations had higher trade barriers than the United States, these trade provisions benefited the United States more than they did Mexico. Much more controversial was the removal of barriers to FDI; firms were to be guaranteed national treatment, and performance requirements were to be eliminated. The Agreement also included provisions to liberalize financial, telecommunications, and other service markets. A dispute mechanism and safeguards for intellectual property rights were established.

With the Agreement, the regionalization of services and production has accelerated in a number of key sectors. For example, the flow of American-made components to Mexico, assembly of the finished product in Mexico, and marketing of the completed product in the United States and elsewhere have given a considerable stimulus to the regionalization of production, especially in automobiles, electronics, and textiles. The increased effort to integrate the continent physically through development of cross-border transportation systems is a notable example of this restructuring of the continental economy. Historically, the Canadian railway system has run east and west in order to unify its economy and polity. However, since NAFTA was created, Canadian National Railway has purchased Illinois Central to create a north-south linkage, and some infrastructure is being built across the U.S.-Mexican border, although at a very deliberate pace. Other initiatives will eventually forge a North American transportation system, and that will lead to a more integrated North American continental market.

Efforts to make accurate assessments of the short-term economic consequences of the Agreement should be received with skepticism. Not only do economists admit they lack the necessary tools, but also a number of other developments have blurred NAFTA's impact on trade flows, employment, and other factors. In the years since NAFTA was approved, the economies of both Mexico and the United States have been affected by economic forces far more powerful than NAFTA itself; for example, the Mexican peso crisis beginning in December 1994 cost Mexico about one million jobs and resulted in a 25 percent fall in wages. At the same time, the United States enjoyed an economic boom that had nothing whatsoever to do with NAFTA. Although NAFTA critics point to the increased American trade deficit with Mexico, that is actually explained by the 1990s boom in the American economy.

Common sense suggests that the positive or the negative impact of the Mexican economy—which is less than a twentieth the size of the American economy—on the American economy would be negligible. Because the Mexican economy is so very small, NAFTA's impact there has been important; it has also been positive.

To a large degree, differences in macroeconomic performance account for what critics label NAFTA's negative impact on the American trade balance. Macroeconomic policies are the most important determinant of both employment and the overall economic welfare of a society. However, a trade agreement like NAFTA does have an impact on the distribution of jobs across industrial sectors and geographical regions; for example, NAFTA has certainly resulted in the loss of hundreds of jobs in the American garment industry, but new jobs have been created elsewhere in the economy. Overall, the Agreement has had only a small impact on American wages and employment.

NAFTA has speeded the industrialization of Mexico and has accelerated restructuring of the North American automobile industry. Since about 20 percent of the cost of production in the auto industry is labor-related and, in 1998, average salaries at unionized U.S. plants were about $16.75 an hour in contrast to the average wage of $8.60 per day in Mexico, Mexican manufacturing and American consumers have benefited from NAFTA. Japanese auto companies have also moved parts of their production for the North American market to Mexico. Auto parts produced at some 600 plants employing about 150,000 workers account for about 12 percent of Mexico's exports of manufactured goods. However, even though NAFTA has created a much improved environment in Mexico for American and other direct investment, no "great sucking sound" has yet been heard. In the first three years of NAFTA, total American FDI in Mexico significantly increased. Although this FDI is large for Mexico, it is less than 1 percent of the amount that Canada and the United States together have invested every year in plant and equipment. These investments have helped Mexico without significantly hurting the overall American economy.

In retrospect, NAFTA constituted a Pyrrhic victory and a serious defeat for further trade liberalization. The bitter fight over its ratification, and the reckless, ill-informed denunciations of the Agreement by Ross Perot, Patrick Buchanan, and others, poisoned the atmosphere with descriptions of the evils of globalization. The Clinton Administration failed to educate the public on what trade does and does not do when its spokesperson claimed that NAFTA would create "jobs, jobs, jobs." The Administration also made elaborate and as yet unfulfilled claims that NAFTA would create a dynamic and democratic Mexico that would be a strong economic and political partner of the United States. The bitter controversy over NAFTA turned labor, environmentalists, and many others against trade liberalization and became a major factor in the 1997 defeat of the proposed fast-track legislation. And for what? It is difficult to believe that North American regionalism benefited American consumers or the United States as a whole; whether it was more beneficial for Canada and Mexico than multilateral trade liberalization might have been is not certain. What is certain is that NAFTA did greatly benefit the American auto industry and other NAFTA-protected industries. However, the overall American economy would have gained even more benefits if the United States had continued its pursuit of multilateral trade liberalization.

SOUTHERN ENLARGEMENT

By the 1990s, Latin America had become an increasingly important market for the United States, and in June 1990 President George Bush announced his "Enterprise of the Americas" proposal, a vision of a Western Hemisphere free-trade area from Alaska to Terra del Fuego. Despite their continuing high import barriers, especially in automotive and high-tech industries, Latin American governments initially responded enthusiastically to the proposal. The 1980s debt crisis and implementation of structural adjustment policies had caused most countries in Latin America to begin abandoning the strategy of import substitution and to lower their trade barriers. Even Brazil, which had the highest level of import protection and the most aggressive industrial policy in the region, having already undertaken important reforms, expressed interest in Bush's proposal. The possibility of a significant opening of the huge American market to their exports caught the attention of Brazil and other Latin American economies.

After a hiatus of several years during which Americans fought bitterly over NAFTA, the Clinton Administration returned to the idea of hemispheric free trade. In December 1994 at the Miami Conference, the

Administration proposed extension of the NAFTA framework to include the entire hemisphere. At the Summit, national governments agreed to begin negotiations on the creation by the year 2005 of a Free Trade Area of the Americas, technical working groups were established to develop a plan, and negotiations were undertaken. Nevertheless, conditions in Latin America had changed significantly between Bush's 1990 Enterprise of the Americas initiative and Clinton's 1994 proposal of a Free Trade Agreement for the Americas, and Latin American governmental enthusiasm for a Western Hemisphere economic bloc had waned.

Although these Latin American countries still want greater access to the American market, they have developed strong reservations about an intimate association with the United States and about the high costs of accelerated market liberalization. In the late 1990s, Latin America, as Sidney Weintraub has stated, was suffering from "restructuring fatigue." The closing of noncompetitive industries and the effect of lower tariffs on competition had raised the risk of a political backlash. Because of such concerns, Brazil and other countries decelerated the rate of reduction of import barriers, and in 1998 these barriers remained, by global standards, relatively high. Moreover, Latin Americans became more skeptical of U.S. willingness to reduce trade barriers and to forgo punitive use of Section 301 of the American Trade Act of 1974; they were also fearful that closer economic and political ties to the United States would compromise their independence. The United States, for its part, expressed its interest in extending cooperation into such areas as security, the environment, and drug trafficking.

Subregional trade agreements have spread throughout Latin America. With each one involving only a few countries, these agreements reflect the diversity of the Latin American continent and its low level of economic and/or physical integration. By far the most important of Latin America's subregional trade pacts is Mercosur, signed in March 1991 among the core countries of Brazil, Argentina, Paraguay, and Uruguay, along with other associated members. A loose agreement was more attractive to the economies of the region than was the tight structure of NAFTA, and its acceptance represented a major political change in the region. While one of Mercosur's purposes was to moderate the historic rivalry between Brazil and Argentina, Mercosur may also be interpreted as an expression of Brazil's ambition to establish its hegemony over its Latin American neighbors. Brazil has also given strong support to creation of a South American Free Trade Area (SARTA) that would integrate the many other subregional arrangements with Mercosur. Whether SARTA was motivated more by the desire to increase Latin America's bargaining position in an eventual negotiation with the United States or by the desire to create a South American economic free-trade area independent of the United States is not completely clear. At the least, it can be said that Brazil has strongly resisted American efforts to incorporate Latin America into an enlarged NAFTA.

The Clinton Administration's proposal for a Free Trade Agreement for the Americas was dependent on congressional passage of fast-track legislation to enable the Administration to begin negotiations with Chile for that country's accession to NAFTA. However, a fast track was eventually blocked by the political stalemate over trade policy that had emerged during the conflict over NAFTA ratification. A powerful coalition of organized labor, environmental groups, and protectionist business interests allied with important elements in the Democratic Party agreed to support fast track only if the Free Trade Agreement for the Americas and all future trade agreements included strong and binding provisions regarding labor rights and environmental protection. On the other hand, Republican congressional leaders vehemently opposed fast-track authority unless provisions for workers' standards and environmental protection were omitted. Faced with such a stalemate, President Clinton withdrew his request for approval of fast track in the fall of 1997 and thus ended, at least for the immediate future, the effort to extend NAFTA southward.

Conversion of the Clinton Administration from reluctant supporter of NAFTA to enthusiastic advocate of its expansion to include the entire Western Hemisphere deserves attention. The Reagan and Bush Administrations' initial views of NAFTA as a bargaining device to encourage West European participation in the Uruguay Round were good economics and good politics; the threat of North American regionalization did catch the attention of Europeans and led to a successful round of trade negotiations. The subsequent conversion of the Clinton Administration to North American regionalism as an end in itself and not as a stepping-stone to a multilateral trading system was an unfortunate development; most NAFTA benefits accrue only to a limited number of entrenched American, Canadian, and Mexican producer interests. Enlargement of NAFTA to include Latin America would be a further policy blunder unless such an initiative were designed as part of a continuous movement toward a multilateral trading system.

CLINTON'S ECONOMIC STRATEGY

Upon his inauguration as President, Bill Clinton pursued an economic strategy to rejuvenate the flagging American economy and to make America competitive again in world markets. Whereas the policies of the Reagan and Bush Administrations had been designed to increase reliance on the market, Clinton's strategy was based on the assumption that the federal government should play the central role in the search for solutions to America's economic and social problems. His Administration believed that the expensive and wasteful national systems of health care (Medicare and Medicaid) and of social welfare should be reformed, the industrial base (which had begun to atrophy due to the high dollar and Japanese imports) should be rebuilt by a national industrial (or technology) policy, and Vice President Al Gore's "information highway" should be employed to energize the "information economy," just as President Dwight D. Eisenhower's national highway system had stimulated the mass production economy in the 1950s.

Secretary of Labor Robert Reich took office with an ambitious plan for massive investments in education and worker training to elevate the skills of the American workforce. The Administration's overall strategy of economic renewal and increased international competitiveness was to be implemented by a newly created general economic staff, the National Economic Council, headed by Robert Rubin, a successful Wall Street investment banker later to become Secretary of the Treasury. Alas! Things did not work out as the newly elected President and his team had planned. As Bob Woodward documented in his best-selling book, *The Agenda: Inside the Clinton White House* (1994), the Administration's ambitious plans for remaking the American economy collided with economic reality, and within a year the Administration re-treated to a more modest domestic economic agenda.[56]

The President's foreign economic policy grew out of the doctrine of geo-economics that greatly influenced national thinking in the late 1980s and early 1990s. Advocates of geo-economics proclaimed that, in the post–Cold War era, the economic struggle among nations had displaced previous concerns over military security; they argued that Japan's huge trade surplus with the United States was the most serious threat faced by this country. Japan, they alleged, had been intentionally attempting to destroy one American high-tech industry after another. Important members of Clinton's economic team shared many of these ideas and advocated strong economic measures against the Japanese. Resultant threats to Japan of severe retaliation if it should fail to open its automobile and other markets greatly increased the conflict between the United States and Japan and also appealed to organized labor, high-tech industries, and other domestic interests. Eventually, following a bitter and near-disastrous economic conflict with Japan, cooler heads in the Administration prevailed, and security concerns were reaffirmed as central to American foreign policy.

Triumph of Geo-Economics

The Clinton Administration's original emphasis on economic security reflected the intellectual climate of the times.[57] A spate of alarmist books such as Lester Thurow's *Head to Head: The Coming Economic Battle among Japan, Europe, and America* (1992), Jeffrey Garten's *A Cold Peace: America, Japan, Germany, and the Struggle for Supremacy* (1992), and Clyde Prestowitz's *Powernomics: Economics and Strategy after the Cold War* (1991) argued that international economic issues had supplanted the military security concerns of the Cold War era. These books reflected an American economy apparently suffering from "deindustrialization," a huge Japanese trade/payments surplus, and a serious recession. Decisive action was deemed necessary to overcome the decline of the American economy and to make America competitive once again. Many American leaders and intellectuals, including key members of the Clinton Administration, believed that geo-economics had replaced geopolitics in the post–Cold War world. In a major speech, the President told his audience that the United States was like a giant corporation locked in a fierce competitive struggle with other nations for economic survival and that, therefore, the central task of the federal government was to increase the international competitiveness of the American economy. President Clinton believed that international economic competition would increasingly determine a nation's position in the world.

Trade policy reformulated to promote America's economic and political interests provided the key component of the Administration's economic strategy. Officials believed that the principal goal of trade policy should be to promote America's high-tech industries and to create better high-paying jobs for American workers in the new information economy. Moreover, trade policy should advance the Administration's newly conceived foreign policy agenda. High Administration officials believed that trade should be used to refashion the world in America's image; this idea became more and more important in the Administration's calculations. Referring to the effort to transform China into a democracy and a market economy, Mickey Kantor, Clinton's first trade representative, stated that "trade and economics are no longer a separate sphere from the rest of American foreign policy." This policy change resulted in the Administration launching a powerful economic offensive against Japan that threatened the security ties of these two very important political allies.

American-Japanese Trade Dispute

The Clinton Administration included a number of revisionists who believed that the Japanese played the economic game according to their own rules and that their rules were unfair. These officials argued that, as the Cold War was over and Japan needed America more than America needed Japan, the United States should adopt a tough stance toward Japan and other unfair traders. They argued that the United States should use its economic might to transform Japan and make it "more like us," and that this goal should be central to the Administration's economic strategy. The end of the Cold War and the demise of the Soviet threat had led many Americans to identify Japan and its persistently huge trade/payments surplus as an economic and even a security threat to the United States. Such revisionist beliefs that Japan had to be changed for America's good contributed significantly to toughening the American attitude toward Japan.

The principal objectives of the Clinton Administration's trade offensive against Japan were to decrease Japan's trade surplus and open the Japanese economy to American goods, especially to its high-tech exports. A more assertive trade policy was also intended to end the free ride provided to Japan and other nations when the United States had accepted the closed markets of its allies in the interest of solidarity against the Soviet threat, while leaving the American economy open and largely unprotected throughout the Cold War. This had permitted West European discrimination against American agricultural products and Japanese discrimination against American manufactured goods. With the end of the Cold War, many argued that the United States should use access to its market as a lever to pry open closed economies. The shift to an aggressive trade policy was also strongly influenced by domestic politics. Japan bashing, the Administration believed, would pay off handsomely with the American electorate and would appeal, in particular, to organized labor and America's high-tech industries such as those in Silicon Valley that had strongly supported Clinton's election and were suffering from intense Japanese competition. The Administration's tough policy toward Japan tended to subordinate international commitments and foreign policy concerns to the exigencies of domestic politics.

The theory of strategic trade provided the intellectual rationale for the Administration's aggressive support of managed trade and export promotion. Important members of the Administration believed that Japan's economic success was due to its effective use of strategic trade policy and that the government's trade and industrial policies had been responsible for Japan's rapid industrialization and outstanding international competitiveness. They therefore advocated that the United States imitate Japan's strategic use of trade in its efforts to advance America's economic and political interests. Many argued that the Administration should support "strategic trade-type" industries—those industries in which economies of scale require larger markets than individual countries and where producers gain learning-curve advantages that enable them to "leapfrog" over their competitors from one generation of products to the next.[58]

Proponents of this trade/industrial policy connection believed that strategic industries comprising the "commanding heights" of the information-age economy should be protected against the unfair and predatory policies of Japan and other countries. Clearly, the important task of safeguarding America's threatened strategic industries could not be left solely to the WTO and international civil servants. As Laura D'Andrea Tyson has argued, the slow resolution of trade policy disputes can be devastating for American firms and industries. The Clinton Administration contended that the United States had no alternative than to pursue a results-oriented trade policy that would guarantee both speedy and unambiguous outcomes of trade negotiations. They believed, moreover, that the Administration had to prevent Japan from utilizing its home market as a protected sanctuary for Japanese producers, a policy that enabled those producers to achieve economies of scale and the high profits that were making them capable of capturing one high-tech industry after another.

Several aspects of Administration policy toward Japan are worthy of special attention. At the same time that it continued to impose quotas or "voluntary export restraints" on Japanese imports into the United States, the Administration intensified demands for "voluntary import quotas" or "voluntary import expansion" of American goods into the Japanese market. These demands demonstrated a more self-centered American approach to trade issues. In the past, the United States had pressured Japan to open its markets, but it had done so in the interest of all countries then shut out of that market. Opening the Japanese beef market, for example, had been of considerable benefit to Australian exporters. In this way, for some time American leverage on Japan to open its closed markets actually contributed to a multilateral trading system. The Clinton Administration's results-oriented trade policy, on the other hand, was intended to force Japan to import specific amounts of American products.

Whereas the Reagan Administration's emphasis on managed trade, intended to appease protectionist interests, had been somewhat sporadic, the Clinton Administration enthusiastically adopted managed trade as a key component in its overall economic and political strategy. It is noteworthy that the results of earlier American efforts to open the Japanese economy had been beneficial for Japanese consumers and certain important sectors of the Japanese economy. American pressure to overturn the "big store" law, which discriminated against large stores, had been successful because many powerful Japanese domestic interests supported that reform. The Clinton Administration's approach, however, was specifically designed to benefit American exporters. Its self-serving policy meant that, despite the Administration's expectation of wide support for its trade offensive against Japan, it soon found itself without support either from other countries or from important interest groups within Japan, and it also became the object of severe criticism from most American economists.

The Administration's tough stance toward Japan was enunciated forcefully at the Clinton-Miyazawa Tokyo Summit (Summer 1993). American demands, paradoxically incorporated in the proposed *U.S.-Japan Framework for a New Economic Partnership*, included economic and institutional reforms that would significantly reduce Japan's trade surplus and increase Japanese imports of American manufactured goods. To accomplish the first of these goals, the United States demanded that Japan pursue a much more expansionary economic policy. The Administration also wanted a Japanese commitment to import a specific amount of American goods in particular economic sectors. To prevent Japan from once again agreeing to American demands and then failing to implement the agreements, U.S. officials proposed that the two governments establish objective and quantifiable means to measure progress in opening the Japanese market to American goods. The key component of this American demand for results-oriented or managed trade was that Japan should significantly increase its importing of American-produced automobiles and automotive parts.

A bitter American-Japanese conflict over automobile/auto parts imports was triggered in the late spring of 1994, when Trade Representative Kantor issued an ultimatum that Japan either import a specified number of American automobiles and auto parts or the United States would impose a 100 percent tariff on certain luxury models of Japanese automobiles. These demands were modeled on the 1986 Semiconductor Agreement that had benefited American producers and convinced the Administration that setting a very specific and measurable import target would force the Japanese to abide by the Agreement. This tactic reflected the prevailing sentiment in Washington expressed by C. Fred

Bergsten, director of the Institute for International Economics, that, although it had significantly lowered formal trade barriers, Japan still engaged in extensive exclusionary practices and collusive relationships that effectively restricted imports into the Japanese market. (A telling example at the time was the import barriers against apples from the state of Washington that the Japanese claimed had introduced plant diseases into Japan.) The newly favored tactic for solving the "Japan problem," therefore, was to use American economic leverage to force import targets—tangible goals with tangible measures of success or failure—on the Japanese rather than hope that Japan eventually would live up to its commitments.

Because the largest portion of the American trade deficit with Japan was in automobiles and auto parts, the dispute over automobiles was extremely important to the Administration. Whereas Japanese firms had won 22 percent of the American auto market, American firms had gained only about 1 percent of the Japanese market. Over and over again, Japan had promised, and then subsequently failed, to open its markets in automobiles as well as other sectors. Through establishment, and especially through enforcement, of an objective measure of Japanese compliance, the President expected to be able to prove to the American people, particularly to organized labor and other constituents of the Democratic Party, that he had succeeded where his five predecessors had failed. Clinton's policy was shaped in large part by a desire to build a new coalition supporting the Democratic Party to replace the crumbling New Deal amalgam; managed trade appealed to a number of different constituencies (e.g., high-tech industries as well as trade unionists in heavy industry).

The strategy also appealed to hard-core Democrats who wanted an activist government. In addition, the Administration could "send a message" to the newly industrializing economies of Pacific Asia that the United States would not tolerate repetition of Japan's export-led growth strategy in which unlimited access to the American market was attained without reciprocal opening of home markets to American products. The Administration, believing that a major cause of the perceived industrial decline of the United States was the Japanese economic model and its trade policy, wished to prevent the spread of that model and that trade policy throughout East and Southeast Asia.

The Japanese vehemently rejected the American argument that the Semiconductor Agreement had guaranteed American firms a numerical percentage of the Japanese computer-chip market and thus constituted a precedent for import quotas in automobiles and auto parts. They regarded Clinton Administration demands as a concerted effort to undermine key elements of their economic strategy and strength. Realizing that Japan's economic success since the end of World War II had been confined to only a few, albeit very important, sectors, particularly automobiles and consumer electronics, negotiators knew that Japanese acceptance of numerical quotas would give the United States effective control over development of a critical sector of the economy. Clinton's demands for a guaranteed share of the Japanese market posed a threat to the very nature of the Japanese productive system, with its emphasis on tight industrial groupings (keiretsu) and the just-in-time inventory system. In fact, many Japanese believed that the ultimate purpose of the Administration's policy was to undermine such sources of Japanese economic strength and domestic political stability as the keiretsu and lifetime employment. Any concession in the automobile sector, they believed, would only encourage further American demands. Thus, the Japanese strongly opposed any compromise. Indeed, Japan and the United States found themselves involved in more than a trade or economic controversy. The clash between the two allies had escalated into a political conflict in which both felt that fundamental issues of national power and economic security were involved. Each side believed that its economic and political future was at stake in the automobile dispute.

Despite the seriousness of this dispute, the controversy evaporated almost as quickly as it had arisen, and both sides claimed victory. The compromise agreement had only a modest impact on the automobile trade between the two countries. Most of Japan's concessions, such as increasing the production of Japanese cars in the United States, probably had more to do with the high value of the yen and increasing wage costs in Japan than with American pressures. The United States called off the battle, perhaps because Japan bashing had achieved its domestic political objectives. In addition, the takeoff of the American economy and renewed prosperity in the early 1990s moderated protectionist pressures and caused Americans to become less concerned about their huge trade/payments deficit.

An equally important reason for calling off the trade conflict with Japan was that American security and foreign policy officials had become alarmed over the impact of the trade dispute on U.S. security interests. Statements from high Administration trade officials, that if Japan did not surrender to American demands, the entire American-Japanese security relationship would be undermined, had alerted the Pentagon that things were really getting out of hand and that deterioration of American-Japanese security relations should be stopped. The renewed Japanese-American security understanding, set forth in February 1995 by Joseph Nye, Assistant Secretary of Defense for International Security Affairs, signaled the end of the American-Japanese trade dispute and the beginning of a more balanced American foreign policy attentive to both economic and security interests. The United States, led by the Treasury, also shifted to an aggressive policy of opening East Asia to American investment.

ECONOMIC CAUSES

It is important to understand the sources of the U.S.-Japan trade conflict not only because the conflict posed a serious threat to the global economy, but of equal importance because the underlying causes have not disappeared and are likely to resurface in the future. First, one should ask, Why does Japan have an enormous and continuing trade/payments surplus and the United States, an enormous and continuing trade/payments deficit? Also, Why does Japan have what appears to be a distinctive trade pattern in which it imports a relatively small percentage of the manufactured goods that it consumes? The debate between revisionists such as Chalmers Johnson and Clyde Prestowitz and mainstream economists indicates some answers to these questions. Revisionists believe the explanation is that Japan plays by different and unfair rules. Mainstream economists argue that the trade/payments imbalance between Japan and the United States and Japan's trade pattern can be explained by the conventional principles of economics.

JAPAN'S TRADE SURPLUS/AMERICAN TRADE DEFICIT

Revisionists attribute Japan's continuing surplus to that country's neo-mercantilist economic strategy. They argue that Japanese policy has been designed to generate a trade/payments surplus and to make Japan the world's dominant industrial and technological power. Japan's large trade surplus is cited as ipso facto proof that Japan has unfairly kept its economy closed to non-Japanese goods, protected its domestic market, and employed other devices such as export subsidies and dumping to achieve a trade surplus. They point out that, even though Japan has lowered its formal tariff barriers and, in fact, has the lowest tariffs overall of any industrialized economy, both the Japanese government and business interests maintain a number of discriminatory informal and nontransparent barriers that keep imports out. The mechanisms accused of being informal trade barriers include detailed specific product standards, the distribution system, and the *keiretsu* system.

On the other hand, American economists and the Japanese themselves argue that Japan's trade/payments surplus and America's corresponding deficit can be explained entirely by macroeconomic factors. A nation's balance of payments (current account) is equal to the difference between national savings and domestic investment; thus, a nation with a savings rate that exceeds its investment rate will inevitably have a trade/payments surplus, and a nation with a low savings rate is likely to have a trade/payments deficit. Whereas Japan's national savings rate in the mid-1990s was very high, the American rate was extraordinarily low; such a large difference between the savings rates of the two countries has existed at least since the 1960s. These differing macroeconomic situations, according to economists, clearly explain the Japanese trade surplus and America's deficit; they argue that, therefore, it is inappropriate to blame Japan for America's trade deficit. As figures 8.2 and 8.3 inform us, the gap between total domestic investment and total savings equals the American current account or trade/payments deficit. Thus, even if the United States were to bar all imports from Japan, the overall American trade deficit with the rest of the world would not decrease; Americans would simply import more goods from other countries. The deficit will disappear only if and when Americans save more. Japan, on the other hand, will have a trade surplus unless it greatly decreases its population's extraordinarily high savings rate.

JAPAN'S TRADE PATTERN

The other major issue in the American-Japanese trade dispute has been Japan's trade pattern. Japan imports remarkably few of the manufac-

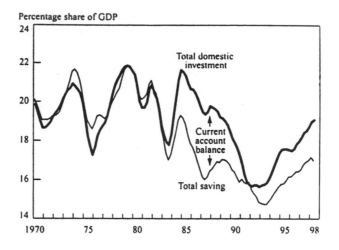

Fig. 8.2. U.S. Investment and Saving.
Source: U.S. Council of Economic Advisors.

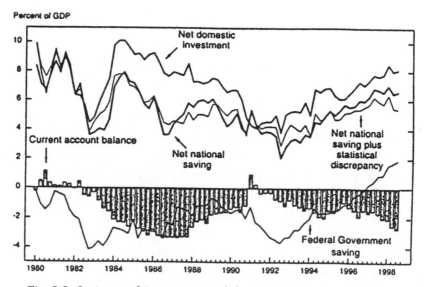

Fig. 8.3. Savings and Investment and the Current Account Balance.
The current account deficit grew in the mid-1980s as savings fell faster
than investment. In the 1990s, both investment and savings have increased.
Source: U.S. Council of Economic Advisors.

260

tured goods that it consumes. Or, to put the matter another way, only a small portion of Japanese trade is two-way trade within particular industries. Or, as economists would say, a substantial portion of American and European trade has been intraindustry trade, but Japanese trade has been largely interindustry. The United States and Western Europe trade many manufactured goods with one another; for example, the United States and Europe export cars and auto parts to one another. Japan, on the other hand, imports mainly commodities (food, raw materials, and fuels) while exporting primarily manufactured goods (motor vehicles, electronics, and other high-tech products). Although Japan began to import more manufactured goods following the revaluation of the yen in 1985, many of the imports were from subsidiaries of Japanese multinational corporations located overseas.

For revisionists, Japan's distinctive trade policy provides evidence of its neomercantilistic economic strategy. Laura Tyson has argued that conventional trade theory does not apply to Japanese trade behavior. Instead, Japan's trade surplus and distinctive trade pattern are due to its policies of trade protection and industrial targeting.[59] Foreign manufacturers, revisionists charge, have been systematically denied access to the Japanese market at the very same time that Japan has carried out a trade offensive against other countries. Japan, they argue, has pursued a strategy of "preemptive investment," excluding foreign goods and investment from its domestic market until Japanese firms have become sufficiently strong to defeat foreign competition anywhere in the world.

Rejecting charges of neomercantilistic trade practices, mainstream economists note that conventional trade theory tells us that Japan's trade pattern is a product of its factor endowments; for example, a shortage of raw materials, a highly skilled labor force, and abundant capital. Other countries with similar endowments such as Italy, they point out, exhibit a similar trading pattern; thus, it is quite natural for Japan to export automobiles, consumer electronics, and auto parts and to import only a small percentage of the manufactured goods that it consumes. Moreover, it is equally natural for Japan to export these types of goods to the huge American consumer market. Economists are convinced that Japan's distinctive trade pattern does not result from predatory Japanese government economic policies.

Assessment of the Debate

Both revisionists and economists provide valuable insights into the American-Japanese trade conflict; indeed, the two positions are more complementary than contradictory. As economic theory informs us, America's low and Japan's high savings rates largely account for America's trade deficit and Japan's trade surplus. Similarly, Japan's distinctive pattern of interindustry trade can be explained largely in terms of Japan's comparative advantage as a capital-rich but resource-poor country. However, one must probe these economic explanations and inquire why Japan does possess such an extraordinarily high savings rate and why it has a comparative advantage in high-tech products and imports so few non-Japanese manufactured goods. These distinctive features of the Japanese economy, as the revisionists argue, have a great deal to do with Japan's neomercantilistic economic policies.

The extraordinarily low American savings rate can be explained by a number of economic policies and a national psychology that has encouraged consumption rather than savings; for example, the American system of Social Security, which has assured Americans that they did not need to save for their retirement, has discouraged savings. Similarly, the extremely high savings rate in Japan has been due to government policies that have deliberately suppressed domestic demand and encouraged saving. Indeed, the government-engineered savings rate helps to explain the more than thirty-year-long Japanese trade surplus. Restrictive macroeconomic policies and overregulation of the economy have further suppressed Japanese domestic consumption and left the standard of living far below what it should be for such a wealthy country.[60] This situation has meant that Japan has suffered from underconsumption, and that has limited the prospects for domestic-led economic growth. In addition, strict capital controls and the postal savings system, along with the lack of an adequate national system of social security, have also encouraged Japanese to save. Although saving for old age has been part of the reason for Japan's high savings rate, policies supporting high savings and underconsumption have been used to promote Japan's overall strategy of rapid industrialization, a trade surplus, and export-led economic growth. However, I would emphasize that Japan's trade/payments surplus is *not* responsible for America's trade/payments deficit.

As economists have argued, Japan as a capital-rich and resource-poor nation has a comparative advantage in manufacturing. However, the revisionist argument that Japan has promoted manufacturing and discriminated against non-Japanese imports through its industrial and protectionist policies is also well grounded. As the revisionists have argued, the strong belief that Japan's comparative advantage is and must continue to be in the manufacture of quality goods in high volume at competitive prices explains Japan's emphasis on industrial production. The commitment to manufacturing has been supported by the fact that an increase in productivity is much more easily attained in manufacturing than in services, and this makes the Japanese extremely reluctant to follow the example of the United States and become a service economy. In addition, the strategies of export-led growth accompanied by a trade surplus enable Japanese manufacturing firms to reach a high volume of output and thus to achieve economies of scale that increase their competitiveness in high-tech industries. The argument is that if Japanese business is to have a high rate of productivity and economic growth, then Japan must maintain a strong manufacturing base. Thus, while it is true that Japan's comparative advantage lies in manufacturing, this advantage has been strongly influenced by the quite visible hand of the Japanese state rather than by the invisible hand of the market alone.

The principal causes of the continuing American trade and payments deficit are to be found in the American economy itself. At the core of the problem is America's propensity to overconsume and undersave. Nevertheless, while Japan is not wholly to blame for America's trade/payments problems, Japan must share part of the blame. Its emphasis on export-led growth and a trade surplus in high-tech products has contributed to Japan's distinctive trade pattern and restricted importing of American high-tech and other industrial goods. In addition, Japan's economic strategy has imposed a large burden on most of Japan's trading partners by limiting their access to its market; this burden has proved especially painful for the rapidly industrializing emerging markets. While this neomercantilistic trade strategy might have been justifiable for a weak war-torn Japan seeking to reestablish itself as an industrial power after World War II, it is hardly appropriate for a mature and, despite its serious economic problems in the late 1990s, a very strong industrial power.

CONCLUSION

Following abandonment of its ill-considered Japan policy, the Clinton Administration committed itself to promoting an open world economy. Strongly influenced by Treasury Secretary Rubin, the Administration became converted to the ideology of unregulated, free markets and the belief that an open world economy was in America's economic interest. The Administration began to pursue this goal aggressively, especially with respect to the dynamic emerging markets of East Asia, where the United States pushed hard for these countries to open their markets to American goods and investment. Although an open world economy is certainly in America's and the world's interest, the East Asian financial crisis proved that pressuring countries to open their markets before they are ready can result in disaster.

Asian Regionalism

FROM THE MID-1980s until the financial crisis struck in the fall of 1997, the Pacific Asian region, an arc of countries from Japan and Korea in the northeast to Indonesia, Thailand, Singapore, and southern China in the southeast, was the fastest-growing region in the world economy. Some have estimated that these economies were growing at 8 percent a year and accounted for approximately one-quarter of world output and almost two-thirds of world capital spending. Indeed, the spectacular economic growth of the emerging markets of East Asia transfixed the rest of the world. Before the 1997 financial crisis, it seemed possible and even probable that these economies would become the center of the world economy early in the twentieth-first century.

During the past quarter century a number of significant developments within this vast and extraordinarily diverse area transformed the region and its place in the global economy. Steady development of a regional economy and regional identity under Japanese leadership, rapid industrialization of southern China, and the financial crisis that suddenly enveloped the region in the fall of 1997 were particularly important. Japan has played an increasingly central role in the region as an economic and, to a lesser extent, a political power. Japanese trade, investment, and Official Development Assistance (ODA) have been crucial to the dynamism of the region and to emergence of a Pacific Asian regionalized economy. The long-term importance of Japanese initiatives, however, will be greatly affected by the future role of China as a regional and global economic power and by the ultimate consequences of the East Asian economic crisis. These developments—the increasing role of Japan in the region, the rapid industrialization of China, and the financial crisis— have significant implications for the future of the region and its place in the larger global economy.

CHARACTERISTICS OF THE PACIFIC ASIAN REGION

Pacific Asian regionalism has several distinctive features that have set it apart from both West European and North American regionalism. Yet these differences can be misleading. The East Asian region is different from others because there is no hegemon or core alliance of major powers. American leadership in North America and the French-German core alliance in Europe have guided the integration of those regions. In the Pacific Asian region there are three major powers—the United States, Japan, and China—with interests and ambitions that vary considerably from one another. Even though Japan has been playing an increasingly central role in the economic affairs of the region, both China and the United States are also powerful actors. The economic development of the region has been largely market-driven as trade flows, foreign direct investment, and the activities of multinational firms (especially Japan's) have been integrating forces.

Despite the increasing integration of certain aspects of the region, its immense economic, cultural, and political diversity has significantly inhibited the development of a regional mentality and of regionwide institutions. While Asian nations share some important characteristics, the region is deeply riven by cultural differences, differences in economic systems, and serious political conflicts. The most important regional institutions have been the subregional Association of South East Asian Nations (ASEAN), composed of Brunei, Indonesia, Malaysia, the Philippines, Singapore, Thailand, and Vietnam, and the Asian-Pacific Economic Cooperation (APEC), composed of Australia, Canada, Chile, China, Japan, Mexico, New Zealand, the United States, and other countries of Pacific Asia. Neither group, however, has been really central to the organization and functioning of the overall Pacific economy. The lack of an effective political structure in the region, the apparently predominant role of economic forces in integrating the region, and the increasing integration of the region with the rest of the world have produced an "open regionalism"; in contrast to the EU's customs union and NAFTA's free-trade area, the Pacific Asian region does not have any regionwide trade or investment barriers. Individual countries, on the other hand, still have high barriers to both imports and foreign investment.

Although Japan does not exercise political hegemony over the region, the economic expansion of Japanese multinational corporations and Japanese economic influence throughout East and Southeast Asia have propelled change in the region. Through a national strategy of foreign direct investment, intrafirm trade, and ODA, Japan has forged a regionwide economy that integrates the economies of East and Southeast Asia with the Japanese home economy. Over the long term, the possibilities of success for this Japanese strategy are, of course, highly dependent on the recovery of Asia from its financial crisis and on the activities of China and the United States in the region. If China continues to grow economically and to modernize its military, it will certainly eventually become the dominant military and economic power. Meanwhile, the East Asian financial crisis has seriously undermined, but not overthrown, Japan's strategy in the region.

JAPAN'S ASIAN STRATEGY

Japan's efforts to create and lead a Pacific Asian economy are crucial to developments throughout the region. In fact, the dynamics of the region cannot be properly understood without appreciation of the re-Asianization of Japan's economy and of its national orientation. While Japan intends to maintain a strong presence in the global economy, it has regained its former interest in East and Southeast Asia. Both Japanese trade and foreign direct investment have been important factors in the industrialization of that region, especially southern China. And because of Japan's huge stake in East and Southeast Asia, the East Asian economic crisis has posed an extremely serious threat to Japan. Japan, of course, has had its own and largely self-inflicted economic crisis; since the collapse of its bubble economy in the early 1990s, Japan has been in a troubled financial condition, and, more recently, the Japanese economy has slowly sunk into a serious recession. The fate of Japan and the region are closely linked.

Prior to the mid-1980s, postwar Japan had demonstrated little interest in the East Asian and Pacific Basin economies. Japanese trade with the region was minuscule, especially when compared to its trade with the United States and other Western countries. There was no large consumer market in the region for Japanese automobiles, electronics, or other sophisticated exports. The Japanese thought of their Asian neighbors primarily as sources of agricultural products and raw materials, and Japanese corporations made few significant long-term investments in the region. Direct investments were almost completely in extractive industries, with few in manufacturing and almost none in high-tech industries. Japanese foreign aid to the region was relatively insignificant and was given primarily as reparations to victims of Japan's wartime atrocities.

Japanese indifference to the region came to an abrupt end with the substantial appreciation of the yen (*endaka*), following the Plaza Agreement of September 1985. The approximately 30 percent appreciation of the yen vis-à-vis the dollar had sudden and dramatic effects as the high yen significantly reduced the profitability and international competitiveness of many Japanese exports, especially in more traditional industries, depressed the Japanese economy, and transformed Japan into the world's foremost financial power by greatly increasing the value of its financial assets. In addition, rising Japanese wage rates and production costs began to undermine the competitiveness of many industries. The Japanese Ministry of Finance responded with a significant economic stimulus to balance the deflationary impact of *endaka*. It was this shift in Japanese macroeconomic policy that resulted in the bubble economy of rampant financial and real estate speculation. When the bubble economy eventually collapsed in the early 1990s, Japan was plunged into a severe recession from which it has not yet recovered (at least not by 1999). Appreciation of the yen also undermined Japan's postwar economic strategy based on export-led growth. And, perhaps most important of all, it led to the re-Asianization of Japan.

Endaka's undermining of Japan's highly successful export-led growth strategy confronted the Japanese elite of political leaders, government bureaucrats, and business executives with two broad policy alternatives. One option was to follow the recommendations of the Maekawa Commission.[61] In its report released on April 7, 1986, the Commission had proposed drastic reform of the Japanese economy and reformulation of domestic and foreign economic policies in order to shift emphasis away from export-led growth toward a much greater emphasis on domestic-led growth; it also recommended that Japan open its economy to imports from other countries. Following the recommendations of the Maekawa Commission would have entailed extensive deregulation and decreased the role of the state in the economy, and would thus eventually have led to a more market- and consumer-oriented economy similar to that of the United States and Western Europe. Many Western experts predicted that *endaka* and the crisis of the economy would cause the Japanese economy to converge with the Western model. However, as has happened several times in postwar Japanese history, the elite chose an alternative strategy.

The chosen alternative can aptly be called "Japan's Asian strategy." This strategy required a concerted effort by the governing elite to use Japan's huge capital and superior technological resources to create an East Asian economy integrated with and dominated by Japan's home economy. Japan's East Asian strategy has been motivated not only by desires to maintain and strengthen its economic position but also by other concerns. As a consequence of American trade protectionism and demands for "managed" trade in automobiles and other sectors, the Japanese had become increasingly wary over their heavy reliance on the United States as an economic and political partner; an Asian strategy could lessen their dependence on the American market. The Japanese had also become increasingly concerned about the emergence of exclusive regional blocs from which they might be excluded. Finally, and not least, the Japanese are intensely worried about China; through trade, investment, and foreign aid, the Japanese hope to transform China into an economic partner more interested in peaceful economic coexistence than in military expansion and political confrontation.

While appreciation of the yen and rising domestic costs provided a powerful incentive for Japanese corporations to decrease their production costs through relocation of production to the low-cost labor economies of Southeast Asia, the financial windfall from that appreciation also gave these firms and the government the necessary financial wherewithal to invest heavily throughout East and Southeast Asia and to substantially increase foreign aid to the economies within the region. Initially, renewed interest in the region was concentrated on Japan's immediate neighbors—Taiwan, South Korea, and Hong Kong. However, as rising wage rates and currency appreciation soon made the Northeast Asian economies less attractive outlets for investment, the

Japanese began to concentrate on Southeast Asia, especially south China. In effect, as Walter Hatch and Kozo Yamamura argue in their book *Asia in Japan's Embrace: Building a Regional Production Alliance* (1996), Japan has tried to maintain its export-led growth strategy by "regionalizing" it.[62]

Foreign direct investment by Japanese *keiretsu* (or industrial groups) has been the principal means employed by Japan as it has expanded economically in East Asia and extended its influence throughout the region. Following the Plaza Agreement and appreciation of the yen, Japanese investment in the region soared. Initially, the investments were placed in the most advanced economies (South Korea, Taiwan, Hong Kong, and Singapore) and in Southeast Asia. Later, Japanese foreign investment shifted toward mainland China and away from the rest of East Asia. Although American FDI in the region has remained substantial, in the 1990s Japan became the largest supplier of FDI to the region. Despite this important shift, Japanese FDI in the United States and Western Europe has continued to reach even higher levels than in Asia. However, in relation to the size of the economies involved, Japanese investment in East Asia is huge.

By the late 1990s, Japanese firms had invested approximately $100 billion in the region. More than forty-five hundred Japanese firms, either alone or in joint ventures, employed nearly one million workers throughout the area. This Japanese investment was accompanied by a huge technology transfer valued at about $1 billion. By the late 1990s, a large percentage of the production of Japanese MNCs was located in Pacific Asia. This development caused one Japanese economist to say that Asia outside Japan had become the "workshop of the world." It is worth noting that there was also increasing FDI in the area from Taiwan, Hong Kong, and South Korea. Foreign direct investment by Japan and other Asian countries in the industrializing economies of Pacific Asia profoundly reshaped the economic structure of the region and the relationships among the economies.

The virtual explosion of FDI in the region and the activities of Japanese firms significantly altered Japan's trade pattern along with the trade patterns of other nations in the region. In the early 1990s, Pacific Asia actually overtook the United States as Japan's largest export market, and Japan surpassed the United States as the principal trading partner with the region. Japan's trade surplus with the region soared and exceeded its trade surplus with the United States. Although the region's trade with the larger world economy remained greater than intraregional trade, intraregional trade also surged, at least until the 1997 financial crisis. Yet, I emphasize that the United States remained the most important export market for Pacific Asian exports and that exports to the United States grew more rapidly than did American exports to the region. As these export economies pegged their currencies to and/or slightly below the dollar, their exports were highly competitive in the American market. All the economies in the region, especially China, have had a huge and growing trade surplus with the United States.

Throughout these years, Japan and its corporations were implementing a deliberate strategy to create a vertically organized regional division of labor under Japanese leadership, even though some American economists and the Japanese themselves have disputed this contention. Based on their examination of trade data, some economists have argued that geographic proximity and such market factors as the comparative advantage of Japan and other economies in the region can fully explain the pattern of trade and investment within that region. Furthermore, they argue that there is no evidence of a deliberate Japanese effort to create some kind of economic bloc. The Japanese themselves argue that the expansion of their firms throughout the region and the interlocking production networks have resulted merely from business firms' responses to market forces. It is probable that Japanese dislike the term "strategy" because it is too reminiscent of Japan's pre–World War II effort to create an East Asian Co-prosperity Sphere, and because it may seem to imply that Japan is attempting again to create an East Asian empire or exclusive sphere of influence, albeit this time through the peaceful tools of trade, finance, and investment rather than military conquest.

Hatch and Yamamura argue convincingly that economists' conclusions and those of the Japanese are based on the false premise that Japanese public policy and private initiatives are separate rather than closely tied to one another.[63] There are literally dozens of ways, they point out, in which the economic bureaucracies (Ministry of International Trade and Investment, Ministry of Finance and Economic Planning Agency) have designed and coordinated an overall Japanese policy toward the region and have fashioned mechanisms to carry out this policy to integrate the other economies with Japan's home economy. Japanese multinational firms and Japanese official foreign aid, they note, have had a profound impact on trade patterns, investment flows, and financial interdependence in the Pacific Asian region. In particular, Japanese multinationals, with the strong support of the state, have created "regional production alliances" composed of parent Japanese firms, Japanese subsidiaries located throughout the region, and subordinate indigenous firms, and these regional production networks have been utilized as export platforms for Japanese firms in the intensifying competition for world markets.

The purpose of its Asian strategy has been to enable Japan to continue its postwar export-led growth. Both the trade and growth strategies were threatened by the substantial appreciation of the yen, increasing domestic production costs, and the spread of trade protectionism in the United States and Western Europe. Although this Pacific Asian strategy has indeed provided Japan with insurance against the continuing threat of Western protectionism, Japan's overall economic strategy has also reduced the costs of Japanese exports to the West, increased the international competitiveness of Japanese firms through integration of the East and Southeast Asian economies into a vertical multilevel regional production system, and incorporated these economies into a division of labor organized and managed by Japanese multinational firms.

The regional division of labor consists of vertically organized production networks in such industrial sectors as automobiles and electronics. The parent firms, located in Japan, produce the most technology-intensive components and are at the vertex of the organization. On the next rung are Japanese subsidiaries in economies within the region and below that are the firms of the more industrialized economies of Northeast Asia. At the lowest rung are the indigenous firms in the low-wage and less-industrialized economies of Southeast Asia. The overall result of this strategy is an East Asian integrated system of "network capitalism" managed by Japanese corporations with the Japanese home economy at its core.[64]

According to Hisahiko Okazaki, one of Japan's most distinguished and outspoken postwar diplomats and former Japanese Ambassador to

Thailand, Japan has been creating an exclusive Japanese market by incorporating the Asia-Pacific nations into the *keiretsu* system.[65] Regionalization of the *keiretsu* system through creation of regional production networks enables Japanese firms to avoid the major restructuring of their economy proposed by the Maekawa Commission. The home-based firms in these regionalized *keiretsu* export high-tech and high-value-added components to their affiliates in the region for assembly into finished goods for local consumption, export back to Japan itself, and/or export to the West. Such a corporate strategy enables the parent Japanese firm to cut costs and maintain the high returns on the firm's investments in technological innovation for as long as possible, thereby retaining Japan's monopoly and comparative advantage in high-tech industries. Many local firms are, in fact, Japanese component suppliers associated with *keiretsu* members in Japan that have also established plants to supply the parent firm's subsidiaries in one or more of the economies in the region.

This Japanese corporate expansionism throughout East and Southeast Asia has been accompanied by an important shift in foreign policy toward the region. Japan has greatly intensified its involvement and increased its various links to the states there. The Japanese emperor and one Japanese prime minister after another have made state visits, and Japan has even created the post of "ambassador for Asia-Pacific cooperation." However, the most important manifestation of the re-Asianization of Japan is found in the substantial increase of Japanese Official Development Assistance (ODA). Japan, in fact, has become the largest donor of aid to the region. In 1991–1992, Japan allocated about 35 percent (about $4.5 billion) of its total foreign aid budget to six countries in the region; Americans allocated 2 percent of theirs (about $342 million) to two countries in the region! Japan's financial assistance has been largely in the form of "soft" loans and typically has been targeted to large infrastructure projects, thus assisting infrastructure development that will support Japanese-led industrialization in the region, strengthening Asian regional integration under Japanese leadership, and, despite their strong denial, awarding almost all contracts to Japanese firms or their Asian corporate partners. Thus, the Japanese government has fashioned ODA and a broad array of other policy instruments to promote the interests of Japan and Japanese firms in the region.

Peter Drucker has pointed out that Japan's Asian strategy has been based on two fundamental premises. The first premise has been that comparative advantage in labor-intensive industries has largely shifted to the industrializing economies of Southeast Asia, making attempts to retain low-value-added industries in Japan wasteful of valuable productive resources and even harmful to the more advanced Japanese industrial economy; in these conditions it would be a gross misallocation of corporate and national resources, Drucker suggests, to perform blue-collar manufacturing work in Japan. The second premise has been that economic leadership in the emerging high-tech world of the new millennium rests on the control of brain power and technological superiority rather than on such traditional cost advantages as low-cost labor. Comparative or competitive advantage in the advanced and high-value-added industries of the modern economy has become based on technological leadership and organizational skills. Japan, therefore, should use its scarce economic resources (capital and skilled labor) to increase its technological capabilities through continuously moving up the technological ladder.

Following this logic, Japanese firms have been abandoning assembly or manufacturing within Japan itself of more traditional, labor-intensive products and moving such operations overseas to Asian subsidiaries tightly linked to their home industrial base in Japan. Consequently, skilled labor and other resources have been released to move up the industrial/technological ladder and produce more technologically advanced and higher-value-added finished products and components to be assembled in overseas subsidiaries by lower-wage and lower-skilled labor in Southeast Asia. In effect, the Japanese have organized to combine their own technology and expertise with the low-cost labor of their neighbors in order to capture markets in the rest of the world. In its most crude formulation, this strategy means that, in the international division of labor being fashioned by Japanese corporations with the support of the Japanese government, Japan will furnish the "brain" and the other Asian countries will furnish the "brawn."

Before the financial crisis, the extensive regional production networks were sending an increasing proportion of their output to markets within the region. Rapid growth of these economies led to expansion of a wealthy middle class with an enormous appetite for Japanese consumer goods. But a significant portion of the goods produced by regionalized *keiretsu* was destined for the Japanese home market, where these products have helped to meet demands for increased consumption of imported manufactured goods. Although American, Asian, and other non-Japanese firms have increased their manufactured exports to Japan and Japan's trade pattern has become more "normal"—that is, more like the intraindustry pattern of other advanced industrial countries—Japan continues to be distinctive in that it does not import significant amounts of manufactures produced by non-Japanese firms. And the largest portion of the output of these Asian production networks is still sent to the United States, Western Europe, and other Western economies. These exports have become a source of friction between the United States and the economies in the region.

Production networks located throughout the region have helped Japanese firms to maintain their market share in Western markets despite appreciation of the yen; the networks have also provided a significant competitive advantage in the intensifying struggle for world markets. Japanese firms have been able to exploit the particular comparative advantage of the economies in which they have set up production or assembly operations, advantages such as local raw materials, a depreciated currency, or low-wage labor. However, low-wage labor has not been as important as many critics have presumed, because Japanese firms tend to use the same "lean production" techniques overseas as those that have made Japanese firms at home such formidable competitors. The regional networks, however, have had the advantage of concentrating production and assembly of particular products or components in plants throughout the region, thus enabling firms to achieve economies of scale and other production efficiencies.

Furthermore, exporting goods to the United States or Western Europe with labels such as "Made in Thailand" or "Made in Malaysia," even though many of these products contain a substantial fraction of Japanese-made high-value-added components, has, in reality, increased "Japanese" imports into the United States and Western Europe while avoiding negative reactions to such an increase. Moreover, the fact that most Asian countries have had undervalued currencies pegged to the dollar has been an added bonus to Japanese corporations that have to deal with an overvalued currency at home. In these ways, Japan's

Asian strategy has assisted Japan's own firms to maintain a strong competitive position in world markets while limiting Japanese fears of deindustrialization.

The ideological rationale of Japan's Asian strategy is found in the "flying geese" theory of economic development set forth in the 1930s by economist Kaname Akamatsu.[66] In this model, economic development is promoted by diffusion to the rest of the region of capital, technology, and managerial skill from Japan, the most advanced economy in the region. Economic and technological diffusion enable industrializing economies to continuously upgrade their export and industrial structures. As these countries industrialize, they will export increasingly sophisticated goods to Japan and other countries. The theory envisions a cooperative pattern of economic development and regional integration in Asia that benefits both Japan and the economies in the region.

As early as the late 1970s, Saburo Okita, then Japan's foreign minister, popularized the idea that East Asian countries should follow the flying geese pattern. Okita's formulation (which has become very popular with Japanese commentators) posits Japan as the leading goose in this regional flight; it leads the way in industrialization and economic development. Other Asian countries, from the more advanced industrialized economies of Northeast Asia to the lower-income countries of Southeast Asia, then arrange themselves in the flight pattern according to their economic strength and technological development. In descending order, Japan is followed by the more advanced economies such as Taiwan and Korea and the ASEAN members. As more advanced economies lose comparative advantage in particular products, production of that good passes to the "goose" or "geese" immediately behind it. Successive waves of industrializing geese thus gain from the leaders, and, in time, every economy in the region will develop. Eventually this process of technological catch-up will transform the vertically structured regional division of labor into a horizontal regional structure composed of equal and independent economies.

Despite this depiction of a horizontal and egalitarian economic order in the region in which Japan eventually becomes only the first-among-equals, a cursory examination of Japanese policies and practices makes it clear that Japan fully intends to remain the lead goose. The Japanese political and business elite believe that it is imperative for Japan to continue to be a manufacturing center of technologically intensive and other increasingly sophisticated exports. As Hatch and Yamamura have argued, Japan's mercantilist inclinations mean that it will try to be the "factory to the world" and not become a service economy importing foreign-made manufactured goods (i.e., goods other than those produced at home or abroad by Japanese firms). Japan has encouraged the industrializing economies of East Asia to export their manufactured goods to the United States and Western Europe rather than to Japan, and it is significant that both the government and major firms have implemented a wide array of policies and practices to prevent diffusion of Japan's most important industrial secrets and technological know-how to other countries. In fact, other Asians complain bitterly about Japan's refusal to share its more advanced industrial technology.

Nevertheless, through its investments, trade policies, and foreign aid, Japan has been transferring to East Asia its postwar formula for export-led growth, a development strategy based on technological catch-up and on an infant-industry industrial policy. And the East Asian economies have been developing through adopting those industries already proven successful in Japan and the West. The East Asian economies have also adopted such other important elements of Japan's economic model as an activist role for the state in the economy. Also, in some economies, large industrial conglomerates have developed that are similar to the *keiretsu*, for example, the South Korean *chaebol*. Moreover, these societies have given Japan and its firms a key role in their industrialization. Although the technological sophistication of these economies has been rising, the technological base of the region and the high-tech components of its manufactured products continue to be largely Japanese. For example, despite its remarkable success, the South Korean automobile industry could not survive without key Japanese-made components. Until and unless these economies become more innovative, their role in the global economy will remain subordinate.

JAPANESE REGIONAL LEADERSHIP

Japan's leadership ambitions in Pacific Asia were set back by the East Asian economic crisis. The initial Japanese government reaction to the crisis was confused and has been severely criticized within and without the region. While expressing sympathy for the plight of the afflicted economies, the Japanese government in effect threw up its hands and informed other Asians that Japan could not provide any assistance because of its own economic problems. Eventually, however, Japan did make substantial financial contributions to the IMF's several rescue efforts; it even became the largest national donor. Japan has also maintained its ODA to the region. In addition, much to the annoyance of U.S. Treasury Secretary Rubin, Japan in the fall of 1997 proposed establishment of a $100 billion Japanese-led Asian Monetary Fund (from which the United States would be excluded) to help the troubled economies manage their debts. Although this initiative was strongly rejected by China, the United States, and others, many experts believe that the proposal should have been modified and then pursued further. (Indeed, a modified version proposed a year later was given a more kindly reception by the United States.) However, the most important contribution that Japan could make to the solution of the region's economic problems would be to achieve a rapidly growing Japanese economy that could absorb imports from the region.

Japanese leadership within the region, and even in the global economy, will not succeed unless there is a major overhaul of their economy. Since the collapse of the bubble economy in the early 1990s, Japan has suffered from a severe financial crisis that has discouraged both investment and consumption; one estimate was that, in 1998, the banking system alone was carrying approximately $1 trillion in bad (or nonperforming) loans. After suffering from slow growth throughout most of the 1990s, during the first quarter of 1998 the Japanese economy plunged into a serious recession, the worst since the Great Depression. Stocks dropped precipitously. Although Japanese officialdom, especially the powerful Ministry of Finance (MOF), was very slow to acknowledge the crisis, it was clear to American and other foreign observers that the Japanese economy, especially the banking system, needed drastic changes. The Clinton Administration was adamant that Japan had to pursue expansionary fiscal and monetary policies. In the succeeding months, important Japanese economic interests, especially its large corporations, were converted to the idea that radical action was needed. However, the MOF remained very reluctant to acknowledge the crisis and strongly resisted American pressures for reform and stimulation of Japan's stagnant economy.

Japanese, American, and other experts believed that Japan had to attack its dire economic problems on three broad fronts. Implementation of ambitious measures to stimulate the economy was necessary. The banking and financial system, which had become a serious drag on the economy, also had to be reformed. And a thorough overhaul of the bureaucracy and economy must be carried out if any efforts are to bear fruit.

Economic Stimulus

The Clinton Administration, most American economists, and even many Japanese believed that the Japanese government had to do much more to stimulate its stagnant economy. Whereas many U.S. Administrations had pressured Japan to open its economy to American goods and services, during the late 1990s the American motive changed. Then the United States began to pressure Japan to import more goods from the economies of East Asia. Such a move would have helped the East Asian economies and would also have relieved pressures from imports that were stimulating protectionism in the United States. Nevertheless, the Japanese government remained reluctant to take meaningful action and instead attempted one palliative after another. The MOF strongly resisted creation of a large government spending program because the government was already deeply in debt and facing increased social security costs due to a rapidly aging population. Nevertheless, between October 1997 and late April 1998, the government did announce about half a dozen packages of economic measures to stimulate the economy. The response of both American and Japanese economists in each case was that these efforts would do little to pull the economy out of recession, and that a much more ambitious approach to Japan's recession was required. Arguing that Japan was in a "liquidity trap" (the economic equivalent of astronomy's "black hole" from which escape is difficult), Paul Krugman in a series of articles in May and June 1998 and on his Website (www.mit.edu/krugman/www) made the highly controversial proposal that the Bank of Japan implement a radical program of reinflation by printing lots of money to encourage Japanese consumers and businesses to start spending again. Krugman's classic Keynesian proposal to increase "effective demand" through the threat of inflation was ridiculed and unceremoniously rejected by MOF officials, who retorted that Krugman was ignorant of the ways in which the Japanese economy works. Presumably, one reason for this official resistance was that a higher rate of inflation would have harmed Japanese pensioners.

After Prime Minister Keizo Obuchi assumed power in mid-1998, the Japanese government announced in mid-November a program to re-energize the Japanese economy; it was billed as the "definitive" rescue effort. The nearly $200 billion stimulus package, which included a combination of tax cuts, loans, and government spending, was the largest in Japanese history. Although many experts doubted that even this stimulus package would make a real difference, by the early summer of 1999 signs of an economic rebound were clearly evident.

The long-term revitalization of the economy will also necessitate reform of Japan's financial system. Because the banking system is central to Japan's economic troubles, no amount of money or liquidity provided by the government will work unless the banks are able and willing to channel new funds to consumers and investors—which they have not yet been able to do. Until banking reforms are implemented, banks will not be in a position to make effective use of additional capital. Indeed, Japanese banks have stopped loaning too freely and in early 1999 were not loaning enough.

Reform of the Banking and Financial System

Despite the long simmering financial crisis and its negative impact on consumption and investment, the MOF and the Japanese government have been reluctant to take decisive remedial action. This hesitancy has been due in part to the fact that every solution would be costly for banks, depositors, and/or, ultimately, taxpayers. The MOF has also been reluctant to acknowledge its own failures (including corruption) regarding the banking system because that could cause a loss of public confidence in the banking system. In their system based on social harmony and protection of losers, the Japanese government has found it difficult to follow American advice to simply permit insolvent banks and financial institutions to fail; a system of fewer and stronger banks, American experts have proclaimed, would resolve the problem.

Over many years, the Japanese government and the MOF have tried various rather timid measures to salvage the banking and financial system. Fortunately, in October 1998, following months of debate and parliamentary action, the Obuchi government took decisive action and created a new structure to handle bank failures and instituted a new mechanism to recapitalize those banks with a large number of non-performing loans. A crucial and quite controversial element in this scheme was use of public funds to save failed banks. Although this important move was welcomed by most observers, critics noted that it failed to make the nation's banking practices more transparent when it did not require banks to make their financial positions public. It remains to be seen whether or not these reforms will be adequate to revitalize Japan's ailing banking system.

Institutional Reform

Foreign and Japanese experts believe that a major reform of both the Japanese economy and government bureaucracy is essential to real economic success because the overall productivity of the economy (in contrast to that of the export sector) is low and because of the necessity to support the aging Japanese population. Even the export sector itself is characterized by overcapacity and low profit margins. Government regulations and traditional ways stifle innovation and entrepreneurship. Proponents of drastic reforms are fully aware, however, that any meaningful reform will be extremely difficult to achieve. Partially because of the power of domestic interests that seek protection, the Japanese economy is one of the most heavily regulated in the world. The emphasis on social harmony and the safeguarding of the weak has also contributed to overregulation. Many economists believe that overregulation stifles initiative and prevents labor and capital from moving freely to new, more efficient industries, and that burdensome regulations are largely responsible for the low level of productivity frequently found in non-export sectors of the economy. Deregulation of the economy, most economists believe, would stimulate entrepreneurship and increase productivity; it would also be an important step toward opening the Japanese market to imports, and that would further increase overall

281

efficiency. However, truly meaningful reform of the economy would entail closing thousands of firms and putting hundreds of thousands of Japanese out of work; therefore, it is almost a certainty that public and vested interests would be overwhelmingly opposed to such action. Moreover, as deregulation would weaken the power of the Ministry of Finance and other state bureaucracies, these agencies would also be likely to oppose such reforms. Real reform of the Japanese economy will be slow and limited at best.

Most American economists and public officials believe that the solution to Japan's economic problems is to transform Japan into an American-type market economy. However, the Japanese, like other Asians and most continental Europeans, are fearful of the possible consequences of an American-style market-oriented economy. Most reject "Anglo-Saxonization" of their economy as a threat to social peace and to economic/political independence. Japanese society, they fear, would be torn apart by the ruthlessness of such an economy and its tolerance of economic insecurity and of the large number of losers frequently generated by such systems. For these reasons, Japan strongly resists conversion to the American economic model. Transformation of Japan into a Western-style economy would entail a fundamental shift in relationships between individuals and social institutions and would change Japan from a corporatist to a pluralist society. One must conclude again that major reform of the Japanese economy is unlikely.

EMERGENCE OF CHINA AS AN ECONOMIC POWER

China's future economic and political role in the region is among the most important issues facing East Asia and, over the long term, the entire world. China's rate of economic growth in the 1990s has been astounding. In 1992 and 1993, China grew by 13 percent before inflation forced the government to apply brakes. Measured by overall GNP, China's economy has become the second- or at least the third-largest in the world and, by some estimates, will surpass the United States early in the twenty-first century. As China's economy has grown and industrialized, its economic presence in the region, and in the world economy more generally, has become more and more imposing. In addition,

"Greater China" (the increasingly intertwined economies of mainland China, Hong Kong, Taiwan, and the expatriate Chinese communities of Southeast Asia) has also become an important economic force throughout the region. Chinese military capabilities have expanded, and, with the declining military significance of Russia in East Asia, China looms as the dominant Asian military power. Whether or not China can continue its rapid growth and how it ultimately chooses to exercise its expanding economic and military power will be important not only in East Asia but everywhere.

Due to the financial troubles of other economies in the region along with Japan's economic malaise, many American and other observers believe that China has become the leading power in the region. Certainly, China's impressively rapid industrialization and extraordinary rise as an exporter support the contention that China is "another Japan" or even a "super Japan." However, this characterization of Chinese economic development must be qualified in certain ways. For example, although China's trade surplus with the United States of $40 to $50 billion annually is approximately the same as Japan's, such export success does not make China an economic superpower. China's economic success has been heavily dependent on its access to foreign capital and technology, as well as on its access to the American market. Moreover, China's industrial economy is to a large extent a "hollow" economy. A substantial portion of China's trade surplus with the world has been generated by non-Chinese firms; large exporters from China are in many cases subsidiaries of foreign MNCs (American, Japanese, and Taiwanese). Also, considerable credit for mainland China's economic success belongs to Hong Kong as the greatest supplier of capital to China. The dynamism of the Chinese economy has been fueled largely by FDI and exports as well as by domestic capital accumulation and/or an expanding domestic market.

Foreign firms, either directly or indirectly, have accounted for approximately three-fourths of China's exports. The largest sneaker factory in China and the world has Taiwanese managers, is financed by Goldman Sachs, and produces Nike, Reebok, and Adidas shoes under contract. Foreign businesses and foreign-owned factories have increased at a rapid pace, and between the mid-1980s and mid-1990s, Chinese exports attributable to foreign firms rose dramatically. These foreign subsidiaries have been primarily process or assembly plants in low-tech and low-value-added industries, and many of the components in these products have been imported. Consequently, most of the profits from these firms actually have accrued to other nations while China has gained only a relatively small percentage in taxes and wages. Whereas Japanese exports have been among the most technologically sophisticated in the world, Chinese exports have consisted primarily of such products as toys, low-end consumer electronics, textiles, and footwear, and these exports have usually been marketed under non-Chinese brand names (Nike, Reebok, Sony). Even though China has been steadily climbing the technological and value-added ladder, the Chinese export sector remains largely an enclave economy with only limited spillover into China's huge continental economy.[67]

Despite the limitations on China's economic achievements, China's immediate neighbors in the ASEAN have good reason to view that country as an economic challenge in the present and as a possible military threat in the future. The ASEAN countries have been particularly upset by the speed with which China has become an industrial power, especially in some high-tech products. For example, in 1993 China produced more automobiles than all six ASEAN countries combined; it has also become the largest producer of color televisions in the world. China's southern coastal region threatens the ASEAN's cost competitiveness in such products as semiconductors, audiovisual devices, and cameras. China has displaced Taiwan as the second-largest computer producer in the region. China's ASEAN neighbors in general have been concerned that China has been absorbing FDI that otherwise might have been theirs, and the industrial rise of China has stimulated ASEAN countries to increase economic cooperation with one another.

Since the Chinese economy is still in transition from the command economy of the immediate past to a more market-type economy, assessment of China's accomplishments and its potential is difficult and perhaps impossible. Although economic liberalization has progressed considerably, in mid-1999 the state bureaucracy still weighs heavily on the economy. Moreover, approximately half of China's factories are state owned (many by the military), and many industries receive generous subsidies from the government that are critical to their survival. Although in 1997 the government announced ambitious plans to privatize the huge public sector, accomplishing this task will be particularly difficult politically because so many firms are owned by the military. Moreover, the firms that are nationalized at present are the only source of economic security for hundreds of thousands of otherwise redundant employees. Wide-scale unemployment and huge inequalities from one region to another pose extraordinarily serious threats to Chinese political stability. If laid-off workers cannot be absorbed by a rapidly expanding private sector, public sector downsizing will inevitably lead to serious social tensions and political conflict.

The shift from a state-run to a private, market-oriented economy will create many winners but also many losers. Such a transformation could also entail a profound shift in the Chinese power structure, from bureaucrats and party officials to private business; however, it is important to note that in China, bureaucrats, party officials, and private business people may be one and the same. At this writing, it is not certain that China can carry out its planned transition, but at present it is somewhere between the command economy of the past and the market economy of the future. As Hatch and Yamamura have suggested, this situation has created a painful neither-nor existence combining the worst of both systems.

China has become a dual economy pervaded by huge and threatening inequalities. The four Special Economic Zones (SEZs) along the seacoast, in which China's economic growth has been highly concentrated, are dynamic and highly industrialized. Guangdong Province (Canton), for example, with just 6 percent of China's population, is responsible for 21 percent of its economic growth. The bulk of the economy is still located in farming by hundreds of millions of Chinese peasants living in the countryside. While China is the world's third most wealthy country in terms of overall GNP, on a per capita basis it continues to be one of the world's poorest countries. It will be many years before the country will have a sizable wealthy middle class that can sustain an economy based on domestic-led growth. More ominously, income inequality has been increasing among different regions, between rural and urban dwellers, and between winning and losing industries, and this necessarily carries the danger of serious instability. Beijing must wrestle with the dilemma that, while freeing the market from bureaucratic restrictions generates wealth, accompanying relaxation of political controls could lead to internal fragmentation and, as in the Soviet Union, even to overthrow of the Communist regime.

Understanding of China's future role has been limited by myths about "Greater China." Many observers are apprehensive that ethnic Chinese capitalists on the mainland, in Taiwan, and throughout Southeast Asia will join to create a financial and manufacturing network that would be a formidable force and counterweight to Japan in the region. Such fears greatly exaggerate the importance of Greater China, even though it is true that the linkages among mainland China, Taiwan, and the Chinese communities of East Asia have become extremely important to China and the rest of the area. Taiwan and expatriate Chinese communities, for example, have supplied much of the investment capital and economic expertise, and many marketing channels, that have fueled Chinese industrialization. However, connections among the Chinese communities are generally ad hoc and largely commercial. Expatriate Chinese firms are usually family-owned commercial enterprises, interested mainly in quick profits and lacking in organizational capabilities to create regional production networks similar to those forged by huge Japanese conglomerates. Furthermore, few of these firms have become important technological innovators.

In April of 1999, China had not yet become a member of the World Trade Organization, and its access to the crucial American market remains dependent on its status as a "most favored nation"; this status must be renewed annually by the U.S. Congress, and approval has been usually accorded only after fierce controversy, a situation that is and probably will remain highly tenuous, certainly at least through the next U.S. election and the beginning of a new administration. The long-term prospects of China's joining the WTO are clouded by a host of troublesome political and economic issues. The issue of Chinese-human rights abuses has been highly contentious; many Americans and West Europeans consider China's refusal to grant basic freedoms and political rights to its people to be a genuine and legitimate concern. In addition to this humanitarian issue, such other issues as the status of Taiwan's membership in the WTO have blocked Chinese membership. It is also unclear whether or not China is prepared to accept such membership obligations as unrestricted openness to trade and FDI and complete disclosure of economic data. In the late 1990s, the issues of China's membership in the WTO and China's relations with the United States were greatly complicated by allegations that China had stolen American military secrets and by the unfortunate, inadvertant NATO bombing of the Chinese embassy in Belgrade.

Fear of China as an economic and military power has become an important issue, and it is not necessary to accept Samuel Huntington's apocalyptic vision of a "clash of civilizations" to share such concerns. Political leaders, the business community, and organized labor in a number of countries are very worried about competition from low-wage Chinese workers; opponents of China's WTO membership also point out that both foreign firms operating in China and Chinese firms themselves have been able to operate without concern for labor and environmental standards. Many opponents fear that WTO membership would further enable cheap Chinese exports to inundate world markets, lead to mass unemployment in the West, and further damage the environment.

Some American political leaders even fear that the eagerness of American and other firms (Boeing and Loral, for example) to gain access to the government-controlled Chinese market has led these firms to supply China with such dual-purpose technology, possessing both commercial and military significance, as that for aircraft design, computers, and satellites and thus have greatly strengthened China's military potential. Other critics point to Chinese behavior that violates international commercial norms such as intellectual piracy, high import barriers, violations of the international textile and other agreements, restrictions on foreigners, and failure to provide accurate statistics about the economy. Furthermore, China has strict rules of secrecy on matters that the international community considers to be normal business and economic information. Although many concerns in the West have been motivated by domestic politics or narrow economic interests or have been just plain misguided, the overall Chinese record does raise doubts about China's readiness and willingness to assume the responsibilities of membership in the WTO and to become an acceptable member of the world economic system. Although China is undoubtedly destined to be a major military power, its economic role in the region and around the world will remain uncertain until many such issues have been resolved.

Asia-Pacific Economic Cooperation (APEC)

An Asian Pacific identity and institutional framework have been slowly evolving, and several regional organizations have been formed at both private and intergovernmental levels. However, efforts to create a formal multilateral Asian Pacific institutional structure comparable to the EU and NAFTA have faced immense obstacles. The diversity of the region, existing political conflicts, and intense competition among economies have complicated political and economic cooperation. In addition, the major powers of the region—the United States, Japan, and China—have quite different economic and political agendas. For example, whereas the United States wants all trade and investment barriers in the region to be eliminated, the nations in the region have been very reluctant to open their economies.

In 1989, the Asia-Pacific Economic Cooperation (APEC) was created and held its first meeting in Canberra, Australia. APEC emerged from an Australian initiative intended in part to increase the bargaining position of the East Asian/Pacific region in the Uruguay Round of trade negotiations. The European Single Market Act (1986) and acceleration of the movement for greater European integration were important stimulants of this initiative. The Japanese strongly supported the formation of APEC, in part to gain leverage vis-à-vis the EU in the Uruguay Round and at the same time to have a fallback position if the GATT Uruguay Round negotiations should fail. In the decade since APEC's creation, there have been many efforts to strengthen the organization, yet APEC has remained primarily a forum for intergovernmental discussions among almost all the nations in the region. The institutional underdevelopment of the region is signified by the very name of APEC itself; because the member nations cannot reach agreement even on the basic character of the organization, there is no term such as "forum," "organization," or "council" to complete the organization's name.

APEC proponents have reasoned that, given the size of the region, APEC should and could play a major role in the world economy. However, organizational effectiveness has been limited by the absence of strong leadership and the diversity of culture, political interests, and economic development among the member countries. Progress has also

been blocked because APEC has been divided into at least two opposing camps. One group, led by the United States, has wanted to break
down trade and investment barriers; the United States and its principal
supporters (Australia, Canada, and Singapore) would like to make
APEC into an institution possessing some binding force to achieve this
objective. Another group, composed of the less developed countries of
East Asia and led by Malaysia and China, has remained suspicious of
APEC's goal of free trade; they have preferred an organization without
any binding commitments. While Japan has frequently taken positions
close to this latter group, it has usually tried to avoid offending either
side. APEC will remain a minor player in the region and in the larger
global economy unless these problems are solved and fundamental
changes are made in the organization.

Most Asian countries have had quite ambiguous attitudes about
APEC. The Chinese have chosen to participate but are very suspicious
that APEC might infringe on their interests by pressuring them to open
their economy. The Japanese have regarded APEC primarily as a means
to increase Asia's bargaining position in international negotiations and
to ensure that the United States will continue to play a major military
role in the Pacific. APEC has also secured access to the American market for Asian exports, but Japan, China, and others have strongly resisted the idea that APEC, rather than the WTO, should become a
forum for trade negotiations. Although the members of the ASEAN
have supported APEC, they remain suspicious of any regional organization subject to domination by either the United States or Japan. Fear of
American or "white" domination has encouraged Prime Minister Mahathir Mohamad of Malaysia to propose a unified Asian political bloc,
the East Asian Economic Caucus, that would exclude the United States
and other "white" powers.

The American attitude toward APEC has been ambiguous from the
very beginning of the organization. The original Australian proposal
would not have included the United States, but then Secretary of State
James Baker demanded its inclusion. The Bush Administration, like
Japan, believed that a regional Asia-Pacific organization would be a
bargaining chip in the Uruguay Round as well as a fallback position if
the negotiations should collapse. Also, APEC might provide a means
to pressure Japan and East Asian emerging markets to open their

economies to American goods; furthermore, APEC membership would fit America's multitrack trade strategy. The United States wanted "in" even though it had no plans of its own for the organization. However, this situation changed, at least temporarily, with the advent of the Clinton Administration and its realization that APEC might become a vehicle to lower trade barriers throughout East Asia and the Pacific.

The major Clinton Administration APEC initiative was the 1993 Seattle Summit, billed as representing a significant U.S. commitment to the region. Whereas previous American Administrations had preferred a bilateral approach to nations in the region, the Seattle meeting was intended to acknowledge the importance to the United States of the region as a whole and the beginning of a multilateral American approach to the region. This elevation of the Asian/Pacific region in American foreign policy was signified by the fact that, whereas previous APEC meetings had been held at the foreign-minister level, the Seattle conclave of eighteen members was the first APEC summit attended by heads of state. President Clinton also signaled his heightened interest in East Asia by speaking of an "Asian-Pacific Community." Although the agenda prepared by a group of experts from member countries, chaired by Fred Bergsten, director of the Institute of International Economics in Washington, expressed ambitions to transform APEC into "a negotiating forum rather than a purely consultative body," the Summit was actually dominated by an American-led effort to forge a common position toward the Uruguay Round, and it was quite obvious that the major item on President Clinton's agenda was that APEC's Asian members should lower their trade barriers to American goods. The major accomplishments of that Summit were that Mexico and Chile were admitted to the organization and an agreement to create a "community of Asia Pacific economies" was reached.

The question of lowering trade barriers in the region was postponed to the subsequent summit held in November 1994 at Jakarta, Indonesia, where member countries pledged themselves to achieve "free and open trade and investment" by the year 2010 for industrialized APEC members and by 2020 for other members. At the 1995 Summit in Osaka, the blueprint for liberalizing trade and investment was agreed upon, but the other accomplishments of the Summit were modest. It is noteworthy that President Clinton, much to the annoyance of the Japanese hosts, chose to stay in Washington because of a budget crisis. At the November 1996 Summit in Subic Bay, in the Philippines, the United States successfully pressured APEC members to endorse trade liberalization and to support the American-sponsored Information Technology Agreement. At the 1997 Summit in Vancouver, which took place in the early days of the East Asian financial crisis, the organization endorsed the American-sponsored IMF bailout of those nations in crisis and again expressed support for free trade. However, the most interesting event of that summit was the Japanese proposal for an Asian Monetary Fund to assist the troubled Asian economies, a fund from which the United States would have been excluded. Emphasizing the primacy of the IMF in financial matters, the United States scuttled that Japanese initiative. The 1998 Summit in Kuala Lumpur, Malaysia, can only be described as a disaster. Controversial remarks made by Vice President Albert Gore (substituting for President Clinton), in which he attacked the host government and appeared to invite public insurrection, shattered the decorum of the occasion and may have severely damaged the modest effectiveness of the organization.

Despite the Clinton Administration's rhetoric regarding the importance of APEC, its true attitude has been well summarized by a former Administration official. In response to a question about the President's thinking about Asia, the official stated that the President thinks about Asia on the day before he is scheduled to visit the region. The Administration's principal interest in APEC has been as a vehicle to open the economies of the region to American exports and investments. The United States is likely to oppose APEC or any other Pacific Asian organization that it cannot control or at least prevent from taking actions judged contrary to American interests.

Conclusion

At the opening of the twenty-first century, the Asia/Pacific region remains in economic turmoil, East Asia is only slowly emerging from a severe economic crisis, and Japan remains in a serious recession. Yet the region is rich in such economic fundamentals as an excellent labor force and large pools of national savings that propel economic growth over the long term. For all its troubles, Japan continues to lead the world in a number of important technologies and high-tech industrial sectors. The region's problems are primarily political. The one nation that could lead the region, Japan, is in a political stalemate and is unable to take the economic and/or political initiatives that could lift the region out of its economic troubles. Nevertheless, despite its ample supply of problems, the region is slowly regaining its strength.

CHAPTER TEN

Globalization and Its
Discontents

GLOBALIZATION of the world economy has affected and will continue
to affect almost every aspect of both domestic and international affairs.
Growth of international trade, massive international financial flows,
and the activities of multinational corporations are tying national economies more tightly to one another, thus making globalization an important and highly controversial feature of the world economy. Although a
few prominent economists believe that unregulated international finance poses a serious threat to the world economy, almost all economists and other proponents of free markets believe that globalization
promises a world of increasing prosperity and international cooperation; they argue that no obstacles should be allowed to prevent the free
flow of goods, services, and capital.

Critics of globalization, on the other hand, foresee a very different
world; they fear that increased trade, foreign investment, and financial
flows are producing powerful negative consequences for their societies.
Many envision the triumph of a ruthless capitalist system characterized
by exploitation, domination, and growing inequalities within and
among national societies. Alarmist books portray a bleak world of cultural homogenization, rampant commercialism, and even destruction
of Western civilization. Public opinion polls show that at least half the
American people believe that globalization lowers wages, causes unemployment, and has other serious harmful effects. Europeans are even
more skeptical of world economic integration than are Americans, and
in many other industrialized countries popular opinion is equally hostile to it.

Limited Nature of Globalization

Many of the assertions of both proponents and opponents of globalization are either untrue, exaggerated, or just plain silly. While economic globalization is indeed very important, the world is not nearly as integrated as many believe, nor is globalization irreversible; globalization rests on a political foundation that could disintegrate if the major powers fail to strengthen their economic and political ties. Moreover, integration of the world economy has been highly uneven, restricted to particular economic sectors, and not nearly as extensive as many believe. As some writers have noted, the postwar international economy has simply restored globalization to approximately the same level that existed in 1913. *The Economist* has pointed out that France and Great Britain are no more open to trade in 1999 then they were in 1913, and that Japan is even less open. Even the increasingly integrated American and Canadian market is still significantly limited by the border between the two nations. Although the technology leading to increased globalization may be irreversible, the national policies responsible for the process of globalization have been reversed in the past and could be again in the future.

Paul Krugman has noted that the world economy in the late 1990s is even less well integrated in a number of important respects than it was prior to World War I. Under the gold standard and the influential laissez-faire doctrine, for example, the decades prior to World War I were an era when markets were truly supreme and governments had little power over economic affairs. Considered in relation to the size of national economies and of the international economy, trade, investment, and financial flows were greater in the late 1800s than they are at the end of the 1900s. During the twentieth century there certainly has been a great increase in the speed and absolute magnitude of economic flows across national borders; yet the economic impact of globalization has been largely confined to the Triad (the United States, Western Europe, and Japan) and to the emerging markets of East Asia. And even though the industrial economies have become much more open, imports and inward investments are still small compared to the size of each domestic economy. The American economy has "globalized" more rapidly than other industrialized economies, yet trade (imports and exports) in the mid-1990s was only 24 percent of GNP, up from 11 percent in 1970. While this is indeed a significant increase, the American economy is still largely domestic-driven. Moreover, economic integration among the Triad countries in tradable goods, services, and financial markets is more limited than many assert. National borders continue to be important barriers to international economic flows.

Labor globalization was actually much greater prior to World War I than afterward; international migration declined considerably after the war. In the second half of the nineteenth century, approximately 60 million Europeans emigrated to the New World and to such other "lands of recent settlement" as Australia, New Zealand, Argentina, and other temperate regions. Large numbers emigrated from China and British India to the European colonies in Southeast Asia and to other tropical lands like East Africa and the Caribbean. These large moving streams of labor had powerful consequences for the world economy. With the outbreak of World War I, mass migration ceased, and it has never really recovered. Try telling a Mexican or North African low-skilled laborer that we now live in a global economy in which national boundaries have ceased to be important! In fact, much of the globalization rhetoric is no more than the conceit of a rich and industrialized country.

Although the number of political refugees has remained large ever since World War II, few have been granted citizenship in their lands of refuge. The United States is the only country that has welcomed large numbers of new citizens in this period. Western Europe has accepted a flood of refugees and thousands of "guest workers," but it has been much less generous than the United States in extending citizenship to any substantial numbers. In the late twentieth century, therefore, labor migration is not a central feature in the world economy. Indeed, labor migration is relatively low even among members of the European Union.

At the opening of the twenty-first century, we should remember that many important aspects of globalization are not novel developments, and we should recognize that most of the world's population is excluded from a globalization associated primarily with the industrial-ized economies and the industrializing economies of East Asia and Latin America. We should also realize that, despite its importance, eco-nomic globalization is limited and cannot possibly possess either all the negative or all the positive consequences attributed to it.

PERSPECTIVES ON GLOBALIZATION

In the industrialized economies, three different perspectives are appar-ent in the growing debate over globalization and its consequences. Economists, most business and political leaders, and other proponents of globalization share a "free market" perspective opposed to strict reg-ulation of the world economy. Many individuals and such interest groups as organized labor, businesses facing competition from imports, and economic nationalists share a "populist" perspective, and strongly oppose globalization while advocating restrictions on free trade and on the activities of investors and multinational firms. Overlapping some-what with the populist perspective, but more to the political left, are "communitarians"—environmentalists, human-rights advocates, and others who believe that globalization is creating an environmentally polluted, hierarchic, and exploitive world order. These groups advocate a more just, environmentally sound, and egalitarian world order.

Free Market Perspective

Most economists and business leaders believe that globalization and the growing worldwide adoption of American values (social, economic, and political) are releasing pent-up economic forces and leading to more efficient use of the world's scarce resources, and that this will result in maximization of global wealth and enable all peoples to benefit eco-nomically. In addition, they expect that commercial and other bonds among democratic market-oriented societies will be strengthened, thus promoting world peace. Belief in the enormous benefits of globalization has been enthusiastically elucidated by Lowell Bryan and Diana Farrell in their book *Market Unbound: Unleashing Global Capitalism* 1996).[68] These business consultants proclaim that globalization is leading to an era of unprecedented prosperity as more and more nations participate in the global economy, and as financial and technology flows from developed to less developed countries lead to equalization of wealth and development around the world.

Populist (Nationalist) Perspective

Members of this group blame globalization for most of the social, economic, and political ills afflicting the United States and other industrialized societies. One or another member of this group attributes the following unpleasant developments to globalization: growing economic inequality and high levels of unemployment within the industrialized economies, shrinkage or demise of social programs and the welfare state in the name of international competitiveness, destruction of national cultures and of national political autonomy, illegal migration, increasing crime, and on and on. In the United States, Ross Perot and Patrick Buchanan on the political right and organized labor on the political left subscribe to such beliefs; both right and left have denounced free trade and multinational corporations for having caused or at least compounded America's social and economic problems. In Europe, both neofascists and socialists have expressed antipathy toward economic opening and the feared loss of national self-determination. Even such a successful capitalist as the late French-British financier James Goldsmith warned against the dangers of free trade with low-wage countries in East Asia and advocated high barriers to restrict exports from less developed countries (LDCs) from entering Europe. These critics have supported trade protectionism, regional economic blocs, and limitations on the activities of multinational corporations.

Communitarian Perspective

The third position is a melange of dependency theory, Gandhian economics, and the "limits to growth" thesis. The term "communitarianism" is borrowed from Dani Rodrik's book *Has Globalization Gone Too Far?* (1997) and suggests that the central goal of this group is to return to local, independent, and close-knit communities.[69] The members of this diffuse group, which includes Zapatista guerrillas of the state of

Chiapas (Mexico), anticorporate crusader Ralph Nader, and financier George Soros, denounce globalization for foisting a brutal capitalist tyranny, imperialist exploitation, and environmental degradation upon the peoples of the world. They fear a world dominated by huge multinational corporations that will remove all obstacles limiting economic growth, free trade, and pursuit of corporate interests. Such critics maintain that, in the name of international competitiveness and profit maximization, social welfare programs in the industrialized countries are being eliminated and peoples everywhere are being homogenized into passive consumers. Like the populists, this group believes that large multinational corporations, unregulated capital markets, and faceless international bureaucrats in such organizations as the World Trade Organization and the International Monetary Fund do the bidding of capitalists and run the world in ways that destroy national independence and democratic self-rule everywhere.

Communitarians, like many populists, also believe that globalization is responsible for almost all of the world's economic and political ills, including income inequality and chronic high unemployment; as one critic has put it, the poor in the rich countries subsidize the rich in the poor countries. Communitarians differ from the populists, however, in their orientation to the political left. For example, Richard Falk in his *Economic Aspects of Global Civilization: The Unmet Challenges of World Poverty* (1992) blames globalization for much of what's wrong with the world from the economic plight of the South to the Gulf War.[70] Believing that globalization is ultimately unsustainable because of its devastation of the environment, many communitarians advocate return to a world of self-sufficient closed communities.

ISSUES IN THE DEBATE

The diversity, wide-ranging nature, and imprecision of the definitions of globalization used by both proponents and critics complicate evaluation of the issues involved in the debate. Many, if not most, of the "blessings" and "evils" attributed to globalization are really due to such other factors as technological developments, historical accidents, and reckless or dubious national policies unconnected to globalization. West Europeans, for example, blame high rates of unemployment on globalization, when the real culprits are inflexible labor markets and the economic policies associated with creating a regional and not a global economy.

As already stated, I shall use the term "globalization" to refer to the increasing linkage of national economies through trade, financial flows, and foreign direct investment (FDI) by multinational firms. The debate encompasses many issues and provides an important vehicle for understanding both the real and the alleged consequences of economic globalization. However, because the issues are so wide-ranging, and in some cases so speculative, I shall concentrate just on those particularly relevant to domestic and international economic affairs, and I shall not directly address contentions that globalization poses a serious threat to democracy, destroys local autonomy, and homogenizes societies into a formless mass. However, my discussion of the alleged economic effects of globalization is relevant to consideration of these political and social issues. If, as I believe, the present and future economic consequences of globalization have been greatly exaggerated, then its social and political consequences have also been exaggerated. There are many extremely serious social and political problems in the world at the turn of the century, and changes in policies are needed if these problems are to be solved or even ameliorated. However, blaming globalization and wishing that it would go away does not solve these problems, while changed national and regional policies could assist the poor and the downtrodden.

International Distribution of Wealth and Power

Proponents and opponents of economic globalization differ considerably in their expectations of its effects on the distribution of wealth and power within and among national economies. Proponents argue that globalization will eventually achieve greater equality and convergence of performance among national economies. Integration of the less developed economies (of the South) into the world economy will lead to great increases in their rates of economic growth and levels of productivity. In fact, the farther behind an economy is, the faster that economy could grow until it catches up with the more advanced countries. More rapid rates of economic growth will tend to "lift all boats" in these societies and will, in time, benefit the entire population. Indeed, most American economists and other commentators believe that developing countries will adopt the American model of a market-oriented economy and that globalization will increase worldwide acceptance of individualism and political democracy.

Populist and communitarian opponents of globalization present a very different assessment of its consequences. Populists believe that, although the economic and technological flows from developed to less developed countries may indeed be beneficial to the latter, they are harmful to the former. The process of convergence, they proclaim, has already seriously undermined and will continue to weaken the power, wealth, and security of the United States and other industrialized countries. Investments in LDCs by American and other multinational corporations (MNCs), they allege, cause workers in developed economies to lose their jobs and their wages to fall.

Communitarians argue, on the other hand, that globalization creates an hierarchical international economic and political system composed of the rich core of developed economies and the exploited, impoverished periphery of less developed economies. Globalization, they argue, is leading to a massive concentration of corporate power within and across national boundaries, a concentration supported by the World Bank, the IMF, and other American-dominated international organizations. The communitarians (among whom one should include Pope John Paul II) argue that international trade and the activities of multinational corporations are leading to increased international inequality. As the Pope told his receptive audience in Cuba during his January 1998 visit, the rich everywhere are growing richer while the poor are growing poorer. In words reminiscent of now defunct dependency theory, communitarian critics charge that globalization is resulting in a "global apartheid" that is enriching developed countries and impoverishing less developed countries.

Such populists as Ross Perot, Patrick Buchanan, and the late James Goldsmith have expressed fear that diffusion of technology from developed to developing economies will increase the productivity and the competitiveness of the low-wage developing economies. Rejecting this argument, economists point out that wages and productivity have historically risen together. As the productivity of low-wage workers in developing countries increases, their wages will also rise, and thus their alleged threat to high-wage workers in the developed countries will be reduced; for example, as Korea has industrialized, the wages of South Korean workers have risen considerably and have approached Western levels. Although the developed countries will lose markets for those products in which the developing countries gain comparative advantage and which they can produce for themselves, the increased wealth of the latter will create enlarged markets for new exports in which the former retain or gain comparative advantage. In this way, both developed and developing economies will benefit from globalization and economic convergence. How is it possible to evaluate these contradictory assessments of economic globalization and its consequences?

It is true that a disturbing concentration of economic power is forming as large corporations merge with one another, engage in takeovers, and ally with one another. This restructuring and rationalization of corporate activities around the world is significantly transforming the global economy. Yet, this development must be kept in perspective. As critics of globalization themselves point out, this corporate restructuring is in response (at least in part) to the intensification of economic competition as trade and investment barriers fall. This increased competition itself constitutes a significant restraint on the exercise of corporate power. The entry of Japanese automobile firms into the American market, for example, has significantly reduced the monopoly power of American car makers and has been of great benefit to American consumers in terms of price and quality. The most disconcerting examples of the concentration of corporate power, such as the rise of immense media and telecommunications giants in the United States, have little to do with globalization, but are instead the consequence of technological and domestic economic developments. Insofar as the concentration of corporate power is a serious problem, it should be dealt with by strict enforcement of antitrust and competition laws and not by erection of trade and other economic barriers.

The impact of globalization on the distribution of power among nations, and especially between the developed and less developed countries, must also be placed in perspective. One must begin with the fact that every international system throughout history has been hierarchical and composed of dominant and subordinate economies; there has never been, and in the future there is not likely to be, an egalitarian and democratic international system, neither with globalization nor without it. In fact, despite the substantial increase in globalization of economic affairs, the distribution of wealth between developed and less developed countries has not significantly changed over the past half-century. The moderate amount of redistribution that has occurred has in fact favored less developed economies, as is exemplified by China becoming the world's third-largest economy as measured by total GNP. Nevertheless, at the beginning of the new century, the largest segment of the world's population has scarcely been touched by economic globalization. Indeed, Africa and other impoverished regions are more threatened by marginalization and neglect than by globalization and exploitation.

In the modern world, the principal determinants of a nation's international standing in the world economy are factor accumulation (capital and skilled labor) and, over the longer term, its rate of productivity growth. With the possible exception of success or failure in war, the rate of productivity growth is more important than anything else in the determination of whether an economy rises or declines in the international hierarchy. Although the level of productivity of an economy is determined by investment, technological innovation, and effective institutions, there is overwhelming evidence that participation in the international economy is highly beneficial for an economy. Yet, even though trade, technological diffusion, and foreign investment can accelerate an economy's rates of economic and productivity growth, they can also make economies vulnerable to domination by foreign MNCs and subject to international financial troubles and other economic risks. However, if they isolate themselves from the international economy, as LDCs did in the early postwar period, they risk falling farther behind and dropping in the international hierarchy. Every country, especially developing ones, therefore, must face this dilemma and weigh the potential costs and benefits of participating in the global economy.

In an open global economy, there is a danger that a country will lose control over important aspects of its economy. If the past is any guide, such a situation gives rise to powerful nationalist reactions and becomes a source of serious political troubles. This possibility is already on the horizon. German investment in the transitional economies of Eastern Europe, American investment in Latin America, and Japanese investment in Pacific Asia could trigger extremist attacks on foreign firms and investors.[71] Such reactions would not only damage these economies but could also threaten the stability of the global economy. It is almost an unavoidable feature of the international economy that peoples will attempt to raise themselves in the hierarchy of nations, preferably through economic means; but, if that fails, through political means.

Assessment of the charge that globalization leads to a hierarchical structure composed of rich and poor must include consideration of the dynamics of the international system and of the ways in which the structure of that system changes over time. As economists emphasize, globalization has enabled a number of developing countries in Pacific Asia and Latin America to begin closing the economic and technological gap with the developed countries. Indeed, the transformation of many of these emerging markets into fierce competitors has provoked many of the strong reactions found among those populists and other economic nationalists in the developed nations who believe that globalization threatens the security and economic well-being of the United States and Europe. Such fears are by no means groundless, but the threat posed by the industrializing countries to the industrialized economies has been greatly exaggerated. The most pertinent danger in such a situation is that governments of developed countries will adopt dangerous and self-defeating protectionist policies.

As the distinguished Swedish economist S. B. Linder observed, the rapid economic rise of new industrial powers and exporters creates several problems for established economic powers.[72] As rising economies gain a greater share of the world economy, the more advanced economies' relative share is inevitably reduced. Also, the rise of new economic powers and the consequent relative decline of established powers raise concerns about the national security of the established powers. Emergence of new industrial powers imposes on established industrial economies the costly task of adjusting to changes in their comparative advantage, and the increasing international competitiveness and enlarged trade share of rising powers intensifies trade friction and frequently results in a search for scapegoats and charges that rising powers are not playing "fair."

The extraordinarily rapid industrialization of the Pacific Asian economies and their emergence as important exporters have forced other nations to confront the problems caused by significant shifts in international competitiveness and in the international balance of economic power. Similar problems have appeared before, with the sudden emergence of Great Britain in the early nineteenth century, the equally sudden emergence of unified Germany and subsequently of the United States as aggressive export economies in the late nineteenth and early twentieth centuries, and Japan's unprecedented export expansion beginning in the 1970s. Each of these significant shifts in economic power and international competitiveness produced severe economic and political tensions; for example, the economic expansion of Great Britain triggered the formation of the German *Zollverein* (customs union) in the early nineteenth century and subsequently stimulated the unification of Germany and its rapid rise as a great power. At the close of the twentieth century, the economic rise of China and other Pacific Asian economies is repeating this familiar pattern. Although it is probably inevitable that shifts in economic power will give rise to economic tensions, such developments do not have to result in serious economic and political conflict.

Although the developed countries' relative share of global wealth has declined moderately in the late twentieth century, they have not suffered absolute decline and their standard of living has continued to rise. While the developed countries have lost markets in some goods, these economies are still the world's largest exporters. American exports of capital goods to both industrial and industrializing economies even increased significantly in the 1990s. A substantial portion of the American economy's high growth rate after 1995 was due to a surge in exports. The export of capital goods increased because many industrializing countries needed to substitute capital equipment for labor in order to reduce their own costs. Despite the loss to the industrializing countries of America's competitive edge in some products, the United States has continued to have a strong comparative advantage in many others, such as computers, agriculture, and aircraft. Continuation of America's successful adjustment to its changed position in the world is largely dependent on the continued inventiveness of the American economy and is by no means guaranteed.

As I pointed out in *The Political Economy of International Relations* (1987), the spread of industry from the industrialized to the industrializing economies produces opposed consequences.[73] On the one hand, the rise of new industrial powers "competes away" the markets and high profit margins of the established industrial powers. On the other hand, the increasing wealth of the rising powers creates new markets for those products and exports in which the older industrialized economies retain or gain comparative advantage. In this way, the rise of Pacific Asia poses both opportunities and challenges to the advanced industrialized economies. Whether the challenges or the opportunities will predominate will not be known for many years or even decades, and a number of different factors will determine whether the trade-creating or the trade-destroying consequences of industry diffusion will ultimately prevail.

The relations of the developed and the developing countries over the long term depend largely on whether or not the older industrial economies remain or become innovative and able to achieve a comparative advantage in new areas to replace exports of products in which rising industrial economies gain comparative advantage and which they can supply for themselves or export to world markets. Whether or not the industrializing economies open their markets to new exports from the older powers will also be very important. If they are to avoid economic tension and political conflict, each side must make compromises with the other and must not resort to protectionist policies except as temporary measures.

The industrialized economies must not only avoid trade protectionism but must also carry out what economists call an "adjustment process"; they must adopt policies that encourage those businesses that lose comparative advantage to "phase out," while implementing policies that facilitate innovation of new economic activities and improve the economic performance of older ones. The American automobile industry provides an example of successful adjustment. Threatened by superior Japanese imports, the American Big Three automobile companies (Chrysler, Ford, and General Motors) greatly improved the performance of their products and regained international competitiveness. On the other hand, certain sectors of the American steel industry that tried to survive through protection alone provided an unfortunate example of what should not be done.

For their part, the industrializing economies must, at least over the longer term, abandon import-substitution and protectionist policies and open their economies to exports from the industrialized economies. This is happening, but slowly. Brazil, for example, has partially opened its market to computer imports, but it has remained largely closed to automobile imports. Fortunately, greater openness is arising in more and more developing countries.

Labor Welfare in Industrialized Countries

Populists and communitarians in the United States have alleged that globalization has resulted in stagnant real wages, increased wage inequality, and job insecurity; many Europeans blame globalization for chronic high levels of unemployment. Populist charges that imports from low-wage economies are inevitably destructive to the welfare of labor are received favorably throughout the United States and Europe. Free marketeers reject these charges.

A comment is in order here regarding the substantial increase in long-term or "structural" unemployment in Europe since the 1970s, particularly in southern Europe, France, and even Germany. The overall rate of unemployment in Western Europe in the 1990s has been approximately 10 to 12 percent, more than twice that of the United States; in some individual countries the rate has climbed over 20 percent. In Europe, it has become almost an article of faith among business, political, and intellectual leaders that imports from low-wage economies have been responsible for this situation. Most American economists, on the other hand, argue that Europe's high unemployment rate has resulted from inflexible labor markets, overly generous welfare programs and nonwage benefits, and the low rates of economic growth associated with efforts to create the Economic and Monetary Union (EMU). The Europeans have created a system that provides excellent benefits to employed and unemployed workers but discourages hiring of new workers, a system that has little to do with globalization.

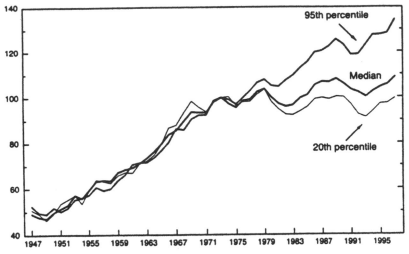

Fig. 10.1. Growth in Real Family Income, 1947–1997. Growth in real family income has slowed and inequality has increased since 1973. *Source*: U.S. Council of Economic Advisors.

Although a number of conservative American economists deny that there has been any significant increase in income inequality in the United States, most economists believe that, while wages have improved in the late 1990s due to robust economic growth, income inequality among workers has increased since the 1970s. Moreover, the overall gap between rich and poor has also increased in Europe and elsewhere. Despite continuous economic growth and a low rate of unemployment (the lowest in twenty-five years), the benefits of economic "good times" in the United States have been distributed unevenly, and many groups have been left behind.

The American situation can be summarized as follows: between the end of World War II and 1973, rapid economic and high productivity growth raised income uniformly for Americans of all income levels, and their incomes approximately doubled. Since 1973, as revealed by figure 10.1, however, the pace of income growth has slowed and income inequality has increased. Whereas median family income increased 10 percent between 1973 and 1999, income in the highest income bracket (ninety-fifth percentile) grew more than a third while income in the lowest income grouping (twentieth percentile) remained virtually unchanged or actually dropped, especially for women. The real earnings of many low-wage and middle-class workers have stagnated or experienced only modest gains, while the more wealthy 20 percent of American families have gained greatly. In addition, corporate "downsizing" and "reengineering" in the 1980s and 1990s greatly increased anxiety and insecurity among all workers, especially those in middle management and those over fifty years of age. In brief, since the 1970s, the standard of living of many American workers has grown very slowly, while income inequality has increased considerably.

Populists ask how an American or European worker earning $20 or more per hour can possibly compete against billions of Chinese, Indians, Indonesians, and Bangladeshi earning less than $.20 an hour. Most professional economists, on the other hand, attribute the relative decline in the wages of low-skilled American workers mainly to technological changes taking place within the industrialized economies themselves. Technological advances, they argue, have decreased demand for low-skilled northern workers while greatly increasing demand for skilled, especially college-educated, workers.

Those who blame globalization for declining real wages and increasing income inequality in the United States maintain that lowered or eliminated trade barriers, improvements in communications and transportation, and the increased imports of manufactured goods from less developed countries have created this problem. All these developments mean that American workers must now compete directly with low-paid workers from the industrializing economies; moreover, problems for the industrialized countries are increased because Mexico, China, and other developing countries have no, or very few, of the labor standards, worker protection rules, and environmental regulations that increase production costs in the United States. Some have alleged that direct investment in the industrializing economies by American and other multinational corporations has made matters worse by equipping these low-wage workers with the most advanced production techniques and thus enabling them to compete on an equal footing with higher-paid workers in the industrialized economies. This "unfair" competition from low-wage countries, many proclaim, has rapidly advanced up the technological ladder so that, at the century's end, it is harming a growing number of white-collar workers. India, for example, has become a world-class center of data processing and software development. Globalization has also increased immigration of workers from poorer countries into the advanced industrial countries, workers who then take jobs away from local workers. Therefore, many critics of globalization charge that increased trade flows, foreign direct investment, and migration are responsible for the deteriorating economic plight of more and more workers in the industrialized economies.

Some prominent economists have broken ranks with their professional colleagues by accepting the globalization explanation of increasing income inequality. These economists point out that international trade rewards an economy's abundant factor of production (capital or labor) and lowers the return gained by the scarce factor.[74] Trade between China with its abundance of low-wage unskilled labor and the United States, for instance, benefits American skilled labor and drives down the real wages of American low-skilled and unskilled labor. Because capital continues to be scarce and labor has become extraordinarily abundant in this open global economy, globalization has also caused a significant shift in the balance of power and welfare away from labor and toward capital in the industrialized economies.

Most American economists argue that the limited trade flows between developed and developing countries cannot possibly explain the roughly 30 percent difference in wages between skilled/college-educated workers and unskilled workers that has emerged in the United States since the 1970s; they believe that growing income inequality is explained by the technological developments transforming industrialized economies. They argue that international trade has had only a small impact on wages, largely because trade between the industrialized and industrializing economies is still minimal when compared to trade among the industrialized economies themselves. For example, imports into the industrialized economies of manufactured goods from less developed countries (LDCs) in the late 1990s have reached only about 2 percent of the combined GNP of the industrialized countries.

Economists point out that such technological developments as automation, "lean production" techniques, and computerization have significantly reduced the demand for low-skilled and unskilled workers. Advanced economies are rapidly shifting from unskilled, blue-collar, labor-intensive industries to service industries and to greater reliance on skilled labor in manufacturing as well as in other aspects of economic life. This structural change parallels the shift from agriculture to manufacturing in the late nineteenth century when, as agriculture became more mechanized, superfluous farm workers migrated from the land to the factory. In the late 1990s, many of the tasks formerly performed by unskilled and less-skilled workers are being carried out by computers and automated processes. The new service- and knowledge-based industries require more highly skilled workers than in the past, and the demand for unskilled workers has declined dramatically throughout the American economy while the demand for skilled workers has increased in almost every sector. The semiskilled assembly-line worker in Detroit or Cleveland who once commanded a high wage in the automobile and other mass-production industries is indeed becoming superfluous in the information economy.

Whereas some critics point out that declining wages and increasing inequality have accompanied the opening of the American economy, most economists believe that openness has not had a big impact. Although the United States has certainly become more open than in the past, imports from LDCs remain just a small percentage of total GNP and therefore cannot produce the large consequences claimed by critics of globalization. However, economists do concede that opening the American economy to significant migration has exerted downward pressure on the wages of lower-skilled labor.

One may inquire why most American economists maintain that technological advances explain the problems of unskilled American workers in the American economy and that imports from low-wage countries do not. It is probable that one reason that economists emphasize technology rather than trade is that they do not wish to give "aid and comfort" to proponents of trade protection. Nevertheless, such a distinction between trade and technology is questionable. Since low-cost imports in many cases motivate domestic producers to decrease their own production costs, and this creates pressures for technological change, it is difficult to understand why so many economists treat technological change as entirely independent of trade. Competition from low-wage countries has definitely stimulated labor-saving technological change in the United States and other high-wage economies, as British economist

Adrian Wood has pointed out.[75] This means that some of the effects on wages attributed to technological changes have actually been due to trade competition, and this indicates that globalization undoubtedly accounts for more of the wage and income problems than most economists have been willing to admit. Yet, it is highly doubtful that imports from low-wage economies are as significant as opponents of globalization claim, while it is certain that trade protection is not a wise solution to the problems of stagnant wages, income inequality, and job insecurity.

"Race to the Bottom," the End of National Sovereignty, and Convergence of Economic Systems

Some allege that the most important result of globalization is the triumph of the market over the nation-state and the consequent end of national sovereignty. Economic forces are said to be eroding national boundaries so that governments lose control over their economies, and national economic systems converge toward a common model. Market-oriented proponents of globalization consider this development as signalling a grand moment in human history: the supremacy of the market over the state and of economics over politics means the end of a human institution and of the political struggles responsible for war, domination, and other ills. For critics of globalization, on the other hand, victory of the market means the end of the state as the protector of the economically weak against the economically strong, and the supremacy of ruthless market forces and those who control such forces. Every value, institution, and human virtue, they fear, will be subordinated to commercial interests and corporate profits.

These differences over the significance of globalization for national policy and sovereignty focus on several issues. The first major question is whether or not globalization has triggered a "race to the bottom" as national governments are forced to strip away business regulations, corporate taxes, and other encumbrances on corporate competitiveness. Does globalization mean the end of the welfare state and of safety nets for those who lose because of economic change? Additional questions

311

arise from the alleged impact of globalization on national economic autonomy: Are governments losing control over their national economies, and is globalization causing national economies to converge toward the American economic model based on openness and the free market? I shall argue that, despite the significance of globalization, it has not replaced the state, national differences, and politics as the really important determinants of domestic and international affairs.

"Race to the Bottom"

Many American and West European critics of globalization charge that, in order to increase the competitiveness of local firms and keep them at home, governments have engaged in a "race to the bottom." They argue that economic policies and the welfare state are being scuttled in the name of higher corporate profits and international competitiveness. Whereas in the past, trade liberalization was accompanied by increases in social insurance and welfare safety nets, critics charge that since the 1980s, social welfare programs have been abandoned, taxes on business have been reduced, and regulation of business practices has been curtailed. Moreover, they note, environmental protection is being cut back to encourage domestic corporate investment and discourage outward FDI. Dani Rodrik even fears that the downsizing of the welfare state in combination with the increased economic insecurity caused by growing fear of low-wage competition could exacerbate class divisions and interclass conflict in Europe and the United States. Over the long term, he suggests, the clash between winners and losers from globalization could lead to social and political disintegration of national societies.

It is indeed true that welfare expenditures in the United States and elsewhere have leveled off and, in some cases, have been reduced. For example, the Clinton Administration decreased spending on the largest American welfare program, Aid to Families with Dependent Children (AFDC). In addition, the Personal Responsibility and Work Opportunity Act, signed in August 1996, requires welfare recipients to work and also severely limits welfare benefits; although this change in the nation's safety net did eliminate a number of welfare "cheats," it did harm many who truly need help without significantly improving the lot of many unskilled individuals unprepared for an increasingly high-tech economy.

It is important to recognize that these welfare reductions can be more accurately explained by the triumph of Reaganesque conservative ideology than by genuine concerns over globalization and international competitiveness, even though international competition has been used to defend these changes in welfare policy. Moreover, the available evidence does not support the charge that welfare expenditures weaken the international competitiveness of American firms. Although globalization and intensified international competition may one day force a severe reduction of social welfare spending, worries about a race to the bottom due to globalization are not yet warranted by the evidence.

Those worrying about a race to the bottom have focused their attention on reductions of welfare programs for the poor. However, examination of expenditures by the American federal government reveals that social welfare expenditures are moderate and impose only a modest burden on taxpayers. Of the approximately $1.5 trillion spent by the federal government in 1995, only 22 percent funded the nation's three most important welfare programs: the AFDC, the Food Stamp program, and Medicaid. On the other hand, the largest federal budget expenditure (33 percent) actually supported middle-class entitlement programs (Social Security and Medicare) in which total expenditures are rising rapidly and do pose a threat to the health of the economy. If one is genuinely worried that excessive taxation and government spending are a large burden on the economy, then reform should begin with these middle-class entitlement programs.

The argument that globalization has resulted in an irresponsible deregulation of American business is also dubious. Since the late 1970s, there has been significant deregulation of many economic sectors, but globalization has played only a minor role. Deregulation has been due both to political conservatism and to economists' findings regarding the high costs to the economy of needless regulation. The argument that regulations have been weakened in order to coddle domestic corporations is a great exaggeration, and furthermore, although employment in manufacturing firms did decline significantly over the final quarter of the twentieth century, the American economy has definitely not experienced serious deindustrialization. Indeed, the contribution of the manufacturing sector to the GNP has declined much more slowly than has employment, because U.S. manufacturing has become more productive and therefore has required fewer workers.

Although American firms have certainly increased their investments abroad and have subcontracted many activities to foreign firms, corporations are not the footloose entities portrayed by their critics. Decisions about the location of a firm's activities are determined by many considerations other than cost and domestic regulations; proximity to the market, access to local technology, and other noncost considerations are of equal or even greater importance. In actuality, most investments by American firms are made within the United States, and only a small percentage of the total is invested in other countries. Moreover, most American FDI goes to America's industrialized competitors, especially those in Europe, Canada, and Japan, all of which are even more highly regulated than the United States. Very little goes to LDCs. Nevertheless, it is undoubtedly true that the threat to move production abroad has to some extent strengthened the bargaining position of capital over labor.

The issue of a race to the bottom is quite different in Western Europe, where both private and public welfare expenditures are much larger than in Japan or the United States. The generous pensions, long paid vacations, health benefits, and other nonwage costs have imposed a huge financial burden on European firms and taxpayers, and the evidence strongly suggests that welfare expenditures and associated costs have reduced the competitiveness of European firms and encouraged many to move production facilities to Eastern Europe and the United States. While few continental Europeans accept the draconian views about welfare held by American conservatives, many do believe that their welfare states have become too expensive and must be scaled back. Nevertheless, it remains very unlikely that Western Europe will participate in any race to the bottom by drastically reducing welfare programs or by adopting what they consider to be the brutal and heartless American reliance on unregulated markets.

Regardless of the strength or weakness of the argument with respect to the effect of economic globalization on safety nets and the welfare state, the United States should do much more to compensate those individuals who lose from the combined effects of globalization, technological change, and other unfortunate consequences of modern economic life. As *Business Week* columnist Robert Kuttner has succinctly stated, capitalism must make the "process of creative destruction" tolerably stable and socially bearable; assistance must be provided for the losers in the process. Even such conservative economists as Milton Friedman and Edmund Phelps, recognizing the significance of the social problems created by what Edward Luttwak has aptly named "turbo-capitalism," have set forth important proposals to compensate the losers from economic change. Surely, the $8 trillion American economy can afford to provide adequate safety nets and retraining programs for those left behind by rapid economic and technological change.

Loss of National Autonomy

Both critics and proponents of globalization argue that the increasing integration of national societies has led to a decrease in the economic, political, and cultural autonomy of nation-states, or the end of their national sovereignty. Various individuals and groups argue that globalization entails the end of economic independence, erosion of political democracy, and a debilitating process of cultural homogenization. They even charge that economic integration of national societies means that domestic groups, and even whole societies, are losing control over their own destinies to powerful outside economic and technological forces. While some regret such a situation, others believe that the "end of the state" is an entirely good thing that will ensure a more prosperous and peaceful world. I shall deal only with the alleged consequences of economic globalization on domestic and international economic affairs, because such other alleged consequences as cultural homogenization and loss of political democracy are certainly not likely to appear if, as I argue, economic globalization has not significantly undermined national economic autonomy.

Globalization opponents argue that the global market has become much more important than have states and national societies in the determination of economic affairs and even of national political affairs. Books alleging a historic transformation in the relationship of state and market have such dramatic titles as *The Retreat of the State*, *The End of Geography*, and *The End of Sovereignty*?[76] Noting that national sovereignty has previously meant unlimited control by governments over their economies, many now view economic affairs as virtually determined by transnational market forces and multinational corporations. The increasing economic integration of national societies allegedly undermines national economic independence and reduces national economic policy autonomy as[77] (1) intensification of trade competition and the need to reduce costs require a significant downscaling of the welfare state and cause governments to engage in a "race to the bottom"; (2) the preponderance of power in the society shifts from the state to the firm, because if its own government does not or can not take actions that reduce the costs of doing business, firms will simply shift activities to other countries; (3) the policy options of governments are limited by their desire to attract foreign capital and their fear of capital flight (some even conclude that international finance now rules the world); and (4) integration of financial markets has undermined the effectiveness of macroeconomic policy (fiscal and monetary) in management of the economy. As I have already discussed most of these points elsewhere in this book and found them to be considerably overstated, I shall concentrate on the alleged impact of globalization on macroeconomic policy.

In an international economy of fixed rates and freedom of movement of capital, it is indeed true, as the "irreconcilable trinity" informs us, that a nation loses the ability to control its economy through macroeconomic policy.[78] However, this constraint is actually a policy option. A nation could, for example, achieve macroeconomic independence by abandoning fixed exchange rates. Such a choice has indeed been made by the United States, whereas the members of Euroland have chosen fixed exchange rates. Moreover, in every society economic expansion is limited by what economists call the "natural rate" of unemployment; the principal constraint on economic growth is the threat of inflation, which is determined by monetary policy and ultimately by supply and demand factors.[79] While globalization or openness to the outside world can obviously affect supply and demand, as it has in the United States in the 1990s, the principal determinants of supply and demand remain primarily domestic.

When assessing the impact of globalization on domestic economic policy, a historical perspective is useful. Those who argue that globalization has severely limited economic sovereignty appear to believe that governments have previously possessed considerable autonomy. They argue as if the nation-state once enjoyed unlimited economic sovereignty and had complete freedom in determining its economic policy; that is, that governments were free because they were not subordinate to transnational market forces. This viewpoint maintains that, in the late twentieth century, government policy has been restricted by the increased integration of national economies; that trade, financial flows, and the multinational firm have led to the loss of governmental control over their domestic economies. Many, having incorrectly assumed that states once had complete economic freedom, exaggerate the changes taking place in the relationship between the state and the economy in the late twentieth century. In fact, the present relationship of state and market that is, the increased importance of the market—is neither particularly revolutionary nor transforming when viewed within an accurate historical perspective.

Prior to World War I, national governments had very little effective control over their economies. Under the classical gold standard of fixed exchange rates, governments were more tightly bound by what Barry Eichengreen has called "golden fetters" than they are in the late-twentieth-century world of flexible rates. Moreover, as Nobel Laureate Arthur Lewis has noted, prior to World War I the economic agenda of governments everywhere was limited to little more than the efforts of central banks to maintain the par value of their currencies. As John Maynard Keynes pointed out in *The Economic Consequences of the Peace* (1919), national economic policy did not concern itself with the welfare of the "lower orders" of society. The minor and highly constrained role of the state in the economy changed dramatically with World War I and subsequent economic and political developments.

Throughout the twentieth century, the relationship of state and market did indeed change significantly as governments harnessed their economies to meet "total war" and to meet their citizens' rising economic expectations; the great wars of the twentieth century and the immense economic demands of the Cold War elevated the state's role in the economy. During periods of intense concern about security, national governments used new tools to manage their economies and began to exercise unprecedented control over their economies. The

Great Depression, the rise of organized labor, and the sacrifices imposed on societies by World War II led Western governments to expand their activities to guarantee the welfare of their citizens. For some years, the perceived success of the Communist experiment also encouraged governments to help Keynes's "lower orders"; and after World War II, governments in every advanced economy assumed the responsibility of promoting full employment, a generous and high level of economic welfare, and an ever-rising standard of living.

Nevertheless, even after World War II the role of Western governments in the economy remained fairly limited; economists exaggerated the role of the government when they argued that they had learned to use Keynesian techniques to "fine-tune" the economy.[80] High rates of economic and productivity growth were required to fulfill the exaggerated expectations of the population, but the rates of economic and of productivity growth declined significantly after 1973 in both the United States and Western Europe. Although American economic and productivity growth rose again in the late 1990s, growth rates in Japan and Western Europe had not risen significantly by the twentieth century's end. And it is questionable whether or not the American economy will continue to grow quickly enough over the long term to be able to meet what might be called the "revolution of rising expectations" of American consumers and wage earners.

With the end of the Cold War and the triumph, at least in the United States, of conservative economic ideology, the interventionist state has come under increasing attack. Indeed, Daniel Yergin and Joseph Stanislaw argue that the market has taken control from the state over the "commanding heights" of the economy, and that the nation-state is finished as an economic actor.[81] While it is true that the state may be reverting to its more modest nineteenth-century role in the economy, this change is due more to developments within national societies and in the international political environment than to the effects of economic globalization.[82] Despite strong frontal attacks on the welfare state by conservatives, the welfare state is only partially in retreat, and government expenditures for welfare purposes have remained large. Thus far, the opening of economies has been accompanied by continuing, albeit declining, state expenditures for social welfare. Any "retreat of the state," at least of the American state, has been due primarily to the end of the Cold War and the defense budget decrease of approximately 30 percent. Although the state at the close of the twentieth century appears to be retreating to its more limited nineteenth-century role, it remains an important actor in economic matters.

Convergence of National Economic Systems

Are the demands of economic efficiency, intensified international competition, and the struggle for ever-greater corporate profitability leading to the convergence of national values, institutions, and economic policies around the world, as some believe? Are economic and technological forces causing nations to cast aside outmoded economic systems and converge toward the common mold of the American economic model based on free markets, openness to the global economy, and minimal involvement of the government in the economy? For some, such a development would produce great joy; for others, this possibility is a source of intense worry.

Proponents of a market-dominated world economy such as Francis Fukuyama and Thomas Friedman foresee all nations converging toward a new world order based on liberal values (free markets, individualism, freedom), spreading global prosperity, and world peace. For these enthusiasts, globalization is here, it is good, and we cannot do anything about it; globalization is inevitable and cannot be reversed. Friedman goes so far as to argue that Margaret Thatcher and Ronald Reagan have set the course for history; together these economic conservatives are said to have fashioned a "Golden Straitjacket" that establishes the primacy of the private sector, removes all restrictions on trade, foreign investment, and the market, and maintains a nearly balanced budget if not a budget surplus![83] Although some observers may find this depiction of President Reagan's economic accomplishments difficult to reconcile with his Administration's huge expansion of the federal budget, frequent concessions to trade protectionists and mammoth budget deficits, Friedman's hyperbole is representative of the globalists' new conventional wisdom.

Critics of globalization, on the other hand, either (like populists and communitarians) fear the consequences of a market-dominated world or reject the idea that convergence of national economies is occurring;

319

this latter position is best represented by Asia expert Chalmers Johnson and political scientist Samuel Huntington, who dismiss the popular American idea that all national economies are adopting the American free-market model. National values, ingrained institutions, and centuries of tradition, they argue, cannot be swept aside as easily as "globalists" proclaim. Furthermore, Johnson, Huntington, and others skeptical of the argument that globalization is leading to convergence and homogenization of national societies believe that political, economic, and security conflicts among nations will remain vital factors in international affairs.

Is globalization forcing or at least encouraging the convergence of national economic institutions and private economic practices? Many argue that intensification of global economic competition, expansion of trade, and foreign direct investment, along with interpenetration of national societies, necessitate that societies adopt similar domestic institutions and economic practices. Many American economists and public officials do argue that the superior performance of the American economy in the 1990s and the contrasting weakness of the state-led Pacific Asian economies, including Japan, and of the welfare state systems of continental Europe, have made the American market-type economy the model for the rest of the world.

The belief that modern technology and market forces are forcing every nation to adopt a common pattern of social, economic, and political organization is an old one. Before "globalism," other "isms" and theories—Marxism, industrialism, and modernization theory—predicted that modern technology and economic developments would destroy all existing societal values and institutions and amalgamate the human race into a uniform and universal pattern of values, beliefs, and institutions. Needless to say, these predictions have not yet been fulfilled. Although national societies have certainly adopted many common institutions, national differences continue to be fundamental and of determining importance in the functioning of capitalist or market economies; market economies come in vastly different shapes and forms and are not converging to a single, uniform type. In fact, even within individual national societies, convergence is limited. For example, even though American institutions of higher learning perform the same functions and are closely integrated with one another by Internet and other means, Harvard, Yale, and Princeton are definitely not converging toward a common model![84]

The impact of the world economy on domestic economics and politics has drawn the attention of scholars of both domestic and international political economy.[85] As Suzanne Berger has pointed out, the world economy impinges on national economies in at least two important ways.[86] Changes in the international economy can decrease (increase) the power and autonomy of particular states, and the world economy can reshape domestic politics and economic affairs through its impact on domestic interests. Through these channels, the global economy can change the behavior and institutions of national societies, but it is not clear whether, or to what extent, external developments associated with globalization are in fact transforming national economies and leading to greater convergence.

The increasing integration of national economies and intensified international competition have certainly encouraged societies to adopt particular institutions and practices that have proved to be especially successful elsewhere; the spread of the Japanese highly efficient technique of "lean" production to the United States, Great Britain, and elsewhere best exemplifies this phenomenon. Yet, the conclusion that economic globalization has been homogenizing domestic economies is not warranted. To my knowledge, the only significant examination of this issue is found in Suzanne Berger and Ronald Dore's edited volume *National Diversity and Global Capitalism* (1996).[87] In a number of case studies, the contributors to this excellent volume (all of whom are experts on one or another of the economies examined) seek to determine whether or not convergence of institutions and domestic practices has been occurring. Berger and Dore draw the following conclusions:

1. Despite some convergence in macroeconomic performance such as growth rates and productivity levels, very little convergence has taken place at the level of national institutions. National institutions tend to be "sticky" or, in the language of economics, "inelastic." Societal changes are usually very costly, strongly resisted, and exceedingly slow.

2. Differing but equally effective systems of corporate and other institutions within national societies limit the need for convergence to achieve particular objectives.

3. External pressures may require some response or outcome, but the character of the response is largely determined by domestic factors and is not limited to a unique or single response.

4. Convergence of national institutions has been a subject of international negotiations; it can seldom be identified as an automatic consequence of globalization.

5. The domestic effects of globalization are largely determined by states themselves.

Although this study does not and could not prove conclusively that globalization will never produce convergence of economic institutions and practices around the world, the evidence does strongly suggest that there has been little or no significant homogenization of national economic and social institutions more generally over the course of the past half-century. Nor is globalization leading to the commercialization of all human affairs. While economic globalization may encourage homogenization of human values and behavior, other factors such as modern advertising and "pop culture" are more important.

International affairs can certainly have a profound impact on national societies and can even force important changes in some aspects of a society's policies and institutions. A notable example was the Meiji Restoration (1868) in Japan. Increasingly besieged by encroaching Western imperial powers, and having witnessed the subjugation of China, the Japanese elite transformed Japan from a feudalistic, fragmented society into a powerful state-centric and highly integrated society. Yet, the fundamental aspects of Japanese society—the subordination of the individual to the group, an intense, tribal nationalism, and a fierce desire to maintain national independence and to "catch up" with the West—remain.

At the end of the century, globalists assert that Japan is at long last being forced to change and to move toward the American free-market economy. It is certainly true that Japan in recent years has experienced a number of noteworthy economic and institutional changes as the overwhelming role of the state in the economy has moderated. The Japanese *keiretsu* system has been strained by economic crisis and has been undergoing a number of modifications, the system of lifetime employment has been weakened due to Japan's recession of the late 1990s, and reforms and deregulation have changed a number of economic sectors and activities, including retailing, which has been opened to non-Japanese. Although the list could be enlarged, those who see radical convergence make a fundamental error.

The social and political purpose of a national economy defines its essential features. Although this purpose may change, it changes slowly and usually in response to a major upheaval; for example, following Japan's defeat in World War II, the purpose of the Japanese economy changed in one important respect as the post-Meiji emphasis on harnessing the economy for military purposes was abandoned and the new goal became the concerted effort to "catch up" economically and technologically with the United States. Despite this important change, the overall political purposes of the Japanese economy remain those of preservation of domestic social harmony and strengthening of national independence. In pursuit of these fundamental social and political goals, the central role of the Japanese state in the economy is very likely to continue, and Japan will strongly resist American-style "marketization" of its economy. Japan's, like Western Europe's, determination not to leave important social and political matters up to the vicissitudes of the unregulated market constitutes a high hurdle to Japan's convergence to Friedman's Golden Straitjacket.

CONCLUSION

Despite the increasing attention given to economic globalization, the world in important ways is actually less integrated in the late twentieth century than it was in the late nineteenth and early twentieth centuries. Recent integration of aspects of the world economy has been highly uneven, limited to particular economic sectors, and not nearly as global as many believe. The one important economic area to which the term globalization clearly does apply, however, is international finance, and the East Asian economic crisis and the global economic turmoil of the late 1990s gave considerable credence to the charge that globalization has significantly increased international economic instability. The experience of East Asia illustrates that when financial speculators move billions of dollars from one economy to another with the push of a button, international financial markets can wreak havoc on national economies and destabilize the global economy. Rapidly shifting international financial flows have indeed become a major threat, and this has intensified the debate over international regulation of the financial system.

CHAPTER ELEVEN

Managing the Global Economy

ON THE THRESHOLD of the twenty-first century, the future of the global economy appears uncertain. During the 1990s, the American economy experienced its longest period of uninterrupted successful and sustained economic growth; income rose for most Americans while inflation and unemployment declined. In Western Europe, on the other hand, economic growth remained sluggish and unemployment was at high levels across the Continent. And Japan was in financial crisis after its "bubble" burst in the early 1990s and it entered a serious recession in the late 1990s. Extricating itself from these difficulties proved exceptionally difficult, but as these lines are written in early summer 1999, there are signs of considerable improvement in the economy. Russia has been in a state of extreme economic distress for nearly a decade. The once-thriving emerging markets of East Asia have struggled with a devastating economic crisis, and Latin America has suffered serious difficulties. Many believe that increasing globalization of the world economy is the culprit behind many, if not most, of these problems.

In the United States, the dominant response to the world's economic troubles and to charges against globalization has been "just follow our example." Most American commentators believe that more open markets and less government intervention will lift the world out of its economic troubles, a belief based on the conviction that American economic success in the 1990s is a product of a recently fashioned New American Economy based on globalization, the computer, and corporate dynamism. Deregulation, privatization, and continuing reduction of the heavy hand of government in the economy have, many argue, paved the way for a streamlined and consequently resurgent American economy. Therefore, Americans believe that the stagnant and troubled economies of the rest of the world should adopt the American system and that free trade, freedom of capital movements, and nonintervention by the state in the economy should be the guiding principles of global capitalism in the twenty-first century.

However, not all agree that this would produce a "streamlined and resurgent" global economy; indeed, some sources of potential difficulty can be identified. The threat of financial turmoil continues, and the United States and the other major economic powers are far from agreement on ways to prevent future financial crises. The movement toward potentially exclusive regional free-trade areas, especially in Western Europe, is also troubling, and at this writing no international agreement on principles to govern economic regionalization has yet materialized. Furthermore, there is a renewed threat of trade protection and significant erosion of the support for open markets.

Creating a "New Financial Architecture"

In the late summer of 1998, the East Asian economic crisis spilled over into the global economy, setting the stage for what President Clinton declared to be the "worst crisis in 50 years." The Russian government's substantial devaluation of the ruble in August triggered that global crisis. For political reasons the Clinton Administration had bet heavily on "saving" Russia and had pressured the IMF to loan Russia tens of billions of dollars that were subsequently squandered. Investors and governments around the world panicked as they witnessed a major nuclear power reneging on its agreements and facing economic and political chaos. Worried that other countries would also default, investors began to withdraw their funds in search of safe havens. Declining corporate profits and investor panic accentuated a steady fall of the American and other stock markets; the threat that the Long-Term Capital Management Fund would collapse deepened the crisis.[88] These events, in turn, set off a serious credit crunch that further slowed global economic growth. In the late fall, some estimated that approximately one-third of the world economy was in recession. Only the United States was still experiencing economic growth. With the depression in East Asia and recession in much of the rest of the world, commodity prices fell considerably, and this caused economic distress in many commodity-exporting sectors, including American agriculture.

American officials had become concerned in the early fall of 1998 that the financial crisis would continue to spread; they focused much of their attention on Brazil. Brazil possessed many characteristics of a developing economy in serious trouble, including a huge budget deficit and sizable international debt. The country's uncertain fiscal situation was causing a heavy capital outflow and putting severe pressure on the Brazilian currency, the real. The Clinton Administration particularly feared that financial collapse in Brazil, a major importer of American products, would seriously damage the American economy and accelerate turmoil throughout the world. As the troubles of the global economy continued to unfold, the Clinton Administration was finally galvanized into action. In a well-publicized speech in mid-September to the Council on Foreign Relations in New York, the President proposed that all the major economic powers stimulate their own economies in order to restore global economic growth; he also proposed that, at the next meeting of the G-7, the major powers should develop a longer-term solution to the problem of global financial instability.

These Clinton initiatives were given a cool reception. Every central bank rejected the suggestion that interest rates be cut so as to stimulate global growth. Subsequently, that autumn, the Federal Reserve, motivated primarily by concerns about the American economy, did cut interest rates three times between September and the end of November; these rate reductions succeeded in reinvigorating the economy. The Clinton proposal for a G-7 meeting had been accepted by other nations, although without enthusiasm; the meeting took place following the annual joint meeting of the IMF and World Bank (WB), held in Washington in October.

Clinton's New Architecture

At the IMF-WB meetings, President Clinton set forth his proposals for a "new international financial architecture" to contain the spreading economic crisis and prevent future crises. The Administration also hoped to forestall efforts by other governments (mainly Western European and Japanese) to impose new restrictions on international capital flows. The President's proposals were considered at the meeting on

October 30 of the major economic powers, and several important decisions were reached. The G-7, assuming that if investors were fully aware of risky situations, they would not repeat the mistakes made in Mexico and East Asia, agreed that much greater transparency of financial conditions in every country was crucial to prevention of future financial crises. To achieve this goal, the G-7 called for much tighter international standards for accounting and for regulation of banks.

The most important G-7 decision was its acceptance of the President's proposal that the IMF should establish a $90 billion contingency fund to provide countries with emergency financial assistance; the fund would help only those countries already carrying out economic reforms and those whose economic "fundamentals" were basically sound. Thus, the IMF could step in before a crisis actually occurred to shore up the country's financial defense of their currencies by providing adequate liquidity and thereby preventing financial panic. When it made this proposal, the Clinton Administration had Brazil in mind, as Brazil required a huge infusion of foreign capital to keep its economy afloat. Following a bruising but ultimately successful battle in the Congress over replenishment of IMF funds, a large part of which had been squandered on Russia, the IMF offered Brazil a large assistance package of over $40 billion. A precondition for the financial support was that the Brazilian economy be overhauled in significant ways. Having failed to improve its economic performance, Brazil suffered a major economic crisis in early 1999.

Debate over Regulation of International Finance

As important as the G-7 decisions had been, they failed to quell the intense controversy regarding the reform and regulation of the international financial system. To deal with destabilizing international financial flows, a number of proposals have been set forth that range from creation of a world central bank to imposition of an international tax on money transfers across national boundaries. Some experts believe that self-imposed national restrictions on financial inflows and outflows are necessary; a number of national governments, such as those of Japan, China, and Chile, have maintained controls on financial flows; and in response to the East Asian crisis and global economic turmoil, Malaysia imposed controls. Moreover, the European Union began consideration of some regionally based capital controls.

Several important proposals for stabilizing international finance have been set forth and debated. A number of economists and others argue that governance of the international financial system should be left entirely up to the market. The Clinton Administration and the IMF favor freedom of capital movements along with greater IMF surveillance over both domestic and international financial matters. A number of countries, including Japan, Germany, and France, believe that stringent international controls over monetary and financial matters are required. Some economists believe that only a "true lender of last resort" will protect the global economy from devastating financial crises.

RELYING ON THE MARKET

A number of economists believe a completely open and unregulated international financial system is the best solution to the problems resulting from international financial flows. They also believe that any other approach necessarily raises the problem of "moral hazard"; that is, if lenders and borrowers believe that the IMF or another official agency will rescue them from their folly, reckless behavior will be encouraged, as happened in the East Asian financial crisis. In an unregulated financial market, the market itself will punish those investors and borrowers who fail to pursue prudent economic behavior. Knowing that no one will rescue them if they get into trouble, international investors will become more cautious. Many proponents of this position regard the term "speculation" as pejorative and argue that what is generally called "financial speculation" is actually the rational attempt by investors to protect their assets from irresponsible government behavior. This position holds that there is no need for international regulation of financial affairs, because truly financially irresponsible lenders and borrowers will be punished by the market and will thereby be deterred from reckless behavior.

Such proponents of this position as Milton Friedman, Walter Wriston, George Schultz, and William Simon argue that the IMF is ineffective as well as obsolete and should be abolished. Friedman considers the role of the IMF in the world economy to be an example of bureaucratic self-aggrandizement. The IMF, Friedman points out, was

329

originally created to supervise the system of fixed exchange rates that collapsed on August 15, 1971, when President Nixon closed the gold window by refusing to continue the U.S. commitment to buy and sell gold. The IMF then found a new function as an economic consulting agency for countries in trouble, offering money to help them in exchange for promises of reforms. In Friedman's opinion, this interventionism by the IMF encouraged countries to continue pursuing unwise and unsustainable economic policies. Russia's failure to make the hard decisions required to salvage its devastated economy, he believes, was a classic example of IMF culpability for encouragement of irresponsible behavior.

For Friedman and fellow conservatives, the IMF response to the Mexican crisis of 1994–1995 represented a quantum jump in the IMF's counterproductive interventionism. Mexico was bailed out by an aid package of $50 billion put together by the IMF, the United States, and other countries. Friedman has asserted that the IMF money actually ended up in the hands of such foreign entities as American banks that had foolishly lent money to Mexico, while Mexico itself was left in recession and saddled with higher prices. However, the Mexican crisis had a longer-term and even more serious consequence because it fueled the East Asian crisis by encouraging investors to again make risky investments. Drawn by high returns and assured that the IMF would bail them out if the exchange rate broke down and governments defaulted, investors poured money into the emerging markets of East Asia. In effect, the IMF and its provision of insurance against currency risk subsidized private banks and investors, a clear example of a policy that encouraged undesirable behaviors. Thus, the solution to financial instability must be through elimination of IMF-induced "moral hazard."

The market-oriented position rests on the assumption that investors are rational and will not invest in risky ventures if they know that they will not be bailed out by the IMF and the American government. Therefore, eliminate "moral hazard," and you eliminate the problem of serious international financial crises. That may be correct, but such an approach has never been tried and there is no empirical evidence to support such a daring policy experiment. Indeed, the available evidence leads to the conclusion that investors are *not* consistently rational but *do* get caught up in euphoria. Indeed, when the speculative bubble bursts, many innocent people will get hurt. For this reason, few governments are willing to risk leaving international financial matters entirely "up to the market," and many governments have installed mechanisms at the domestic level to protect their citizens from financial instability.

STRENGTHENING THE IMF

Others believe that the solution to the problem of international financial instability can be found in strengthening the regulatory role of the IMF. Proponents of this position, especially the United States and increasingly the IMF itself, believe in the freedom of capital movements. However, while agreeing with the market approach about the beneficial nature of free capital flows, they believe that greater supervision of financial matters by the IMF is necessary. Indeed, the IMF has already taken a number of important initiatives to create a regime for international finance. Most important, the IMF charter has been amended to give the IMF greater jurisdiction over financial matters. As IMF's First Deputy Managing Director Stanley Fischer has said, the amendment is intended "to enable the Fund to promote the orderly liberalization of capital movements." He has also noted, however, that achievement of this goal requires continuous and reliable information on the financial conditions in potentially risky economies, development of an effective surveillance system to monitor such economies, and action by the IMF as the lender of last resort.

The following paragraphs indicate some of the difficulties faced by the IMF in its efforts to strengthen its role in preventing financial crises:

1. *Improved Information Gathering.* The 1994–1995 Mexican crisis was indeed deepened by the poor information about Mexican financial conditions supplied by the Mexican government to the IMF and investors. For example, the size of Mexican financial reserves and external debt was kept secret. In 1996, lessons learned from this experience did lead to increased data gathering and its dissemination by the IMF. However, some experts point out that even the improved system of data gathering proved inadequate and clearly did not forestall the 1997 East Asian financial crisis. Although more reliable information on the financial conditions of developing economies would be an important safe-

331

guard against reckless investing, the fact that governments wish to keep financial data secret in order to increase their leverage with foreign investors raises a major hurdle. The predicament is made worse because governments wish to keep their financial condition secret in order to strengthen their relative position in the intensifying competition for capital imports.

2. *Codes of Conduct and Improved Surveillance.* To increase financial discipline at the international level, the IMF has placed much greater emphasis on developing codes of conduct regarding "good practice" in financial affairs that would require upgrading of the Basle Accords regulating international banking.[89] In addition, improved surveillance and monitoring of specific economies for such dangers as high budget deficits and high rates of inflation are required. However, even if a country is warned of impending problems, it may not act to forestall them, and the IMF is powerless to force such action; yet it would not be proper for the IMF to warn investors of potential problems in a particular country.

3. *Lender of Last Resort.* In a world of increasing capital flows and growing numbers of borrowers, it is inevitable that individual countries will occasionally experience serious financial troubles and require international assistance in the form of a large infusion of money to prevent a liquidity or even an insolvency problem. When a sound economy has a temporary cash-flow problem, that is a liquidity problem; but an economy with severe economic problems will have an insolvency problem.[90] Even though the most appropriate agency to perform the role of lender of last resort would be the IMF, the IMF is seriously limited in this capacity, because, unlike a true central bank, it cannot create money and its cumbersome governing mechanism prevents it from acting quickly in a crisis. In addition, the IMF's assumption of the role of the lender of last resort would raise a serious dilemma because the risk of encouraging "moral hazard" increases in proportion to the size of the available resources.

Strengthening the IMF as a means of promoting freedom of capital movements and preventing financial crises has been an important objective for the Clinton Administration. The priority of keeping economies open to international finance reflects the American commitment to a pro-market ideology, the American financial interests to which the Treasury is highly responsive, and the belief that America has a strong comparative advantage in financial services. However, as the intense 1998 controversy over America's $18 billion contribution to the IMF illustrates, the Clinton Administration's effort (backed by export interests) to strengthen the IMF's role in preventing financial crises had many opponents, and the controversy raised serious questions about the ability of the United States to lead in fashioning a "new international financial architecture." In order to win congressional approval of IMF funding, the Administration had to accept a number of Congress-mandated changes regarding the IMF, even though Congress did withdraw its demand for a major overhaul of that institution. Although some of the changes may be helpful, others may considerably complicate IMF functioning. Meanwhile, it is certain that U.S. attempts to transform the IMF unilaterally were not pleasing to other governments.

The changes proposed by the Congress are listed here with my commentary:

1. IMF agreements with recipient countries and such other IMF activities as reports on various nations must be subject to increased disclosure and transparency. (This proposal responds to charges that the IMF is too elitist and secretive. As many developing countries have resisted disclosure of financial information, this requirement would undoubtedly become a source of friction between the IMF and many countries.)

2. The IMF must impose higher market-based interest rates (about 7 percent) that would encourage faster repayment and greater dependence on the private market. (Many conservatives complain that the IMF competes against the private financial sector and demand that the IMF end its practice of lending to foreign governments at below-market interest rates. If the IMF made this change, it would surely blunt any effort to make it the lender of last resort.)

3. The American government must ensure that IMF loans do not harm the poor or the working class, and labor standards must not be violated. (Obviously, this proposed change was a concession to organized labor and the political left.)

4. The U.S. Treasury must certify that IMF loans do not subsidize industries that compete against American industry. (What more can be said than "economic nationalism is alive and well in the U.S. Congress!")

5. There were several other interrelated proposals, including a requirement that the Treasury make a detailed evaluation of the IMF or Congress would significantly increase its oversight of IMF operations and of international finance more generally. (This change would be likely to invite congressional meddling in IMF affairs and lead to politicization of its activities.)

It is unlikely that the IMF can be strengthened sufficiently to be able to deal with future financial crises. Many countries would offer fierce resistance to strengthening the IMF. Bankers and governments in both the industrialized and industrializing world are and will be extremely reluctant to accept IMF supervision. Furthermore, congressional resistance and weak American leadership would have to be overcome. All of this means that the prospects for IMF-based governance of international financial affairs are extremely dim.

Controlling International Monetary and Financial Affairs

Differing with the Clinton Administration, a number of economists and governments favor some controls over international capital movements. Many believe that short-term flows should be controlled. Nobel Laureate James Tobin and some other American economists have proposed a tax on short-term capital flows and on other flows, and Paul Krugman has argued that countries in financial difficulty should consider capital controls. Charles Kindleberger has proposed creation of a true lender of last resort that could step in quickly to arrest a potential financial crisis. The French, German, and Japanese governments have raised the possibility of other measures to tame large swings in global financial markets and currency values. France, Germany, and Japan have proposed that the European Union, Japan, and the United States should manage exchange rates and keep them within specific bands or target zones in order to stabilize the global economy. However, the United States and central bankers have strongly objected to delegating decisions over interest rates and macroeconomic policy to any international authority; they prefer to rely on the market.

The differences between the United States and its principal economic partners over currency and financial matters were the subject of the annual meeting of the G-7 finance ministers and central bankers in February 1999. Creation of a mechanism to regulate international finance was the principal issue discussed at that meeting. On one side of the debate were the German, French, and Japanese governments, favoring increased controls; many European and Japanese officials particularly wanted to control "hedge funds."[91] On the other side were the United States and central bankers who were strongly opposed to an international authority and preferred to leave decision making to themselves. The differences between the United States and the other economic powers partially reflect ideological positions regarding market functioning, but they also reflect the relative competitiveness of American financial institutions and their political strength within the United States. A compromise agreement was reached on establishment of a "financial stability forum" composed of national currency regulators who will meet twice a year to consult and consider ways to improve the quality of financial information. The difficulties experienced by the G-7 in efforts to agree on reforms of international financial affairs does not augur well for the future stability of the global economy.

Creating a True "Lender of Last Resort"

While it is true that many firms and investors, having suffered huge losses, have become more wary, caution will undoubtedly again be thrown to the winds when a new "euphoria" emerges. Some believe that the only viable solution to the problem of international financial crises is creation of a true lender of last resort that could give rapid and substantial assistance to countries in serious financial trouble. Fulfillment of this responsibility would entail liberal provision of money to reassure markets. As the IMF cannot create money, it would have to be heavily endowed with national contributions to perform this role; however, members are reluctant to contribute.

335

The need for such a lender has significantly increased due to the immense increase in "hot money" circling the globe and looking for speculative investments. As financial expert David Hale has pointed out, the unprecedented size of speculative hedge funds operating on a global basis has no parallel in financial history. And the need of highly leveraged investors to sell fast when prices start to move against them contributes considerably to the instability of the international financial system.

Opposing the idea of a lender of last resort, the market-oriented position believes that an emergency fund to bail out errant investors and countries would create a serious problem of "moral hazard." This is certainly a valid concern because such a fund could easily encourage risky speculation. However, as Charles Kindleberger has pointed out, the damage caused by an international financial crisis is much worse than damage to which "moral hazard" might lead. One must inevitably choose, he argues, between one or another of those two evils, and some believe that "moral hazard" is the lesser of the two evils.

THE CHALLENGE OF ECONOMIC REGIONALISM

Economic regionalism has become an increasingly important threat to a unified global economy. In an exhaustive and authoritative study of regionalization, international economist Jeffrey Frankel has concluded (in the prosaic language that economists like to employ) that "bloc effects" are "discernible."[92] Frankel found that formal regional arrangements do noticeably affect trade patterns well beyond the natural tendency for neighbor to trade with neighbor. As the European Union has enlarged and incorporated new members, diversion of trade and/or discrimination has increased. The Mercosur and its effects on imports of automobiles into member countries provide an even more dramatic example of trade diversion, and certain economic sectors such as automobiles and textiles have been particularly subject to the trade-diverting effects of regional arrangements. Continuation of this trend toward economic regionalism and trade diversion could seriously threaten the open, multilateral global economy.

Intensified international economic competition and a growing struggle for technological supremacy have become significant elements supporting the trend toward economic regionalism. In Western Europe, North America, and Pacific Asia, as well as elsewhere, dominant powers and their allies within each region have joined forces to increase their own economic strength and their bargaining leverage in global economic negotiations. The European Union already participates in international trade negotiations as a regional bloc.

Economic regionalization has become a means to increase the international competitiveness of firms within the region. Various forms of trade agreements (customs unions, free-trade areas, and single markets) to some extent provide such advantages of free trade as economies of scale in production while at the same time denying these advantages to outsiders unless they invest in the internal market and meet member-country demands for technological transfers and job creation. Regionalization also facilitates pooling of economic resources and formation of regional corporate alliances; therefore, it has become an important strategy used by groups of states to increase their economic and political power. Whether this development is good or bad has become a contentious matter among economists and other observers.

Debate among Economists

The spread of regional arrangements has led to an important debate among economists over such issues as whether regional arrangements are more effective than global institutions in solving outstanding economic problems and whether regionalism constitutes a "stepping-stone" or a "stumbling block" to an open multilateral world economy. Many economists believe that the debate could be resolved through establishment of an effective international regime to govern the formation and functioning of regional arrangements and thus to increase the likelihood that regional arrangements will become stepping-stones. Even though such a regime could be highly beneficial, to be effective any regime must overcome major political obstacles. However, the prospects for an international regime that would limit possibilities of creating regional arrangements are poor, because these arrangements have been developed to satisfy such political motives as protection of the North American automobile industry and/or support of the political unification of Europe.

Most American economists oppose economic regionalism because it is discriminatory by nature and creates economic distortions. A region-alized world economy, for example, would exclude many, if not most, of the developing countries and could even thwart or at least delay their economic development. Regionalism also leads to both trade and in-vestment diversions that undermine economic efficiency. Furthermore, economists believe that regionalism could reduce the support for global free trade as domestic groups that benefit from regional arrangements would probably resist further liberalization. MNCs that acquire a toe-hold in a closed region with substantial intraregional trade would be less inclined to push for further trade liberalization. Regionalism would also strengthen the ability of the larger economies in a regional arrange-ment to dominate and possibly exploit the smaller. Most economists believe that the international community should concentrate its efforts on creating an open multilateral world economy rather than on making regional arrangements, because a world economy based on principles of comparative advantage and national specialization would not only pro-duce superior economic benefits, but an open and nondiscriminatory economy would also reduce international economic friction and per-haps even promote peace.

Other economists, however, argue that economic regionalism has several important advantages over global multilateralism. Regional ar-rangements can deal with important subjects not covered by the World Trade Organization, issues that are nearly impossible to handle effec-tively through global negotiations; for example, regional arrangements have been able to establish rules governing such difficult matters as foreign direct investment and regulation of the activities of multina-tional corporations. Regional organizations can also be more flexible than global institutions; the European Union, for example, has imple-mented a number of reforms in such areas as deregulation and competi-tion policy, while the WTO with its many constituencies would have great difficulty in carrying out such reforms. Furthermore, a regional arrangement can facilitate free trade among its members and "lock in" economic liberalization; regionalism can also guarantee access for certain smaller countries to the markets of larger countries. Many believe that if a particular region is large enough and diverse enough to achieve economies of scale and dynamic comparative advantage, then a customs union or a free-trade area makes good economic sense and may even reduce political friction within the region.

A number of American economists believe that economic regionalism constitutes, or at least could constitute, an important and perhaps necessary step toward an open multilateral world economy. Removing internal trade and other barriers among the economies within a region, as the European Union has done, could facilitate an otherwise more wrenching decision to open these economies all at once to global competition. Moreover, removal of barriers within a region could release dynamic forces that would support additional initiatives toward open markets that could benefit the whole world.

Other economists believe that regional movements reverse the postwar movement toward an open world economy. They argue that regionalization has been driven by a number of powerful political and economic forces, including declining American leadership, increasingly significant differences among national economic systems, and intensification of international economic competition, differences that lead national governments to pursue economic regionalization as a clear alternative to the Bretton Woods commitment to an open, multilateral global economy. Indeed, many believe that the only realistic alternative to economic regionalism is economic nationalism and not a multinational world economy. For them, regionalism constitutes the "best of all possible worlds."

Yet, one must acknowledge that the policy prescriptions of economics upon which most international regimes rest would be difficult if not impossible to apply in a regionalized world economy. By definition, economic regions surrounded by a customs union (like the EU) or those employing rules of origin (like NAFTA) do discriminate, at least to some extent, against outsiders. Creation of a regime governing regional arrangements could contribute to maintaining the openness and stability of a regionalized international economy. However, regional arrangements are created primarily for political reasons, and even the existing modest rules limiting their activities are almost totally ignored. In such a situation, therefore, the behavior of regional arrangements

339

would be limited only by the benefits that members would gain through economic openness and fears that particular behaviors would result in retaliation.

An International Regime

The spread of regional arrangements and the threats they pose have led a number of economists to propose a new and much more effective international regime to regulate regionalization. Jeffrey Frankel and others have argued that the international community requires more effective rules to govern the formation and functioning of regional trade agreements (RTAs).[93] Indeed, such a regime is required if the movement toward economic regionalism is to result in any benefits for the overall world economy and/or is to constitute a step toward multilateralism. Establishment of an effective international regime governing RTAs would require substantial reform and strengthening of the WTO. At present, the principal rules of the GATT/WTO that govern regional agreements are contained in Article XXIV of the GATT and provide that (1) barriers to trade among the participants must be completely eliminated (no partial preferences) on substantially all the trade among signers of the agreement; and that (2) there can be no overall increase in the duties and other commercial regulations affecting imports from nonmember countries. Prohibition of partial preferences is intended to prevent use of the otherwise lenient GATT provisions regarding regionalism to legitimate trade protection in certain sectors of the market. Furthermore, the rules are supposed to guarantee that a regional trade agreement will not harm either nonmembers or the global trading system as a whole. However, these rules have done little to protect nonmembers or the trading system in general against discriminatory RTAs.

Article XXIV's limitations have become more and more apparent as regional arrangements have spread and as trade has become more closely linked to FDI. For example, existing GATT/WTO rules require that each new RTA be appraised by a committee; but committee procedures, their rulings, and enforcement do not appear very effective. Since committees considering disputes are open to all one hundred thirty or so GATT/WTO members, deliberations are cumbersome and awkward; also, the terms of reference within which rulings can be made are vague. It is thus not surprising that only six of the seventy-odd committees that have been formed to evaluate proposed RTAs since the GATT began have ever reached a firm conclusion. Furthermore, it is extremely difficult to ascertain whether or not the costs of a particular RTA outweigh its benefits; most produce mixed results. Ambiguity in the rules and procedures opens wide the door for RTAs that would damage nonmembers.

Believing that economic regionalism constitutes a serious and growing threat, Frankel and other economists recommend new rules to decrease the likelihood that regionalized organizations will become stumbling blocks to further global liberalization. They recommend, for example, that RTAs should welcome new members that meet such criteria as removal of all nontariff barriers. Other economists have proposed additional reforms that would strengthen the international regime governing RTAs by increasing WTO authority over RTAs and ensuring that RTAs are consistent with an open multilateral trade regime. Such reforms would increase the transparency of RTAs and the probability that a particular RTA would become a step toward multilateralism.[94]

Whether or not GATT rules are revised may not have much impact, because states are seldom, if ever, concerned about the effects of RTAs on the welfare of nonmembers. Despite the considerable thought that went into drafting the Single Market Act and related initiatives, the West Europeans failed to consider the impact of European economic unification on the rest of the world. When reaching agreement within a region, local producers are generally able to use their power and influence to ensure that the rules benefit themselves rather than outside competitors; this happened with NAFTA and the Big Three American automobile corporations. Although economic theory suggests ways in which RTAs could be created without harming outsiders, commentators have concluded that RTA compliance with the principles of free trade can be provided most effectively by "peer pressure" from injured third parties. Such pressure may be the most effective weapon available to prevent the world economy from fragmenting into regional arrangements and to avoid division into antagonistic blocs like those that characterized the 1930s and resulted in World War II. Although international regimes are important elements in the management of the global economy, they are not sufficient in themselves to overcome the efforts of nation-states to seek their own advantage at the expense of others.

From the beginning of the GATT itself, political considerations have taken precedence over such principles of free trade as national treatment and nondiscrimination, and such political considerations are still seriously hampering efforts to limit the damage to nonmembers caused by RTAs. The British government, for example, would not have accepted the Bretton Woods agreement if that agreement had not permitted the Commonwealth and the special economic relationships within the Commonwealth to continue. And the United States supported establishment of the Coal and Steel Agreement and, subsequently, the European Common Market, and it ignored the principles of nondiscrimination and national treatment it had previously upheld, because the United States wanted a united Europe as a Cold War ally. Only in the early 1960s in the Dillon and Kennedy Rounds did the United States begin to attack discriminatory policies of the EEC. And then it belatedly recognized the degree to which its own economic interests were being harmed by the Common Market's External Tariff, particularly by the Common Agricultural Policy. Eventually, GATT Article XXIV fell into general disuse. In such ways, politics have dominated economics in those international regimes that do govern economic regionalism.

Increasing regionalization of the international economy presents a serious challenge to effective governance of the global economy. Although fragmentation into hostile blocs is highly unlikely, a more regionalized world economy relatively closed to imports and investment by nonmembers would have major (and, I believe, negative) implications for international peace and prosperity. It is important that the United States and the other major powers now cooperate to limit regionalization's possible destructive effects. The existing international regimes and institutions for international cooperation and for guiding the functioning of the world economy have become less and less adequate to their tasks; they must be reformed and new regimes created to ensure the continued existence of a rule-based international economy that can promote peace, prosperity, and stability. None of this can be accomplished unless or until effective leadership is provided and the political foundations of the international economy are strengthened.

The enormous economic benefits of an open and integrated world make a highly regionalized and fragmented world economy quite unlikely. Yet, it is important to recognize that no one anticipated the extent to which, and the speed with which, economic regionalism in trade, services, and investment has developed since the mid-1980s. Some analysts had actually denied that a surge in regionalization was even possible; at the opening of the new century, however, the world is caught in a security dilemma in which one regionalization begets another. Return to a rule-based international trading and economic system would provide a solution to this threatening situation. However, that will not happen unless more effective leadership emerges than the world has had since the end of the Cold War.

The future of and the relationship between globalization and regionalization (and protectionism) is not at all clear as the new century opens. Regionalization, like globalization, must rest on a firm political foundation, and its success is no more assured than is that of globalization. Regional integration of national economies suffers from many of the same problems that afflict globalization. Regionalism, too, requires strong leadership, interstate cooperation, and domestic political support, and every regional movement has been troubled by problems in these areas. As the efforts to create a unified Europe have exemplified, regional unification must overcome serious distributive conflicts, concerns over the loss of national autonomy, and the problem of free riders. As long as they continue to believe that their interests can best be served by their own national governments, individual states and powerful domestic groups have resisted and will continue to resist integration within a region as fiercely as they resist integration into the global economy.

Renewed Threat of Trade Protection

At the opening of the new century, unfortunately there is danger that the United States and other countries will return to protectionist policies. The differing rates of economic growth on opposite sides of both the Atlantic and Pacific Oceans have already produced huge trade imbalances between the United States and its trading partners. As an oasis of strong economic growth in a depressed or slow-growth global economy, the United States became the "importer of last resort" for much of the rest of the world, especially East Asia. The trade/payments imbalance between the United States and East Asia, including Japan, has risen and could continue to rise dramatically, at least for the near future. In 1998, the American trade deficit in goods and services surged to $168.6 billion; the merchandise deficit (goods only) was up 25 percent from 1997 and reached $248 billion. Merchandise imports from East Asia were responsible for a sizable portion of this deficit. Much of the trade deficit was with Japan and other East Asian nations; the deficit with Japan was $64 billion, and with China, $57 billion. The United States also had large deficits with Mexico and Western Europe. These deficits have continued into 1999. This situation would of course change radically if American economic growth significantly declined, its ratio of savings and investments shifted toward savings, and/or currency values changed to decrease the value of the dollar.

In a 1999 response to these huge imbalances and to rising domestic demands for trade protection, the Clinton Administration intensified its pressure on both Japan and Western Europe to stimulate their economies and accept more imports from the troubled economies of East Asia and elsewhere. Even though there would be no significant impact from such changes on the United States unless domestic consumption decreases and savings rise relative to investment, the Administration seemed to believe that some pressures on the U.S. economy would be relieved if more imports were admitted elsewhere. It is important to note that the Clinton Administration also again utilized its multitrack trade policy. Responding to increased demands from domestic steel producers for protection against the alleged dumping of steel on the American market, the Administration pressured other countries to accept voluntary export restraints on their steel exports; other economic sectors have also demanded protection. And, although this was not related to the trade imbalance, the United States and the European Union (EU) in the spring of 1999 fought a "banana war" over the latter's preferential treatment of banana imports from former European colonies, a treatment that harmed the interests of American companies exporting bananas from Central and South America. Other battles with the EU were fought over hormone-treated beef, genetic-engineered foods, and the selection of a new WTO director. The list of U.S. conflicts with its trading partners could be greatly expanded, and these growing differences pose a threat to the effectiveness of the WTO and the future of the trade regime. The clamor in the United States for trade protection in an era of unprecedented affluence leads one to ask what may happen if and when an economic downturn occurs.

Although some steel exporters and others have undoubtedly been dumping goods on world markets and some countries have imposed unreasonable restrictions on American exports, the real causes of America's growing trade deficit in the late 1990s are poorly understood, at least as reflected in the public debate, and misunderstanding could result in continuing escalation of dangerous demands for trade protection. The trade/payments surplus, or deficit, of a country is due to a nation's spending patterns and, in particular, to the difference between national savings and domestic investment. In the 1980s, the American federal budget deficit and low savings rate resulted in the huge trade/ payments deficit that triggered the American-initiated trade dispute with Japan. In the late 1990s, the deficit has again soared. However, the 1990s situation is significantly different from that in the 1980s when Americans were borrowing abroad to indulge themselves in a consumption binge. In the 1990s, the combination of extravagant consumer spending, an extraordinary investment boom, and a zero rate of personal savings—and not the nefarious behavior of America's trading partners—was responsible for America's immense trade deficit.

In the late 1990s, the 1980s debate over America's relatively low savings rate also revived. Both net private savings (personal and corporate) and state/local savings had declined considerably during the prior decade. The personal savings rate dropped from about 6 percent in 1993 to zero or negative in 1998. The reason for this precipitous drop in personal savings was that Americans had been spending down their personal savings, and thus had helped fuel high rates of economic growth during the decade. The large decline in personal savings caused considerable concern and controversy over its implications for the economy. However, these concerns were moderated because the net national savings rate as a share of GNP more than doubled in the 1990s, rising from 3 percent to 6.5 percent, the highest level since 1984. This increase was due to rapid economic growth, the elimination of the federal budget deficit, and emergence of a substantial federal budget surplus. This fortunate development meant that usage of the surplus would be the foremost economic issue for the early twenty-first century. Should it be used for large tax cuts, to fund Social Security, to repay the national debt, to fund new spending programs, or for some combination of these purposes? The debate on this issue has just begun, and its outcome will be very important for the American economy and for America's role in the global economy.[95]

Whether or not the overall global economy can regain a higher rate of economic growth is crucial. While rescuing much of the developing world from recession and strengthening economic growth in Japan and Western Europe are important in their own right, a higher rate of global economic growth is also needed to stem the rising tide of protectionism in the United States and elsewhere. Unfortunately, this task faces high political and ideological hurdles. Many developing countries have yet to institute reforms to restore investor confidence and to build the foundations for expansionary economic policies. Fortunately, in Japan, the government's expansionary economic policies appear to be working and the rate of economic growth has begun to increase. In Western Europe, on the other hand, a powerful ideological conservatism reigns. Since the hyperinflation of the 1970s and the resulting "triumph of the central bankers," the primary goal of economic policy in Europe, and indeed in most industrialized countries, has been to win the fight against inflation. However, as Paul Krugman argues, a greater emphasis on expansionary economic policies, which would necessarily be somewhat more inflationary, is required to increase the rate of global economic growth and, I would add, to ward off the encroaching threat of increased protectionism.[96]

REBUILDING THE POLITICAL FOUNDATIONS OF
A GLOBAL ECONOMY

Throughout this book, I have argued that international politics and political relationships significantly affect the nature and dynamics of the international economy. Although technological advance and the interplay of market forces provide sufficient causes for increasing integration of the world economy, the supportive policies of powerful states and cooperative relations among these states constitute the necessary political foundations for a stable and unified world economy. International regimes or other governing mechanisms cannot succeed unless they are firmly grounded on a strong political base, as they were during the Cold War.

At the opening of the twenty-first century, all the elements that have supported an open global economy have weakened. With the end of the Cold War, both the ability and the willingness of the United States to lead declined. Although the formal framework of anti-Soviet alliances continued, the Cold War allies' political unity weakened as the United States, Western Europe, and Japan emphasized their own parochial national and regional priorities rather than their shared interests. Furthermore, the domestic consensus in both the United States and Europe has been eroded by years of increased income inequalities, high unemployment, and job insecurity. Although major structural changes driven by technological change and ill-considered national policies carry a large share of responsibility for these social and economic ills, more and more people in the United States and Europe blame globalization and competition from foreign low-wage labor in particular. Growing concern over economic globalization and increased competition have intensified the movement toward economic regionalism and the appeal of protectionism.

Renewed American Leadership

The basic premise of a U.S. strategy for the twenty-first century should be that a united global economy is in the economic and political interests of the United States, and the strategy should acknowledge that trade protectionism and economic regionalism pose serious threats to those interests. The United States, as the world's largest trading nation, gains enormously from both imports and exports, and America's financial and other service sectors particularly benefit from economic openness. Despite early fears, foreign direct investment in the United States has proved very beneficial. Even though the United States continues to have a large trade imbalance, as indicated by figure 11.1, it has a strong competitive advantage in services. The trade deficit arises primarily

347

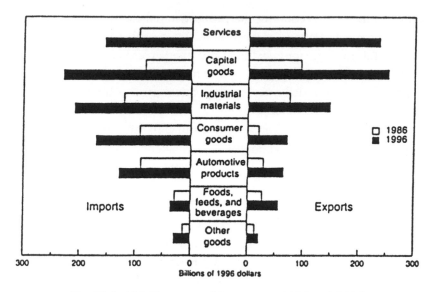

Fig. 11.1. U.S. Exports and Imports in 1986 and 1996.
Both exports and imports, most notably in services and in consumer and
capital goods, have grown rapidly, due in part to market opening.
Source: U.S. Council of Economic Advisors.

from the automobile and consumer electronic sectors in which the
United States has lost much of its former comparative advantage. The
American economy is simply too large to be satisfied with a North
American or even a hemisphere-wide regional trading region, and trade
with Europe, America's largest export market, is of special importance
to the United States.

American political and security interests as well as economic interests are served by a united world economy. As a status quo power, the
United States depends on a stable and peaceful world. To maintain that
situation requires, at the least, a continuing American political and military presence in both Europe and Asia. Also, the possibility of a revived
Russian threat to Europe or of a Chinese threat to Japan and/or other
parts of Asia must not be ignored in the U.S. definition of its national
interests and its policy planning. A regionalized world economy with
large areas closed to nonmembers or one characterized by trade protection would harm American economic and political interests and greatly

348

complicate preservation of the economic, political, and security cooperation between the United States and its principal European and Japanese allies.

For more than four decades, the international political order has supported development of a liberal world economy and encouraged both mutual security and mutual prosperity. Today, that order is changing in many ways. A regionalized world economy would threaten the security and well-being of America's allies as well as those of the United States. Trade protectionism and economic regionalism jeopardize cooperation among the United States and its Cold War allies. While it is uncertain whether or not economic regionalism will prove ultimately to be a stepping-stone or a stumbling block, there is reason to be concerned that a regionalized global economy in which regions are closed to nonmembers could displace a united multilateral world economy. Consider, for example, the potential impact on American public opinion of a highly integrated European Union that discriminated against American goods. I strongly doubt that the United States would continue to maintain a major military presence in an EU inhospitable to American exports and/or investment. Continuation of American military engagement in a Pacific Asia that discriminated against American exports is also unlikely. A regionalized world economy could quite easily lead to a regionalized international political system, and this could undermine the foundations of world peace.

If regionalization were to lead to economic arrangements that exclude goods and investments from nonmembers, there are likely to be serious implications for world peace. The two foremost regional arrangements, the European Union and NAFTA, exclude all other major powers of the world, including Russia, China, Japan, India, Indonesia, Brazil, South Africa, and Pakistan. It is highly unlikely that all these powers will eventually be invited to join these restricted clubs; and if an enlarged EU or NAFTA discriminates against the exports of excluded powers, political tensions will inevitably grow. World peace and economic prosperity could easily be threatened.

A regionalized world is likely to be unstable both politically and economically. At present, American engagement in European security affairs helps preserve the still tenuous rapprochement between a powerful, reunited Germany and its neighbors, particularly France. If American engagement in Europe were terminated, EU existence could be threatened. Furthermore, it is unlikely that a Pacific Asian economic and political community would continue to evolve if the United States really did "go home." The severe political tensions and national rivalries in that region, especially those between China and Japan, make a rupture into hostile camps likely.

If economic regionalism were to strengthen, the relationships among various regions of the global economy would certainly become more important. Would the regional blocs conflict or cooperate with one another? Experts on these matters differ profoundly. One expects that these regions would meet in a "head-to-head" struggle for dominance. A distinguished French scholar and former public official voices a common European opinion when he foresees a clash between the Atlantic and the Pacific regions. An American economist has written that over the long term, Japan and the United States are natural allies against the enlarged and tightly integrated economic bloc in continental Europe. A political scientist largely discounts the possibility of interregional conflict and instead predicts shifting coalitions of states, varying with the issue. Some American economists believe that cooperation is likely or at least possible, provided that the economic policies of each region remain "responsible." A regime governing regional arrangements could affect which of these scenarios, if any, will actually develop.

The continued ability and willingness of the United States to lead the world in the decades ahead are very much in question. Despite the strong belief of American economists that a new trade round is overdue, the United States has made only half-hearted moves toward such a Round. The United States has not pursued the proposal made by EU trade official Leon Brittan to launch a Millennium Trade Round to further reduce trade barriers and deal with other outstanding issues; nor has there been any significant movement toward trans-Atlantic negotiations that would reduce barriers between the world's two largest trading partners. The Clinton Administration's reluctance to lead in these matters is undoubtedly due to the 1997 defeat of the fast-track authorization legislation that would have facilitated further trade liberalization. In addition, the strong congressional opposition in 1998 to IMF financial replenishment and the wariness of the American people toward globalization in general suggest that Americans, or at least powerful groups within the population, are less willing than in the past to play the role of global economic leader.

Nevertheless, the United States is still the only nation capable of providing leadership to avoid the dangers of closed regional arrangements. Even though the American economy has declined relative to others during the postwar era, the United States remains the world's foremost military power, and the size and productivity of its economy make it the only economic superpower. While the role of military power in international affairs has been circumscribed, the military might of the United States remains preeminent. Leadership must be based on power, but American military and economic power are not identical to American leadership. Leadership requires that power be exercised on behalf of some larger political purpose than simply one nation's narrowly defined interests. In the early postwar years, the United States used its power to forge the anti-Soviet alliance and to promote an open world economy to sustain that alliance. At the opening of the new century, however, there is no national consensus on the goals for which American power should be exercised. Or to put the matter another way, in 1999 the United States has not yet formulated a national strategy based on the political realities of the post–Cold War world.

Improved International Cooperation

Although the world needs American leadership, the United States cannot lead alone. Cooperation among the major economic powers has become essential, yet the United States is reluctant to share its leadership role and still assumes that others will follow its lead. The United States must give more attention to the concerns and initiatives of others. For example, during the beginning weeks of the Asian financial crisis, Japan proposed an Asian Monetary Fund, and some East Asian countries expressed interest in such a fund. However, U.S. Treasury Secretary Rubin and Deputy Secretary Summers dismissed the proposal with a brutal rebuff to Japan, apparently fearing that the Japanese initiative would weaken American influence in the region. Although the Japanese proposal was self-serving and probably would not have succeeded, American behavior was certainly not designed to improve American-Japanese cooperation.

Many observers believe that mutual economic interest will ultimately triumph and ensure maintenance of an open global economy. The major economic powers obviously do have a strong political and economic interest in preserving globalization. American business and political leaders regard the movement toward European unity more as an opportunity than as a threat; the huge European market for goods and services and an integrated European capital market could provide great opportunities for exports and foreign direct investment. European monetary and financial unification based on the euro will be a source of capital for American firms and should offer openings for American financial interests. American leaders also expect that a politically united Europe will be a strong and reliable partner. As for Japan and its Asian regional initiatives, Americans at least for the moment, have ceased to fear Japan and have refocused their concerns on China; however as the Japanese economy gains strength, renewed concerns about Japanese competition could be rekindled. On the other hand, mutual economic interests among the three dominant economic powers could provide an excellent basis for a stable global economy.

Nevertheless, there are ample grounds for serious concerns over the American economy, concerns that will affect its policies toward Japan and Europe. The United States, with its addiction to overconsumption, has been living far beyond its means for a very long time. In the 1990s, Americans drew down their personal savings and consumed more than they produced. The country's continuing negative balance of payments resulted in a net foreign debt of approximately $1.5 trillion. (Refer to fig. 8.1.) Although, as these lines are written, the federal budget deficit has become a surplus, the deficit could easily rise again early in the next century when baby boomers retire. The United States cannot go into debt forever; servicing and eventually repaying the large American international debt will require a payments surplus and impose a burden on the economy; the standard of living will necessarily grow more slowly, and this will impose hardships and encourage a search for a suitable scapegoat. In such a situation there would be a need for America's European and Japanese trading partners to become more receptive markets for a great expansion of American exports. In a neomercantilist world where exports are considered good and imports bad, if the United States had to change from a net importer to a net exporter, that could lead to considerable tension both at home and abroad. And in the event of an extended downturn in the world economy, such a problem could become really threatening to stability and even to peace.

The European and Japanese economies are also potential sources of interregional conflict. Europeans, faced with high unemployment and other significant problems, are unlikely to accept America's model of free-market capitalism. Heavily burdened by the tasks of increasing the global competitiveness of their industries, reducing high levels of chronic unemployment, and reforming their extremely costly national welfare systems, Europeans are not likely at this time to lower existing trade and other barriers. Moreover, election of Social Democrat Gerhard Schröder as German Chancellor, and the strengthening of center-left parties in France, Great Britain, and elsewhere on the Continent, mean that Europe is even more unlikely than in the past to adopt the American economic model based on free and unregulated markets.

At the very least, the United States must learn to work with a united, more powerful, and increasingly assertive Europe. Throughout much of the past half-century, the United States has led its divided European allies and has become accustomed to leading without prior consultation with them. For decades, although Europeans may have grumbled about American initiatives with which they fundamentally disagreed, they generally followed the American lead. It is unlikely that a stronger and much more self-confident European Union will continue this practice. In the late 1990s, Europeans have, for example, challenged the American-dominated IMF approach to solving the East Asian economic crisis. It will be very difficult for the United States to accept a united Europe as an equal or superior economic power.

The future of American-Japanese relations is also very much in doubt. Many American commentators believe that a "weak" Japan poses as much of a challenge to the world economy as did a "strong" Japan. Many argue that Japan's economic troubles will force it to move toward the American economic model and will thereby decrease the likelihood of future American-Japanese confrontations. Such a transformation of Japan would necessarily mean extensive deregulation of the economy, opening the economy to manufactured imports and foreign direct investment from the United States and other countries, and shifting from an export-led to a domestic-led growth strategy. A weak Japan is believed to be in no position to challenge U.S. dominance in the global economy. Japan, some maintain, has no choice other than to be America's junior partner in maintaining an open global economy. Perhaps! But several caveats must be considered.

Although Japan is obviously in serious economic trouble at the end of the century, the technological sophistication, productivity level, and international competitiveness of Japanese industry, in the opinion of some experts, has actually improved significantly during the 1990s. In addition, despite its own financial problems, Japan is still the world's foremost financial power. Nevertheless, the nonmanufacturing sector remains weak, and Japan faces the daunting task of providing for a rapidly aging population. While the demands to find solutions for such problems could provoke significant reform of the economy, Japan has long tolerated an inefficient nonmanufacturing sector largely for reasons of domestic social harmony and national independence. The country has financed this economic drain by emphasizing manufacturing, which has a much higher rate of productivity growth than does the nonmanufacturing sector. Manufacturing, in turn, has been promoted by the strategy of export-led growth and, since the late 1980s, by creation of complementary production networks throughout Pacific Asia. Despite its own economic troubles, Japan has been doing everything that it can to maintain its overseas networks. This behavior indicates that it is very unlikely that Japan will adopt the American economic model and open its economy to unrestricted manufactured imports and foreign direct investment.

Over the longer term, dominance of international organizations by Western powers must be reduced. Despite the shift in the international balance of economic and political power toward Japan and the industrializing countries of Pacific Asia and elsewhere, at the turn of the century the institutions governing the world economy are still dominated by the United States and Europe. Although the informal G-5, G-6, G-7, and so forth constitute an effort to broaden representation of important economies, even these groups do not represent the whole world. The G-22, created in the late 1990s and including the major industrializing countries, could become an important instrument to broaden the political base of the system. However, while this informal grouping did draft new rules to regulate international finances, those rules have not been adopted. Indeed, the West Europeans never approved of that organization, which had been sponsored by the United States.

Also badly needed is reform of the World Bank, the IMF, and other international institutions to make them more representative of and responsive to global economic and political realities. If effective governance of the world economy is to be achieved, the disjuncture between the international distribution of economic power and the distribution of rule-making authority in the world's international institutions must be eliminated as soon as practical, and that is unlikely to happen any time soon.

Cooperation between the United States and the industrializing economies is possible only if the United States becomes more tolerant of differences in national economies. As we have seen in the IMF-American rescue efforts in East Asia and in American policy toward Japan, the United States has frequently attempted to impose its own economic policies and institutions on the rest of the world. This effort has rested on the belief that the American or Anglo-Saxon model of free markets is based on the policy prescriptions of economic science and has been proved to be superior to other models. Many countries, however, have strong reservations about the social costs of the Anglo-Saxon model of market capitalism. Also, the United States must cease using trade sanctions as an instrument of foreign policy. By one count, by March 1997 the United States had imposed sanctions sixty-one times on thirty-five countries; such sanctions are deeply resented and not very effective. Another irritant to other nations has been the application of American law to the activities of firms outside American legal jurisdiction ("extraterritoriality").

Although it would be desirable to broaden the international political base of governance, the three dominant economic powers—the United States, the European Union, and Japan—retain primary responsibility for international cooperation. As the Europeans strengthen their unity, they must also maintain openness to the rest of the world economy and resist the temptation to create a closed and exclusive economic bloc from the Atlantic through Eastern Europe. Before Japan can join the other major powers in providing a stable and prosperous world economy, it must address seriously the immense task of domestic economic and political reform and must shift away from an export-led toward a domestic-led growth strategy that will reduce tensions with and ultimately benefit its trading partners as well as Japanese consumers. Yet the greatest responsibility belongs to the United States, because it alone can take the initiatives most essential to strengthening international cooperation. The United States, with its allies, must defend a rule-based international trading and economic order.

Regaining Public Support

Finally, a domestic consensus committed to economic openness and free trade must be reestablished in the United States and in other major economies. The postwar consensus in the United States and Europe on the desirability of free trade has eroded alarmingly. Not only Europeans and Americans but also East Asians had begun, by the end of the twentieth century, to blame their economic troubles on global economic forces over which they have little control. Although the role of globalization in these economic problems has been greatly exaggerated, and although such other factors as technological change, labor market rigidities, and government policies have contributed significantly to the difficulties in each area, the fears arising from globalization must be addressed and must not be rejected out of hand.

More effective national responses to these problems are urgently needed if an open world economy is to be maintained. In the United States, for example, solutions must be devised for the problems of growing income inequality, the plight of low-skilled workers, and job insecurity.[97] Reforms should include strengthened safety nets, greatly expanded job training, and a new social contract between capital and labor. The Workforce Investment Act, signed in August 1998, which unified dozens of federal retraining programs, created individual training accounts, and increased funding of youth training programs among other achievements, was an important step toward preparing Americans for an increasingly competitive and rapidly changing global economy. However, much more needs to be done in the United States and elsewhere to strengthen the domestic political foundations for an open world economy. Newly dominant conservative economic and political ideologies have increased the difficulty of attaining a new national consensus that those who lose from globalization and from rapid economic/technological change must be assisted.

CONCLUSION

The world has enjoyed only two extended periods of liberalized trade and increasing prosperity around the globe. Both of these eras—the Pax Britannica prior to World War I and the Pax Americana following World War II—rested on strong political foundations. The liberal trading system fostered by Great Britain eventually collapsed with the out break of war in 1914. As the twenty-first century opens, the decline of American leadership, fraying economic cooperation between the United States and its Cold War allies, and increasing disillusionment with economic globalization in the United States and elsewhere have weakened the underlying political support for an open world economy. Economic regionalism, financial instability, and trade protectionism all seriously threaten the stability and the integration of the global economy, whose future will depend on the foreign policies, domestic economic policies, and political relations of the major economic powers. If the United States does not resume its leadership role, the Second Great Age of global capitalism, like the first, is likely to disappear.

* Notes *

1. *New York Times*, 4 January 1999, 10.

2. In this legislation, the President submits a bill to Congress implementing an international agreement concerning trade barriers, and the Congress within ninety days must vote the bill up or down with no amendments permitted. This provision not only greatly facilitates enactment of trade legislation, but also assures foreign governments that the Congress will act expeditiously and will not modify trade agreements. This "fast track" authority expired in April 1994. I. M. Destler, *American Trade Policies*, 3d ed. (Washington, D.C.: Institute for International Economics, 1995), 312.

3. John Lewis Gaddis, *The Long Peace* (New York: Oxford University Press, 1987).

4. Proponents of this position include Clyde V. Prestowitz Jr., Ronald A. Morse, and Alan Tonelson, eds., *Powernomics: Economics and Strategy after the Cold War* (Washington, D.C.: Madison Books, 1991); Jeffrey E. Garten, *A Cold Peace: America, Japan, Germany and the Struggle for Supremacy* (New York: Times Books, 1992); and Lester Thurow, *Head to Head: The Coming Economic Battle among Japan, Europe, and America* (New York: William Morrow, 1992).

5. A valuable discussion of this subject is in Henry R. Nau, *Trade and Security: U.S. Policies at Cross-Purposes* (Washington, D.C.: AEI Press, 1995), chap. 2.

6. Gary Burtless, Robert Z. Lawrence, Robert E. Litan, and Robert J. Shapiro, *Globaphobia: Confronting Fears about Open Trade* (Washington, D.C.: Brookings Institution, 1998), 4–5.

7. David B. Yoffie and Benjamin Gomes-Casseres, *International Trade and Competition: Cases and Notes in Strategy and Management*, 2d ed. (New York: McGraw-Hill 1994), 353.

8. Gary Burtless, Robert Z. Lawrence, Robert E. Litan, and Robert J. Shapiro, *Globaphobia: Confronting Fears about Open Trade* (Washington, D.C.: Brookings Institution, 1998), 4–5.

9. Representative of this position is William Greider, *One World, Ready or Not: The Manic Logic of Global Capitalism* (New York: Simon and Schuster, 1997). According to Marxism, capitalism is fundamentally flawed because it produces more goods than workers (consumers) can purchase and thereby causes depressions. John Maynard Keynes (1883–1946) demonstrated that this problem of "effective demand" could be solved by the government's pursuit of expansionary economic policies.

10. Paul Krugman, "Is Capitalism Too Productive?" *Foreign Affairs* 76, no. 5 (September/October 1997): 79–94.

11. The term "revisionism" was first used to characterize the work of scholars discussing the distinctive nature of the Japanese economy. Its leading proponent, Chalmers Johnson, argues that Japan has a basically different type of national economy from those of Anglo-Saxon countries (U.S. and Great Britain) in terms of institutions, the role of the state, and economic nationalism. Japan and other Pacific economies that have adopted the Japanese model of the "developmental"

state do not play by the rules of Western economic orthodoxy and do not possess the latter's strong commitment to the market or its opposition to government intervention in the economy. Chalmers Johnson, *Japan: Who Governs: The Rise of the Developmental State* (New York: W. W. Norton, 1995), 12.

12. Samuel P. Huntington, "America's Changing Strategic Interests," *Survival* 33, no. 1 (January/February 1991): 3–17.

13. Samuel P. Huntington, *The Clash of Civilizations and the Remaking of World Order* (New York: Simon and Schuster, 1996).

14. Several notable examples are Peter F. Drucker, *Post-Capitalist Society* (New York: HarperBusiness, 1993); Alvin Toffler, *The Third Wave* (New York: William Morrow, 1980); and George Gilder, *Microcosm: Economics and Technology* (New York: Simon & Schuster, 1989).

15. The following discussion on technological developments draws heavily on World Bank official Carl Dahlman's "The Third Industrial Revolution: Trends and Implications for Developing Countries" (April 1992), unpublished.

16. Members of the Cairns Group include Argentina, Australia, Brazil, Canada, Hungary, Malaysia, and several other agricultural exporters.

17. Paul Krugman, "The Myth of Asia's Miracle," *Foreign Affairs* 73, no. 6 (November/December 1994): 62–78.

18. C. Fred Bergsten, *America in the World Economy: A Strategy for the 1990s* (Washington, D.C.: Institute for International Economics, 1988), 60.

19. Richard Gibb and Wieslaw Michalak, eds., *Continental Trading Blocs: The Growth of Regionalism in the World Economy* (New York: John Wiley, 1994), 1.

20. Robert C. Altman, "The Nuke of the 90's," *New York Times Magazine*, 1 March 1998, 34.

21. This discussion is based largely on Barry Eichengreen and Peter B. Kenen, "Managing the World Economy under the Bretton Woods System: An Overview," in Peter B. Kenen, ed., *Managing the World Economy: Fifty Years after Bretton Woods* (Washington, D.C.: Institute for International Economics, 1994), 21–27.

22. The term "dollar shortage" referred to the fact that Western countries and others had insufficient dollars to buy the American goods they needed to recover from the war. The problem was largely solved by the Marshall Plan.

23. Benjamin J. Cohen, *Organizing the World's Money: The Political Economy of International Monetary Relations* (New York: Basic Books, 1977).

24. The name of the European community has changed several times during the post–World War II era. In 1957, the European Economic Community (EEC) or Common Market was created. Subsequently in 1967, the EEC was supplanted by the European Community (EC). Finally, in 1993, the EC was replaced by the European Union (EU).

25. Gary Clyde Hufbauer and Kimberly Ann Elliott, *Measuring the Costs of Protection in the United States* (Washington, D.C.: Institute for International Economics, 1994), 11.

26. In 1933, the various strands of trade theory were synthesized by Swedish economists Eli Heckscher and Bertil Ohlin into the conventional theory of trade accepted by most economists today.

27. DeAnne Julius, *Global Companies and Public Policy: The Growing Challenge of Foreign Direct Investment* (London: Pinter, 1990), 3.

28. Paul Krugman, *Geography and Trade* (Cambridge: MIT Press, 1991), 7.

29. Michael E. Porter, *The Competitive Advantage of Nations* (New York: Free Press, 1990).

30. F. M. Scherer, *International Technology Competition* (Cambridge: Harvard University Press, 1992), 5.

31. Jackson's assessment can be found in Peter B. Kenen, ed., *Managing the World Economy: Fifty Years after Bretton Woods* (Washington, D.C.: Institute for International Economics, 1994), chap. 3.

32. Geza Feketskuty, *The New Trade Agenda* (Washington, D.C.: Group of Thirty, 1992).

33. Paul De Grauwe, *International Money: Post-War Trends and Theories* (Oxford: Clarendon Press, 1989).

34. Barry Eichengreen, *Golden Fetters: The Gold Standard and the Great Depression, 1919–1939* (New York: Oxford University Press, 1992).

35. Barry Eichengreen, *International Monetary Arrangements for the 21st Century* (Washington, D.C.: Brookings Institution, 1994).

36. A summary of Williamson's exchange-rate target-zone proposal can be found in *The Economist*, May 8, 1993, 83.

37. Barry Eichengreen, *International Monetary Arrangements for the 21st Century* (Washington, D.C.: Brookings Institution, 1994), 75–78.

38. David Currie and Paul Levine, "The International Co-Ordination of Macroeconomic Policy," in David Greenaway, Michael Bleaney, and Ian Stewart, eds., *Companion to Contemporary Economic Thought* (New York: Routledge, 1991), 482. This article presents an overall assessment of the challenge of international policy coordination.

39. Bretton Woods Commission, *Bretton Woods: Looking to the Future* (July 1994). The Bretton Woods Commission, chaired by Paul Volcker, was a private independent group of senior economic experts.

40. Toyoo Gyohten, in Barry Eichengreen, *International Monetary Arrangements for the 21st Century* (Washington, D.C.: The Brookings Institution, 1994), 142–49.

41. Charles P. Kindleberger, *Manias, Panics, and Crashes* (New York: Basic Books, 1988).

42. Quoted in Joanne Gowa, *Ballots and Bullets: The Elusive Democratic Peace* (Princeton: Princeton University Press, 1999), 3. Gowa's book provides a critique of this attractive idea.

43. This discussion of Minsky's theory of financial crises is based on Kindleberger's *Manias, Panics, and Crashes: A History of Financial Crises*. Minsky's writings on the subject can be found in Hyman P. Minsky, *Can "It" Happen Again? Essays on Instability and Finance* (Armonk, N.Y.: M. E. Sharpe, 1982).

44. The following discussion is based largely on Morris Goldstein, *The Asian Financial Crisis: Causes, Cures, and Systemic Implications* (Washington, D.C.: Institute for International Economics, 1998).

45. "Moral hazard" refers to the effect of some types of financial guarantees that encourage individuals to take actions that benefit themselves at a potential cost to others. An example would be a fire insurance policy that paid the full cost of a building. Most fire insurance policies are written so that a large portion of the replacement cost of a building falls on the owner. A technical definition can be

found in David W. Pearce, ed., *The MIT Dictionary of Modern Economics*, 4th ed. (Cambridge: MIT Press, 1995), 291.

46. Jagdish Bhagwati, "The Capital Myth: The Difference between Trade in Widgets and Dollars," *Foreign Affairs* 77, no. 3 (May/June 1998): 7–16. Also, Robert Wade, "The Asian Debt-and-Development Crisis of 1997–?: Causes and Consequences, *World Development* 26, no. 8 (August 1998): 1535–53.

47. Kenichi Ohmae, *Triad Power: The Coming Shape of Global Competition* (New York: Free Press, 1985).

48. DeAnne Julius, *Global Companies and Public Policy: The Growing Challenge of Foreign Direct Investment* (London: Pinter, 1990).

49. Charles Oman, *Globalisation and Regionalisation: The Challenge for Developing Countries* (Paris: Organization for Economic Co-operation and Development, Development Centre Studies, 1994).

50. Sylvia Ostry, *A New Regime for Foreign Direct Investment* (Washington, D.C.: Group of Thirty, 1997).

51. The members of the EU include Austria, Belgium, Denmark, Finland, France, Germany, Greece, Ireland, Italy, Luxembourg, the Netherlands, Portugal, Spain, Sweden, and the United Kingdom.

52. Commission of the European Community, "One Money, One Market: An Evaluation of the Potential Benefits and Costs of Forming an Economic and Monetary Union," *European Economy* 44 (October 1990).

53. Robert A. Mundell, "A Theory of Optimum Currency Areas," *American Economic Review* 51 (1961): 657–65; and Peter B. Kenen, "The Theory of Optimum Currency Areas: An Eclectic View," in Robert Mundell and Alexander K. Swoboda, eds., *Monetary Problems of the International Economy* (Chicago: University of Chicago Press, 1969). A useful discussion of OCA and its significance for European monetary integration is in Paul De Grauwe, *The Economics of Monetary Integration*, 2d rev. ed. (New York: Oxford University Press, 1994).

54. Jeffrey A. Frankel, *Regional Trading Blocs in the World Economic System* (Washington, D.C.: Institute for International Economics, 1997).

55. An excellent statement of this position is in Richard N. Cooper, "Key Currencies after the Euro," *World Economy* 22, no. 1 (January 1999): 1–23. .

56. Bob Woodward, *The Agenda: Inside the Clinton White House* (New York: Simon and Schuster, 1994).

57. Henry Nau, *Trade and Security: U.S. Policies at Cross-Purposes* (Washington, D.C.: AEI Press, 1995).

58. This definition of "strategic industry" is provided by Theodore Moran.

59. Laura Tyson, in Robert Z. Lawrence and Charles L. Schultze, eds., *An American Trade Policy: Options for the 1990s* (Washington, D.C.: Brookings Institution, 1990).

60. I am indebted to Kenneth S. Courtis, then of Deutsche Bank Capital Markets (Asia), for helping me understand these matters.

61. The Maekawa Commission, which was appointed by then Prime Minister Yasuhiro Nakasone and chaired by Haruo Maekawa, former president of the Bank of Japan, was named the "Study Group on Adjustments in the Economic Structure for International Cooperation." The title of the Commission's report, published in 1986, was *Report of the Advisory Group on Economic Structural Adjustment for Inter-*

national Harmony. A major purpose of the Commission and its recommendations was to decrease the Japanese trade surplus that had become a source of conflict with the United States.

62. Walter Hatch and Kozo Yamamura, *Asia in Japan's Embrace: Building a Regional Production Alliance* (New York: Cambridge University Press, 1996), xi. This chapter draws heavily from the Hatch-Yamamura book.

63. See Hatch and Yamamura, *Asia in Japan's Embrace.*

64. Peter J. Katzenstein and Takashi Shiraishi, eds., *Network Power: Japan and Asia* (Ithaca: Cornell University Press, 1997).

65. Quoted in Hatch and Yamamura, *Asia in Japan's Embrace.*

66. Discussed in Hatch and Yamamura, *Asia in Japan's Embrace.*

67. *Wall Street Journal*, April 7, 1997, 1.

68. Lowell Bryan and Diana Farrell, *Market Unbound: Unleashing Global Capitalism* (New York: John Wiley, 1996).

69. Dani Rodrik, *Has Globalization Gone Too Far?* (Washington, D.C.: Institute for International Economics, 1997), 2. The use of the term "communitarian" refers to those individuals, according to Rodrik, who emphasize "moral and civic virtues" and are very suspicious of market economies.

70. Richard Falk, *Economic Aspects of Global Civilization: The Unmet Challenges of World Poverty* (Princeton University, Center of International Studies, World Order Studies Program Occasional Paper no. 22, 1992), 1.

71. Kazimierz Poznanski of the University of Washington alerted me to this development.

72. Staffan Burenstam Linder, *The Pacific Century: Economic and Political Consequences of Asian-Pacific Dynamism* (Stanford: Stanford University Press, 1986).

73. Robert G. Gilpin, *The Political Economy of International Relations* (Princeton: Princeton University Press, 1987), 114.

74. In technical terms, this idea is known as the Stopler-Samuelson theorem.

75. Adrian Wood, *North-South Trade, Employment, and Inequality: Changing Fortunes in a Skill-Driven World* (Oxford: Clarendon Press, 1994.)

76. Richard O'Brien, *Global Financial Integration: The End of Geography* (London: Pinter, 1992); Walter B. Wriston, *The Twilight of Sovereignty: How the Information Revolution Is Transforming Our World* (New York: Scribners, 1992); Joseph A. Camilleri and Jim Falk, *The End of Sovereignty? The Politics of a Shrinking and Fragmenting World* (London: Aldershot, Hants, 1992); Susan Strange, *The Retreat of the State: The Diffusion of Power in the World Economy* (New York: Cambridge University Press, 1996).

77. This discussion draws heavily on the writings of Geoffrey Garrett.

78. The "irreconcilable trinity" and its significance for economic policy is discussed in chapter 4.

79. The "natural rate," or Non-Accelerating Inflation Rate of Unemployment (NAIRU), hypothesis states that any effort to reduce unemployment below a certain level through expansionary economic policies will result in a higher rate of inflation.

80. Suzanne Berger and Ronald Dore, *National Diversity and Global Capitalism* (Ithaca: Cornell University Press, 1996), 11.

81. Daniel Yergin and Joseph Stanislaw, *The Commanding Heights: The Battle*

between Government and the Marketplace That Is Remaking the Modern World (New York: Simon and Schuster, 1998).

82. Michael Desch, "War and Strong States, Peace and Weak States," *International Organization* 50, no. 2 (spring 1996), 237–68.

83. Thomas L. Friedman, *The Lexus and the Olive Tree* (New York: Farrar, Straus and Giroux, 1999), 86–87.

84. I am indebted to Harvard political scientist Stephen Walt for this pertinent observation.

85. One of the very first writings on this subject was Peter Gourevitch, "The Second Image Reversed: The International Sources of Domestic Politics," *International Organization* 31 (August 1978).

86. Suzanne Berger, "Domestic Politics and the Global Economy" (unpublished 1995).

87. Suzanne Berger and Ronald Dore, eds., *National Diversity and Global Capitalism* (Ithaca: Cornell University Press, 1996), 11.

88. The Long-Term Capital Management Fund had been an extraordinarily successful hedge fund that threatened to go bankrupt and was rescued by the Federal Reserve.

89. Basle refers to the International Bank for Settlements, located in Basle, Switzerland, that sets standards for international banks and other financial institutions.

90. When a sound economy has a temporary cash-flow problem, that is a liquidity problem, but an economy with severe economic problems will have an insolvency problem.

91. A brief and useful discussion of hedge funds can be found in Paul Krugman, *The Return of Depression Economics* (New York: W. W. Norton, 1999), 119.

92. Jeffrey A. Frankel, *Regional Trading Blocs in the World Economic System* (Washington, D.C.: Institute for International Economics, 1997).

93. Frankel, *Regional Trading Blocs in the World Economic System.*

94. The most comprehensive proposals to reform Article XXIV have been set forth in the report of a study group chaired by Jaime Serra, in Valeriana Kallab, ed., *Reflections on Regionalism: Report of the Study Group on International Trade* (Washington, D.C.: Carnegie Endowment for International Peace, 1997).

95. The national savings of the United States are composed of private savings, state and local government savings, and federal government savings.

96. Paul Krugman, *The Return of Depression Economics* (New York: W. W. Norton, 1999).

97. An excellent discussion of required reforms is contained in Gary Burtless, Robert Z. Lawrence, Robert E. Litan, and Robert J. Shapiro, *Globaphobia: Confronting Fears about Open Trade* (Washington, D.C.: Brookings Institution, 1998).

* Select Bibliography *

ALTHOUGH I consulted many sources in the preparation of this book, I have included in this select bibliography only a few references for those readers who would like to pursue further the major subjects that I have covered. The reader's attention is also directed to several major sources consulted in this book: *The New York Times, The Economist, The Financial Times, Business Week,* and *The Wall Street Journal.*

CHAPTER ONE: THE SECOND GREAT AGE OF CAPITALISM

Garten, Jeffrey E. *The Big Ten: The Big Emerging Markets and How They Will Change Our Lives.* New York: Basic Books, 1997.

Gibb, Richard, and Wieslaw Michalak, eds. *Continental Trading Blocs: The Growth of Regionalism in the World Economy.* New York: John Wiley, 1994.

Maddison, Angus. *The World Economy in the 20th Century.* Paris: Organization for Economic Co-operation and Development, Development Centre Studies, 1989.

McRae, Hamish. *The World in 2020: Power, Culture and Prosperity.* Boston: Harvard Business School Press, 1994.

Organization for Economic Co-operation and Development. *The World in 2020: Toward a New Global Age.* Paris: Organization for Economic Co-operation and Development, 1997.

Ostry, Sylvia. *The Post–Cold War Trading System: Who's on First?* Chicago: University of Chicago Press, 1997.

Yergin, Daniel, and Joseph Stanislaw. *The Commanding Heights: The Battle between Government and the Marketplace That Is Remaking the Modern World.* New York: Simon and Schuster, 1998.

CHAPTER TWO: THE COLD WAR INTERNATIONAL ECONOMY

Gowa, Joanne. *Closing the Gold Window: Domestic Politics and the End of Bretton Woods.* Ithaca: Cornell University Press, 1983.

James, Harold. *International Monetary Cooperation since Bretton Woods.* Washington, D.C.: International Monetary Fund, 1996.

Kenen, Peter B., ed. *Managing the World Economy: Fifty Years after Bretton Woods.* Washington, D.C.: Institute for International Economics, 1994.

Ruggie, John Gerard. *Winning the Peace: America and World Order in the New Era.* New York: Columbia University Press, 1996.

Winham, Gilbert R. *The Evolution of International Trade Agreements.* Toronto: University of Toronto Press, 1992.

CHAPTER THREE: THE INSECURE TRADING SYSTEM

Bhagwati, Jagdish. *Protectionism.* Cambridge: MIT Press, 1988.

Esty, Daniel C. *Greening the GATT: Trade. Environment, and the Future.* Washington, D.C.: Institute for International Economics, 1994.

Irwin, Douglas A. *Against the Tide: An Intellectual History of Free Trade*. Princeton: Princeton University Press, 1996.

Krugman, Paul R. *Geography and Trade*. Cambridge: MIT Press, 1991.

————, ed. *Strategic Trade Policy and the New International Economics*. Cambridge: MIT Press, 1996.

Preeg, Ernest H. *From Here to Free Trade: Essays in Post-Uruguay Round Trade Strategy*. Chicago: University of Chicago Press, 1998.

————. *Traders in a Brave New World: The Uruguay Round and the Future of the International Trading System*. Chicago: University of Chicago Press, 1995.

Scherer, F. M. *International High-Technology Competition*. Cambridge: Harvard University Press, 1992.

Schott Jeffrey J., ed. *The World Trading System: Challenges Ahead*. Washington, D.C.: Institute for International Economics, 1996.

Whalley, John, and Colleen Hamilton. *The Trading System after the Uruguay Round*. Washington, D.C.: Institute for International Economics, 1996.

Chapter Four: The Unstable Monetary System

Cohen, Benjamin J. *Organizing the World's Money: The Political Economy of International Monetary Relations*. New York: Basic Books, 1977.

————. *The Geography of Money*. Ithaca: Cornell University Press, 1998.

Cooper, Richard. "Prolegomena to the Choice of an International Monetary System." *International Organization* 29 (1975): 63–97.

DeGrauwe, Paul. *International Money: Post-War Trends and Theories*. Oxford: Clarendon Press, 1989.

Eichengreen, Barry. *International Monetary Arrangements for the 21st Century*. Washington, D.C.: Brookings Institution, 1994.

Henning, C. Randall. *Currencies and Politics in the United States, Germany, and Japan*. Washington, D.C.: Institute for International Economy, 1994.

Kirschner, Jonathan. *Currency and Coercion: The Political Economy of International Monetary Power*. Princeton: Princeton University Press, 1995.

Volcker, Paul A., and Toyoo Gyohten. *Changing Fortunes: The World's Money and the Threat to American Leadership*. New York: Times Books, 1992.

Chapter Five: Global Financial Vulnerability

Bhagwati, Jagdish. "The Capital Myth: The Difference between Trade in Widgets and Dollars." *Foreign Affairs* (May/June 1998): 7–16.

Goldstein, Morris. *The Asian Financial Crisis: Causes, Cures, and Systemic Implications*. Washington, D.C.: Institute for International Economics, 1998.

Helleiner, Eric. *States and the Reemergence of International Finance: From Bretton Woods to the 1990s*. Ithaca: Cornell University Press, 1994.

Kahler, Miles, ed. *Capital Flows and Financial Crises*. New York: Council on Foreign Relations, 1999.

Kindleberger, Charles. *Manias, Panics, and Crashes: A History of Financial Crises*. New York: Basic Books, 1988.

Kristof, Nicholas D., and Sheryl WuDunn. Articles on the East Asian Financial Crisis. *New York Times*, 15–18 February 1999.

Loriaux, Michael, et al. *Capital Ungoverned. Ithaca: Liberalizing Finance in Interventionist States*. Ithaca: Cornell University Press, 1997.

O'Brien, Richard. *Global Financial Integration: The End of Geography*. London: Royal Institute of International Affairs, 1992.

Strange, Susan. *Mad Money: From the Author of Casino Capitalism*. Manchester, England: Manchester University Press, 1998.

CHAPTER SIX: AGE OF THE MULTINATIONAL

Doremus, Paul N., William W. Keller, Louis W. Pauly, and Simon Reich. *The Myth of the Global Corporation*. Princeton: Princeton University Press, 1998.

Encarnation, Dennis J. *Rivals beyond Trade: America versus Japan in Global Competition*. Ithaca: Cornell University Press, 1992.

Graham, Edward M. *Global Corporations and National Governments*. Washington, D.C.: Institute for International Economics, 1996.

Greider, William. *One World, Ready or Not: The Manic Logic of Global Capitalism*. New York: Simon and Schuster, 1997.

Julius, DeAnne. *Global Companies and Public Policy: The Growing Challenge of Foreign Direct Investment*. London: Pinter, 1990.

Moran, Theodore H. *Foreign Direct Investment and Development: The New Policy Agenda for Developing Countries and Economies in Transition*. Washington, D.C.: Institute for International Economics. 1998.

Ohmae, Kenichi. *Triad Power: The Coming Shape of Global Competition*. New York: Free Press, 1985.

Ostry, Sylvia. *Governments and Corporations in a Shrinking World: Trade and Innovation Policies in the United States, Europe and Japan*. New York: Council on Foreign Relations, 1990.

Ostry, Sylvia, and Richard R. Nelson. *Techno-Nationalism and Techno-Globalism: Conflict and Cooperation*. Washington, D.C.: Brookings Institution, 1995.

Ruigrok, Winfried, and Rob van Tulder. *The Logic of International Restructuring*. London and New York: Routledge, 1995.

Sally, Razeen. "Multinational Enterprises, Political Economy and Institutional Theory: Domestic Embeddedness in the Context of Internationalization." *Review of International Political Economy*. 1, no. 1 (spring 1994): 161–92.

CHAPTER SEVEN: EUROPEAN REGIONAL INTEGRATION

De Grauwe, Paul. *The Economics of Monetary Integration*. 2d. rev. ed. New York: Oxford University Press, 1994.

Dinan, Desmond, ed. *Enclyopaedia of the European Union*. Boulder, Colo.: Lynne Reinner, 1998.

Eichengreen, Barry J., and Jeffry Frieden, eds. *The Political Economy of European Monetary Integration*. Boulder, Colo.: Westview Press, 1994.

Henning, C. Randall. *Cooperating with Europe's Monetary Union*. Washington, D.C.: Institute for International Economics, 1997.

Kahler, Miles. *Regional Futures and Transatlantic Economic Relations*. New York: Council on Foreign Relations, 1995.

Katzenstein, Peter J., ed. *Tamed Power: Germany in Europe*. Ithaca: Cornell University Press, 1995.

Kenen, Peter B. *Economic and Monetary Union in Europe: Moving beyond Maastricht*. New York: Cambridge University Press, 1995.

McNamara, Kathleen R. *The Currency of Ideas: Monetary Politics in the European Union*. Ithaca: Cornell University Press, 1998.

Moravcsik, Andrew. *The Choice for Europe: Social Purpose and State Power from Messina to Maastricht*. Ithaca: Cornell University Press, 1998.

Wallace, Helen, and William Wallace. *Policy-Making in the European Union*. 3d ed. Oxford: Oxford University Press, 1996.

Chapter Eight: American Economic Strategy

Bergsten, C. Fred. *America in the World Economy: A Strategy for the 1990s*. Washington, D.C.: Institute for International Economics, 1988.

Bergsten, C. Fred, and Marcus Noland. *Reconcilable Differences?: United States–Japan Economic Conflict*. Washington, D.C.: Institute for International Economics, 1993.

Bhagwati, Jagdish N. *The World Trading System at Risk*. Princeton: Princeton University Press, 1991.

Destler, I. M. *American Trade Politics*. 3d ed. Washington, D.C.: Institute for International Economics, and New York: Twentieth Century Fund, 1995.

Hufbauer, Gary Clyde, and Jeffrey J. Schott. *North American Free Trade: Issues and Recommendations*. Washington, D.C.: Institute for International Economics, 1992.

Krueger, Anne O. *American Trade Policy: A Tragedy in the Making*. Washington, D.C.: AEI Press, 1991.

Krugman, Paul R. *Peddling Prosperity: Economic Sense and Nonsense in the Age of Diminished Expectations*. New York: W. W. Norton, 1991.

———, ed. *Trade with Japan: Has the Door Opened Wider?* Chicago: University of Chicago Press, 1995.

Moran, Theodore H. *American Economic Policy and National Security*. New York: Council on Foreign Relations, 1993.

Nau, Henry. *Trade and Security: U.S. Policies at Cross-Purposes*. Washington, D.C.: AEI Press, 1995.

Weintraub, Sidney. *NAFTA: What Comes Next?* Westport, Conn.: Praeger, 1994.

Chapter Nine: Asian Regionalism

Asia-Pacific Economic Cooperation. *A Vision for APEC: Towards an Asia Pacific Economic Community*. Report of the Eminent Persons Group to APEC Ministers, October 1993.

Bergsten, C. Fred, and Marcus Noland, eds. *Pacific Dynamism and the International Economic System*. Washington, D.C.: Institute for International Economics, 1993.

Das, Dilip K. *The Asia-Pacific Economy*. New York: St. Martin's Press, 1996.

Frankel, Jeffrey A., and Miles Kahler. *Regionalism and Rivalry: Japan and the United States in Pacific Asia*. Chicago and London: University of Chicago Press, 1993.

Funabashi, Yoichi. *Asia Pacific Fusion: Japan's Role in APEC*. Washington, D.C.: Institute for International Economics, 1995.

Gibney, Frank. *The Pacific Century: America and Asia in a Changing World*. New York: Scribner, 1992.

Harding, Harry. *China's Second Revolution: Reform after Mao*. Washington, D.C.: Brookings Institution, 1987.

Hatch, Walter, and Kozo Yamamura. *Asia in Japan's Embrace: Building a Regional Production Alliance*. New York: Cambridge University Press, 1996.

Hellmann, Donald C., and Kenneth B. Pyle, eds. *From APEC to XANADU: Creating a Viable Commmunity in the Post–Cold War Pacific*. Armonk, N.Y.: M. E. Sharpe, 1997.

Johnson, Chalmers. *Japan: Who Governs: The Rise of the Developmental State*. New York: W. W. Norton, 1995.

Katz, Richard. *Japan, the System That Soured: The Rise and Fall of the Japanese Economic Miracle*. Armonk, N.Y.: M. E. Sharpe, 1998.

Katzenstein, Peter J., and Takashi Shiraishi, eds. *Network Power: Japan and Asia* Ithaca: Cornell University Press. 1997.

Lardy, Nicholas R. *China in the World Economy*. Washington, D.C.: Institute for International Economics, 1994.

Naughton, Barry, ed. *The China Circle: Economics and Technology in the PRC, Taiwan, and Hong Kong*. Washington, D.C.: Brookings Institution, 1997.

Posen, Adam S. *Restoring Japan's Economic Growth*. Washington, D.C.: Institute for International Economics, 1998.

Pyle, Kenneth B. *The Japanese Question: Power and Purpose in a New Era*. Washington, D.C.: AEI Press, 1992.

Vogel, Ezra F. *The Four Little Dragons: The Spread of Industrialization in East Asia*. Cambridge: Harvard University Press, 1991.

CHAPTER TEN: GLOBALIZATION AND ITS DISCONTENTS

Burtless, Gary, Robert Z. Lawrence, Robert E. Litan, and Robert J. Shapiro. *Globaphobia: Confronting Fears about Open Trade*. Washington, D.C.: Brookings Institution, 1998.

Friedman, Thomas L. *The Lexus and the Olive Tree*. New York: Farrar, Straus and Giroux, 1999.

Gray, John. *False Dawn: The Delusions of Global Capitalism*. New York: New Press, 1999.

Hirst, Paul, and Grahame Thompson, eds. *Globalization in Question: The International Economy and The Possibilities of Governance*. Cambridge: Polity Press, 1996.

Longworth, Richard C. *Global Squeeze: The Coming Crisis for First-World Nations*. Chicago: Contemporary Books, 1998.

Luttwak, Edward. *Turbo-Capitalism: Winners and Losers in the Global Economy*. New York: HarperCollins, 1998.

Mander, Jerry, and Edward Goldsmith, eds. *The Case against the Global Economy—and for a Turn toward the Local.* San Francisco: Sierra Club Books, 1996.

Pierson, Paul. *Dismantling the Welfare State? Reagan, Thatcher, and the Politics of Retrenchment.* New York: Cambridge University Press, 1994.

Rodrik, Dani. *Has Globalization Gone too Far?* Washington, D.C.: Institute for International Economics, 1997.

CHAPTER ELEVEN: MANAGING THE GLOBAL ECONOMY

Bhagwati, Jagdish, and Arvind Panagariya, eds. *The Economics of Preferential Trade Arrangements.* Washington, D.C.: AEI Press, 1996.

Cable, Vincent, and David Henderson, eds. *Trade Blocs? The Future of Regional Integration.* London: Royal Institute of International Affairs, 1994.

Cooper Richard N. *The Economics of Interdependence: Economic Policy in the Atlantic Community.* New York: McGraw-Hill, 1968.

De Melo, Jaime, and Arvind Panagariya, eds. *New Dimensions in Regional Integration.* London: Centre for Economic Policy Research, 1995.

Eichengreen, Barry. *Towards a New International Financial Architecture: A Practical Post-Asian Agenda.* Washington, D.C.: Institute for International Economics, 1999.

Frankel, Jeffrey A. *Regional Trading Blocs in the World Economic System.* Washington, D.C.: Institute for International Economics, 1997.

Kahler, Miles. *International Institutions and the Political Economy of Integration.* Washington, D.C.: Brookings Institution, 1995.

Keohane, Robert. *After Hegemony: Cooperation and Discord in the World Political Economy.* Princeton: Princeton University Press, 1984.

Lawrence, Robert Z., Albert Bressand, and Takatoshi Ito. *A Vision for the World Economy: Openness, Diversity and Cohesion.* Washington, D.C.: Brookings Institution, 1996.

Oman, Charles. *Globalisation and Regionalisation: The Challenge for Developing Countries.* Paris: Development Centre of the Organization for Economic Cooperation and Development, 1994.

Paarlberg, Robert L. *Leadership Abroad Begins at Home: U.S. Foreign Economic Policy after the Cold War.* Washington, D.C.: Brookings Institution, 1995.

* *Index* *

Names of individuals and cited works omitted in the index.

371